Celeste

Celeste

WRITTEN & ILLUSTRATED BY
I.N.J. CULBARD

SELF MADE HERO

First published 2014
by SelfMadeHero
139-141 Pancras Road
London NW1 1UN
www.selfmadehero.com

Written and Illustrated by: I.N.J. Culbard

Publishing Assistant: Guillaume Rater
Editorial & Production Manager: Lizzie Kaye
Sales & Marketing Manager: Sam Humphrey
Publishing Director: Emma Hayley
With thanks to: Dan Lockwood

A CIP record for this book is available from the British Library

ISBN: 978-1-906838-76-8

10 9 8 7 6 5 4 3 2 1

Printed and bound in China

For Col.

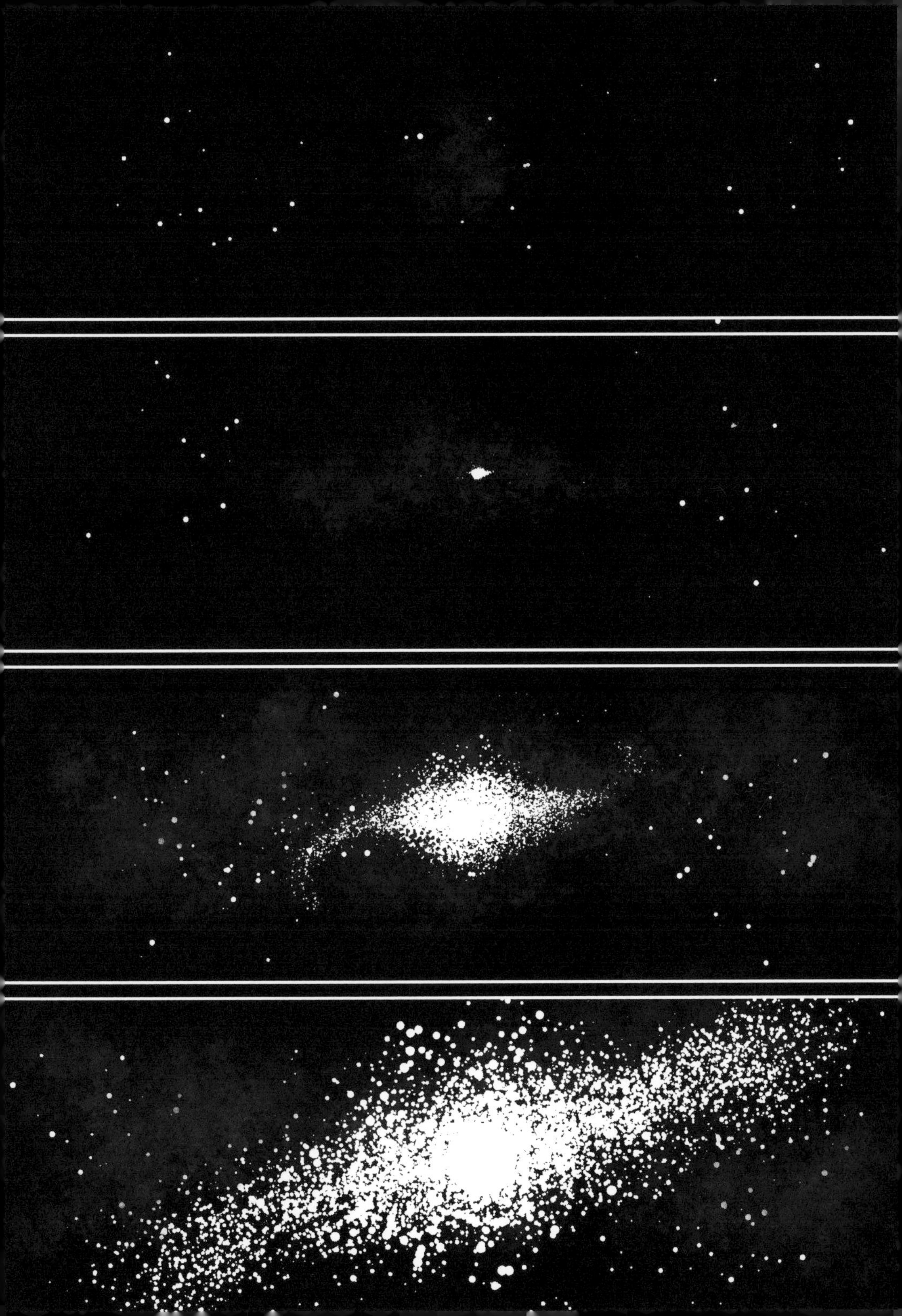

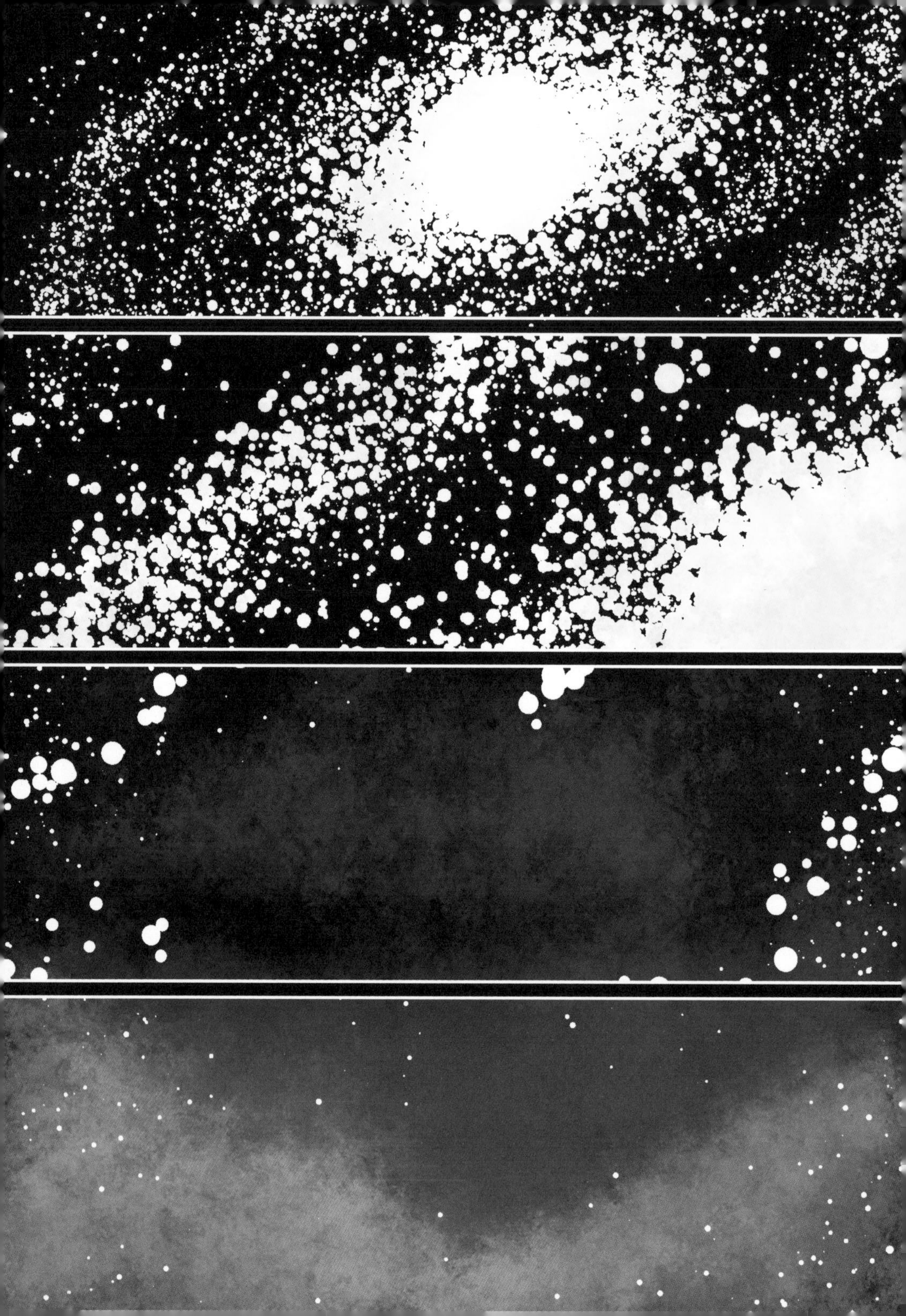

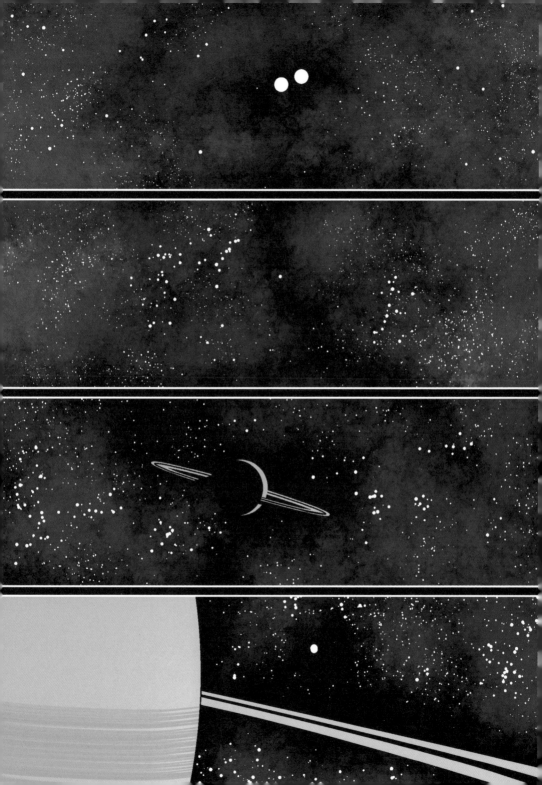

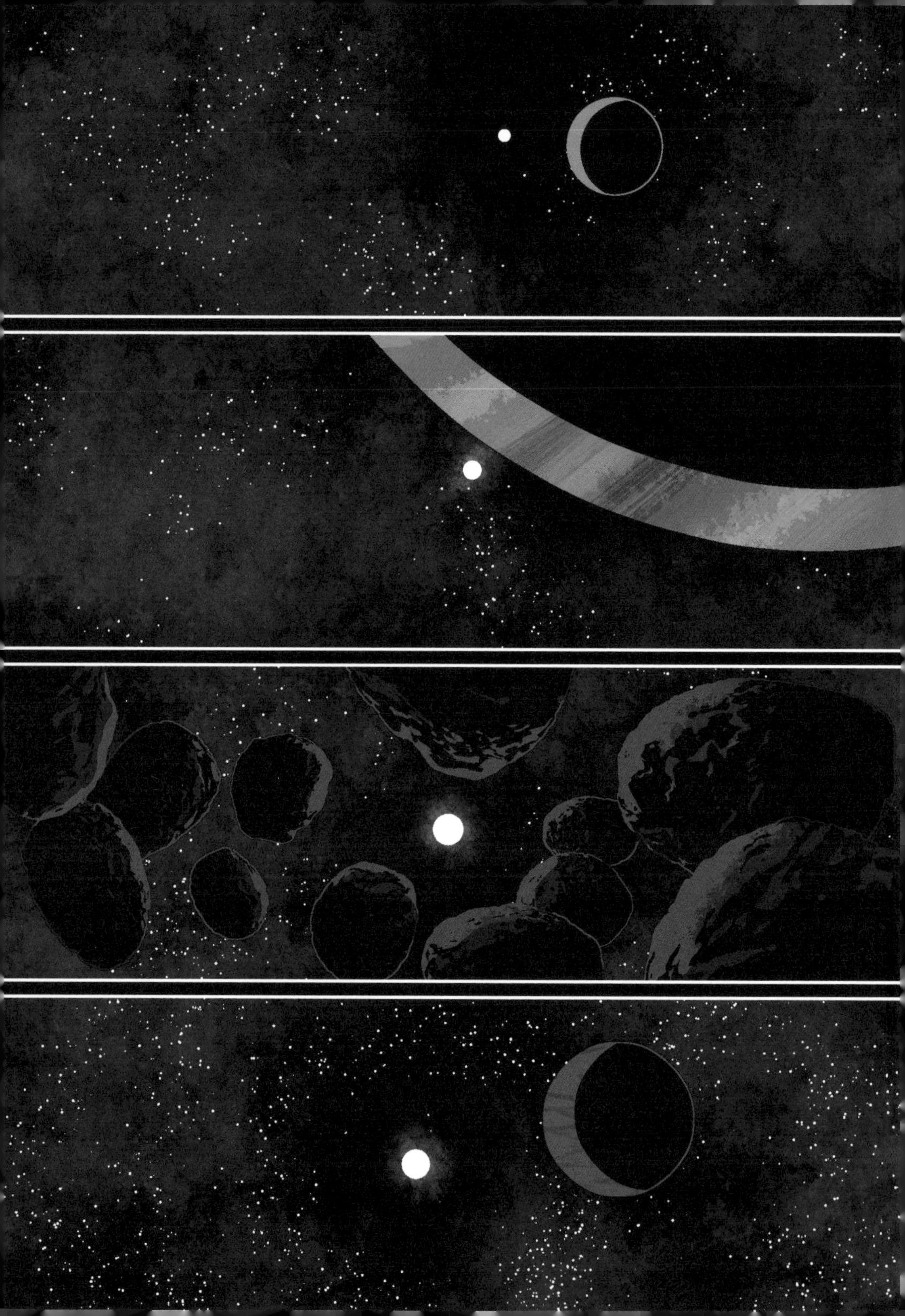

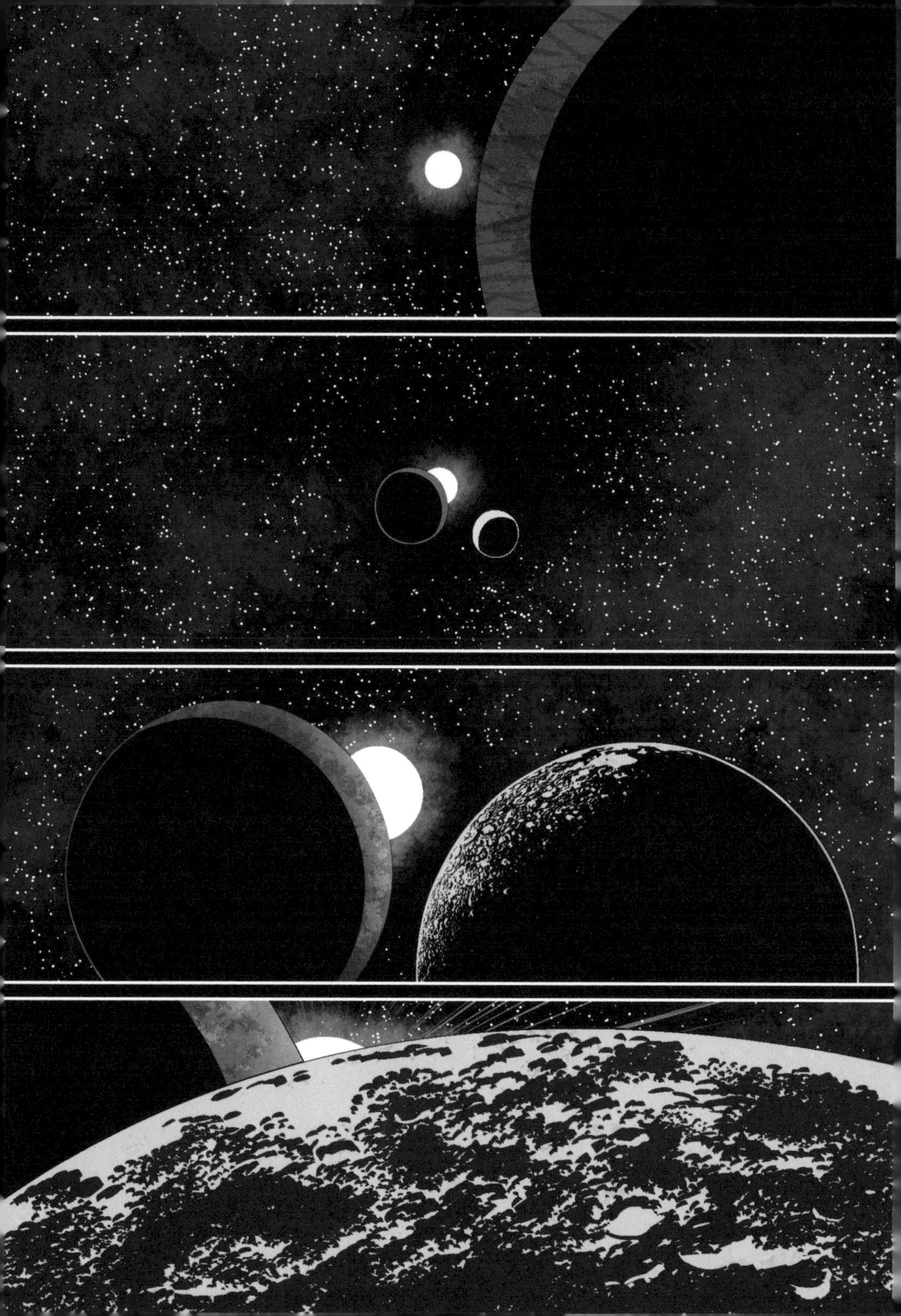

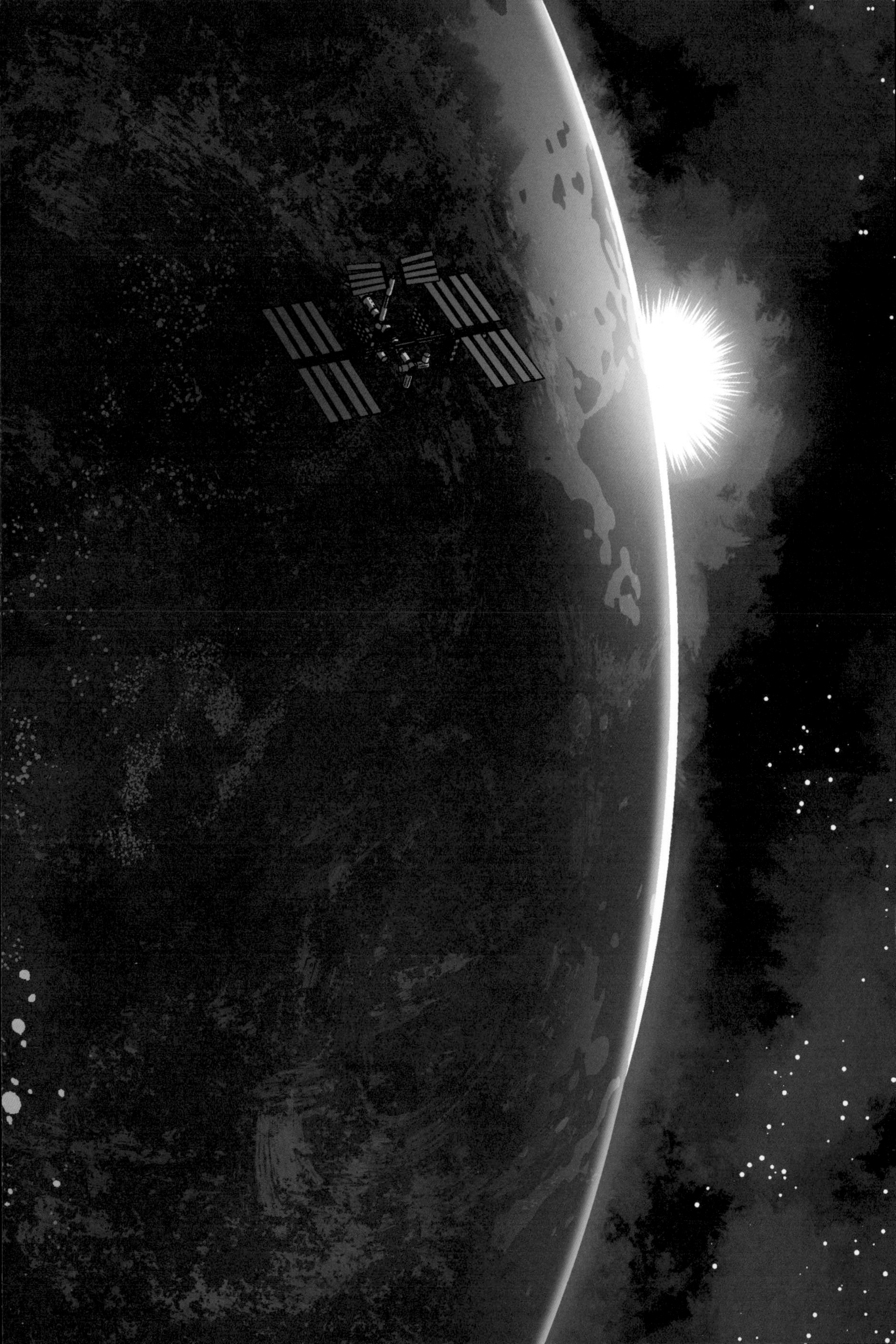

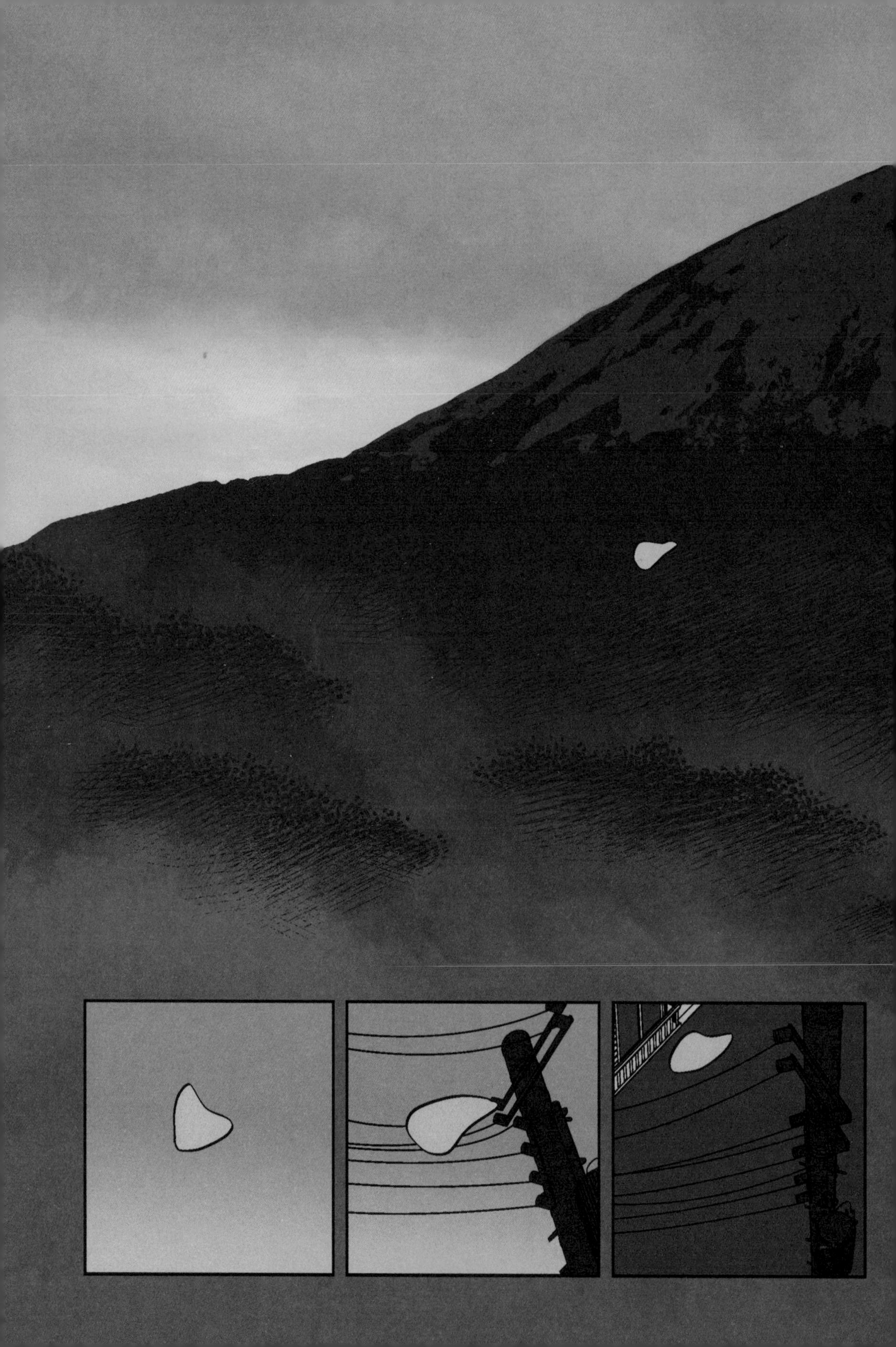

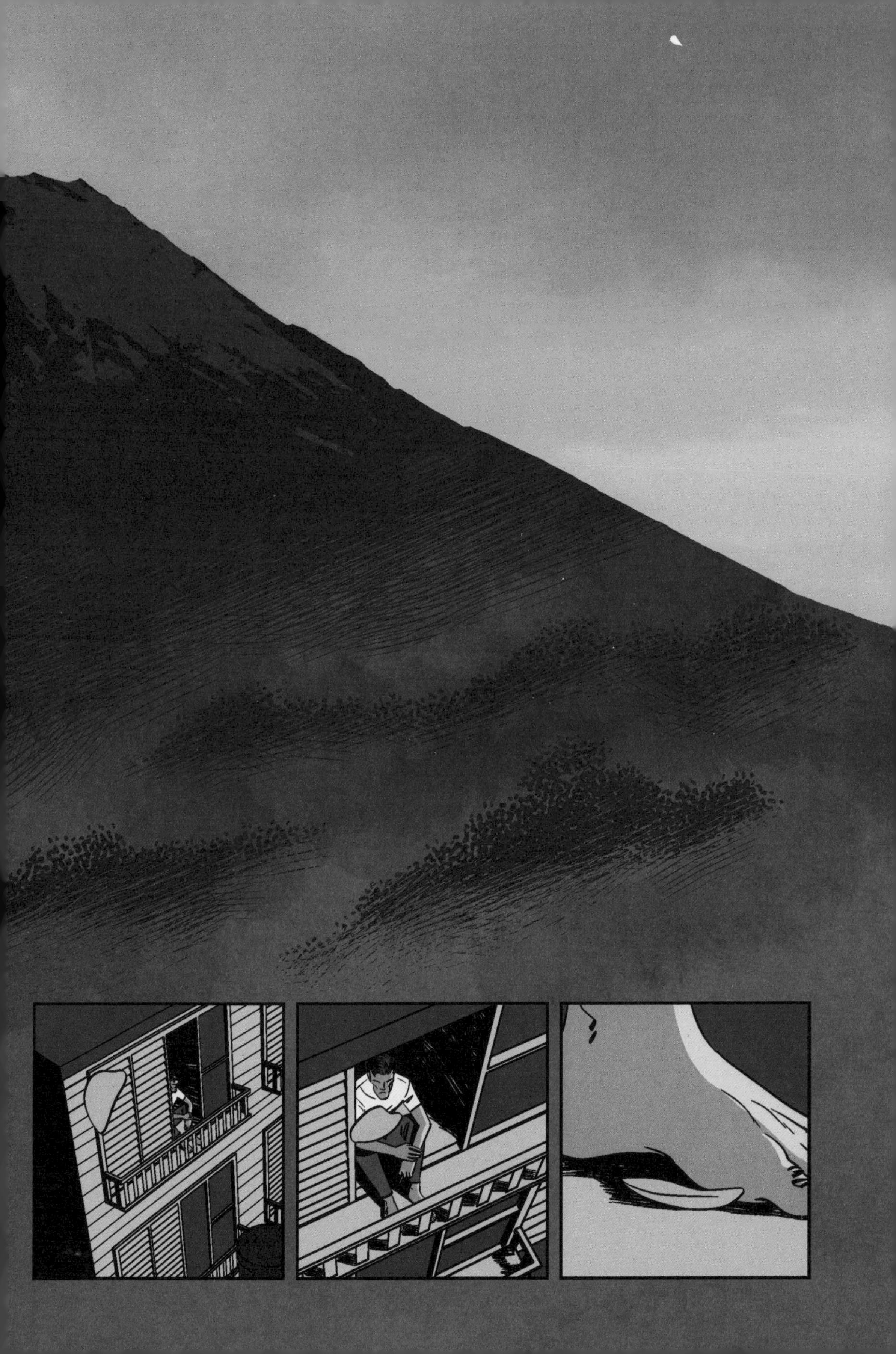

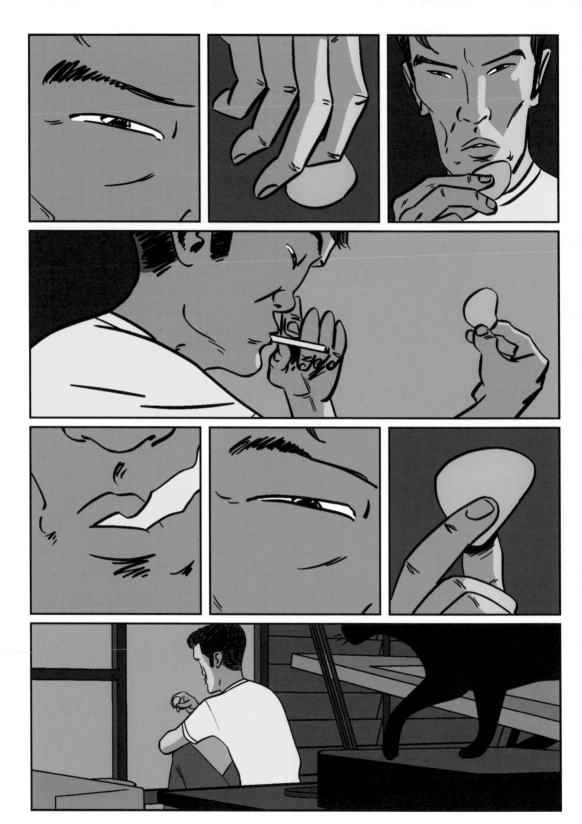

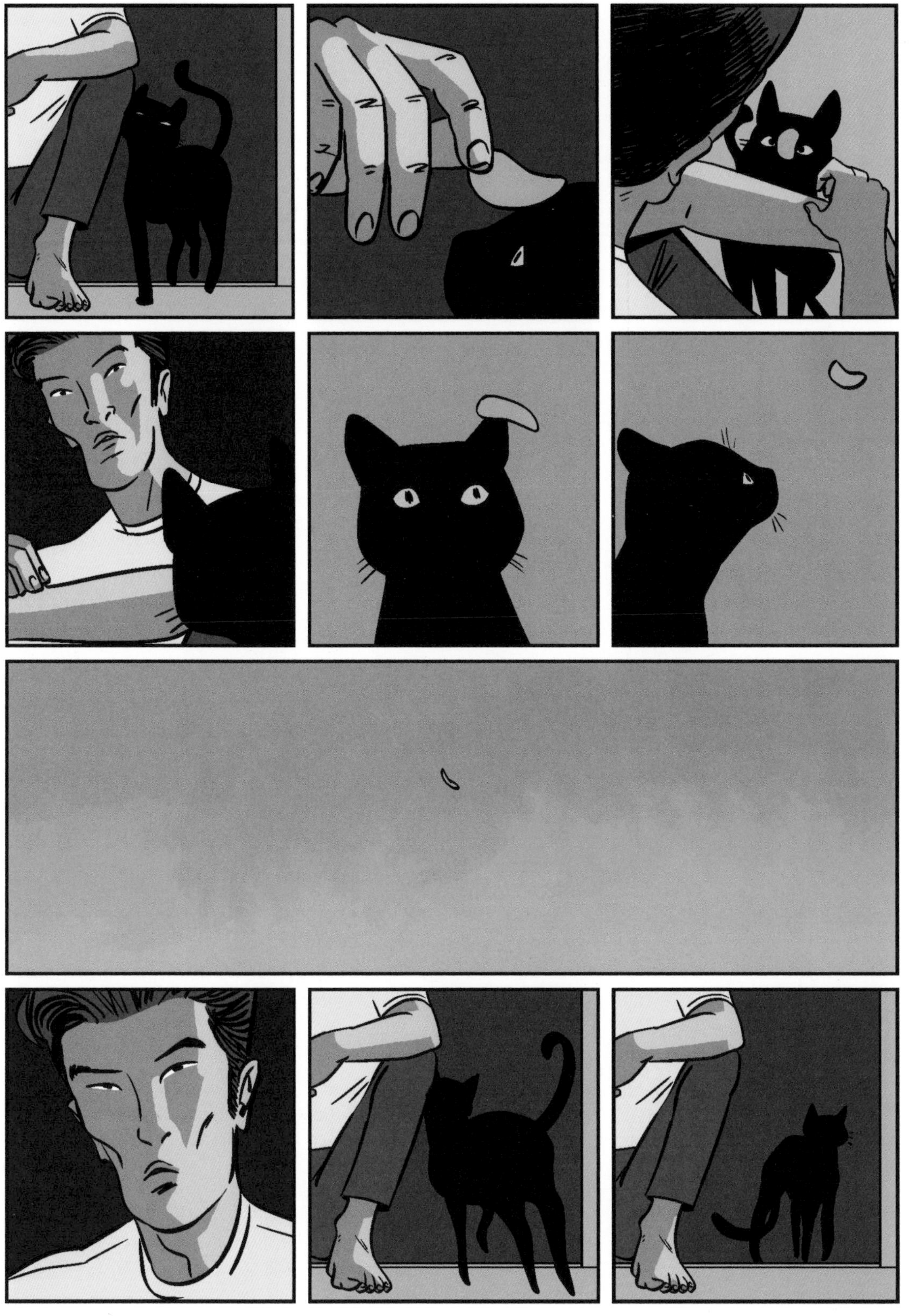

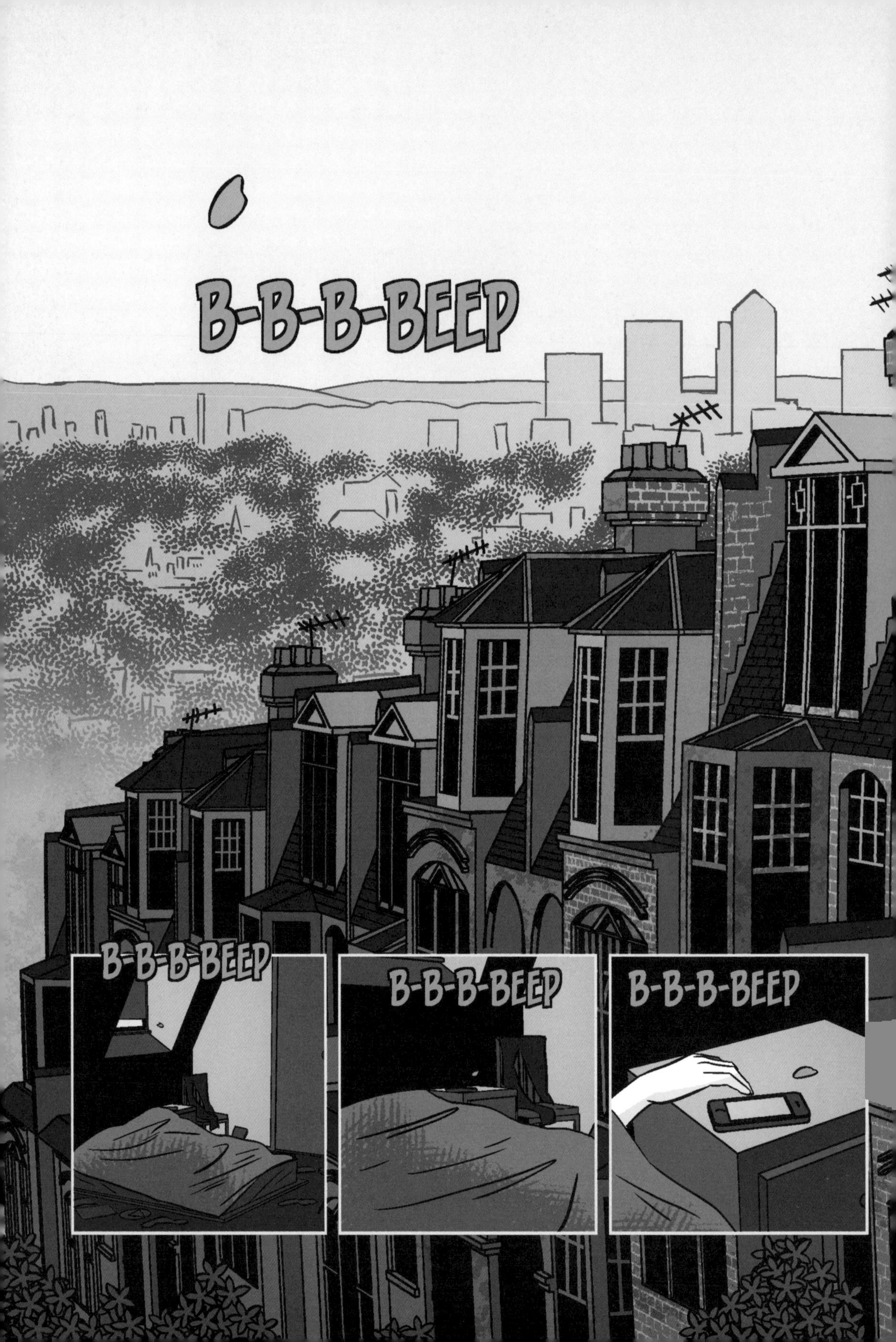
B-B-B-BEEP
B-B-B-BEEP
B-B-B-BEEP
B-B-B-BEEP

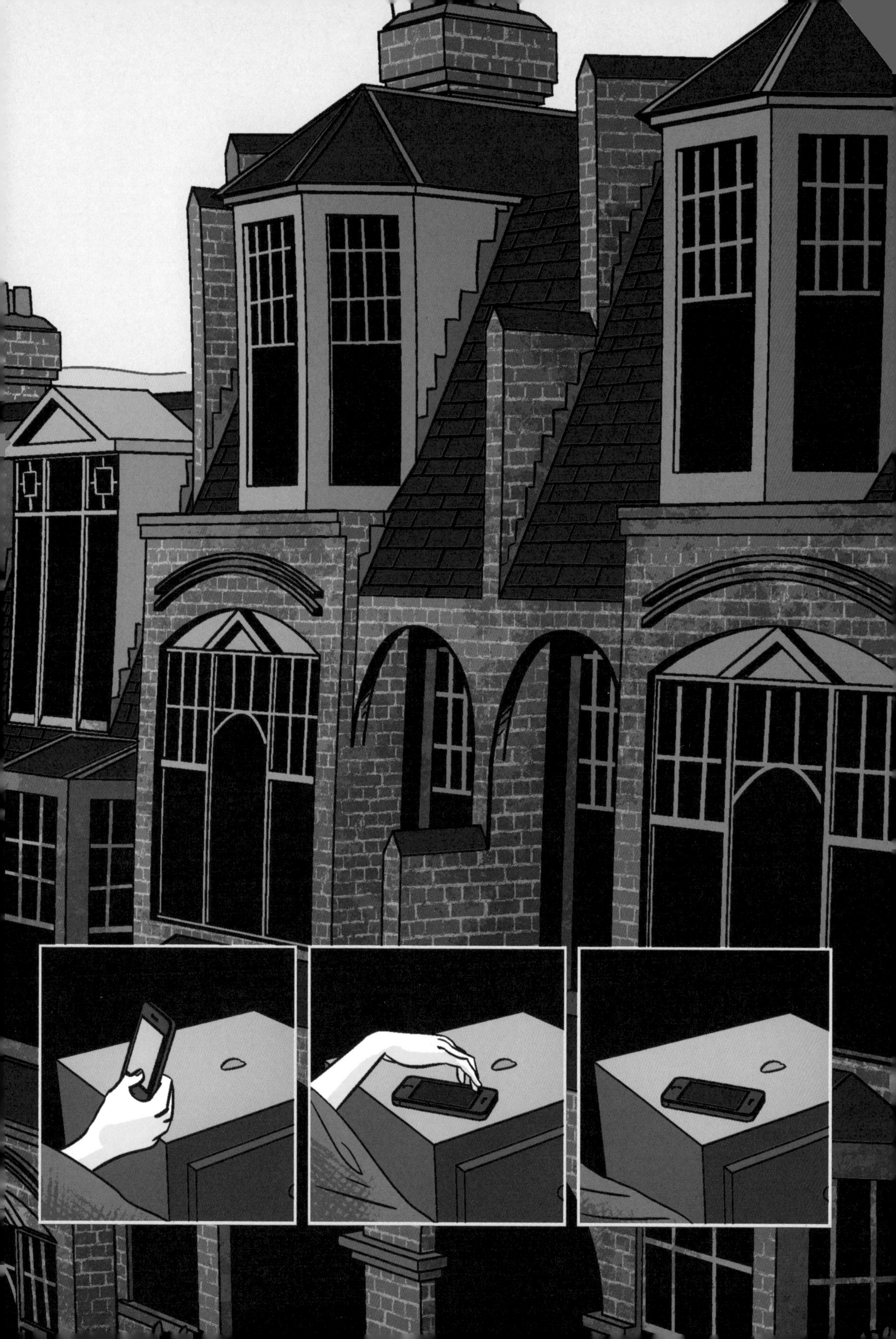

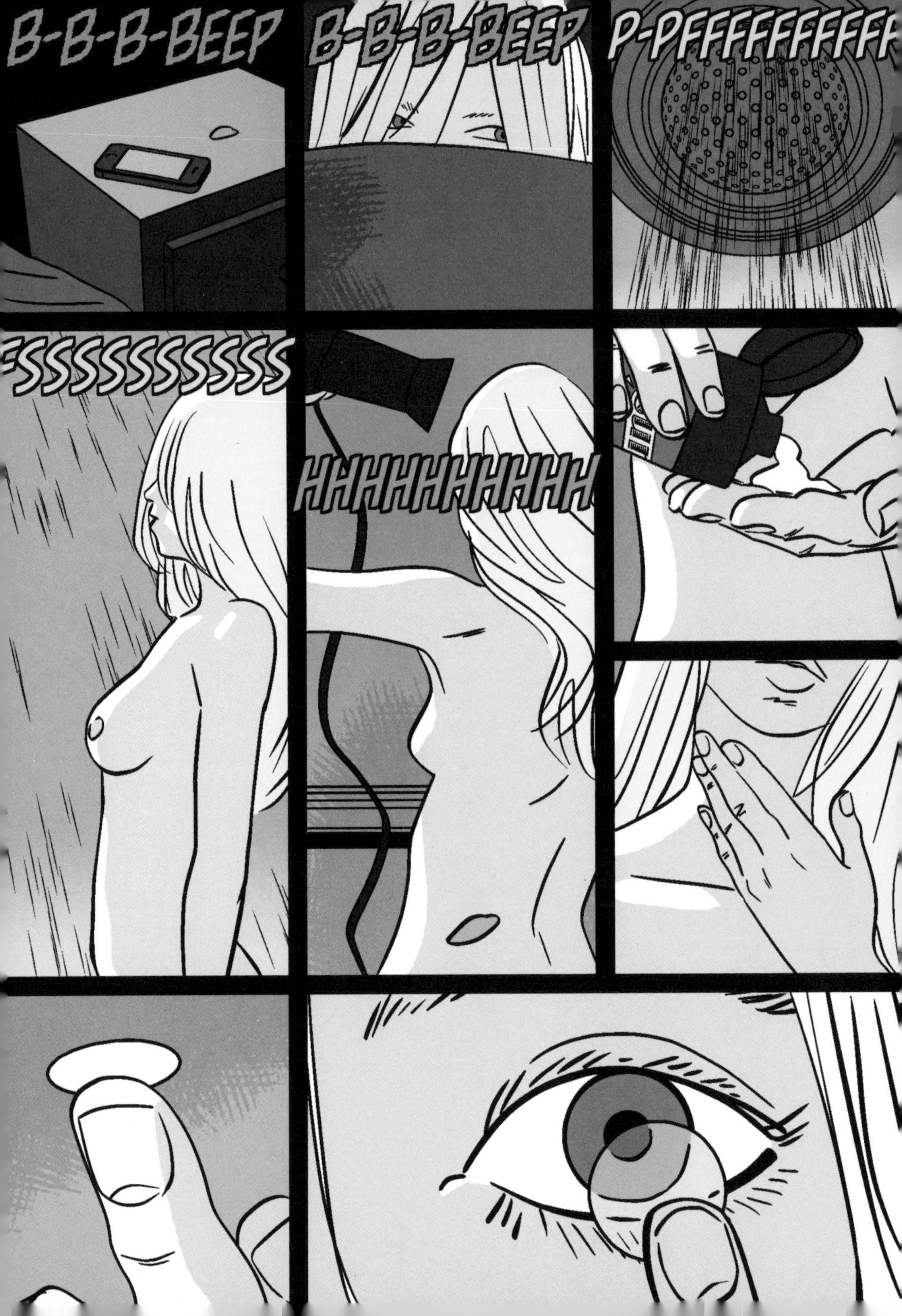
B-B-B-BEEP
B-B-B-BEEP
P-PFFFFFFFFFF
SSSSSSSSSSS
HHHHHHHHHHH

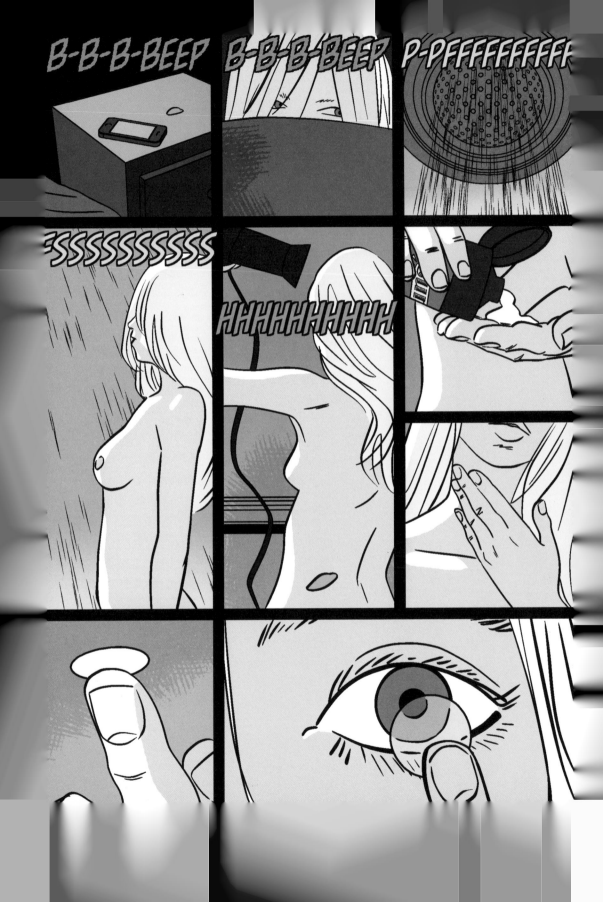

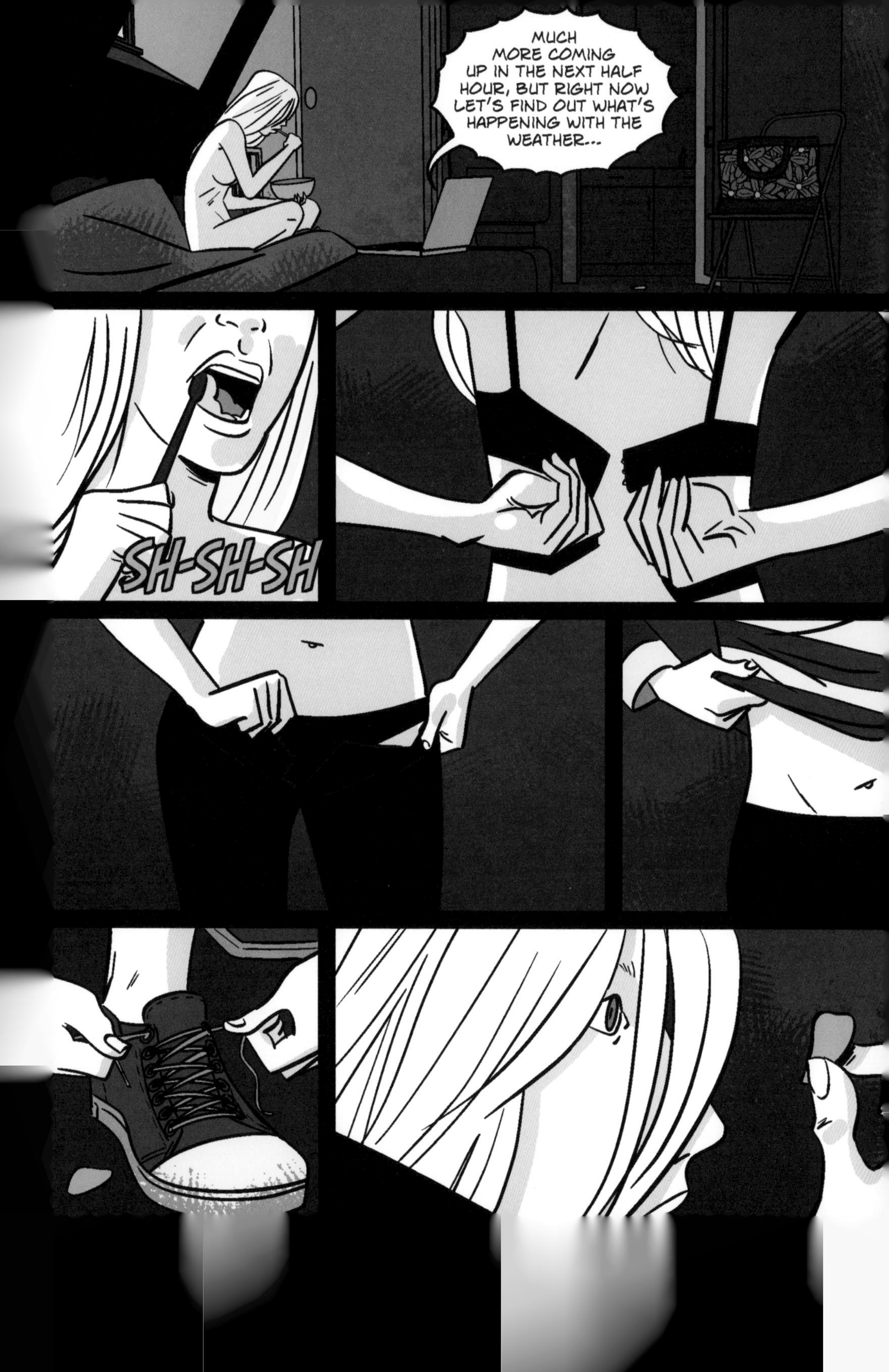
MUCH MORE COMING UP IN THE NEXT HALF HOUR, BUT RIGHT NOW LET'S FIND OUT WHAT'S HAPPENING WITH THE WEATHER...
SH-SH-SH

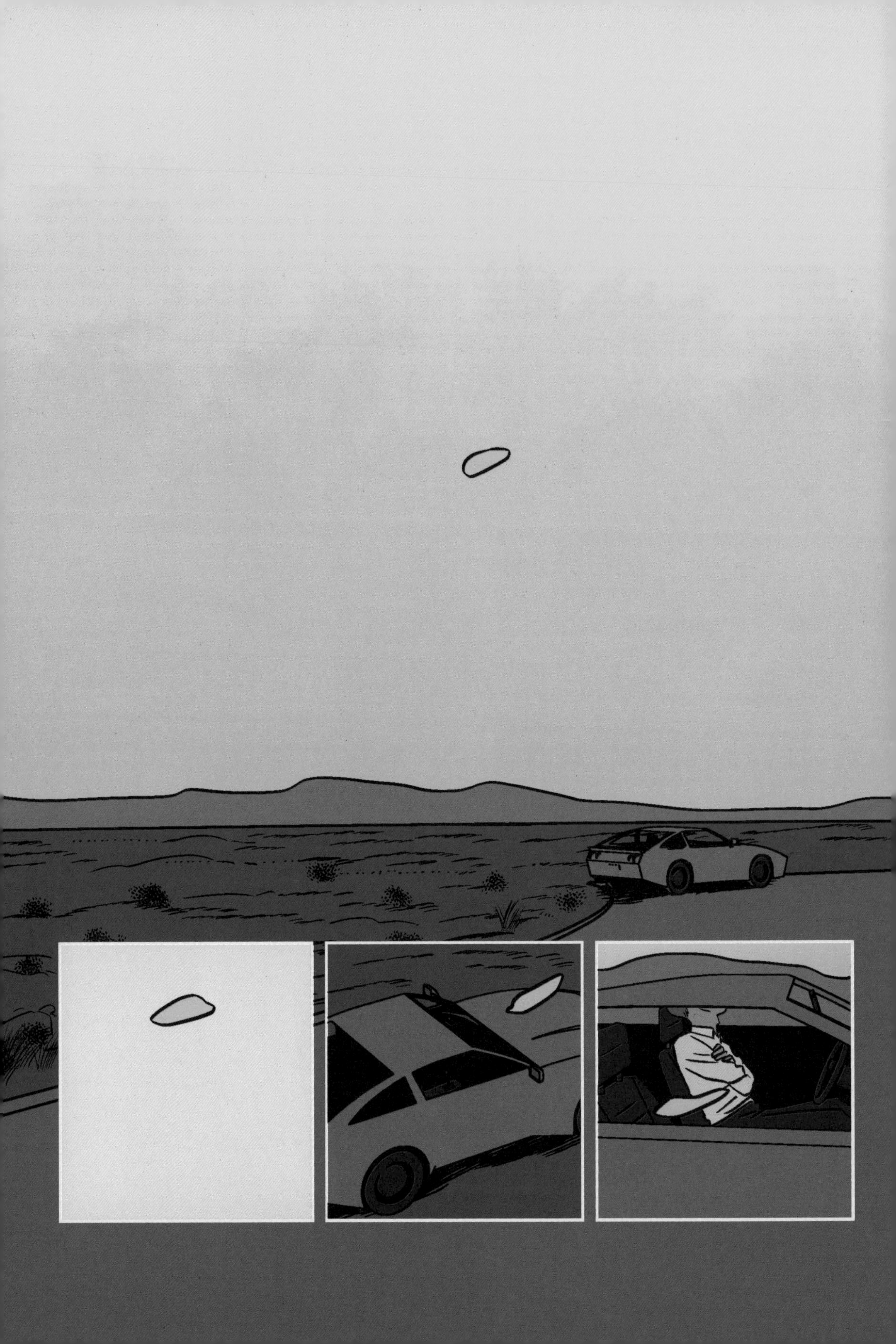

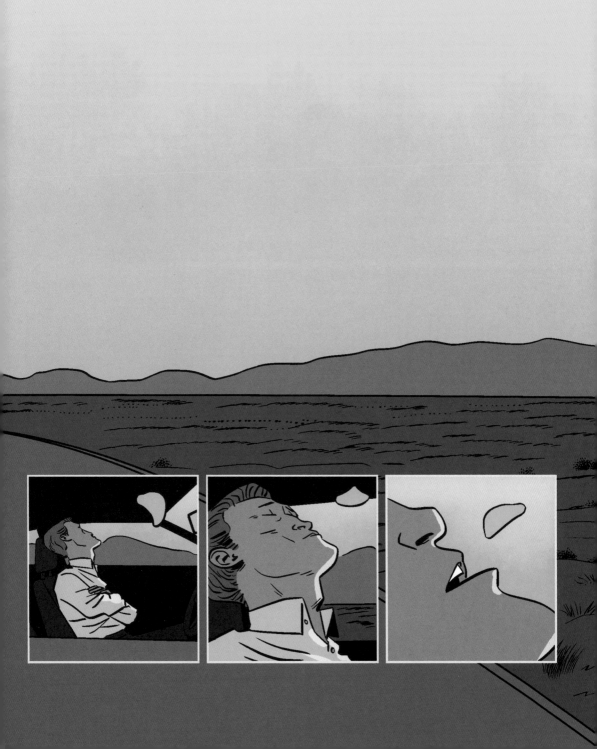

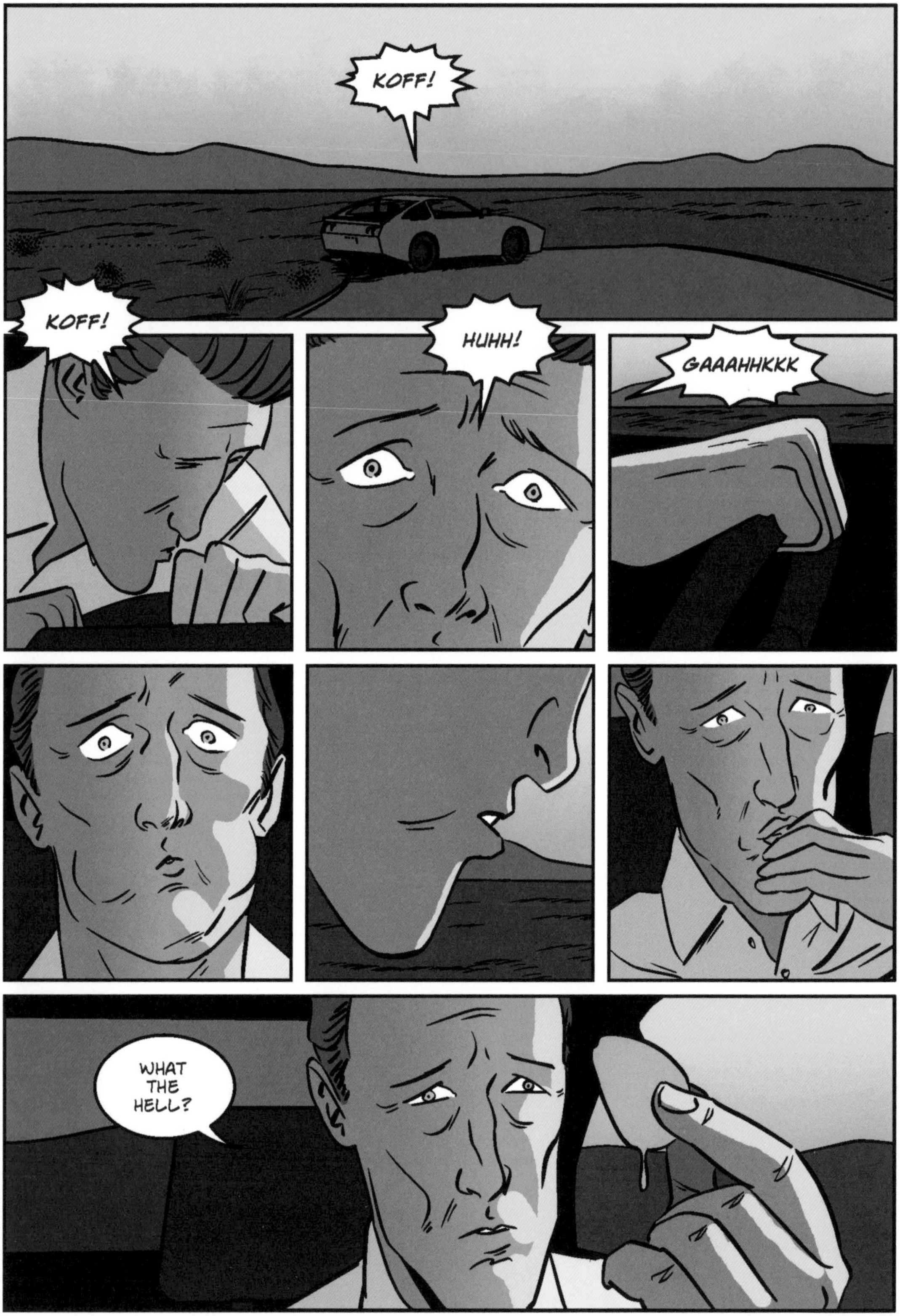
KOFF!
KOFF!
HUHH!
GAAAHHKKK
WHAT THE HELL?

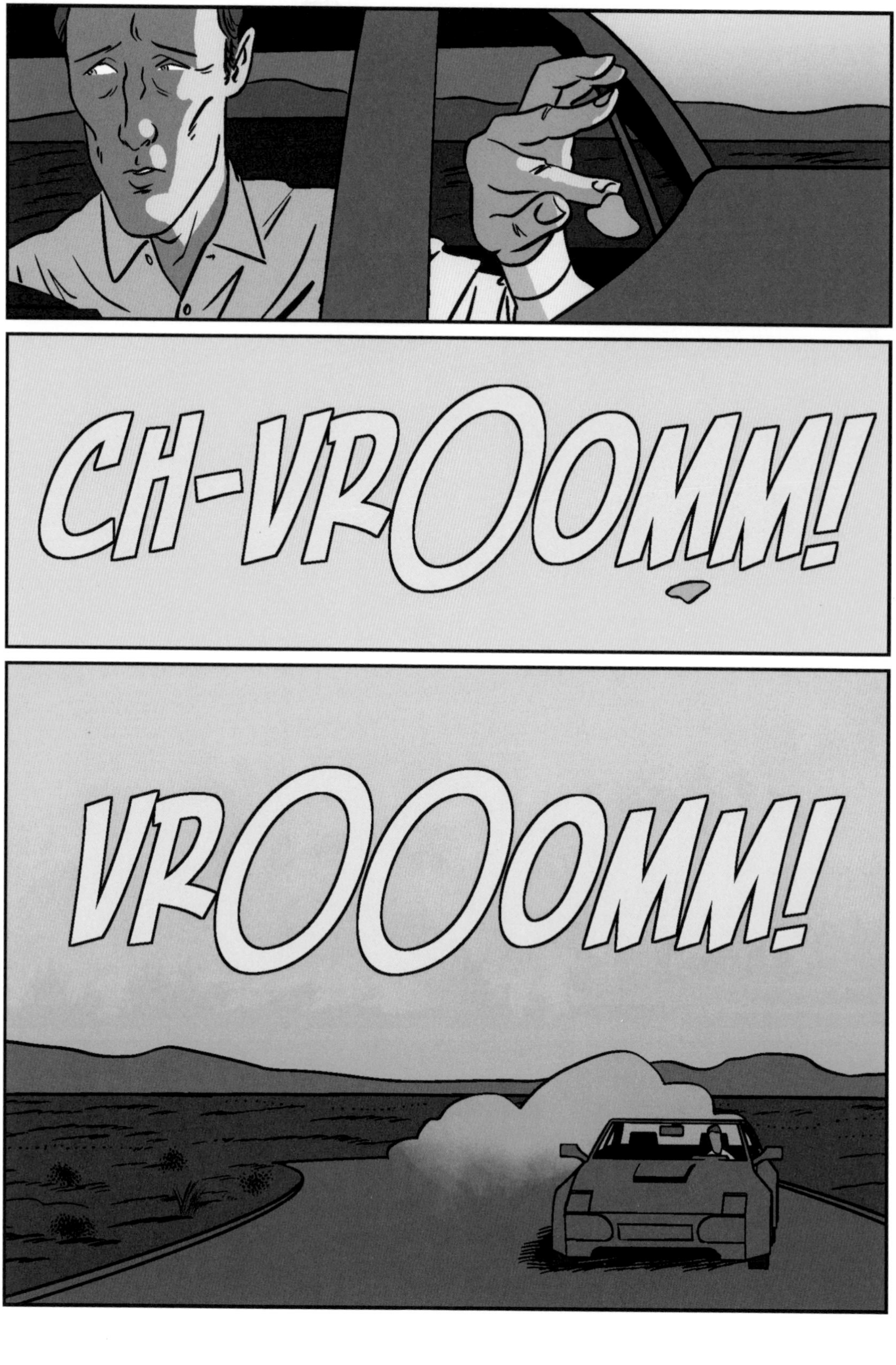
CH-VROOOMM!
VROOOMM!

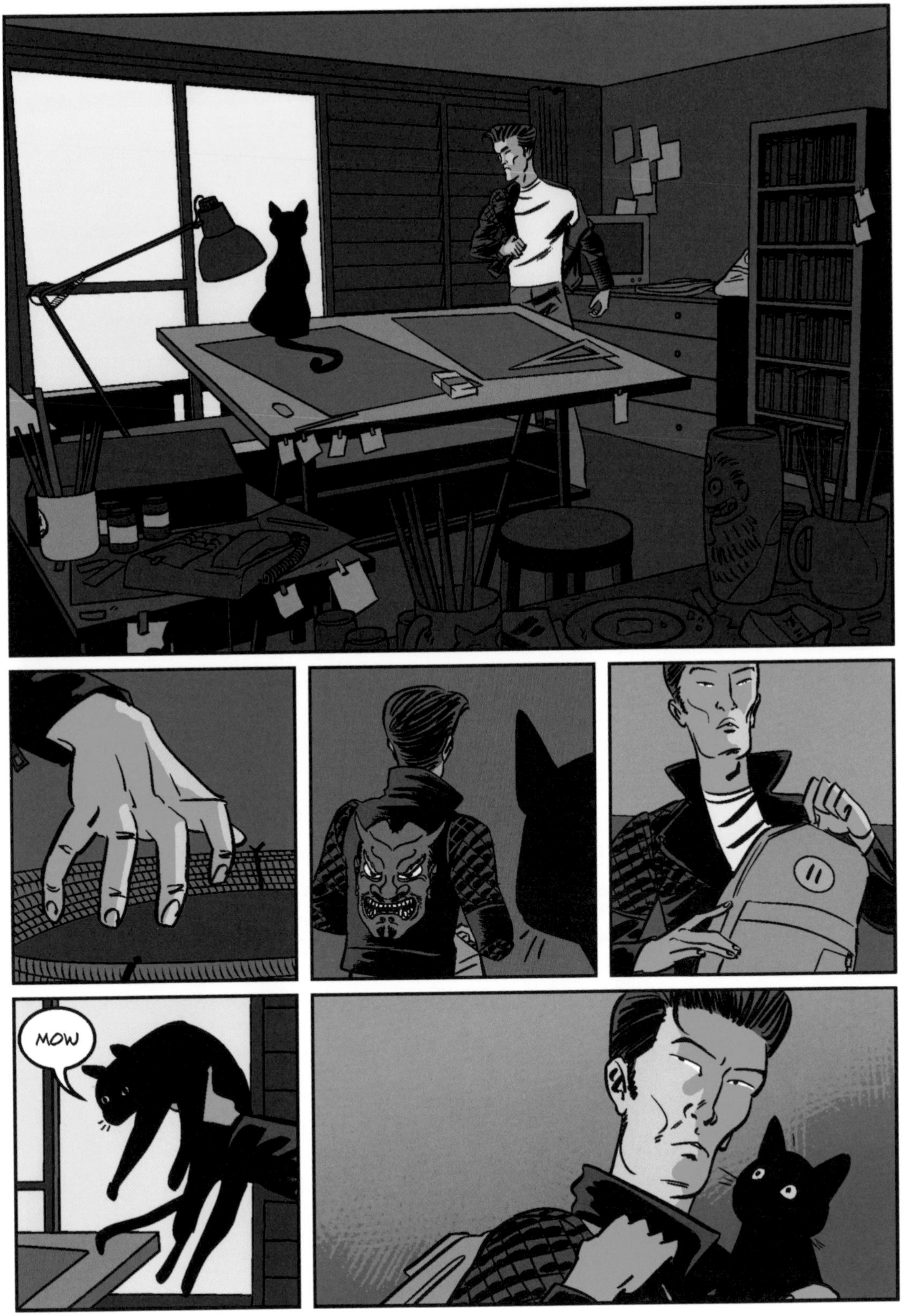
MOW

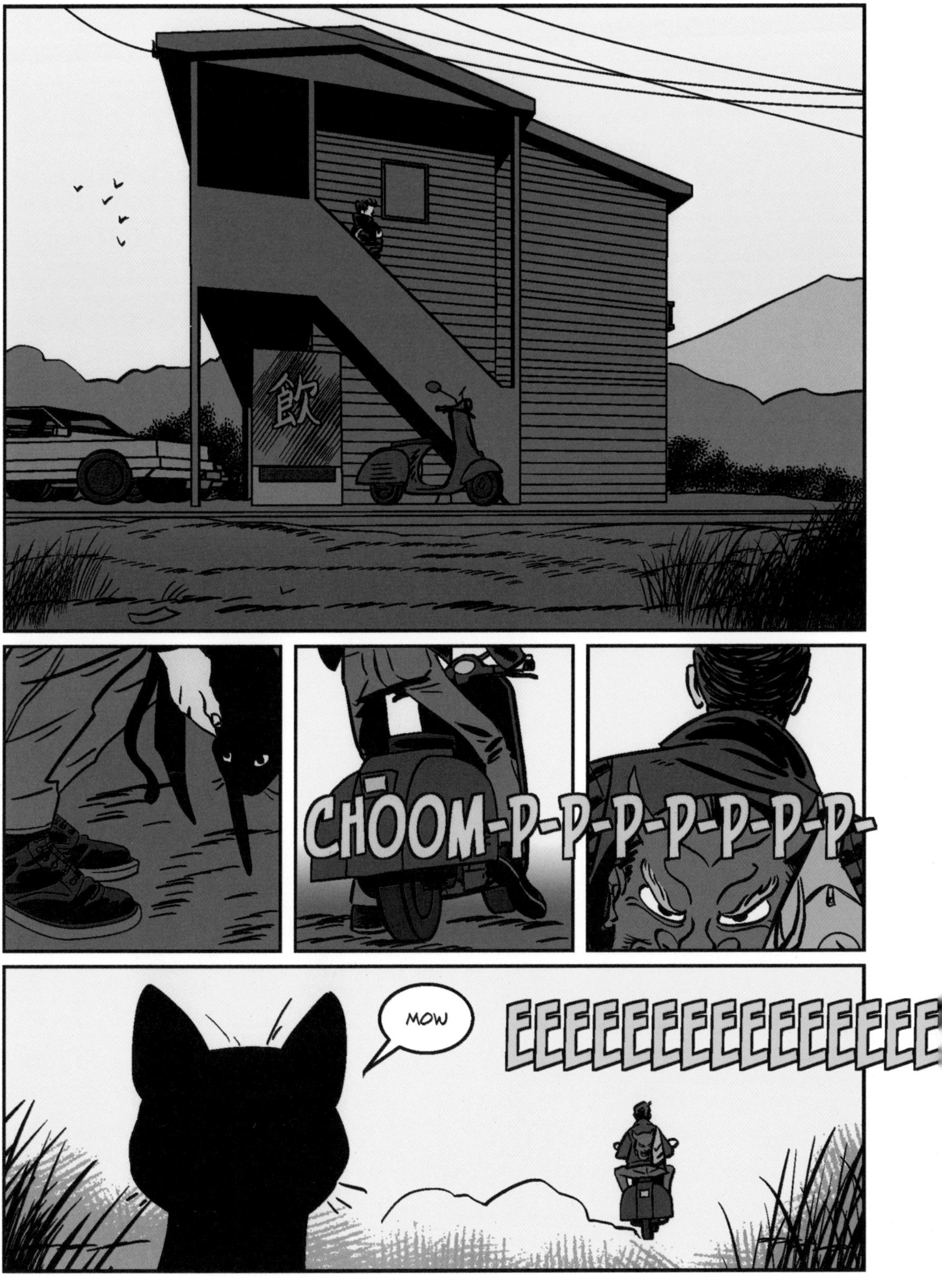
飲
CHOOM-P-P-P-P-P-P-P-
MOW
EEEEEEEEEEEEEEE

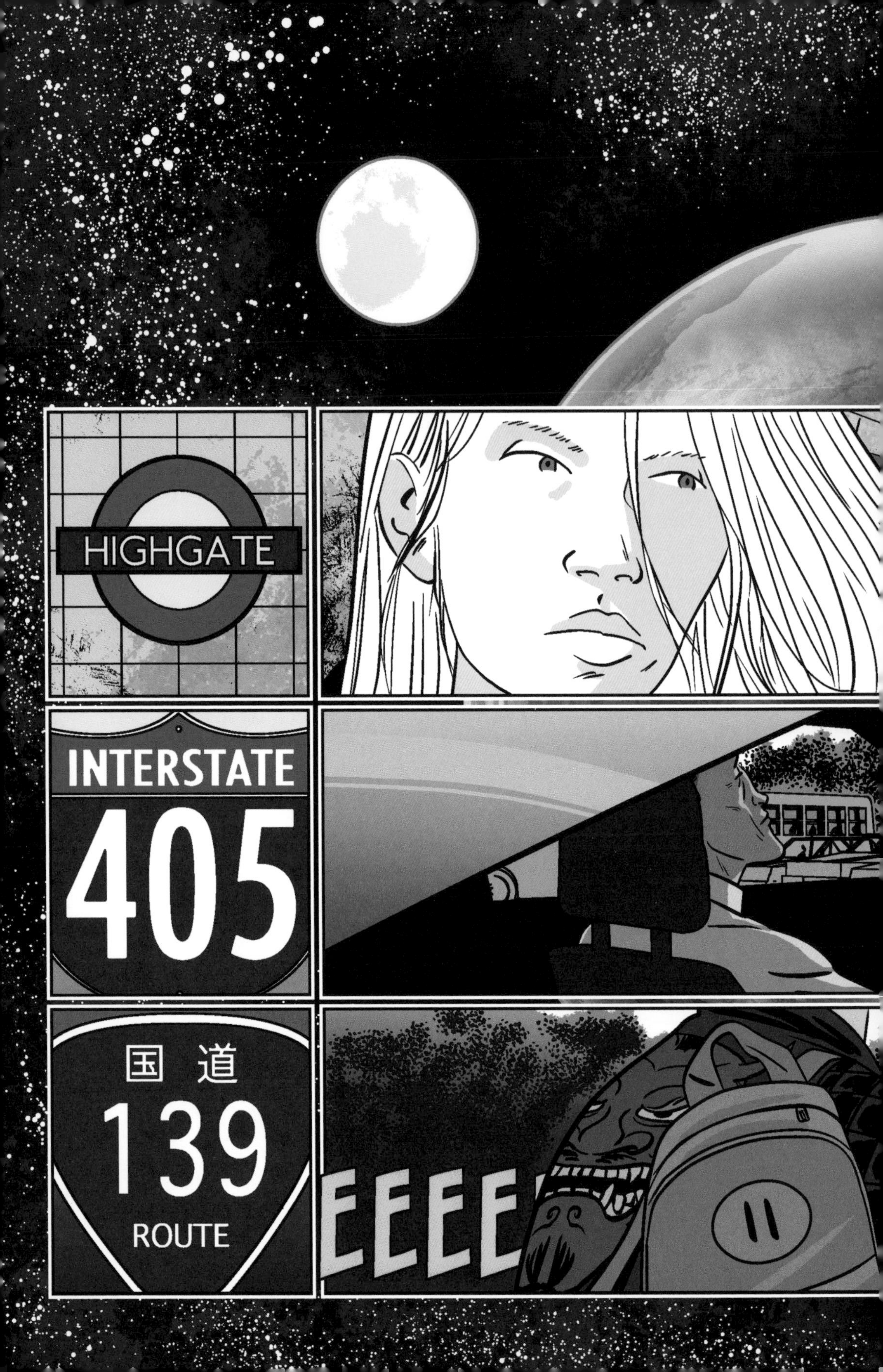
HIGHGATE
INTERSTATE
405
国道
139
ROUTE
EEEE

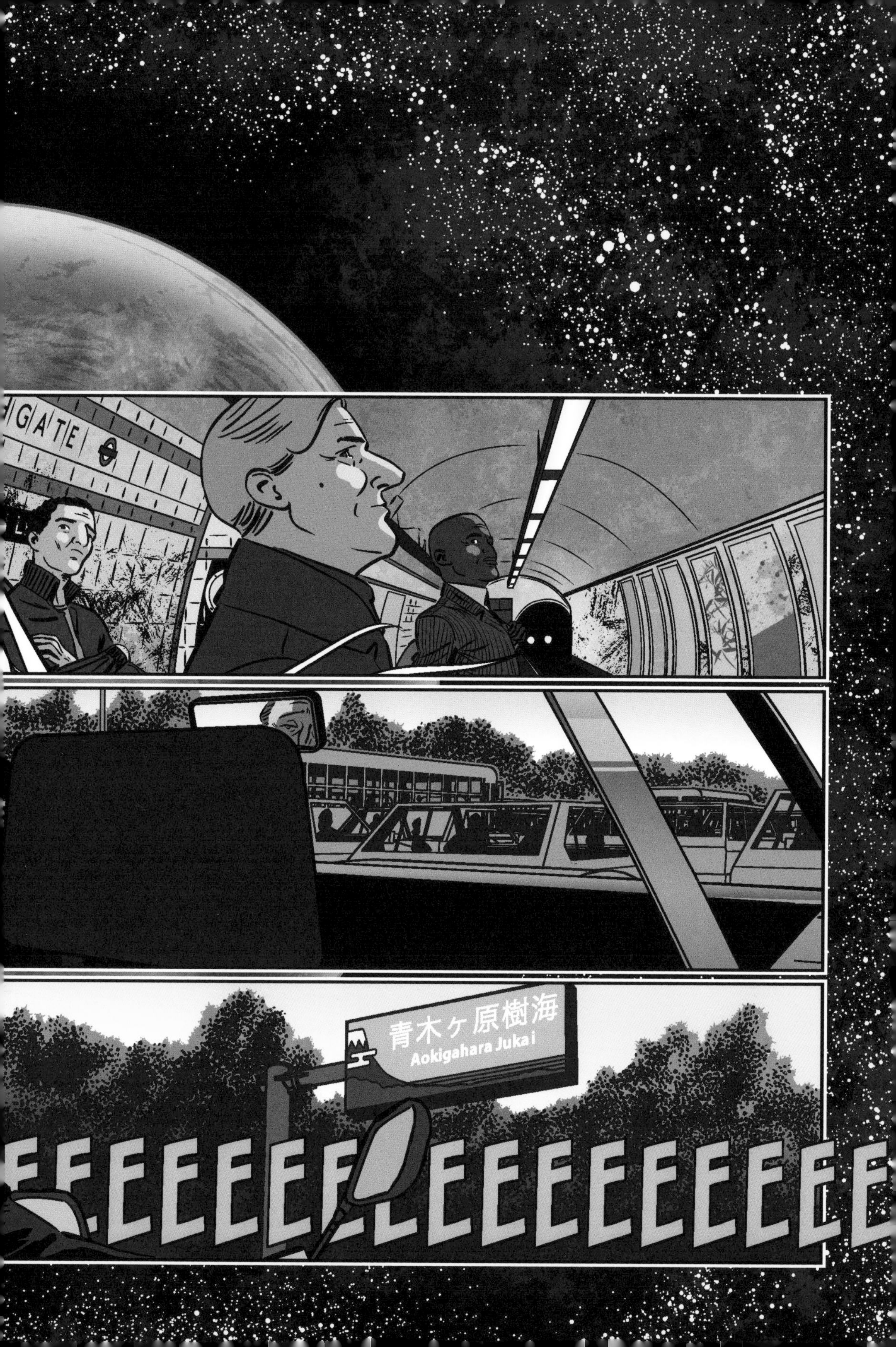

GATE
青木ヶ原樹海
Aokigahara Jukai
EEEEEEEEEEEEEEEEE

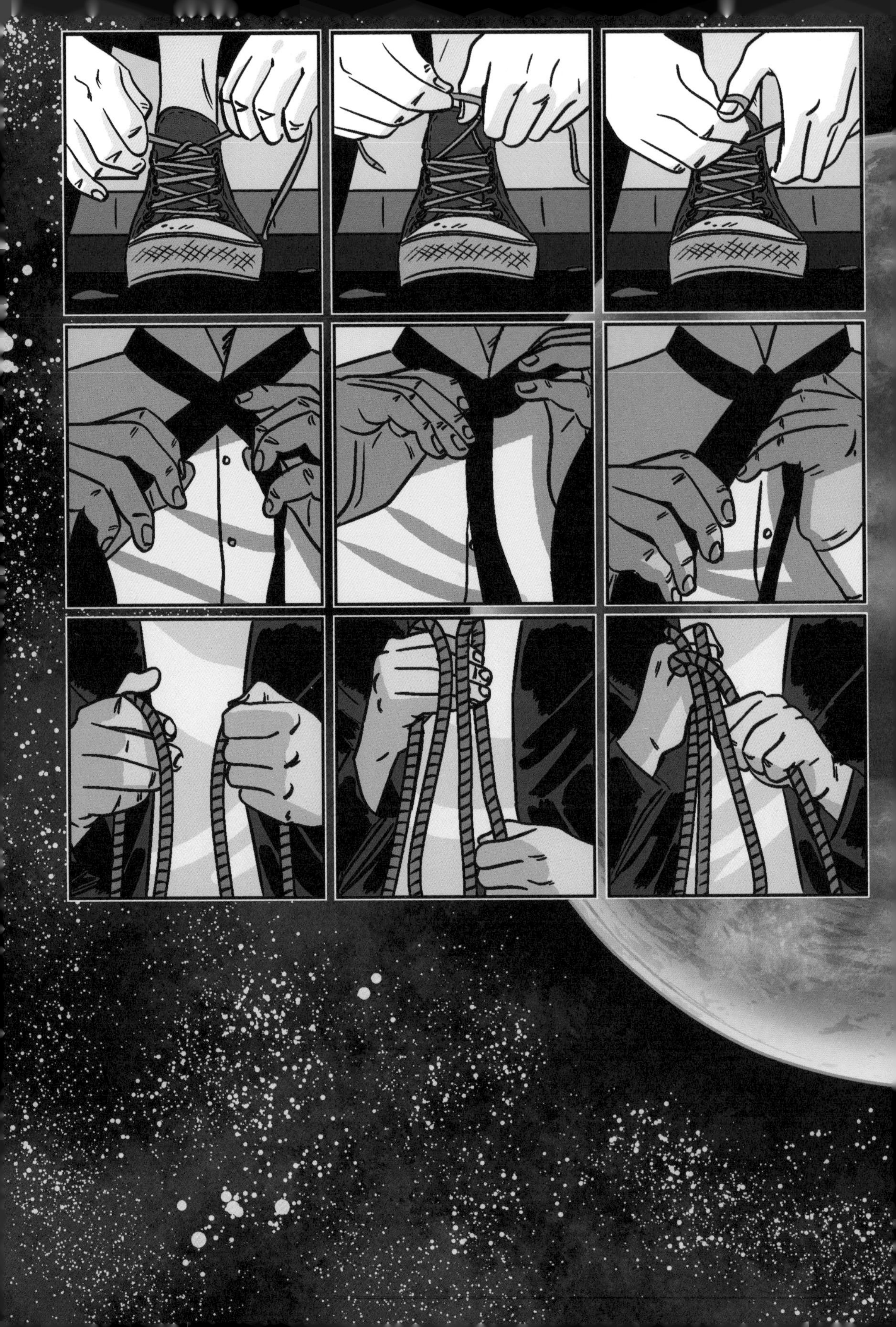

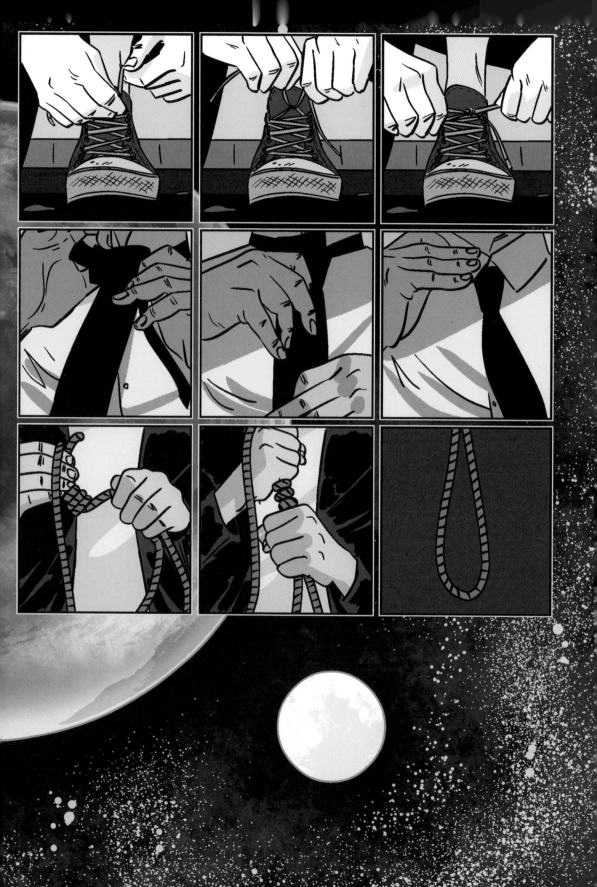

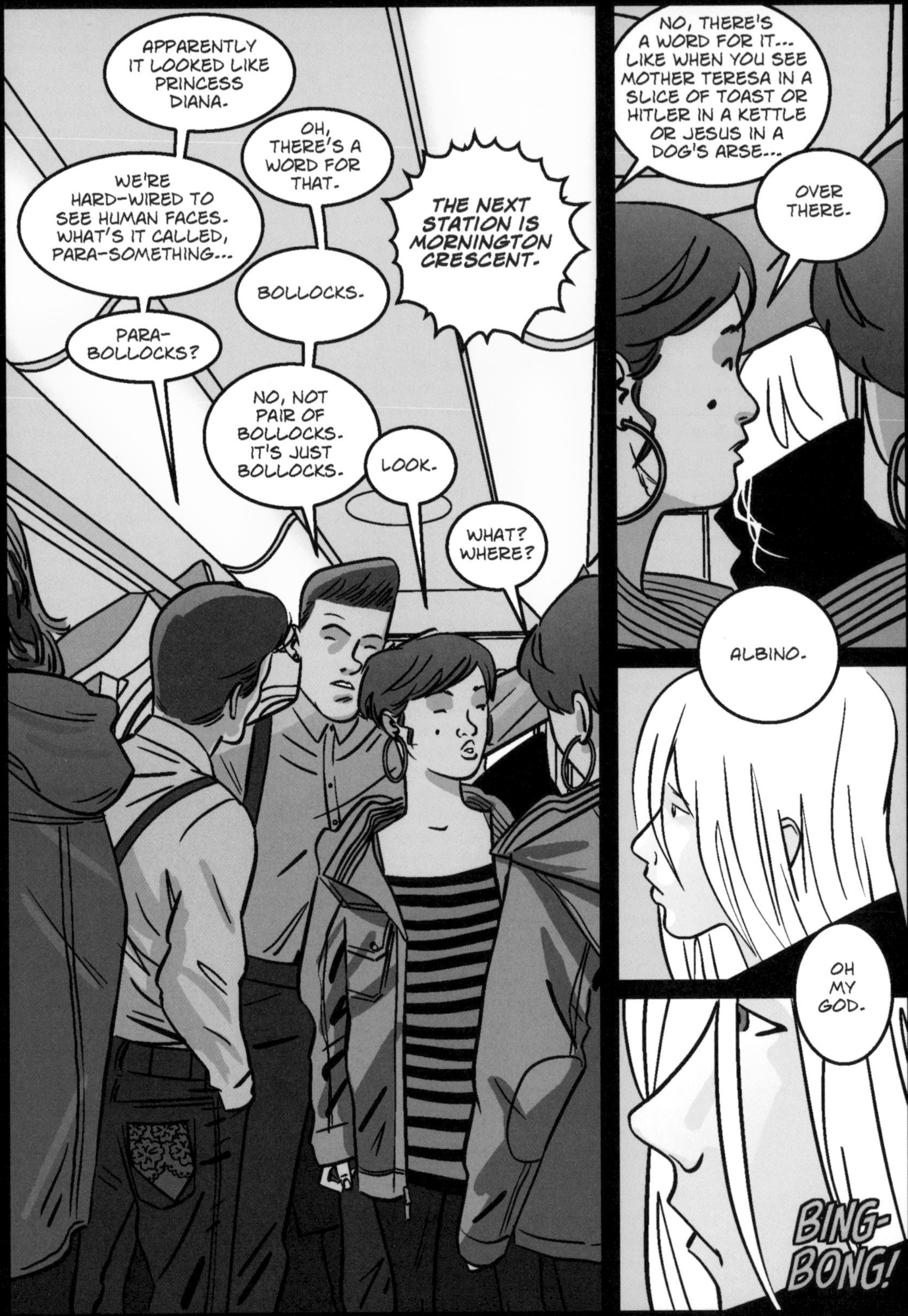
APPARENTLY IT LOOKED LIKE PRINCESS DIANA.
WE'RE HARD-WIRED TO SEE HUMAN FACES. WHAT'S IT CALLED, PARA-SOMETHING...
OH, THERE'S A WORD FOR THAT.
BOLLOCKS.
PARA-BOLLOCKS?
NO, NOT PAIR OF BOLLOCKS. IT'S JUST BOLLOCKS.
THE NEXT STATION IS MORNINGTON CRESCENT.
LOOK.
WHAT? WHERE?
NO, THERE'S A WORD FOR IT... LIKE WHEN YOU SEE MOTHER TERESA IN A SLICE OF TOAST OR HITLER IN A KETTLE OR JESUS IN A DOG'S ARSE...
OVER THERE.
ALBINO.
OH MY GOD.
BING-BONG!

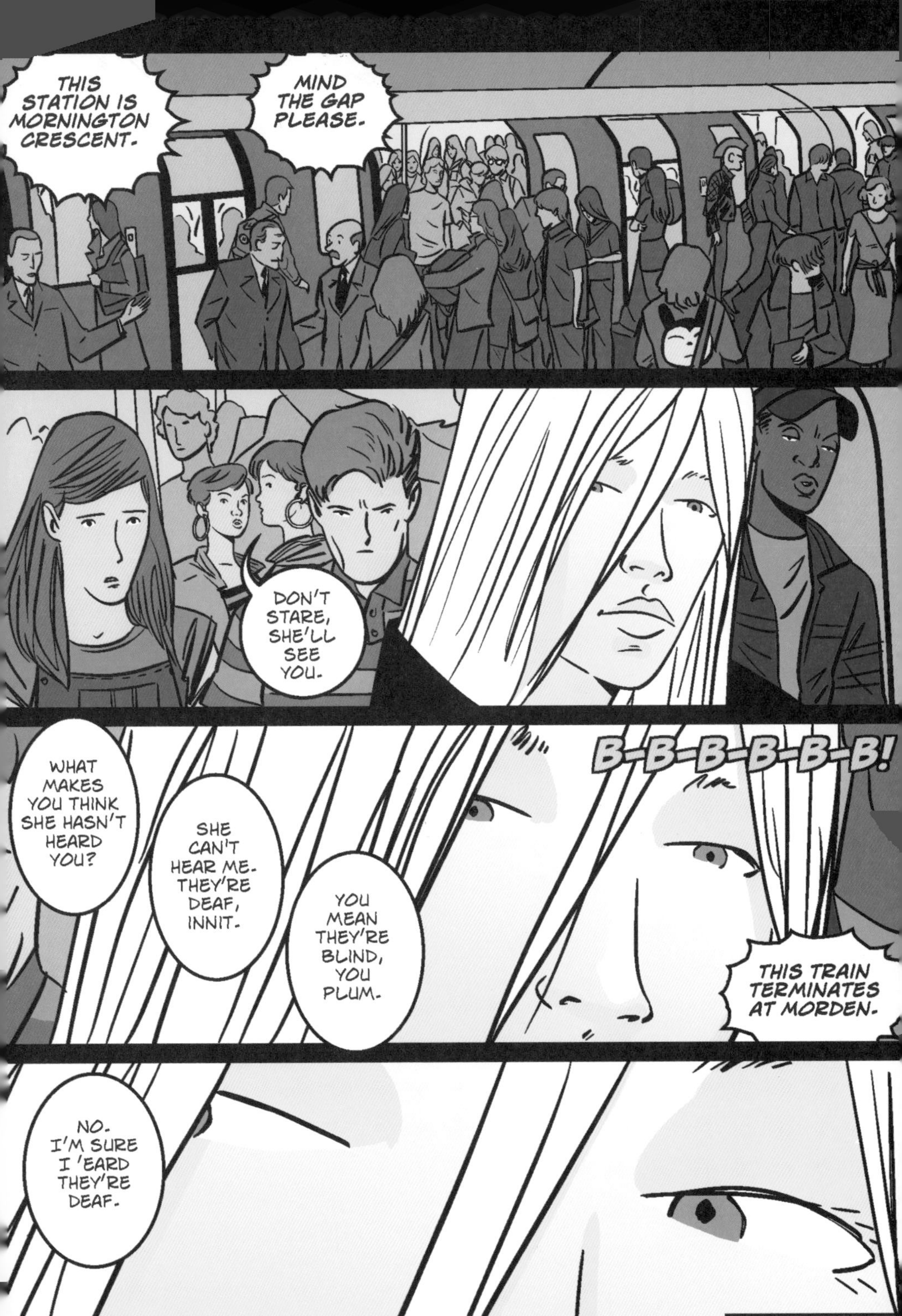
THIS STATION IS MORNINGTON CRESCENT.
MIND THE GAP PLEASE.
DON'T STARE, SHE'LL SEE YOU.
WHAT MAKES YOU THINK SHE HASN'T HEARD YOU?
SHE CAN'T HEAR ME. THEY'RE DEAF, INNIT.
YOU MEAN THEY'RE BLIND, YOU PLUM.
B-B-B-B-B-B!
THIS TRAIN TERMINATES AT MORDEN.
NO. I'M SURE I 'EARD THEY'RE DEAF.
"I'M ALL EARS."

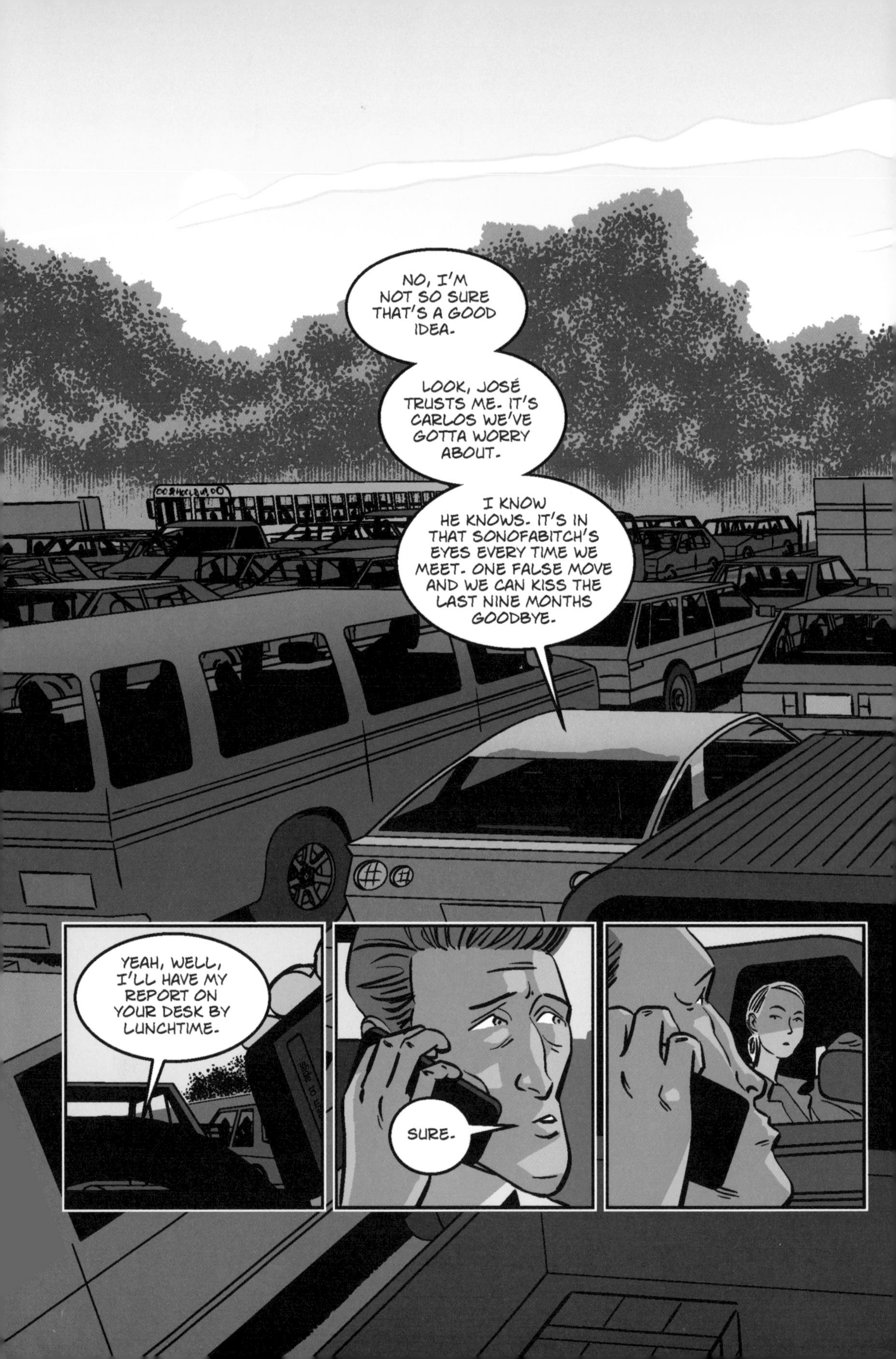
NO, I'M NOT SO SURE THAT'S A GOOD IDEA.
LOOK, JOSÉ TRUSTS ME. IT'S CARLOS WE'VE GOTTA WORRY ABOUT.
I KNOW HE KNOWS. IT'S IN THAT SONOFABITCH'S EYES EVERY TIME WE MEET. ONE FALSE MOVE AND WE CAN KISS THE LAST NINE MONTHS GOODBYE.
YEAH, WELL, I'LL HAVE MY REPORT ON YOUR DESK BY LUNCHTIME.
SURE.

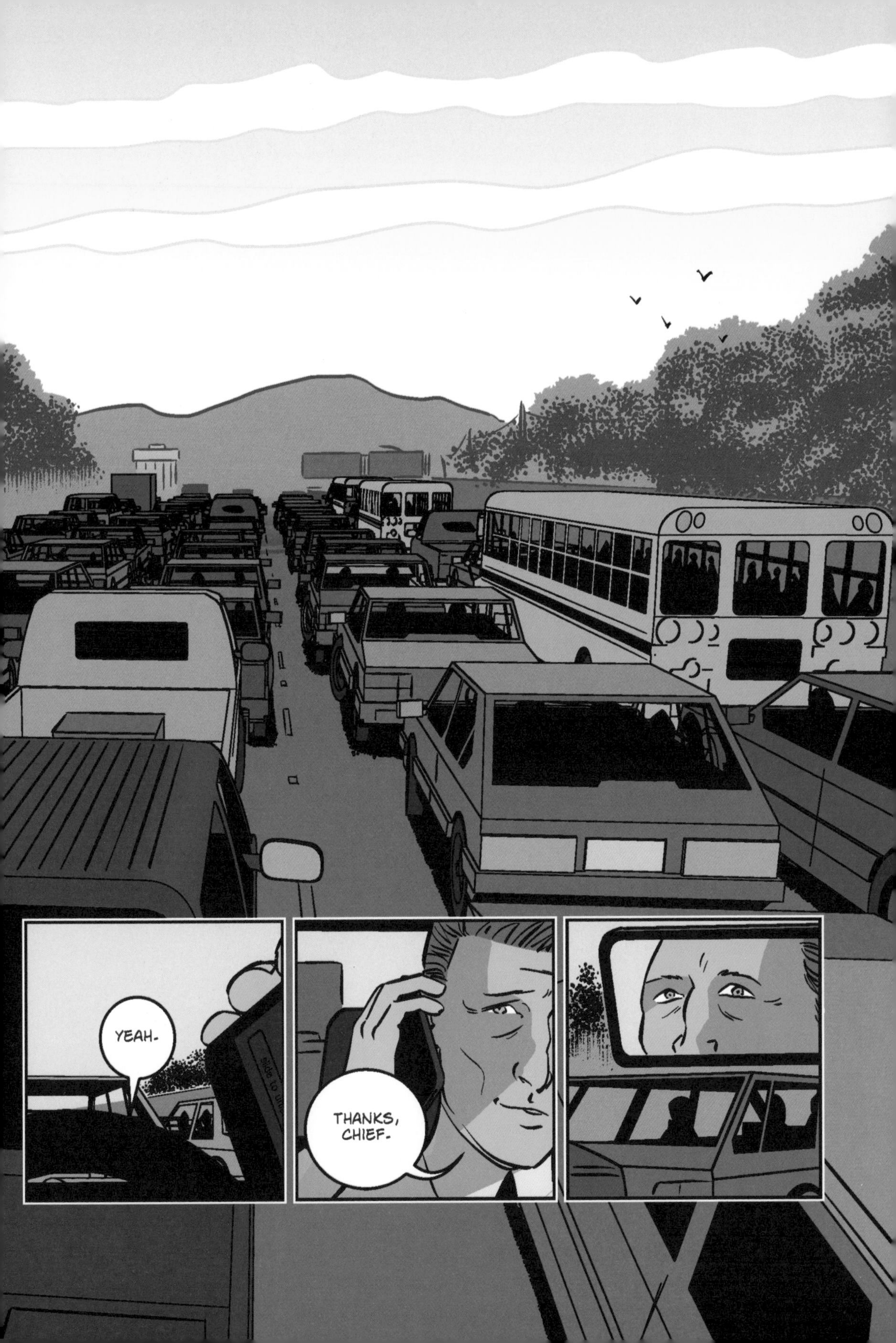
YEAH.
THANKS, CHIEF.

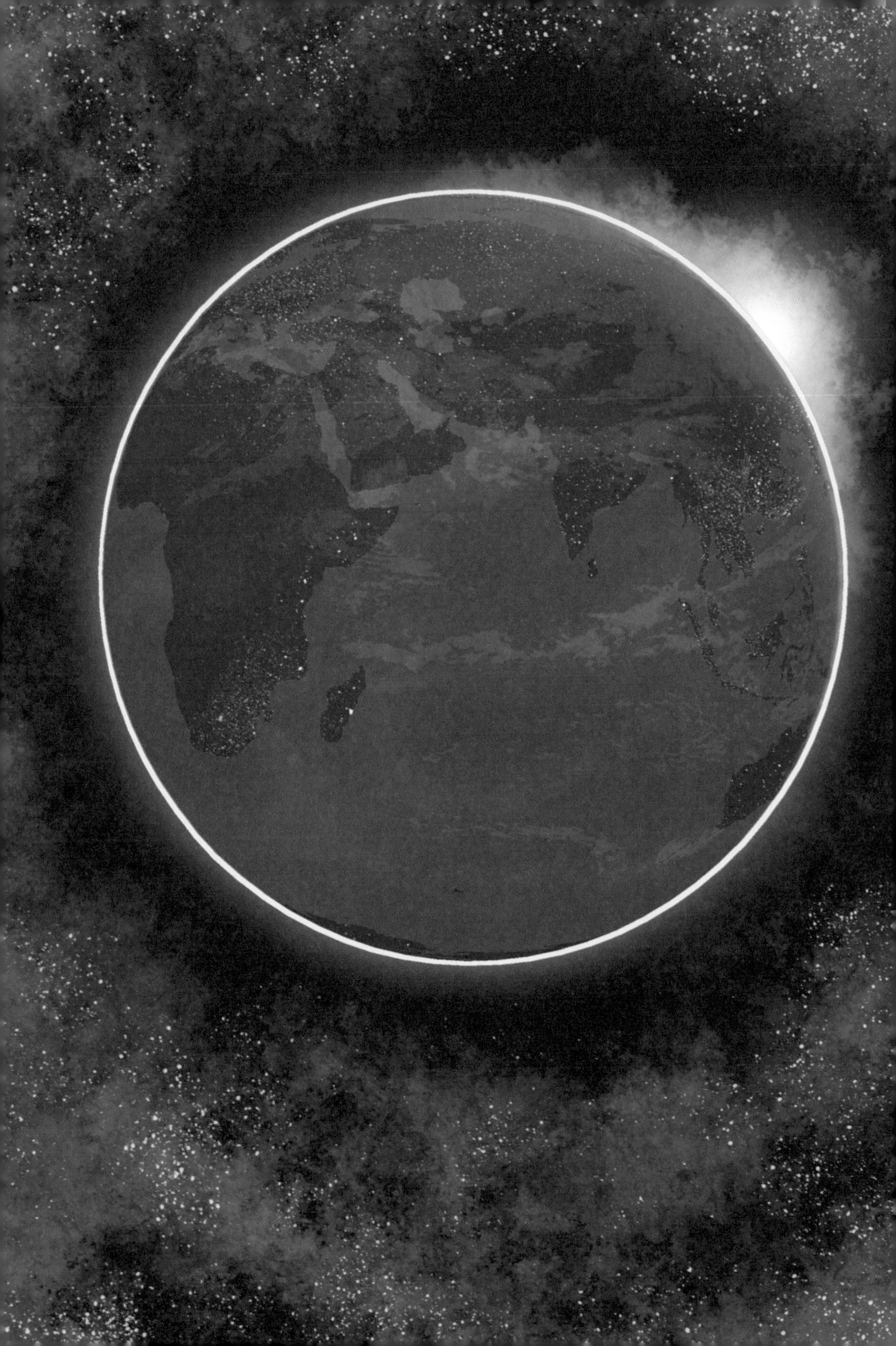

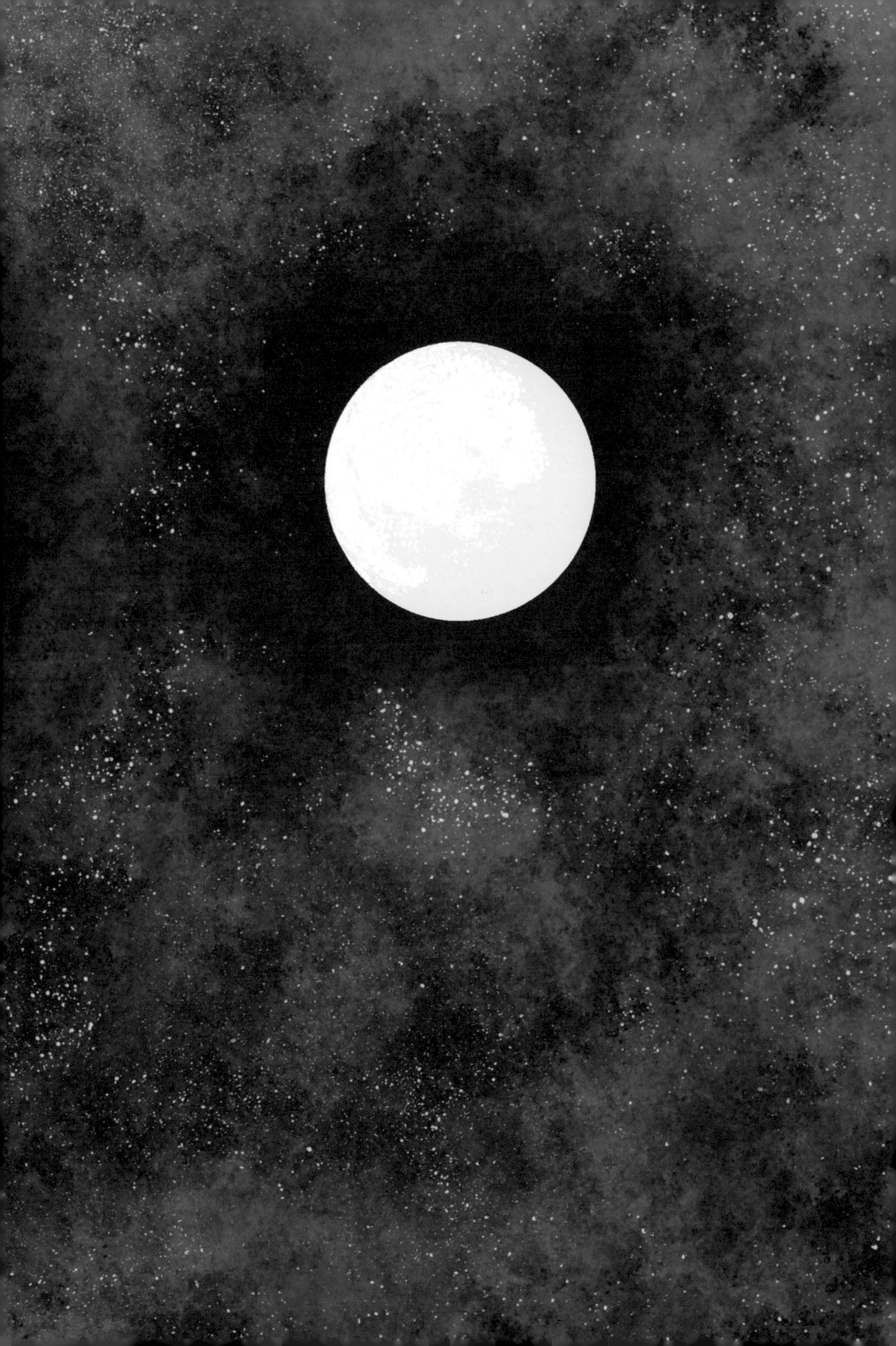

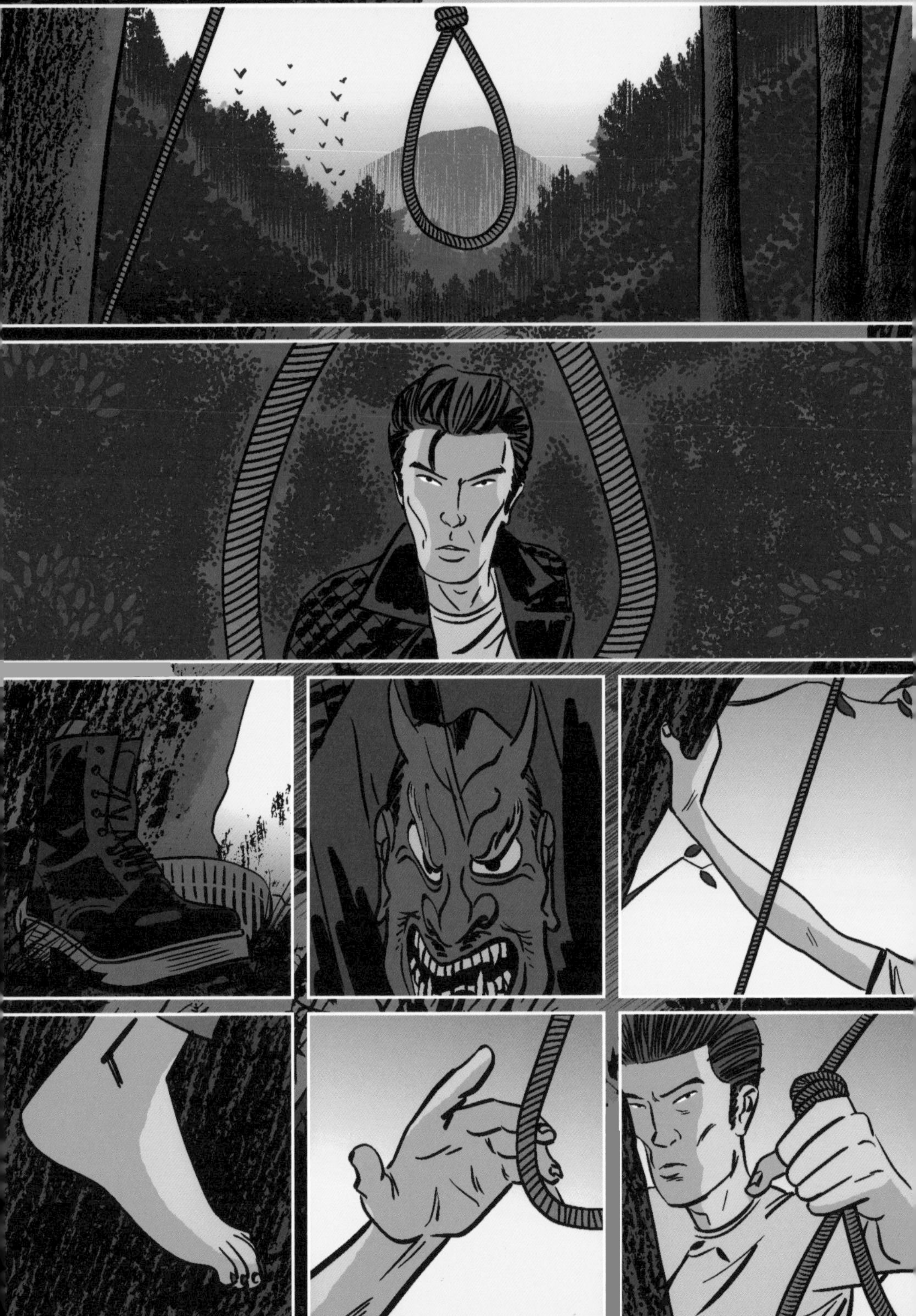

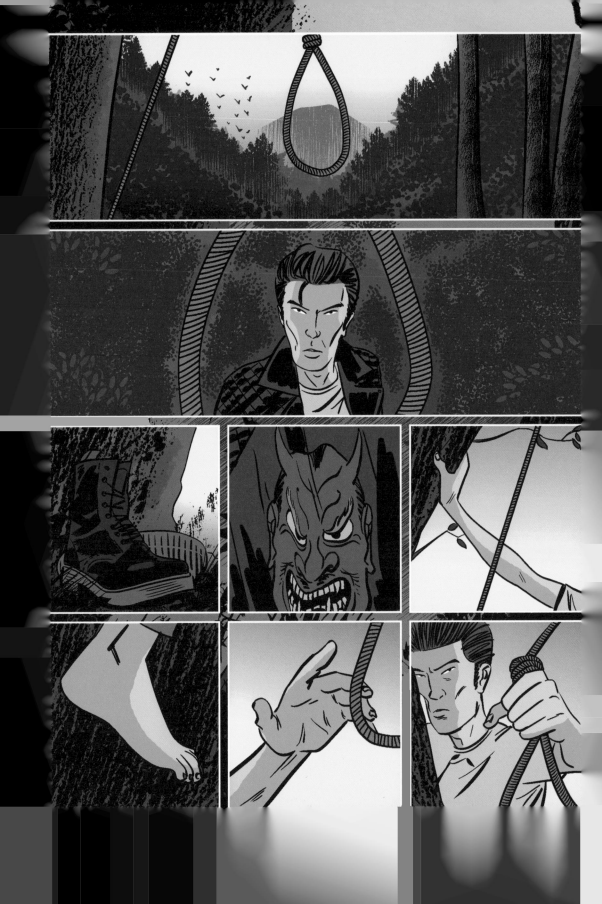

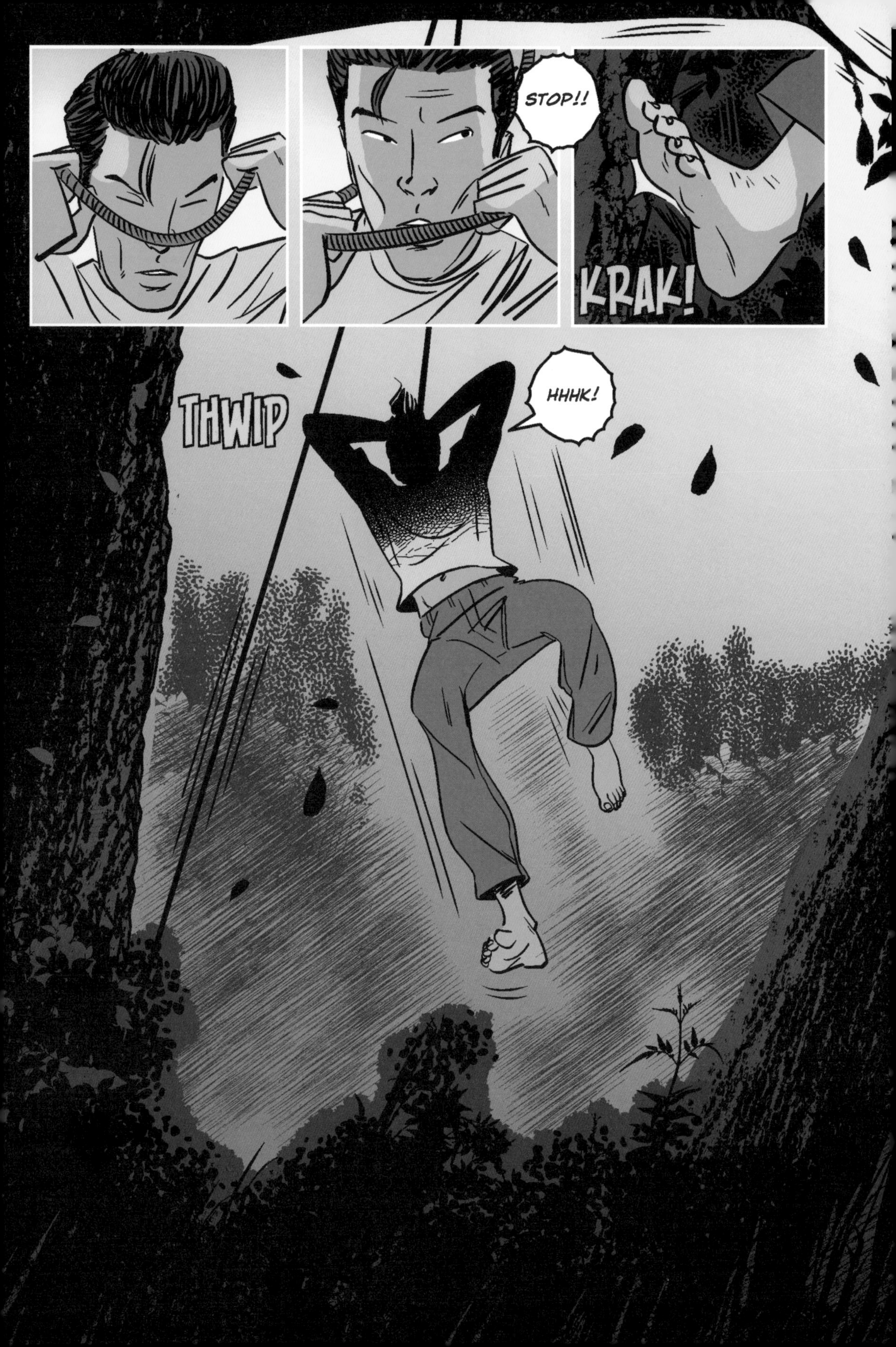
STOP!!
KRAK!
THWIP
HHHK!

THE NEXT STATION IS TOTTENHAM COURT ROAD.
WHAT DOES HE EVEN MEAN 'MIRRORS'?
THAT'S THE REASON I DIDN'T WANT TO SEE HIM ANY MORE... BECAUSE I'D GOT FED UP OF SEEING MYSELF IN HIM.
WHAT A BITCH!
Lower window for ventilation
HE'S SO UP HIMSELF, IT'S UNTRUE.
YEAH, THE FACT HE'D SHAGGED MARTIN, THAT HAD NOTHING TO DO WITH IT...

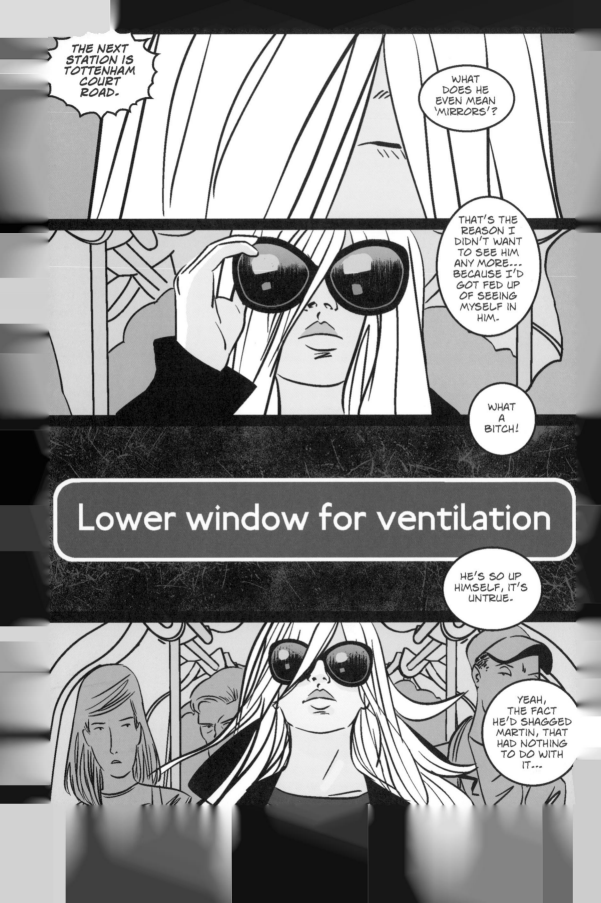

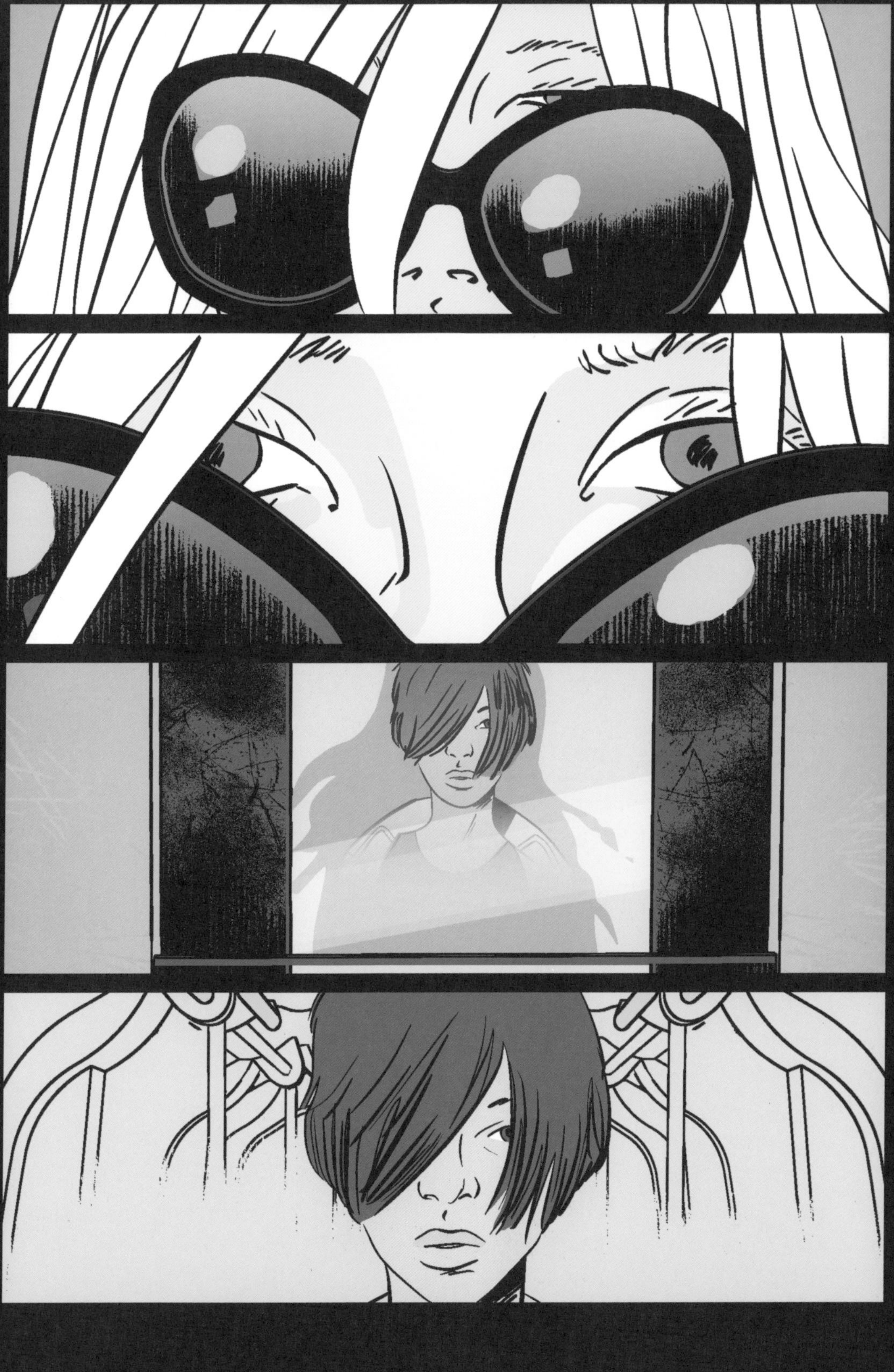

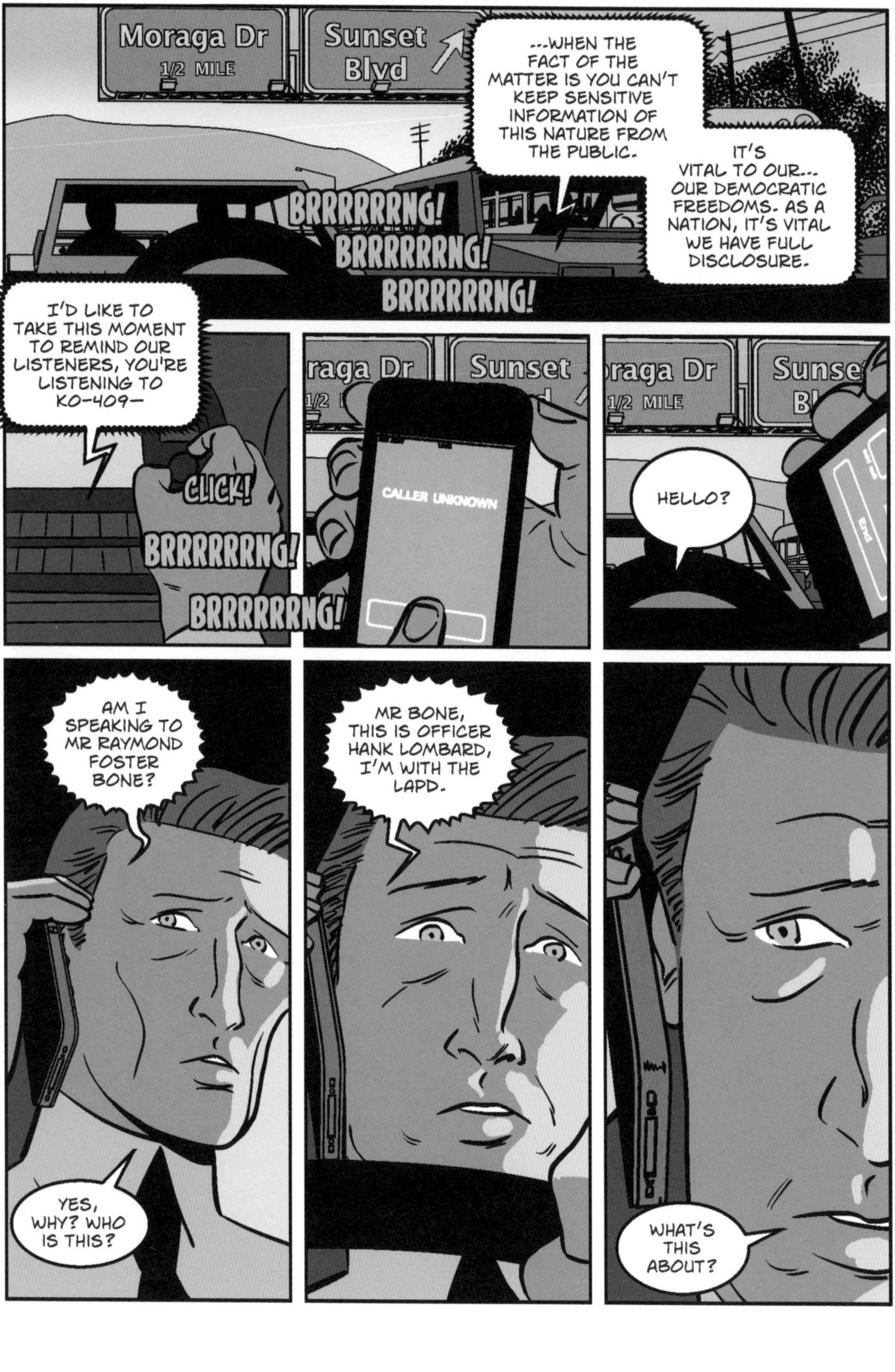
Moraga Dr
1/2 MILE
Sunset Blvd
---WHEN THE FACT OF THE MATTER IS YOU CAN'T KEEP SENSITIVE INFORMATION OF THIS NATURE FROM THE PUBLIC.
IT'S VITAL TO OUR... OUR DEMOCRATIC FREEDOMS. AS A NATION, IT'S VITAL WE HAVE FULL DISCLOSURE.
BRRRRRRNG!
BRRRRRRNG!
BRRRRRRNG!
I'D LIKE TO TAKE THIS MOMENT TO REMIND OUR LISTENERS, YOU'RE LISTENING TO KO-409—
CLICK!
BRRRRRRNG!
BRRRRRRNG!
CALLER UNKNOWN
HELLO?
AM I SPEAKING TO MR RAYMOND FOSTER BONE?
YES, WHY? WHO IS THIS?
MR BONE, THIS IS OFFICER HANK LOMBARD, I'M WITH THE LAPD.
WHAT'S THIS ABOUT?

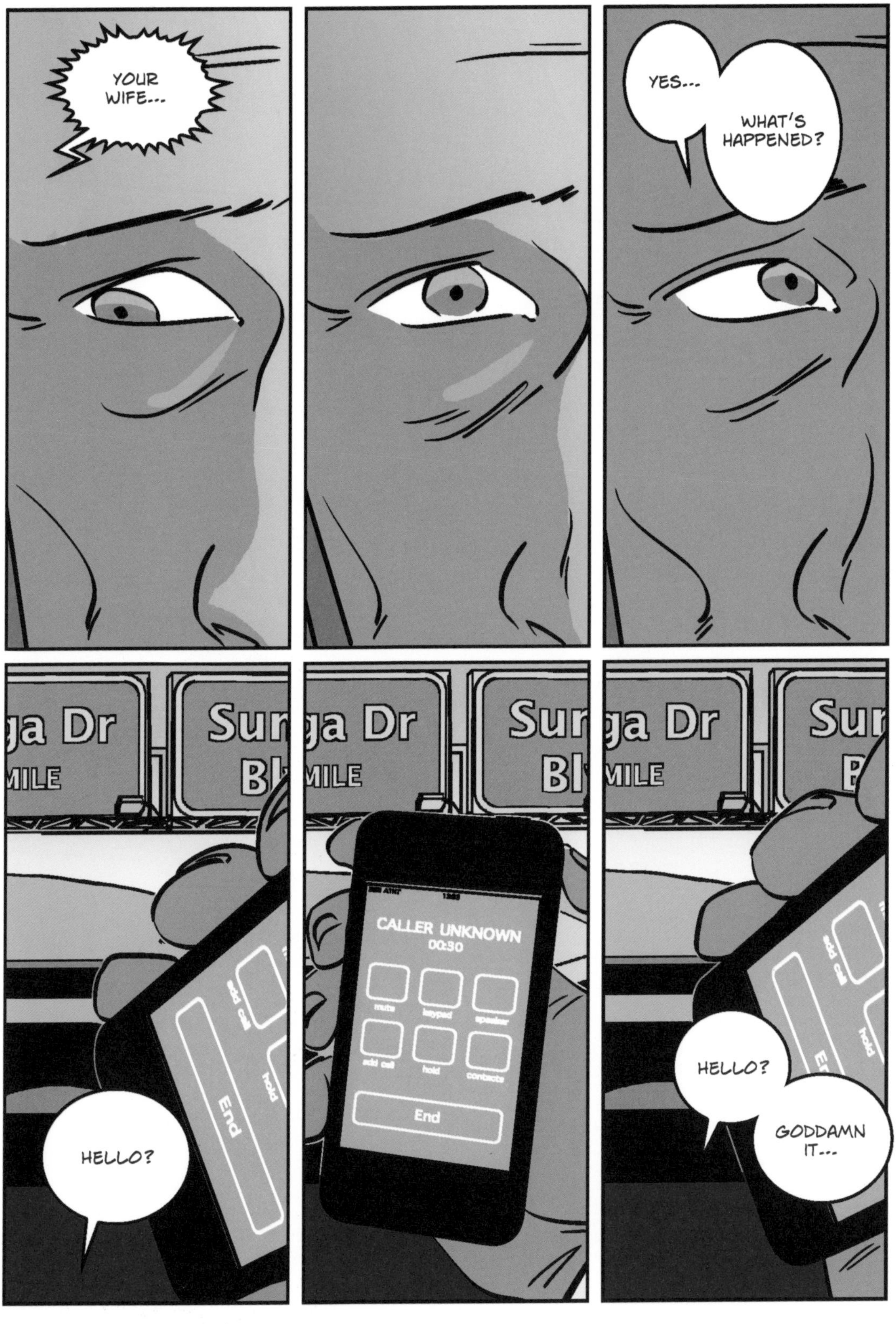
YOUR WIFE...
YES...
WHAT'S HAPPENED?
Surga Dr
MILE
Bl
HELLO?
CALLER UNKNOWN
00:30
mute
keypad
speaker
add call
hold
contacts
End
HELLO?
GODDAMN IT...

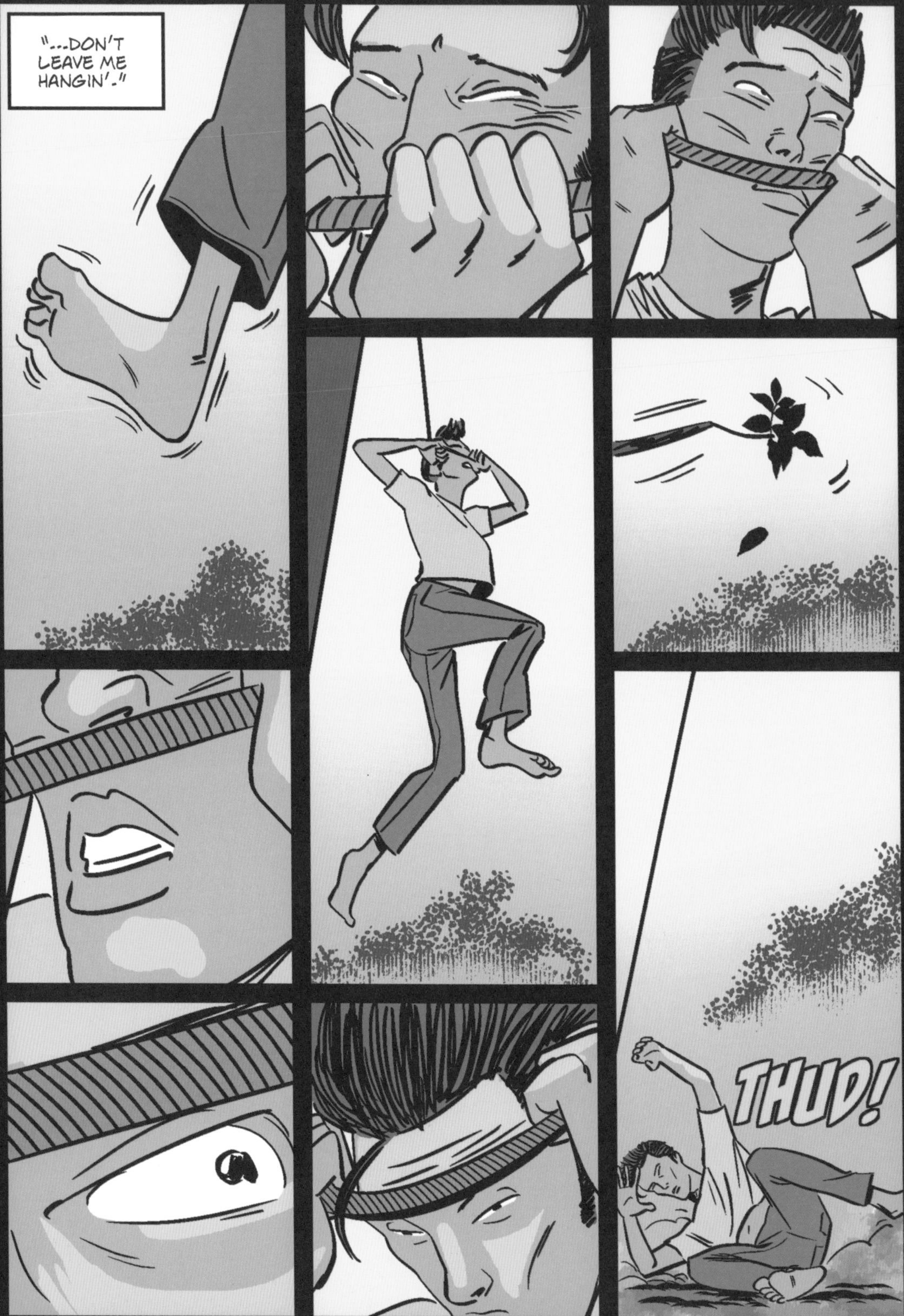
"...DON'T LEAVE ME HANGIN'."
THUD!

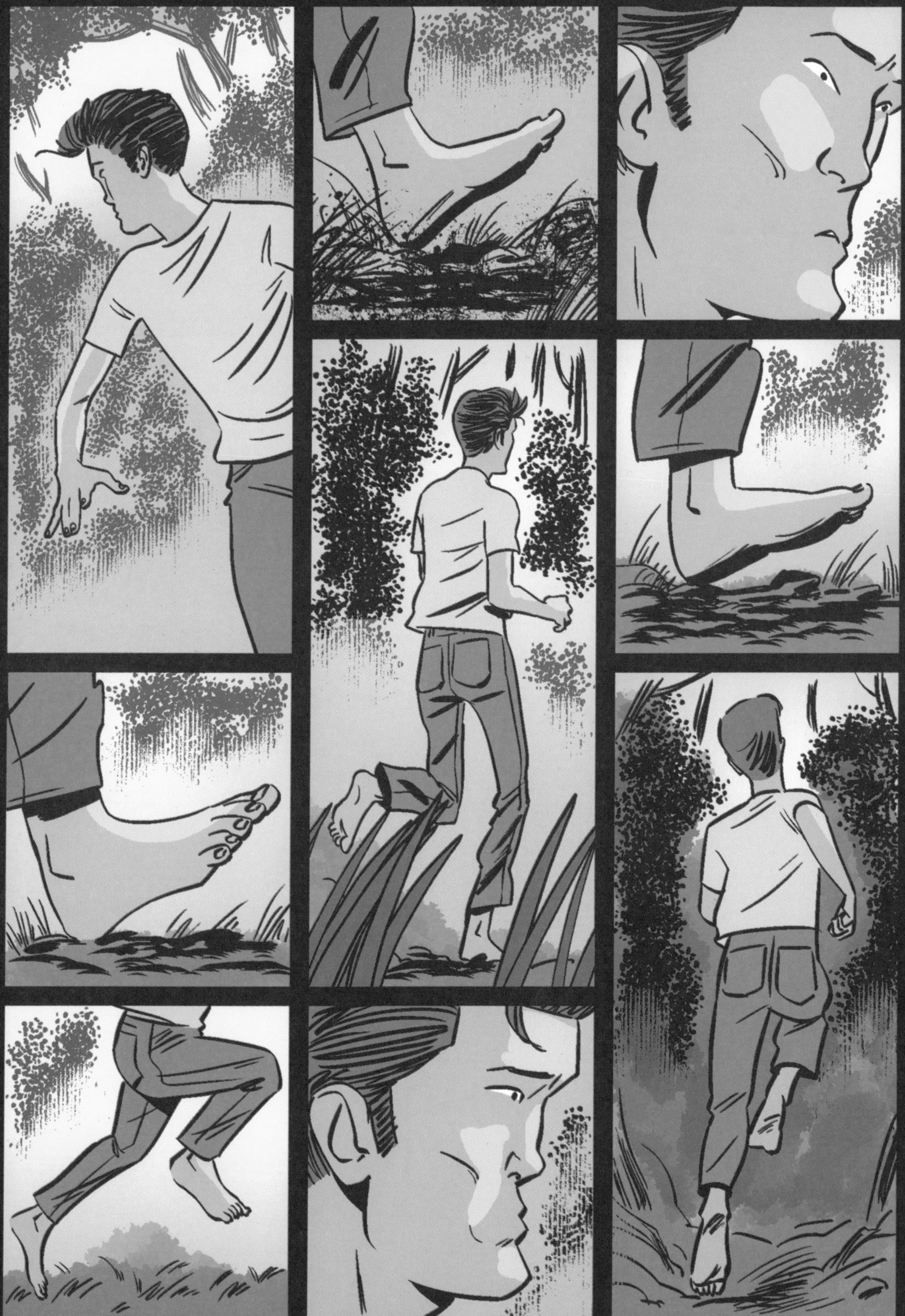

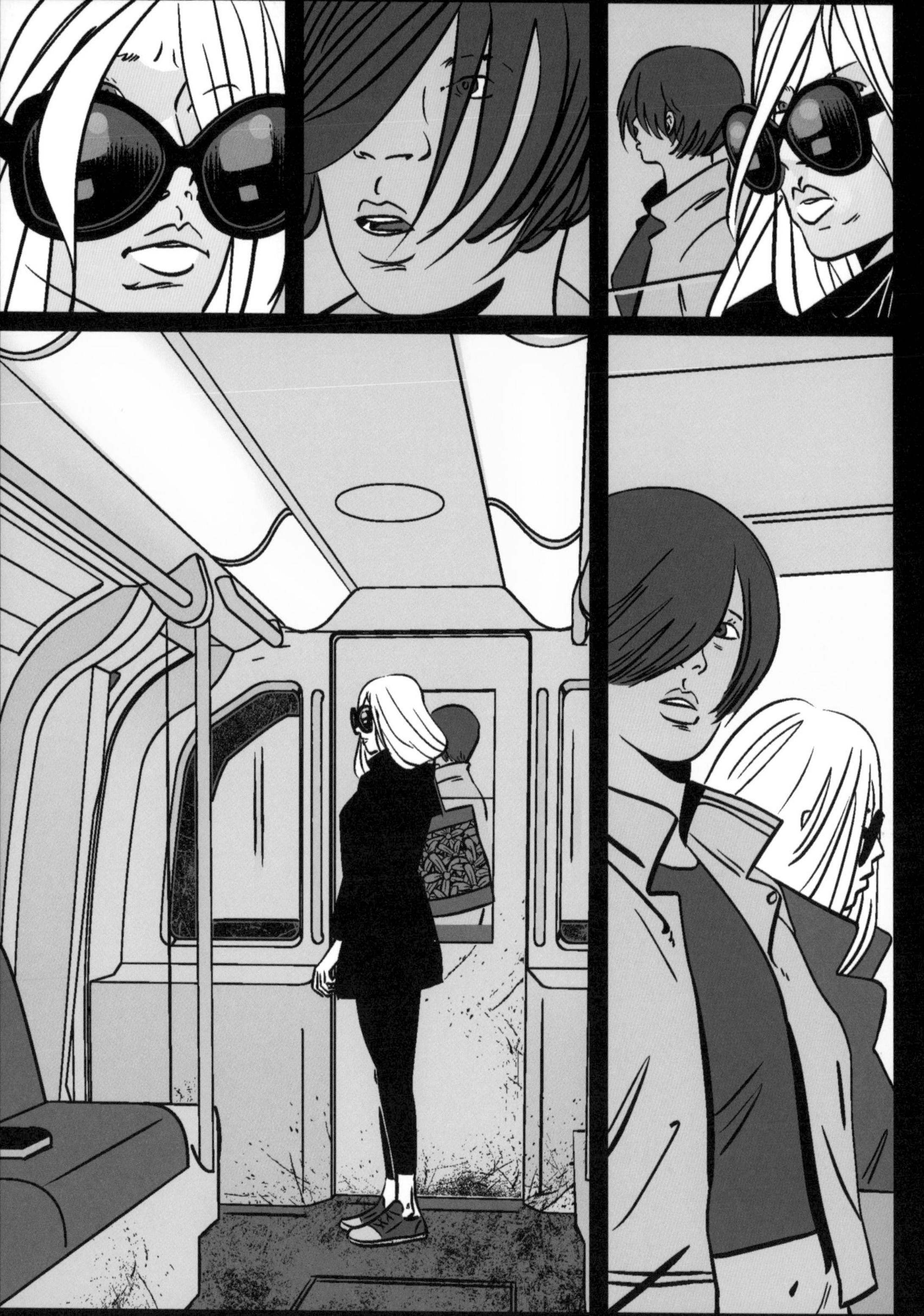

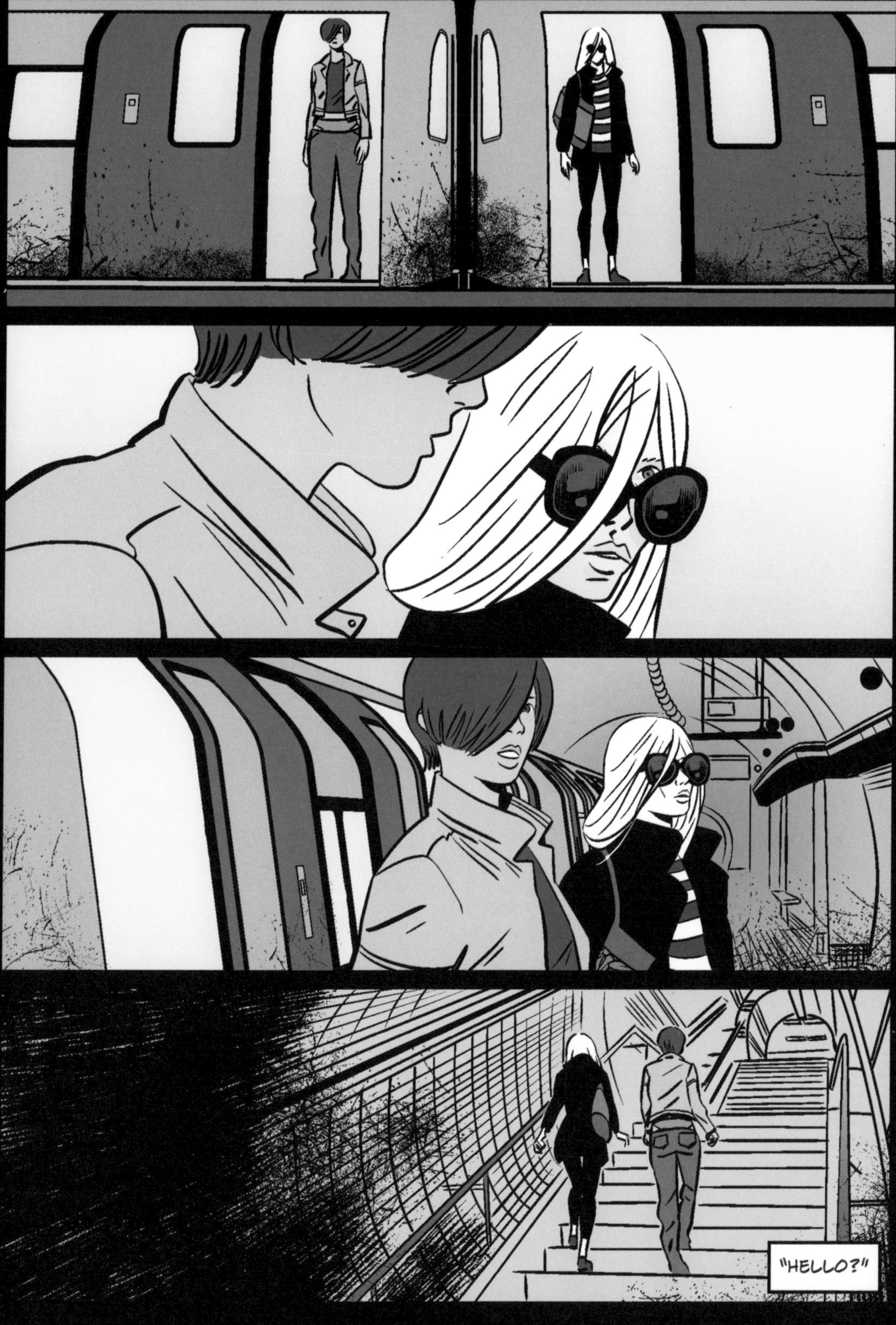
"HELLO?"

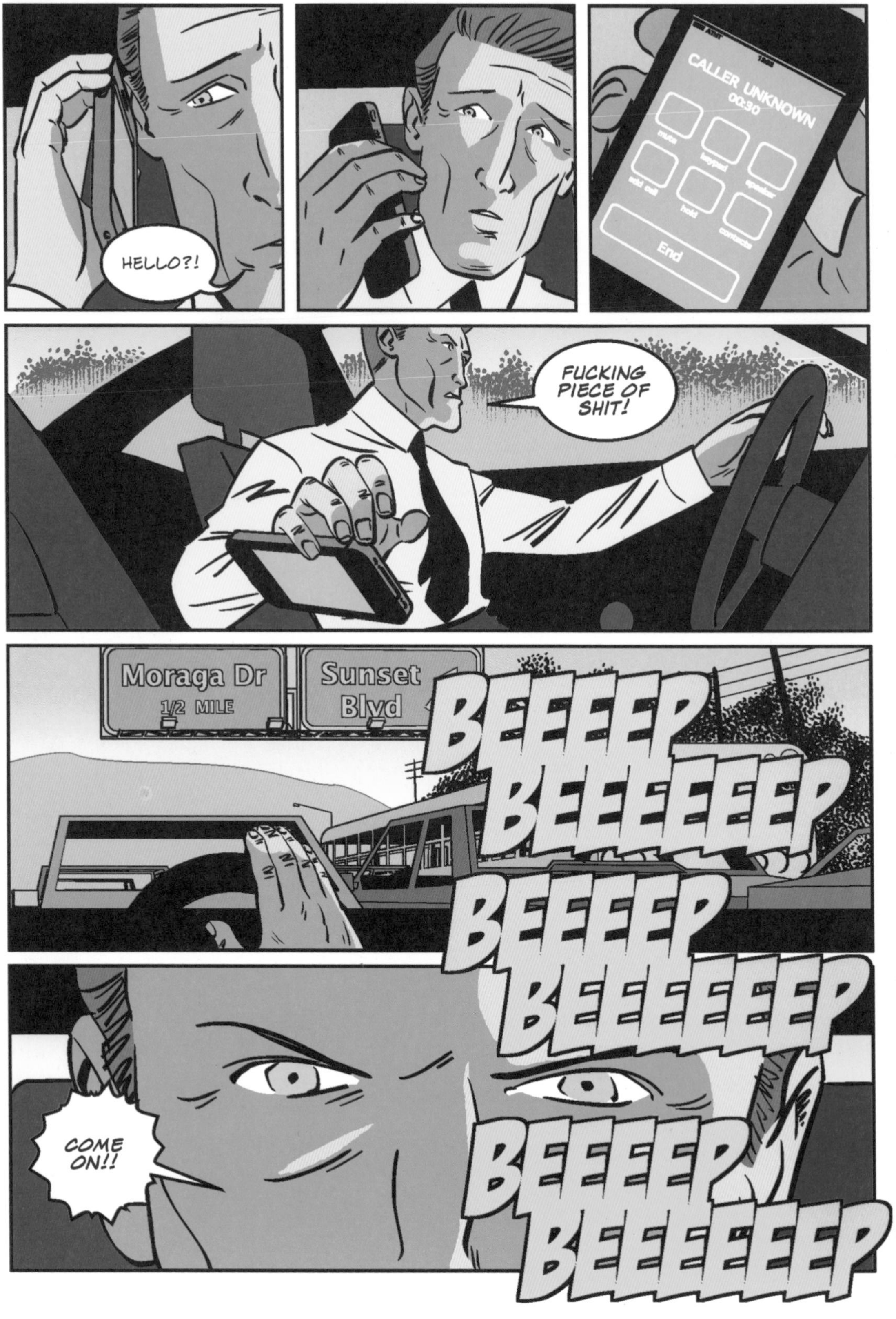
HELLO?!
CALLER UNKNOWN
00:30
mute
keypad
speaker
add call
hold
contacts
End
FUCKING PIECE OF SHIT!
Moraga Dr
1/2 MILE
Sunset Blvd
BEEEEP
BEEEEEEP
BEEEEP
BEEEEEEP
COME ON!!
BEEEEP
BEEEEEEP

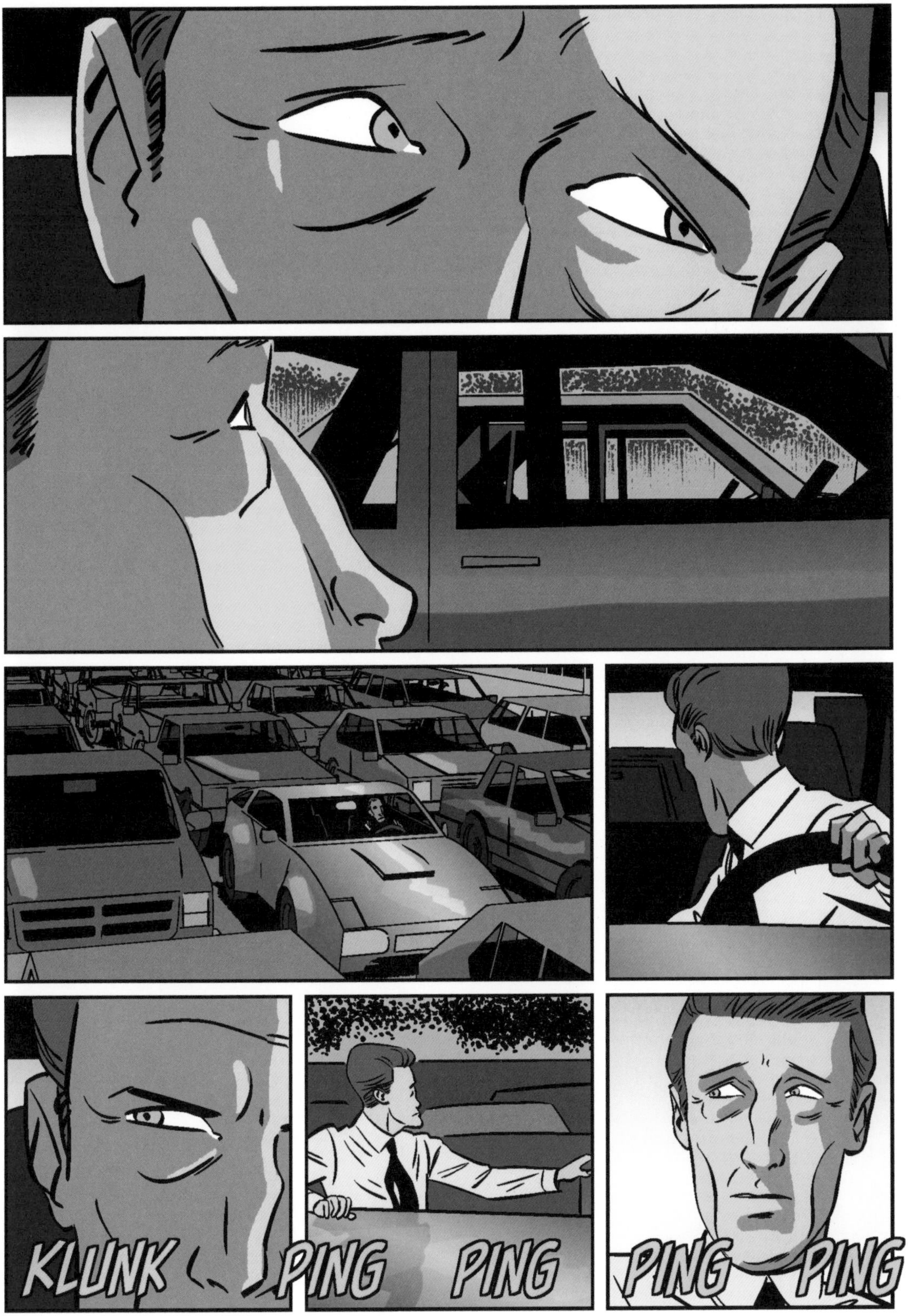
KLUNK
PING
PING
PING
PING

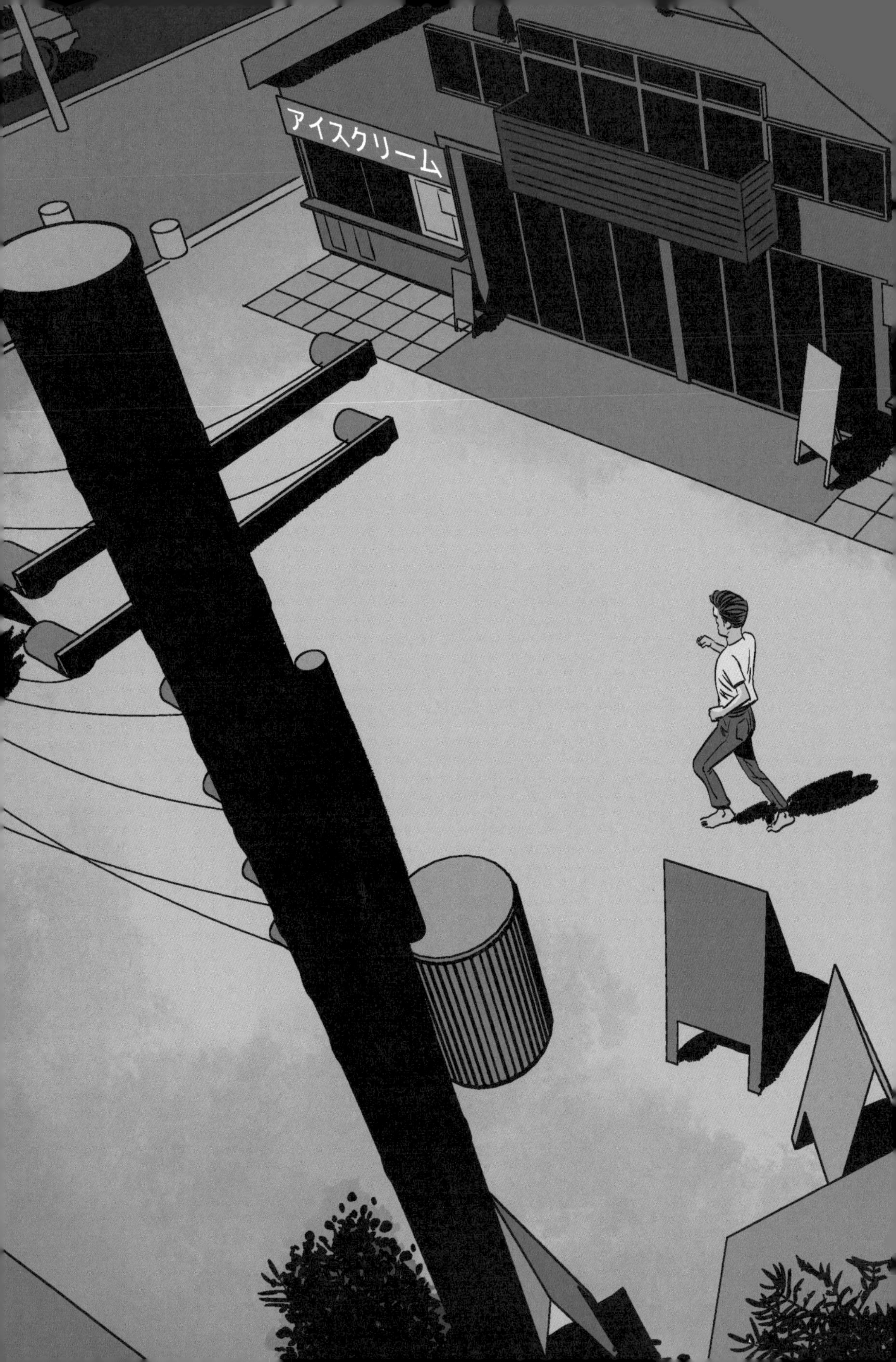
アイスクリーム

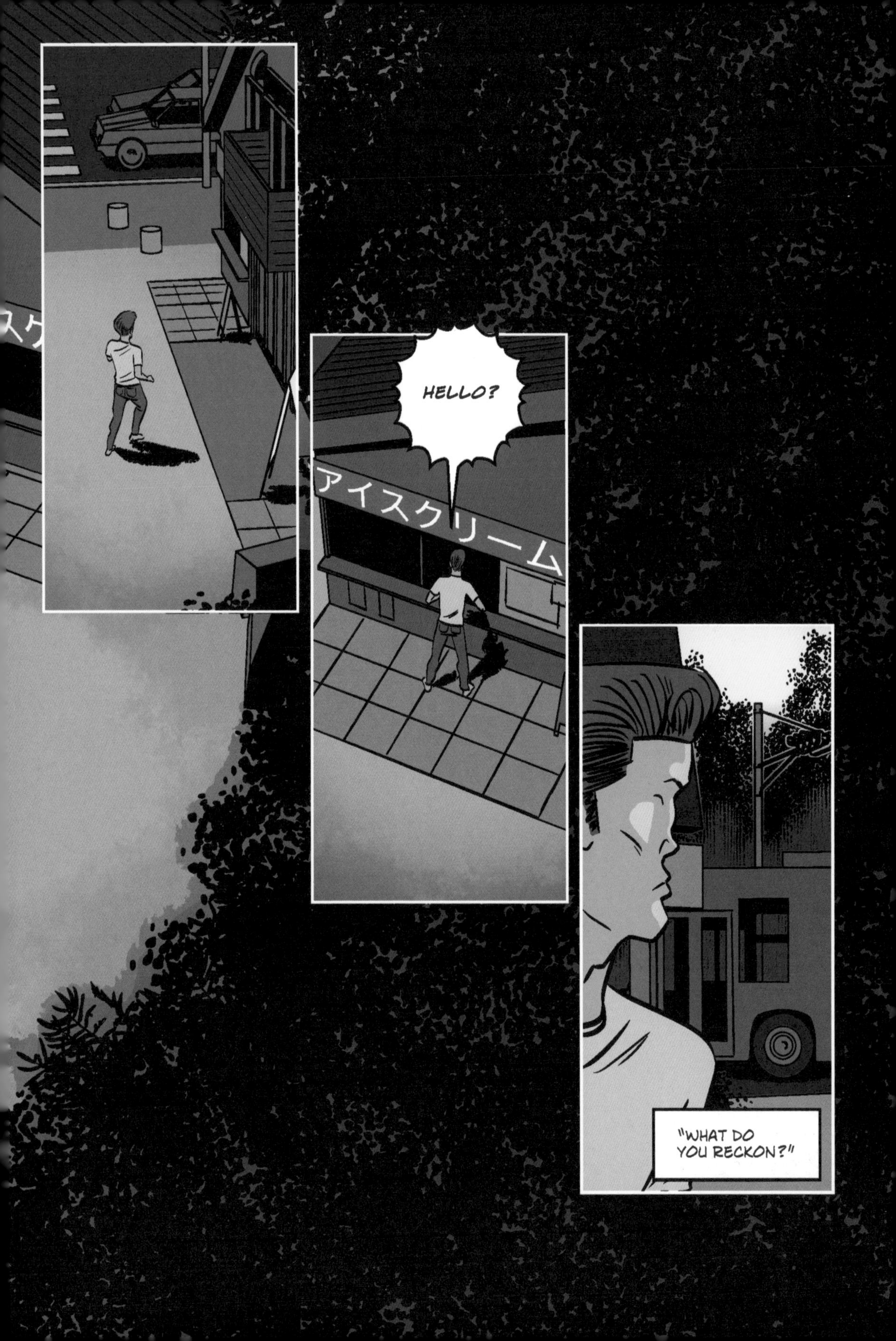
スク
HELLO?
アイスクリーム
"WHAT DO YOU RECKON?"

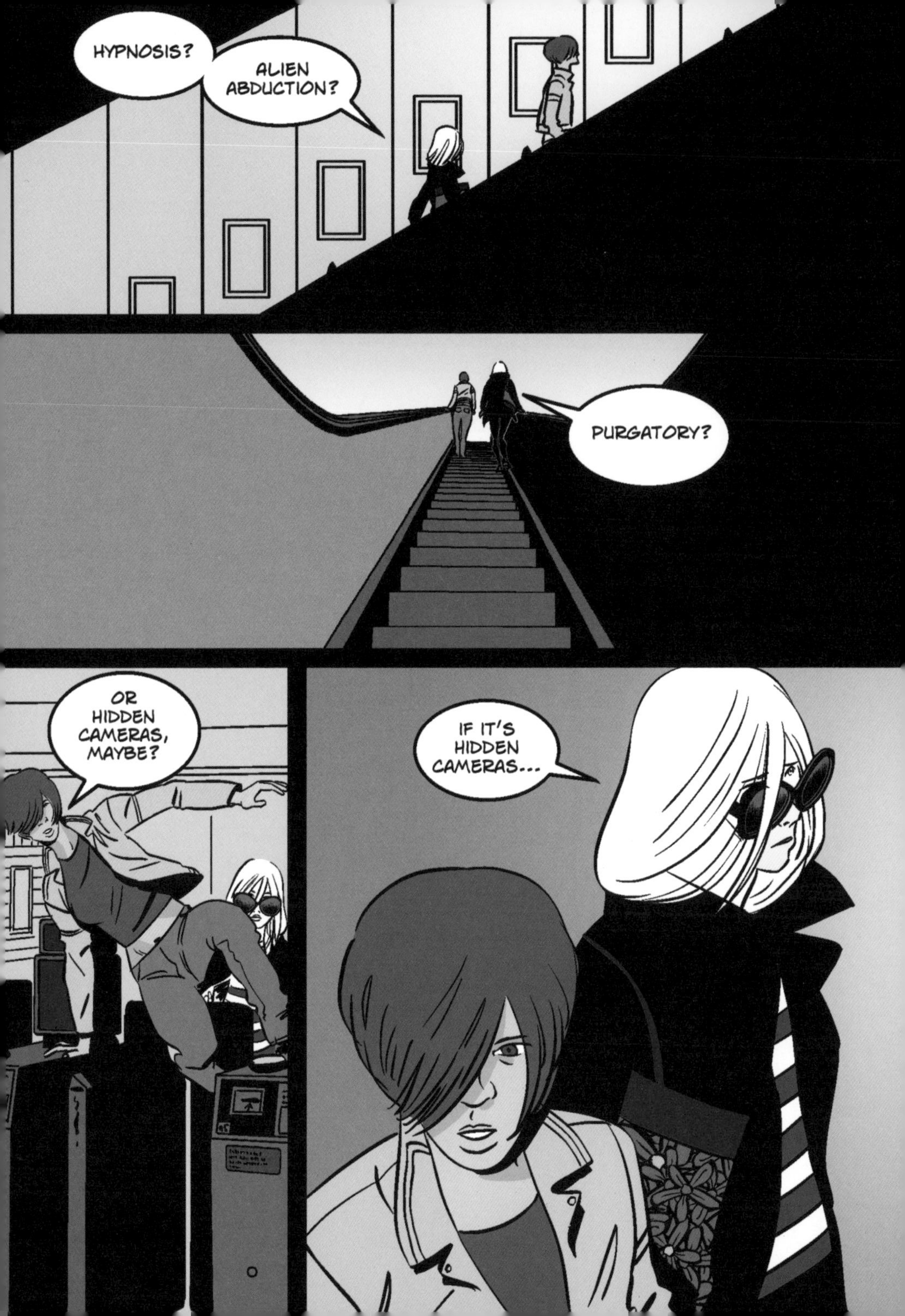
HYPNOSIS?
ALIEN ABDUCTION?
PURGATORY?
OR HIDDEN CAMERAS, MAYBE?
IF IT'S HIDDEN CAMERAS...

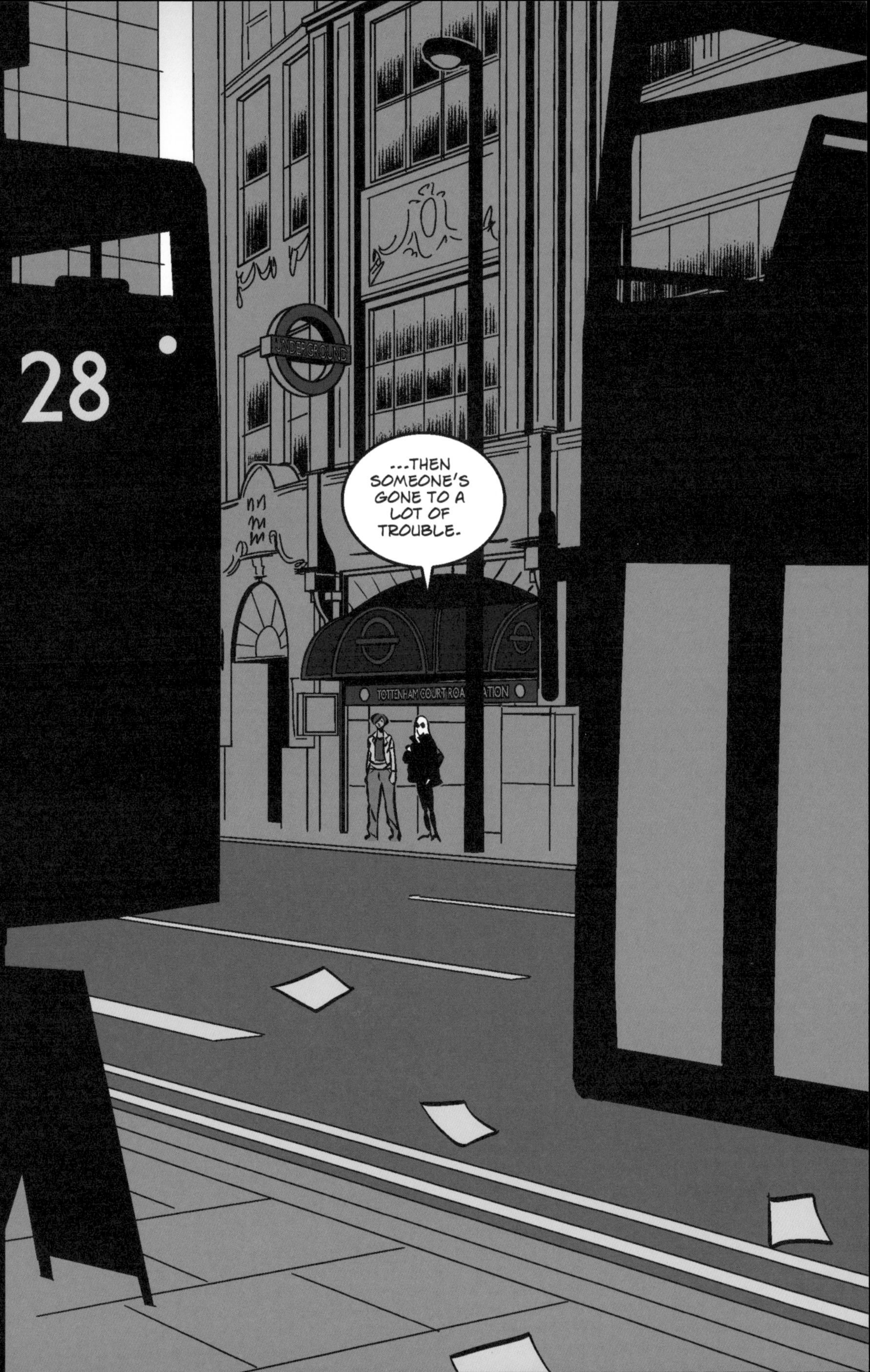
28
UNDERGROUND
...THEN SOMEONE'S GONE TO A LOT OF TROUBLE.

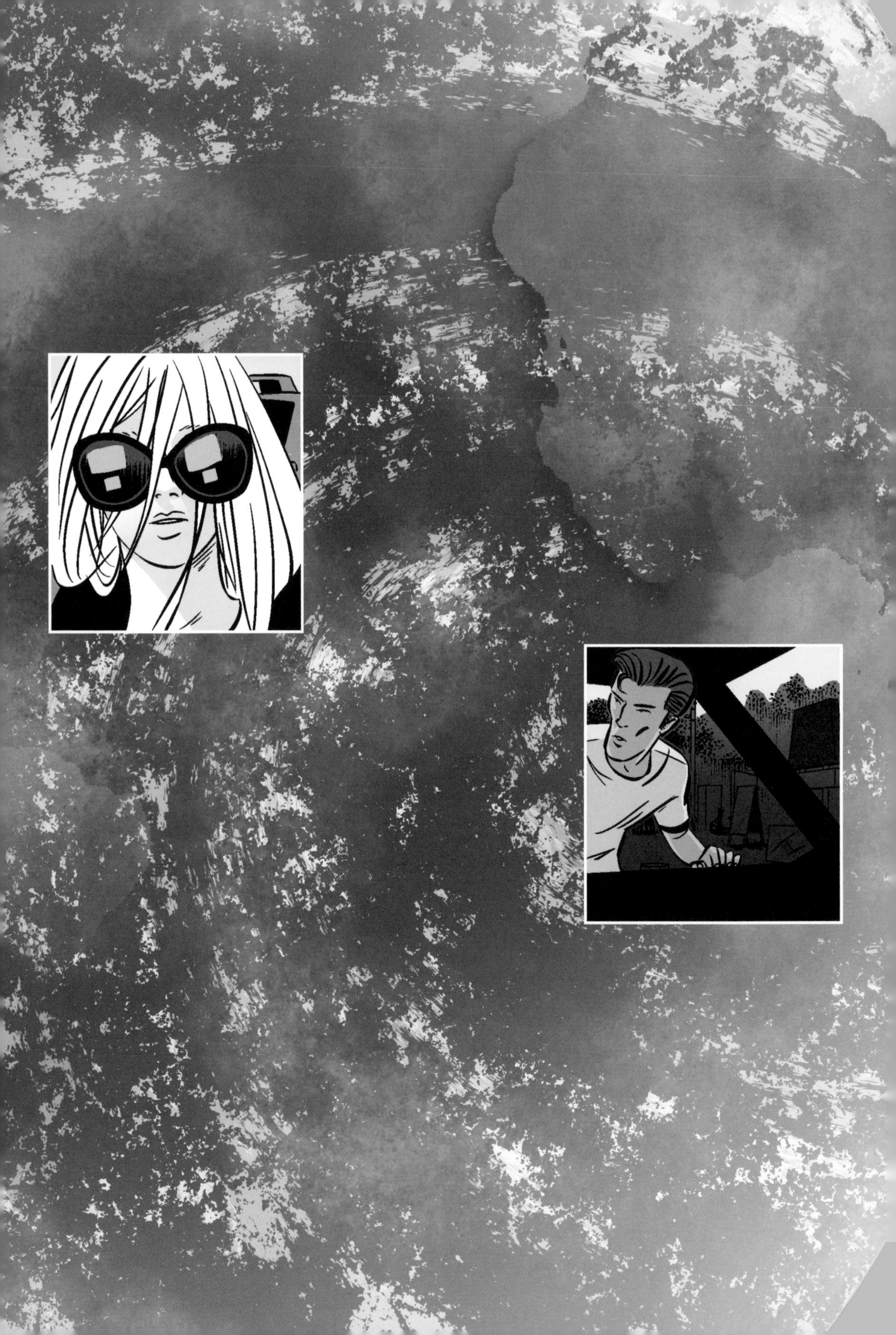

"DO YOU THINK IT'S JUST US?"

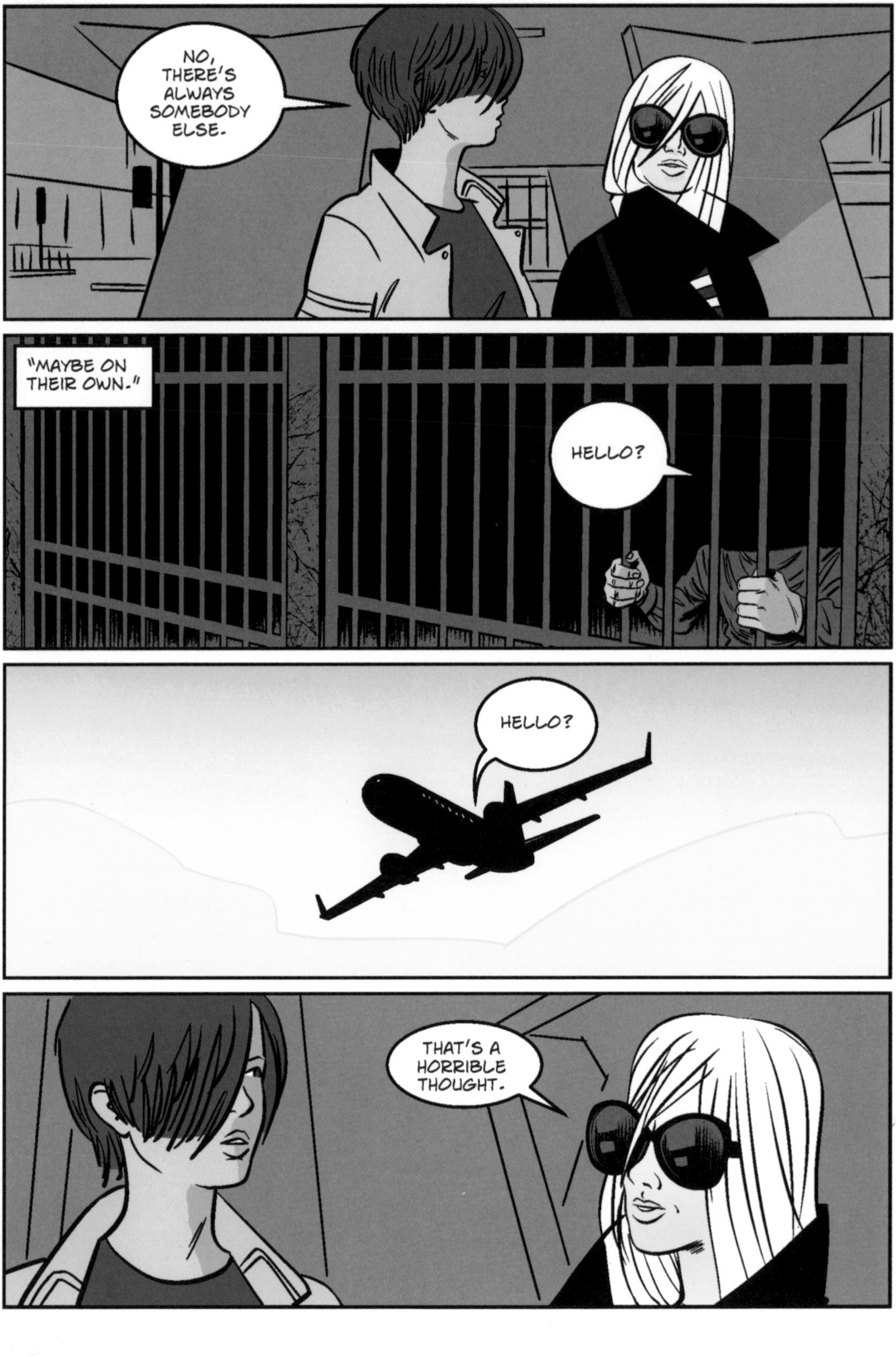
NO, THERE'S ALWAYS SOMEBODY ELSE.
"MAYBE ON THEIR OWN."
HELLO?
HELLO?
THAT'S A HORRIBLE THOUGHT.

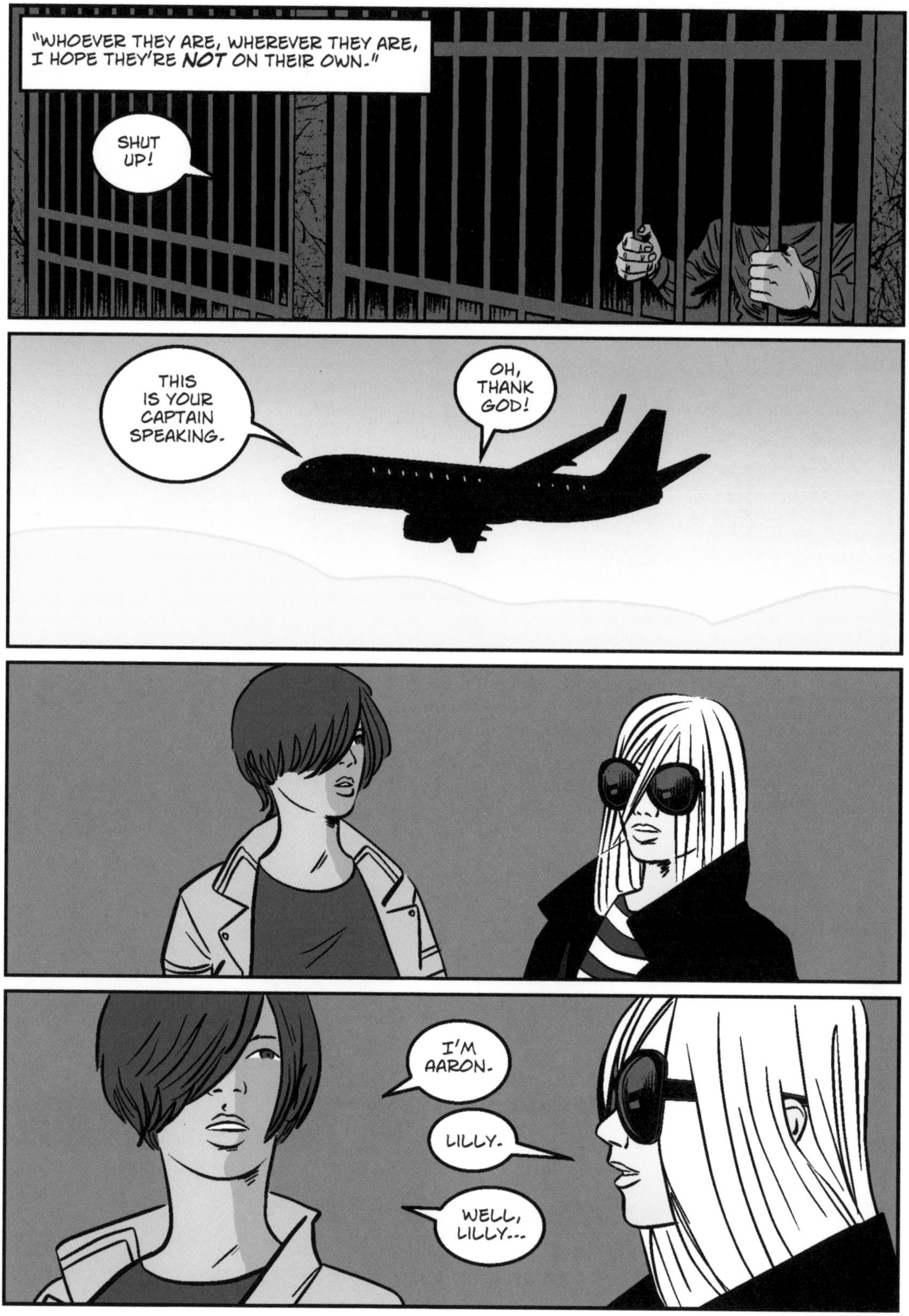
"WHOEVER THEY ARE, WHEREVER THEY ARE, I HOPE THEY'RE NOT ON THEIR OWN."
SHUT UP!
THIS IS YOUR CAPTAIN SPEAKING.
OH, THANK GOD!
I'M AARON.
LILLY.
WELL, LILLY...

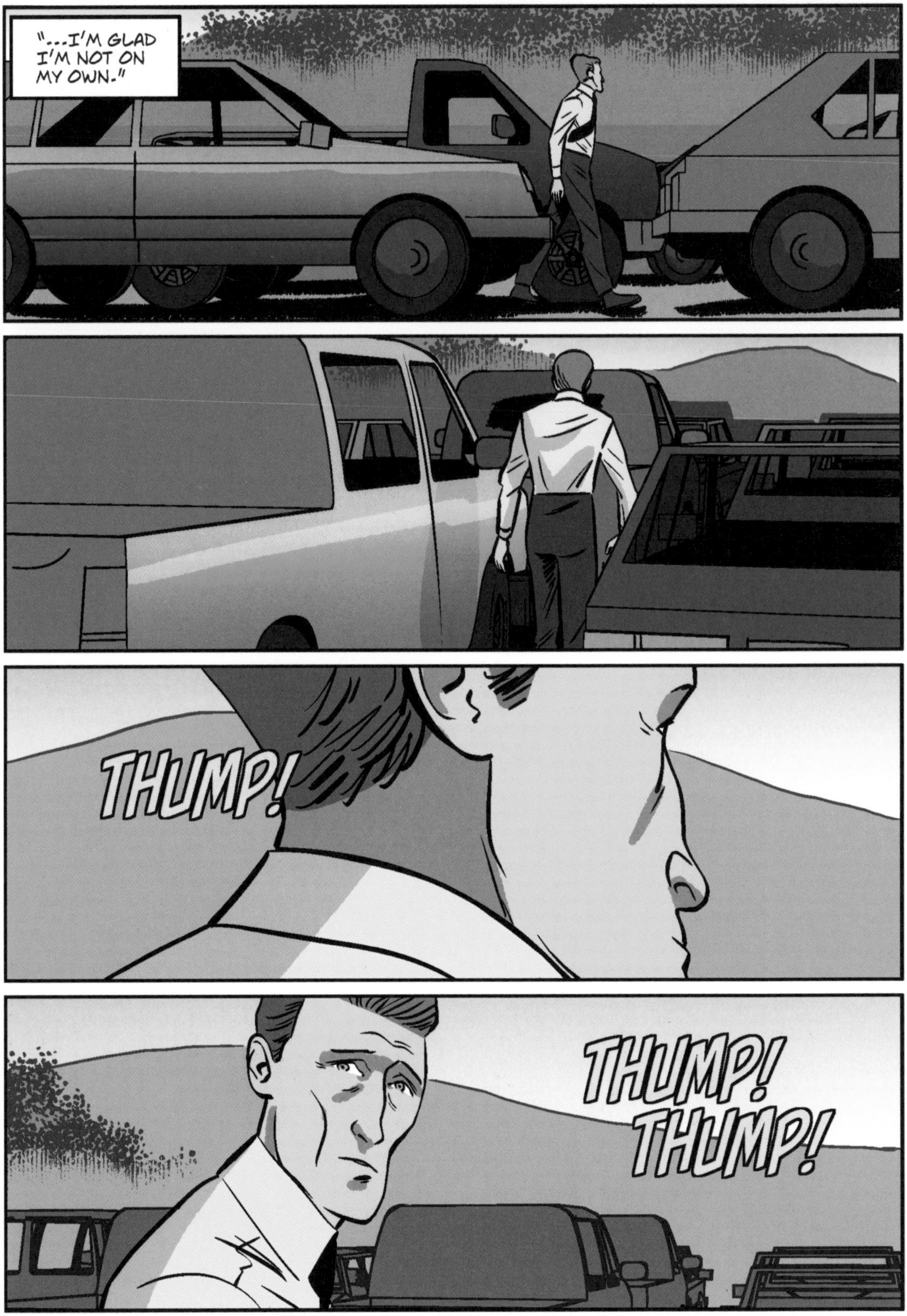
"...I'M GLAD I'M NOT ON MY OWN."
THUMP!
THUMP! THUMP!

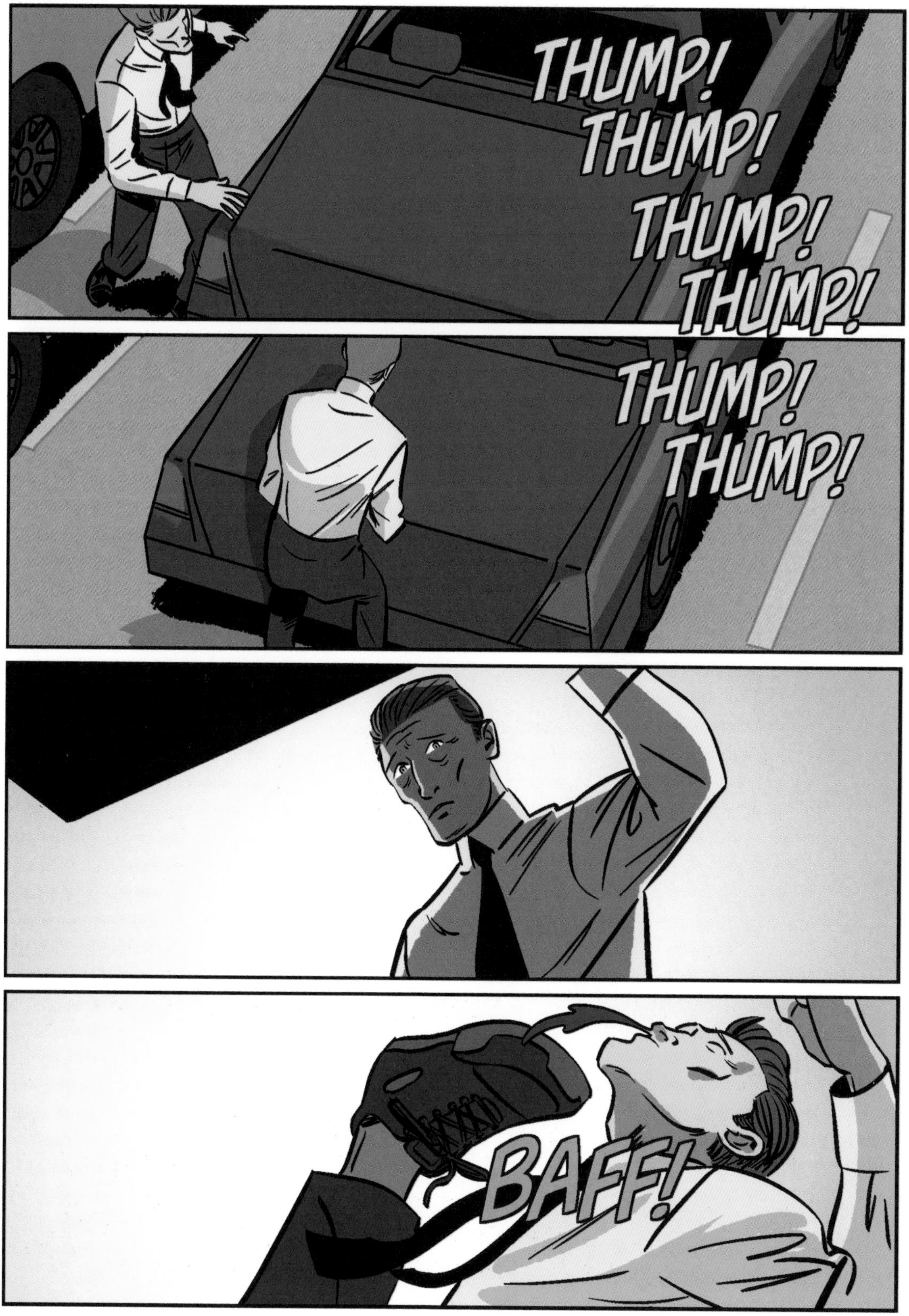
THUMP!
THUMP!
THUMP!
THUMP!
THUMP!
THUMP!
BAFF!

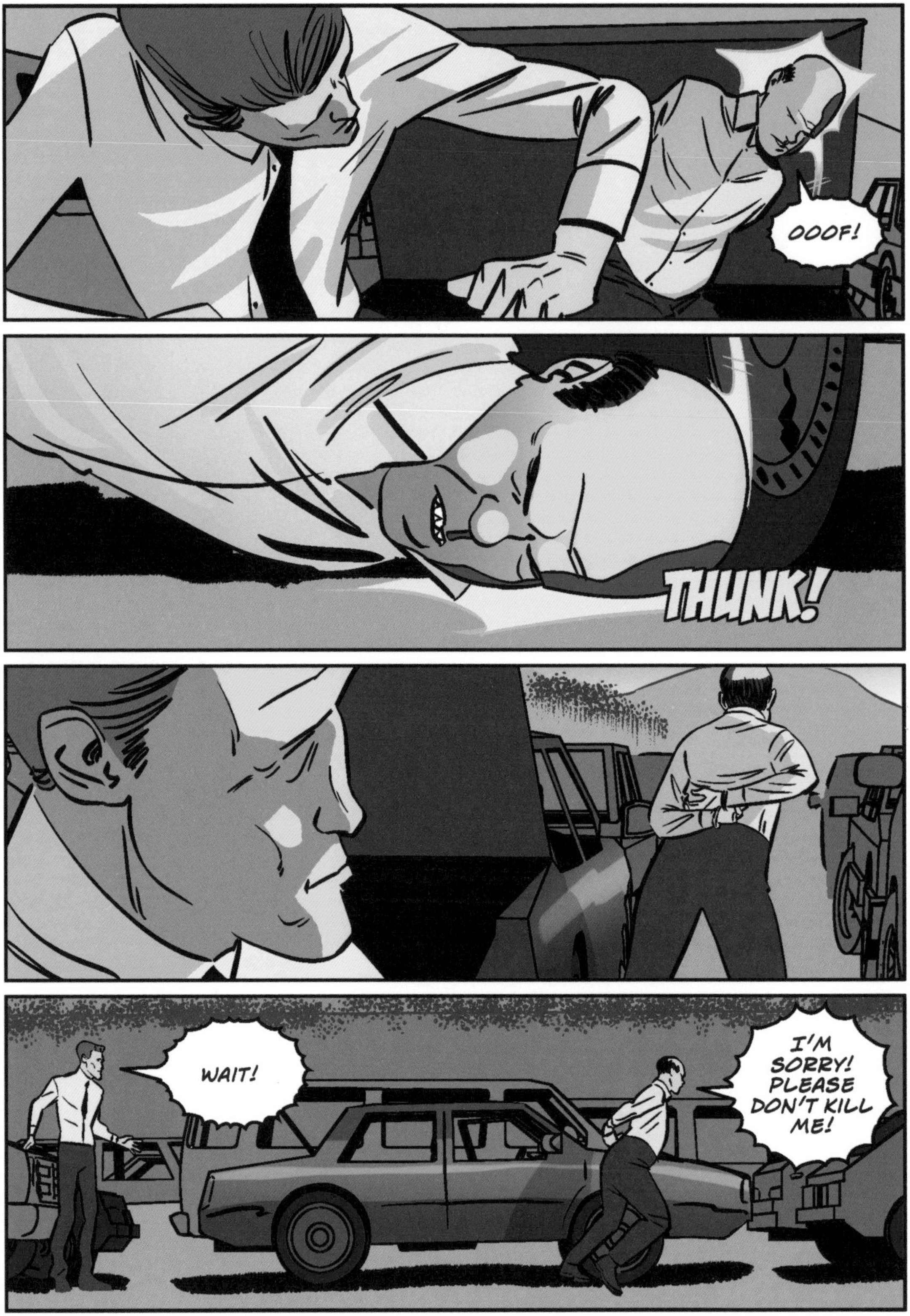
OOOF!
THUNK!
WAIT!
I'M SORRY! PLEASE DON'T KILL ME!

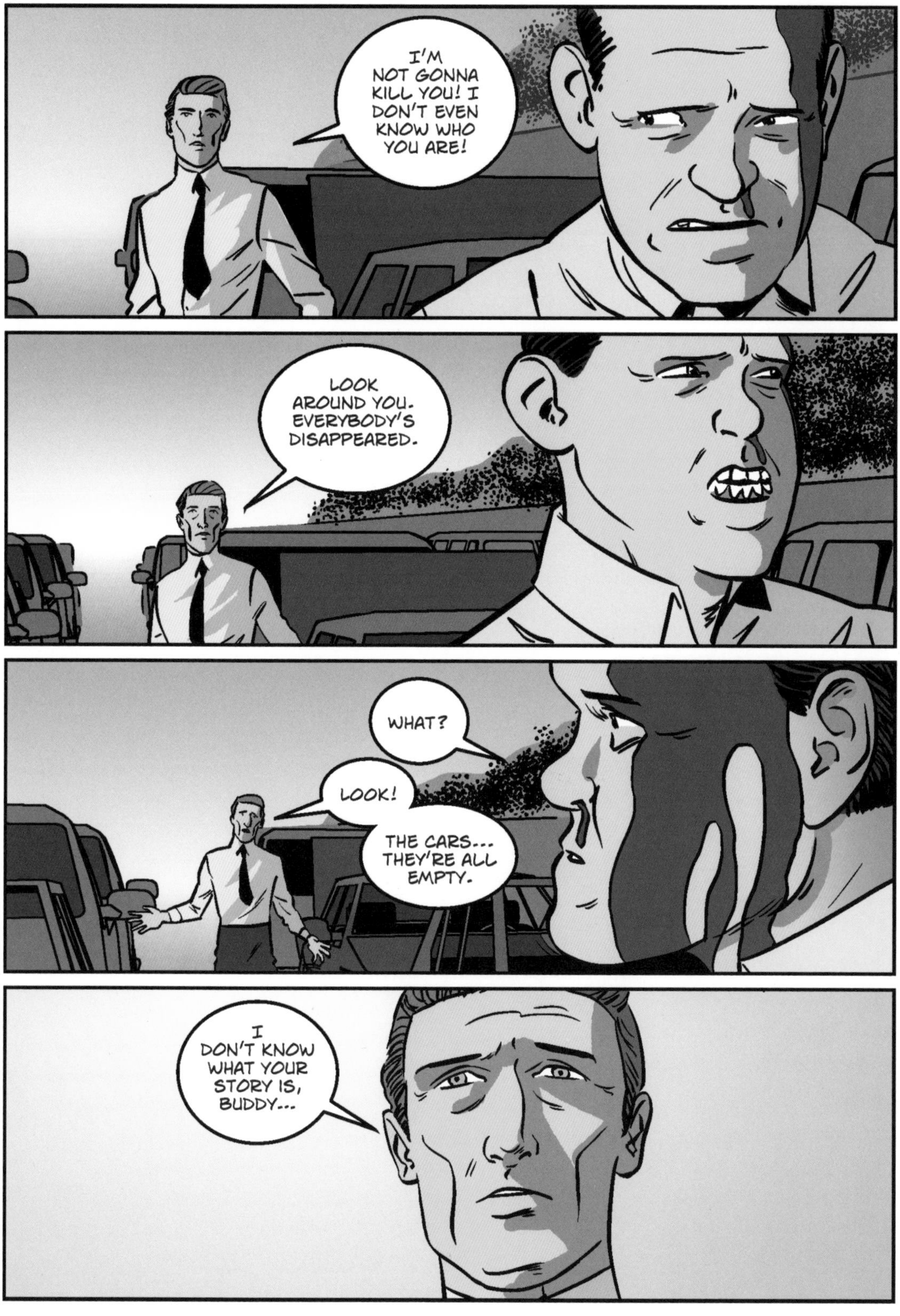
I'M NOT GONNA KILL YOU! I DON'T EVEN KNOW WHO YOU ARE!
LOOK AROUND YOU. EVERYBODY'S DISAPPEARED.
WHAT?
LOOK!
THE CARS... THEY'RE ALL EMPTY.
I DON'T KNOW WHAT YOUR STORY IS, BUDDY...

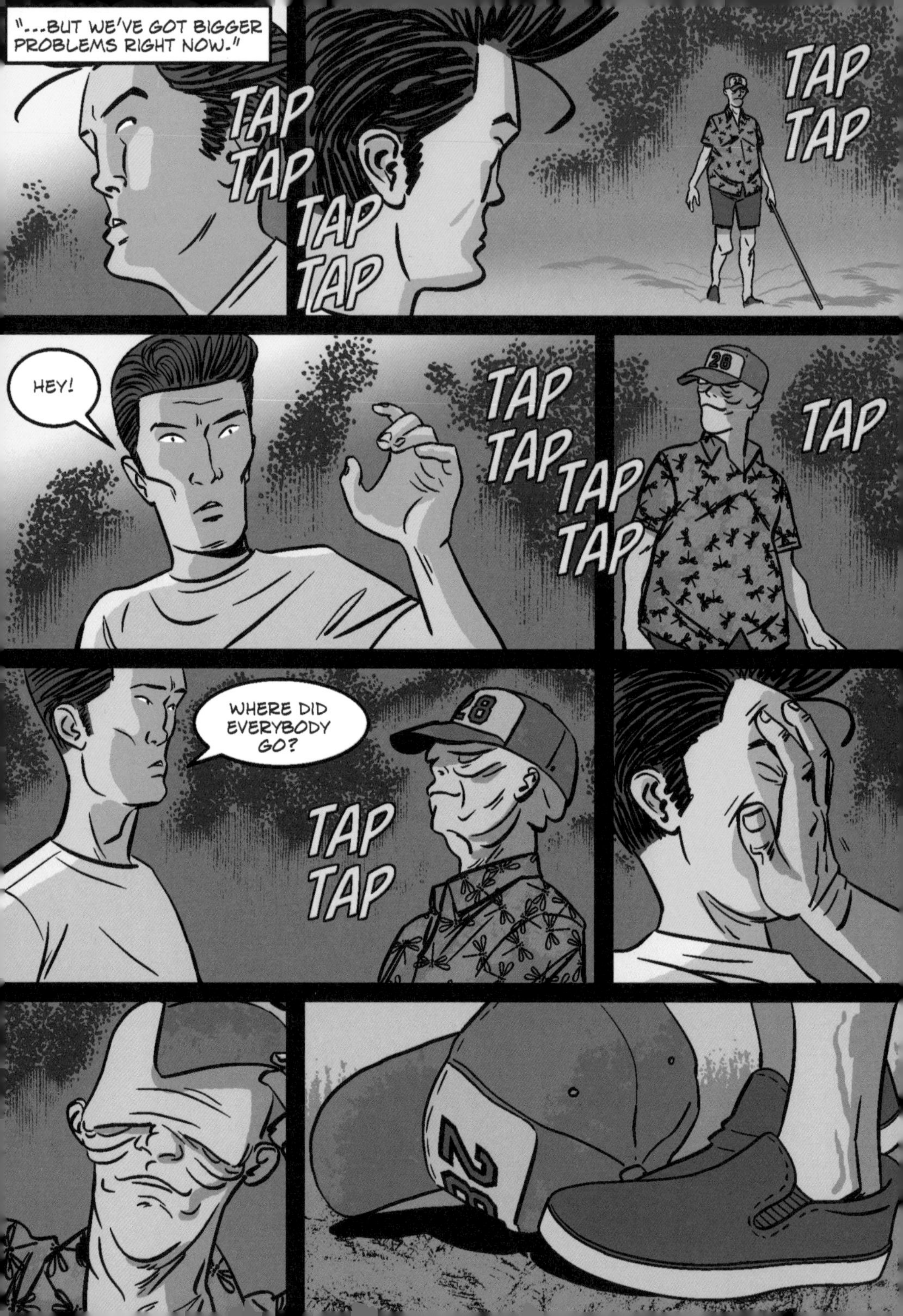
"...BUT WE'VE GOT BIGGER PROBLEMS RIGHT NOW."
TAP TAP
TAP TAP
TAP TAP
HEY!
TAP TAP TAP TAP
TAP
WHERE DID EVERYBODY GO?
TAP TAP

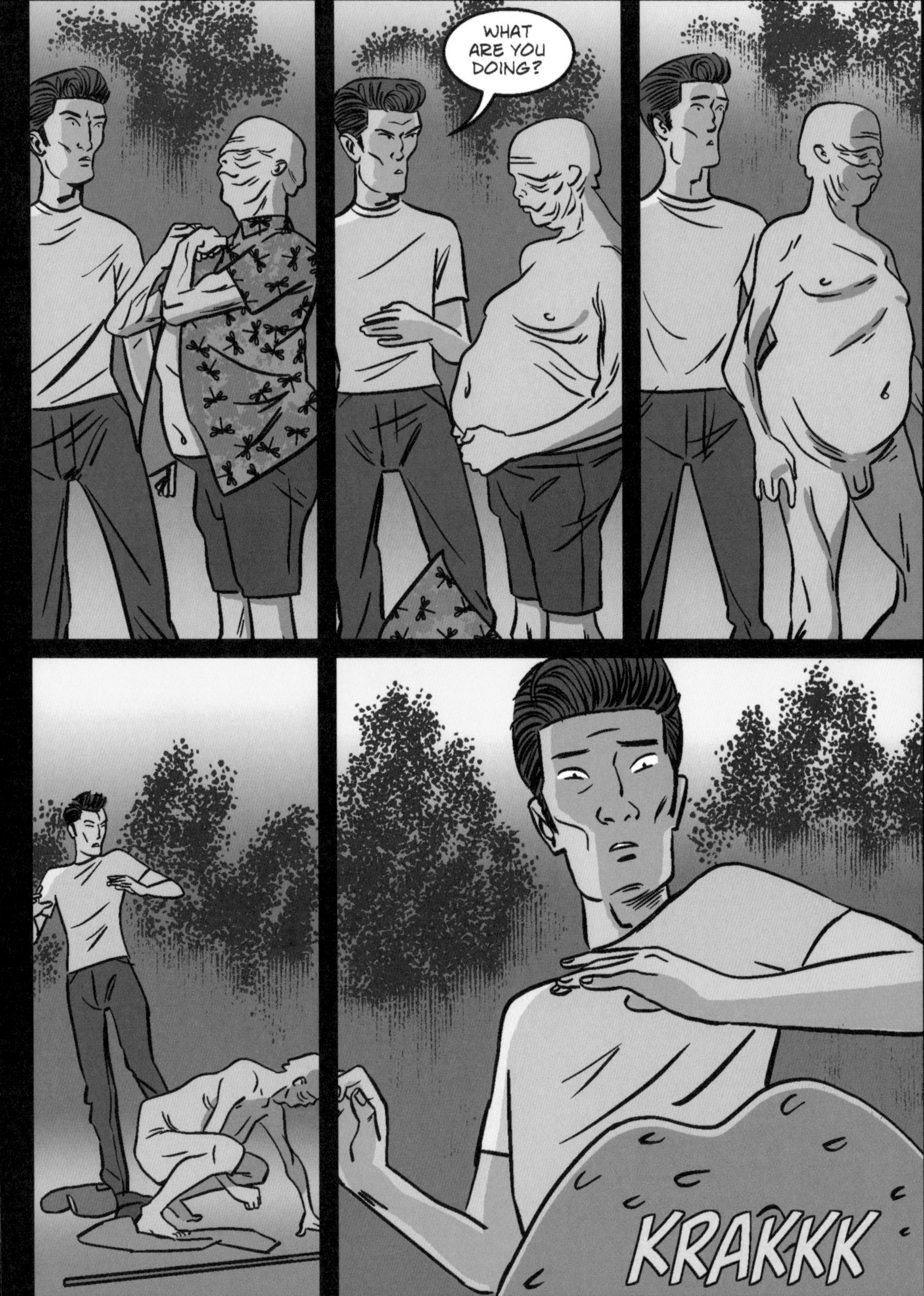
WHAT ARE YOU DOING?
KRAKKK

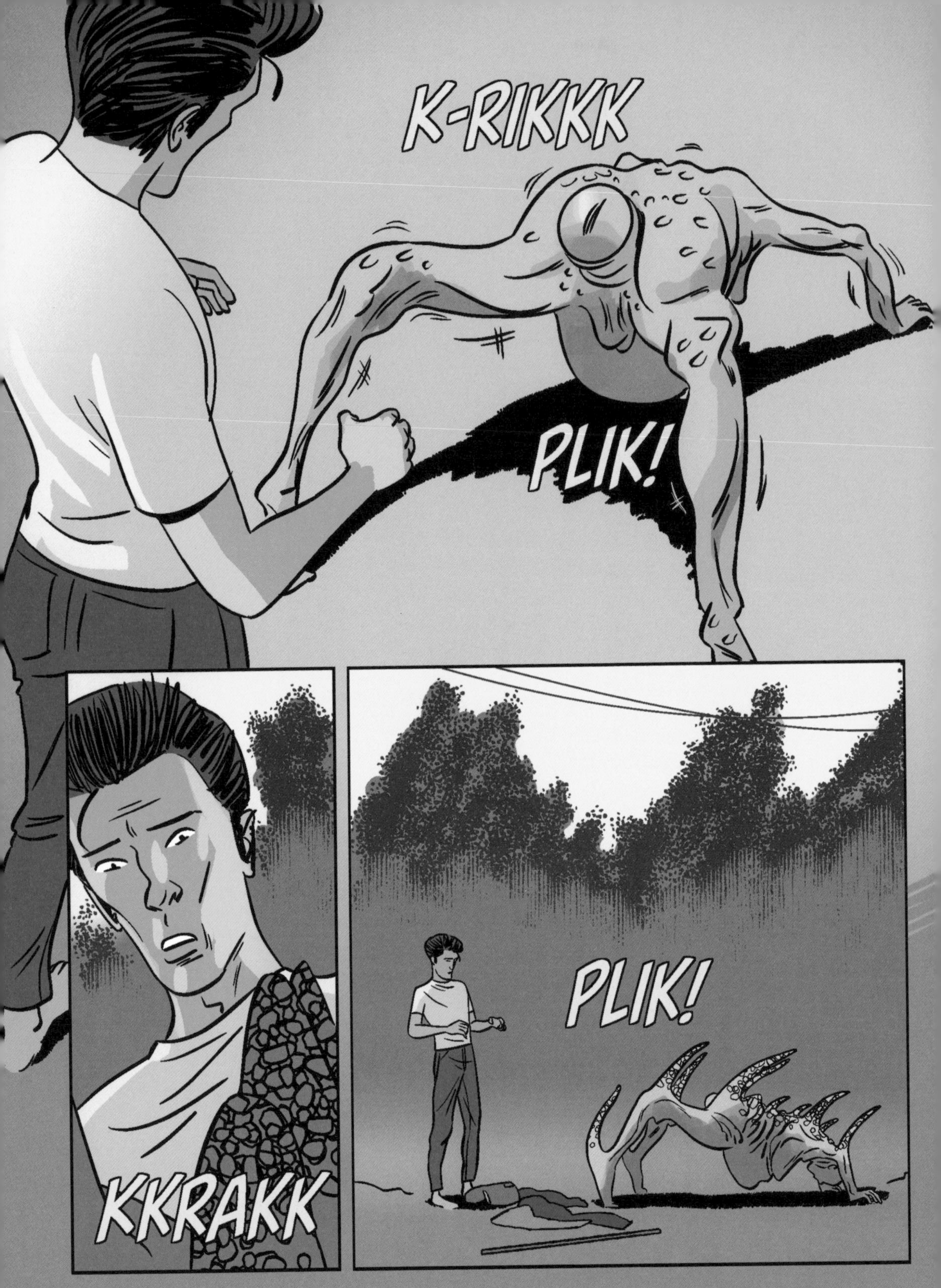
K-RIKKK
PLIK!
KKRAKK
PLIK!

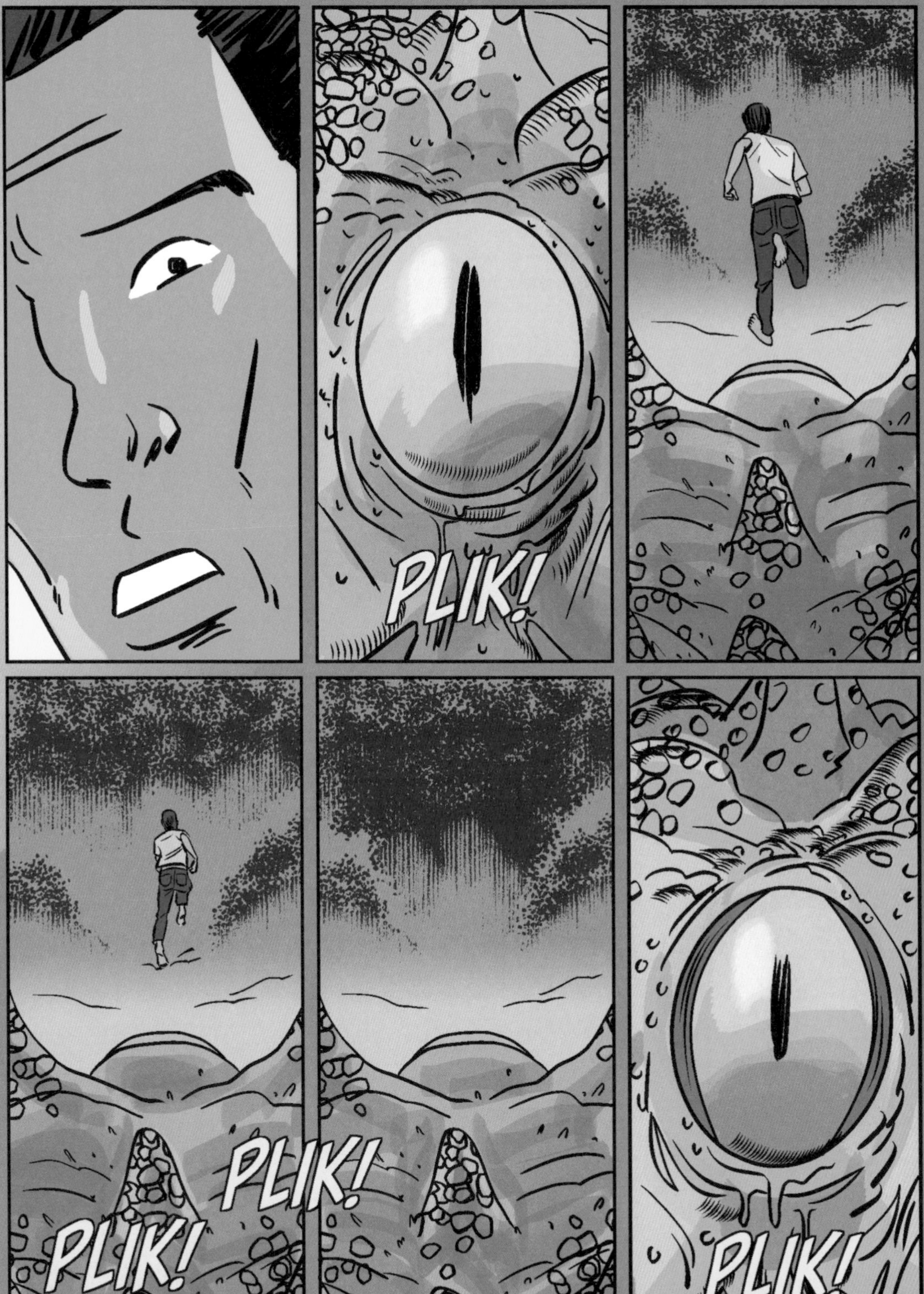
PLIK!
PLIK!
PLIK!
PLIK!

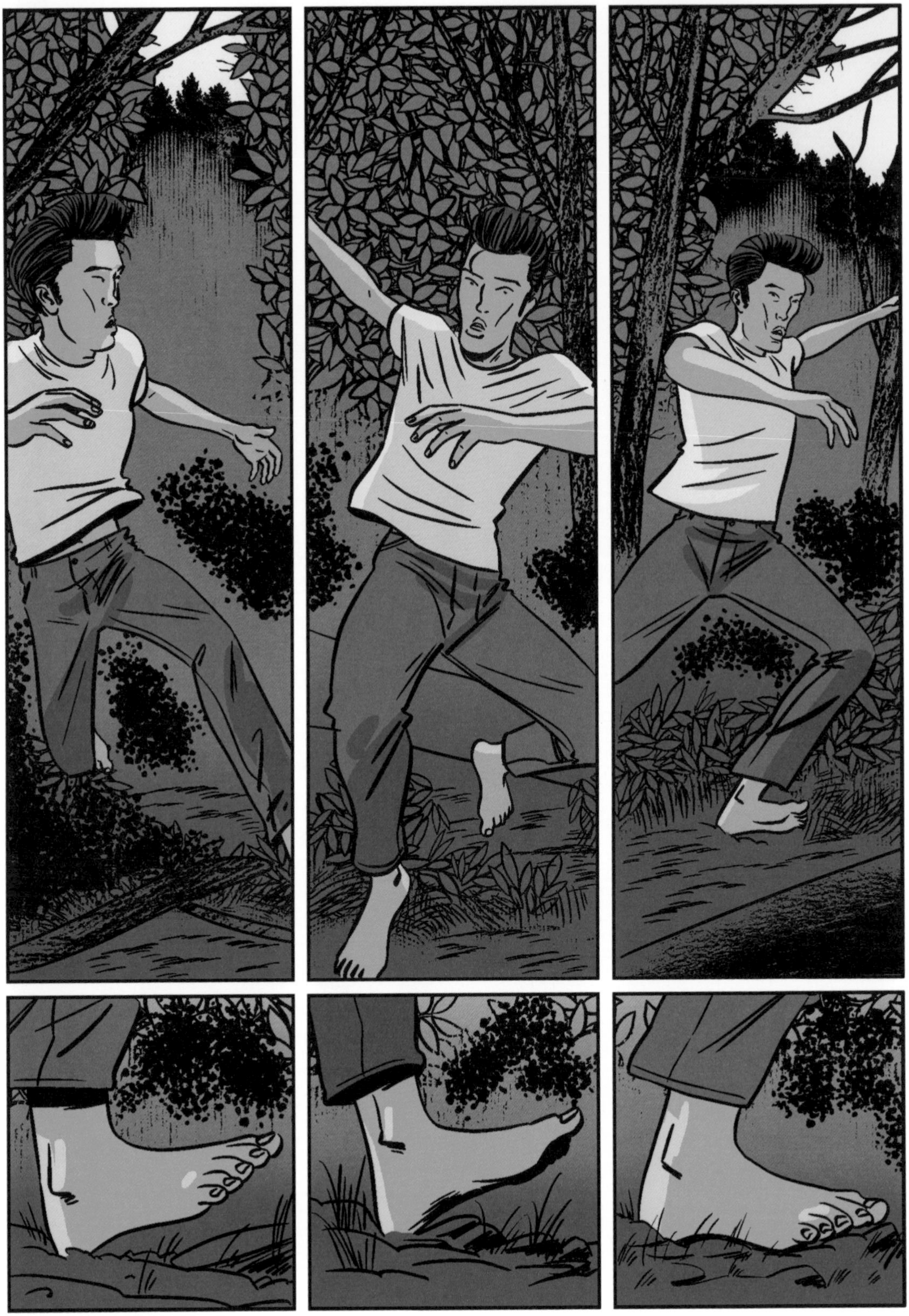

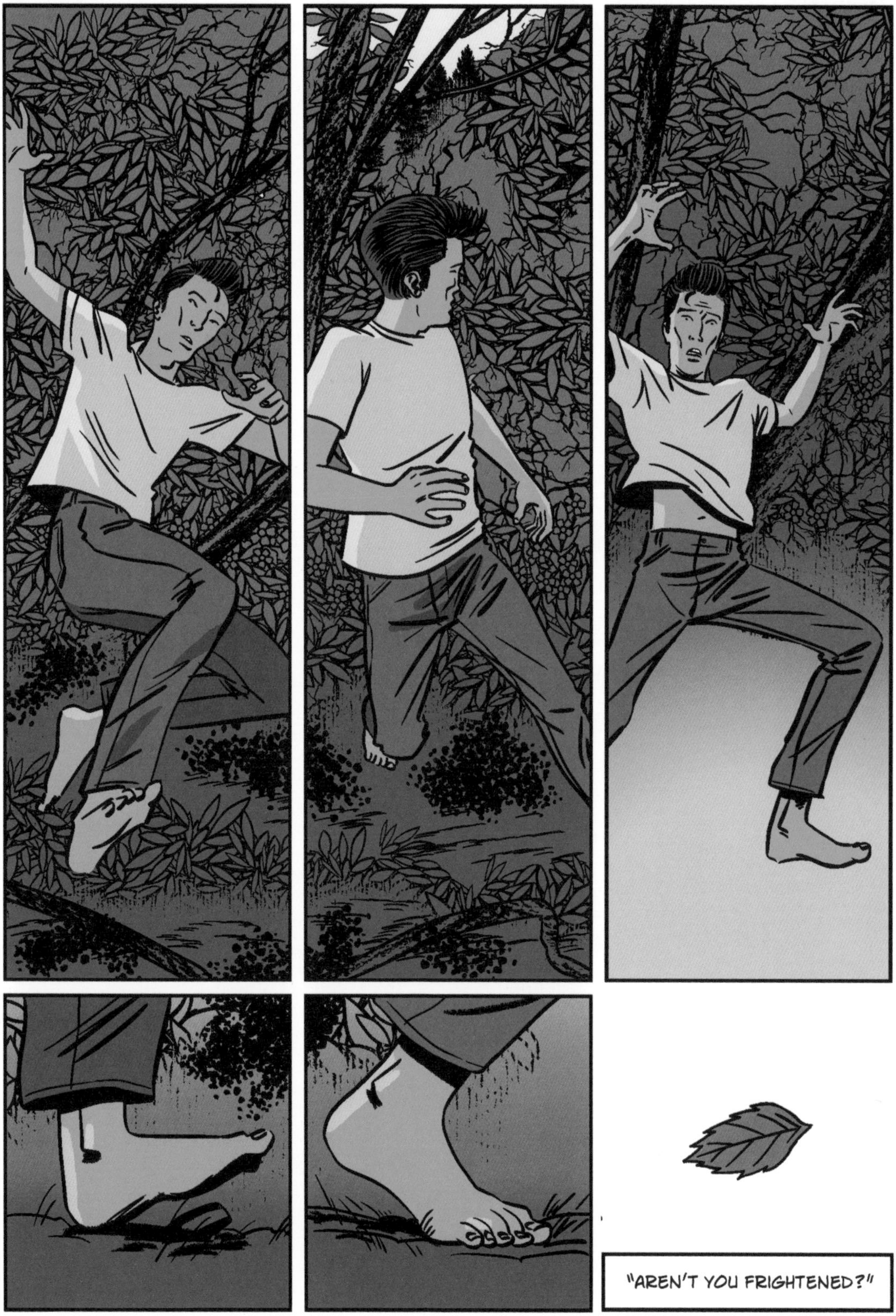
"AREN'T YOU FRIGHTENED?"

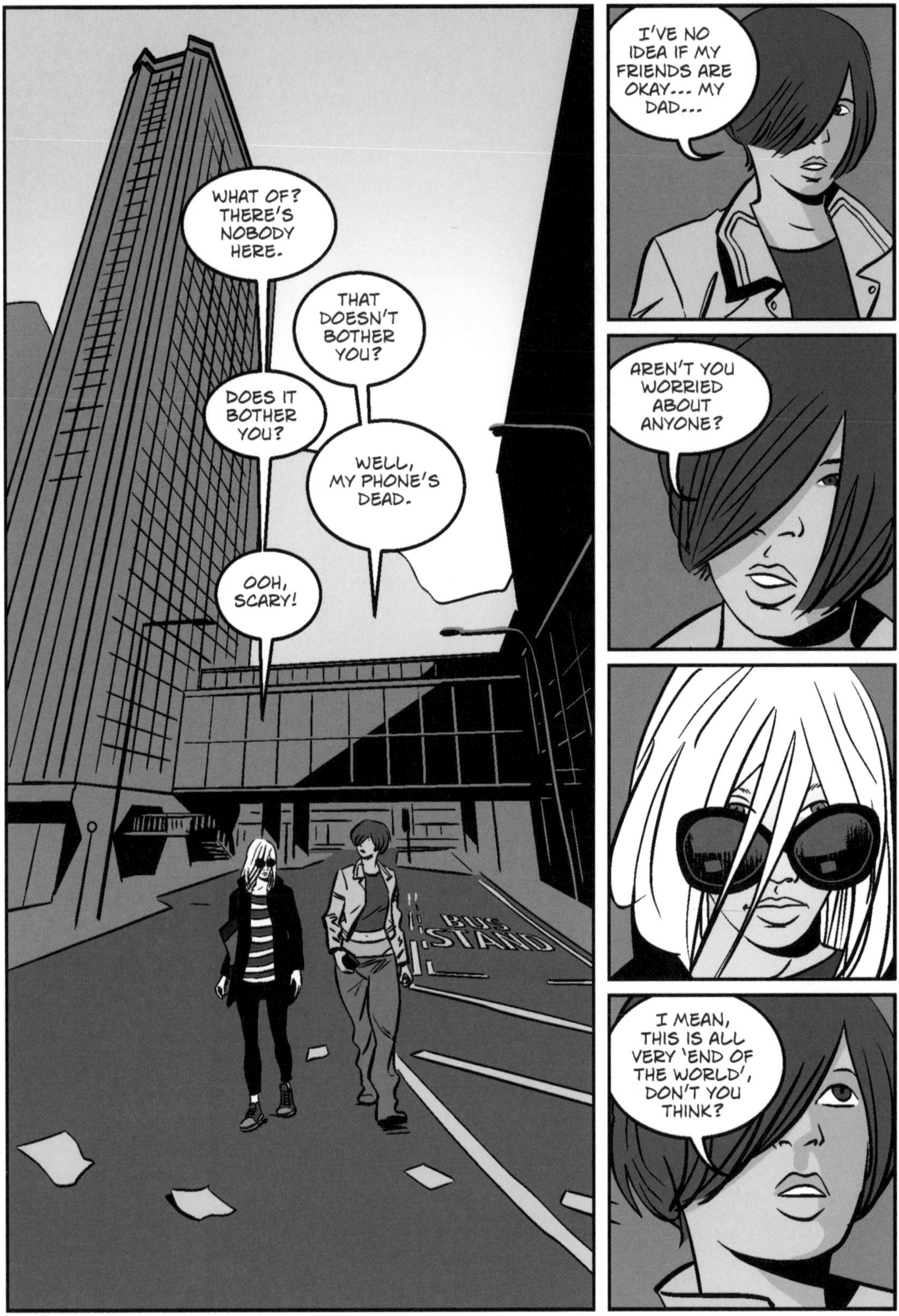
WHAT OF? THERE'S NOBODY HERE.
THAT DOESN'T BOTHER YOU?
DOES IT BOTHER YOU?
WELL, MY PHONE'S DEAD.
OOH, SCARY!
BUS STAND
I'VE NO IDEA IF MY FRIENDS ARE OKAY... MY DAD...
AREN'T YOU WORRIED ABOUT ANYONE?
I MEAN, THIS IS ALL VERY 'END OF THE WORLD', DON'T YOU THINK?

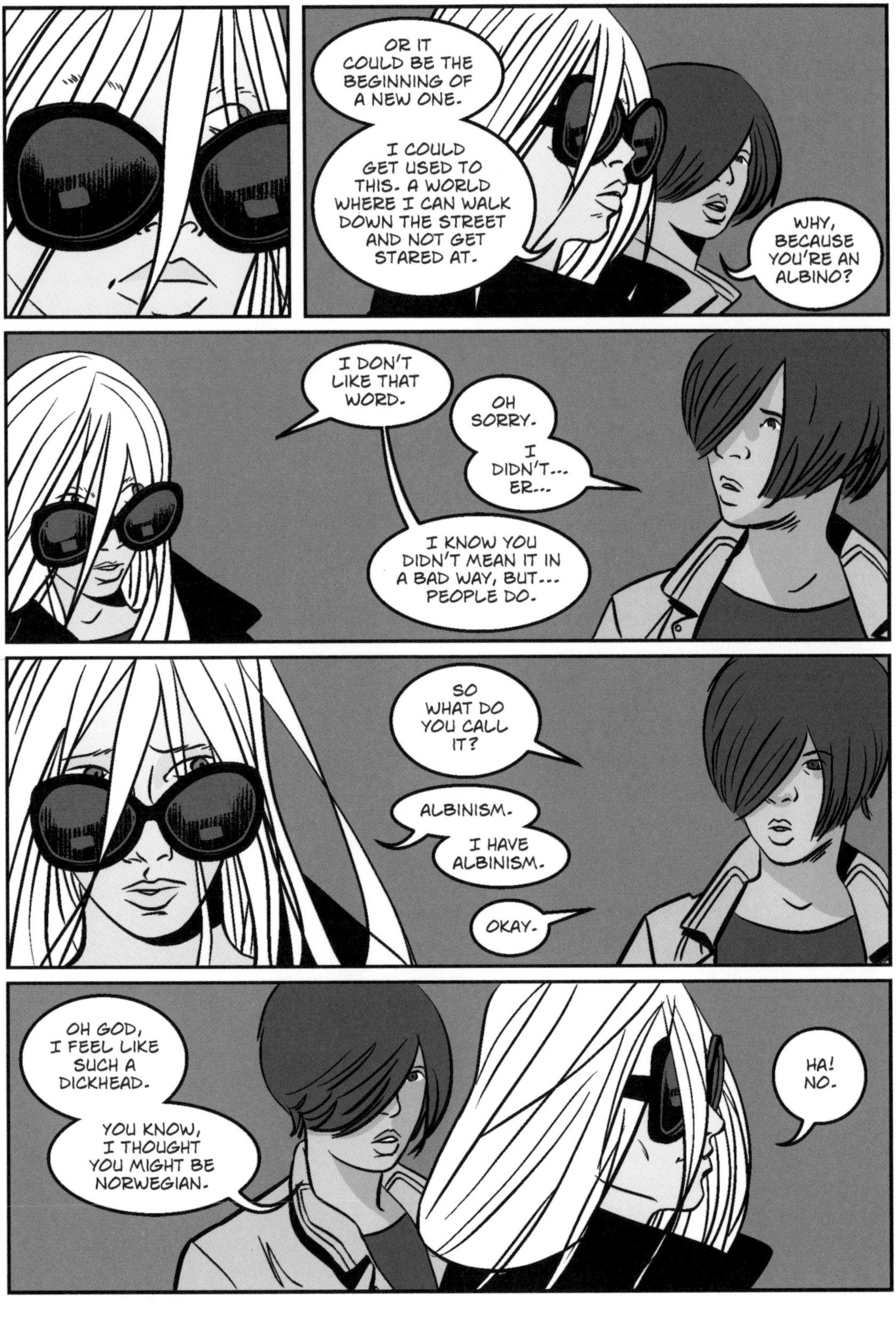
OR IT COULD BE THE BEGINNING OF A NEW ONE.
I COULD GET USED TO THIS. A WORLD WHERE I CAN WALK DOWN THE STREET AND NOT GET STARED AT.
WHY, BECAUSE YOU'RE AN ALBINO?
I DON'T LIKE THAT WORD.
OH SORRY.
I DIDN'T... ER...
I KNOW YOU DIDN'T MEAN IT IN A BAD WAY, BUT... PEOPLE DO.
SO WHAT DO YOU CALL IT?
ALBINISM.
I HAVE ALBINISM.
OKAY.
OH GOD, I FEEL LIKE SUCH A DICKHEAD.
YOU KNOW, I THOUGHT YOU MIGHT BE NORWEGIAN.
HA! NO.

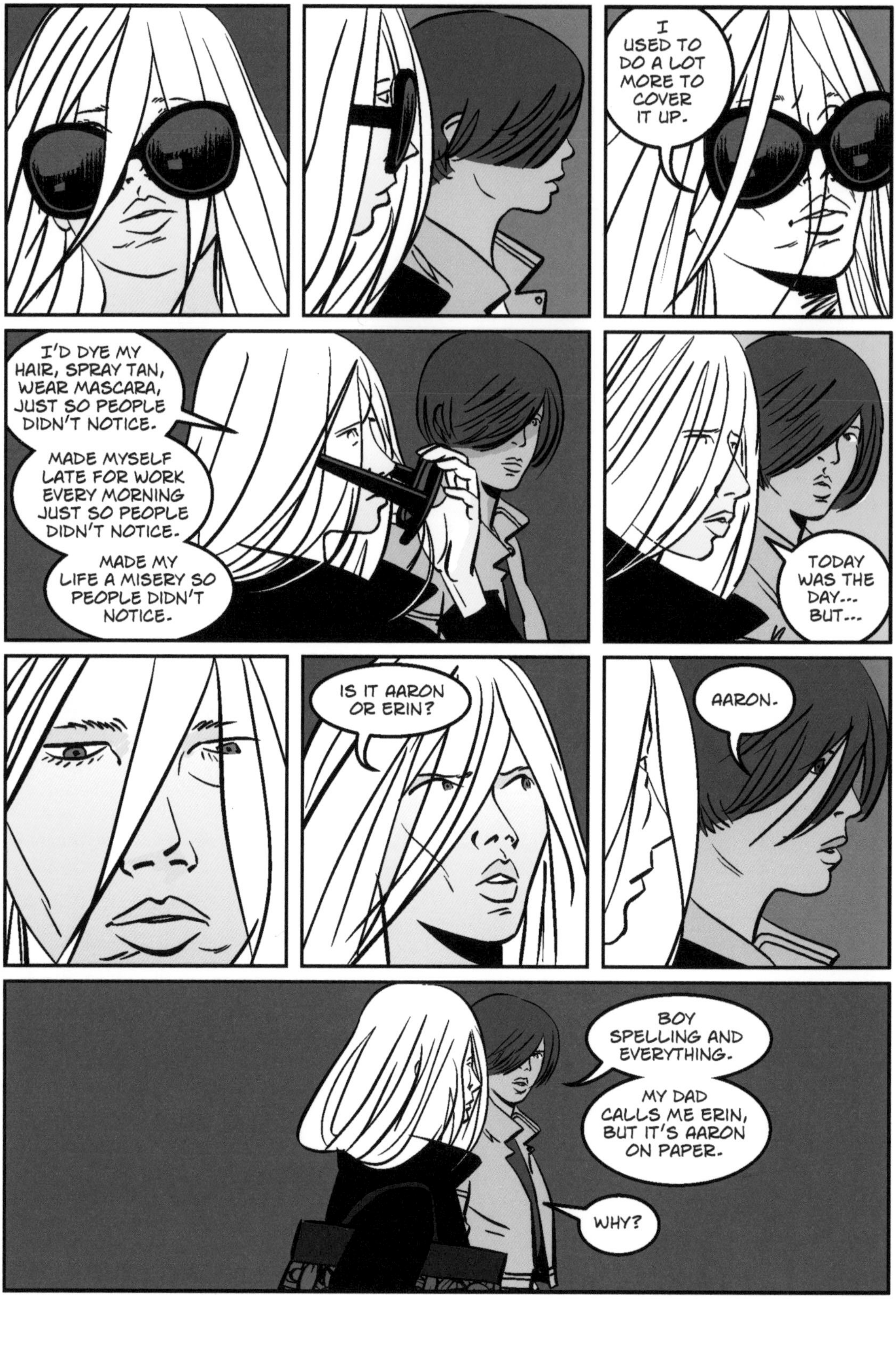
I USED TO DO A LOT MORE TO COVER IT UP.
I'D DYE MY HAIR, SPRAY TAN, WEAR MASCARA, JUST SO PEOPLE DIDN'T NOTICE.
MADE MYSELF LATE FOR WORK EVERY MORNING JUST SO PEOPLE DIDN'T NOTICE.
MADE MY LIFE A MISERY SO PEOPLE DIDN'T NOTICE.
TODAY WAS THE DAY... BUT...
IS IT AARON OR ERIN?
AARON.
BOY SPELLING AND EVERYTHING.
MY DAD CALLS ME ERIN, BUT IT'S AARON ON PAPER.
WHY?

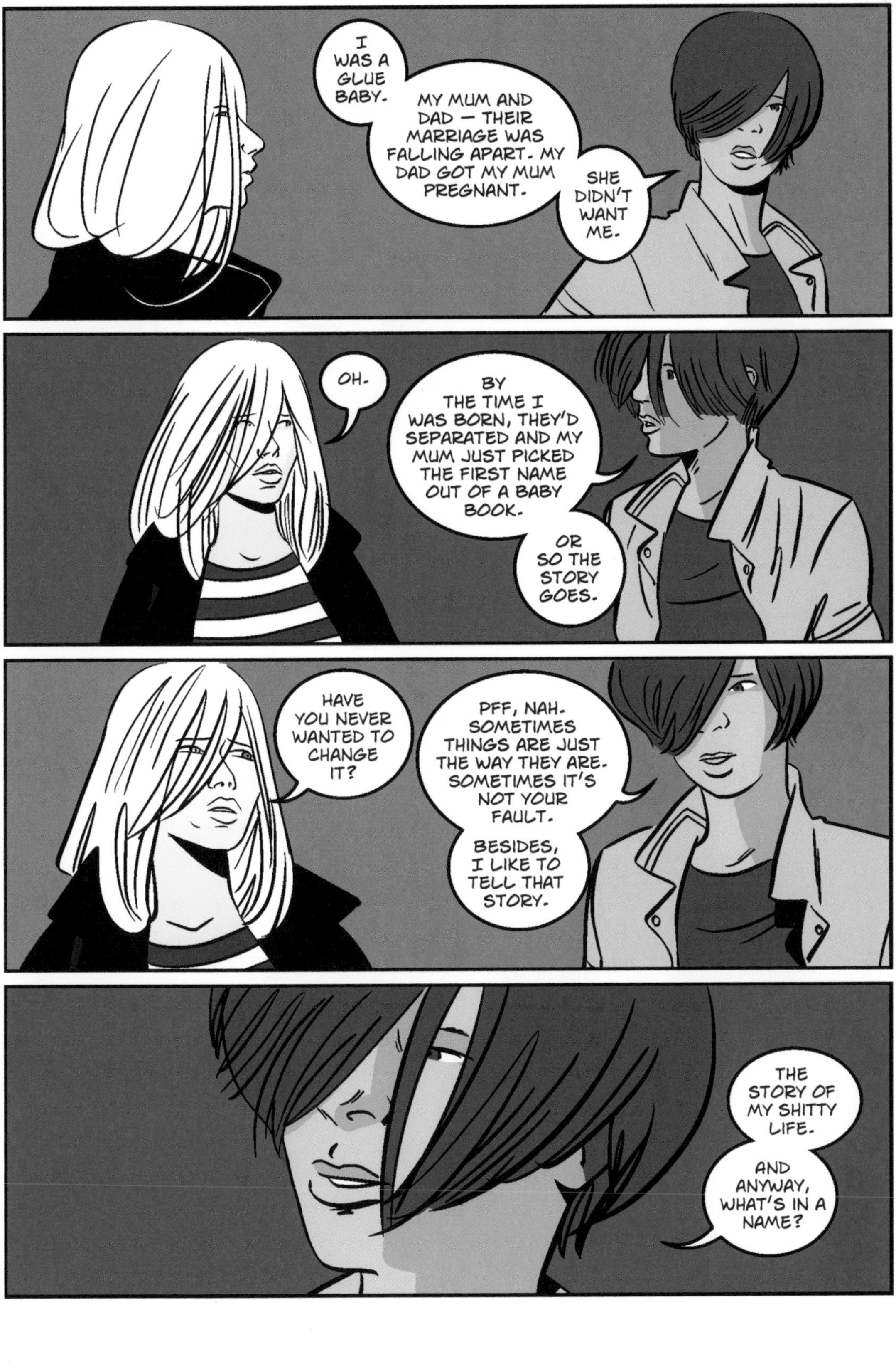
I WAS A GLUE BABY.
MY MUM AND DAD — THEIR MARRIAGE WAS FALLING APART. MY DAD GOT MY MUM PREGNANT.
SHE DIDN'T WANT ME.
OH.
BY THE TIME I WAS BORN, THEY'D SEPARATED AND MY MUM JUST PICKED THE FIRST NAME OUT OF A BABY BOOK.
OR SO THE STORY GOES.
HAVE YOU NEVER WANTED TO CHANGE IT?
PFF, NAH. SOMETIMES THINGS ARE JUST THE WAY THEY ARE. SOMETIMES IT'S NOT YOUR FAULT.
BESIDES, I LIKE TO TELL THAT STORY.
THE STORY OF MY SHITTY LIFE.
AND ANYWAY, WHAT'S IN A NAME?

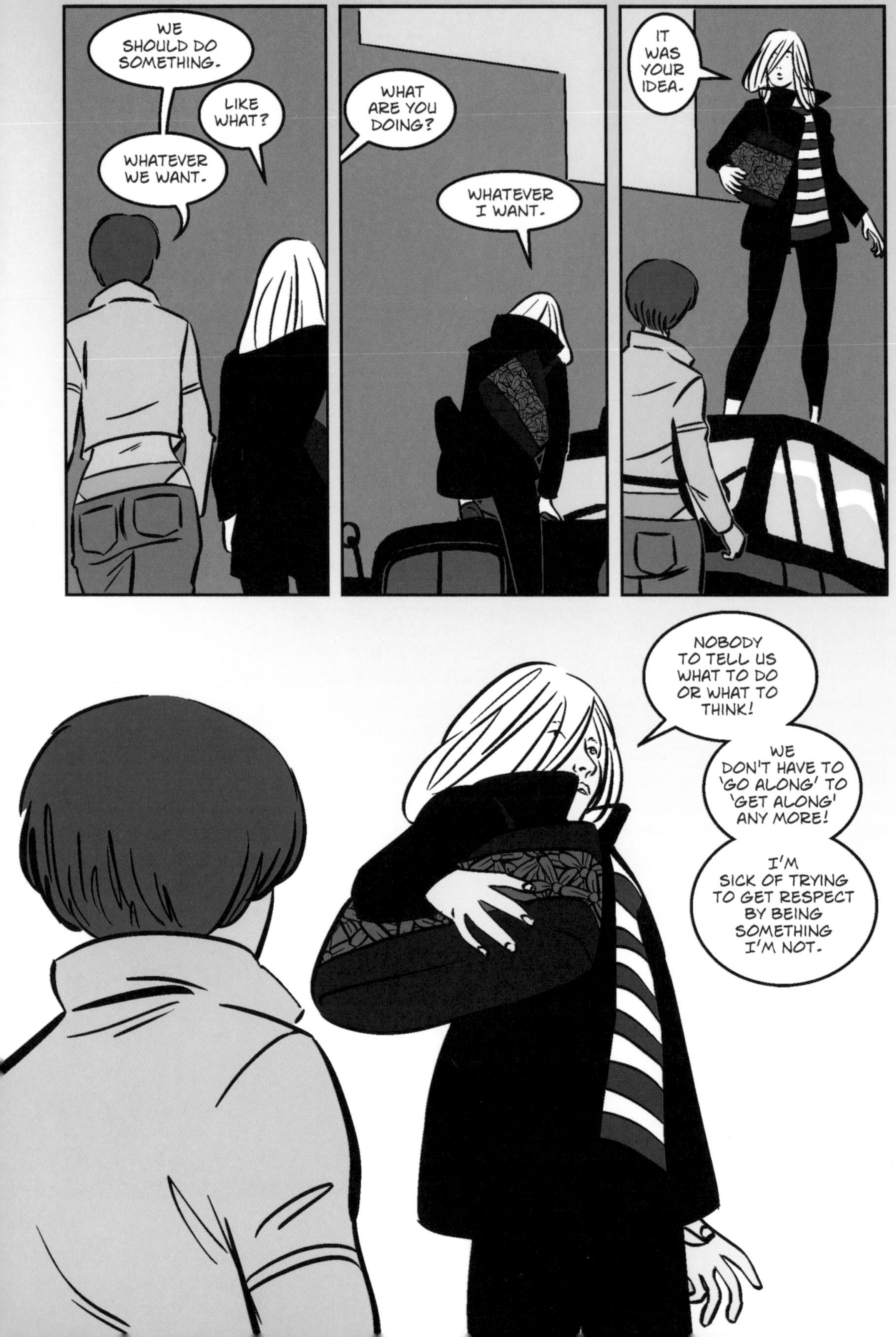
WE SHOULD DO SOMETHING.
LIKE WHAT?
WHATEVER WE WANT.
WHAT ARE YOU DOING?
WHATEVER I WANT.
IT WAS YOUR IDEA.
NOBODY TO TELL US WHAT TO DO OR WHAT TO THINK!
WE DON'T HAVE TO 'GO ALONG' TO 'GET ALONG' ANY MORE!
I'M SICK OF TRYING TO GET RESPECT BY BEING SOMETHING I'M NOT.

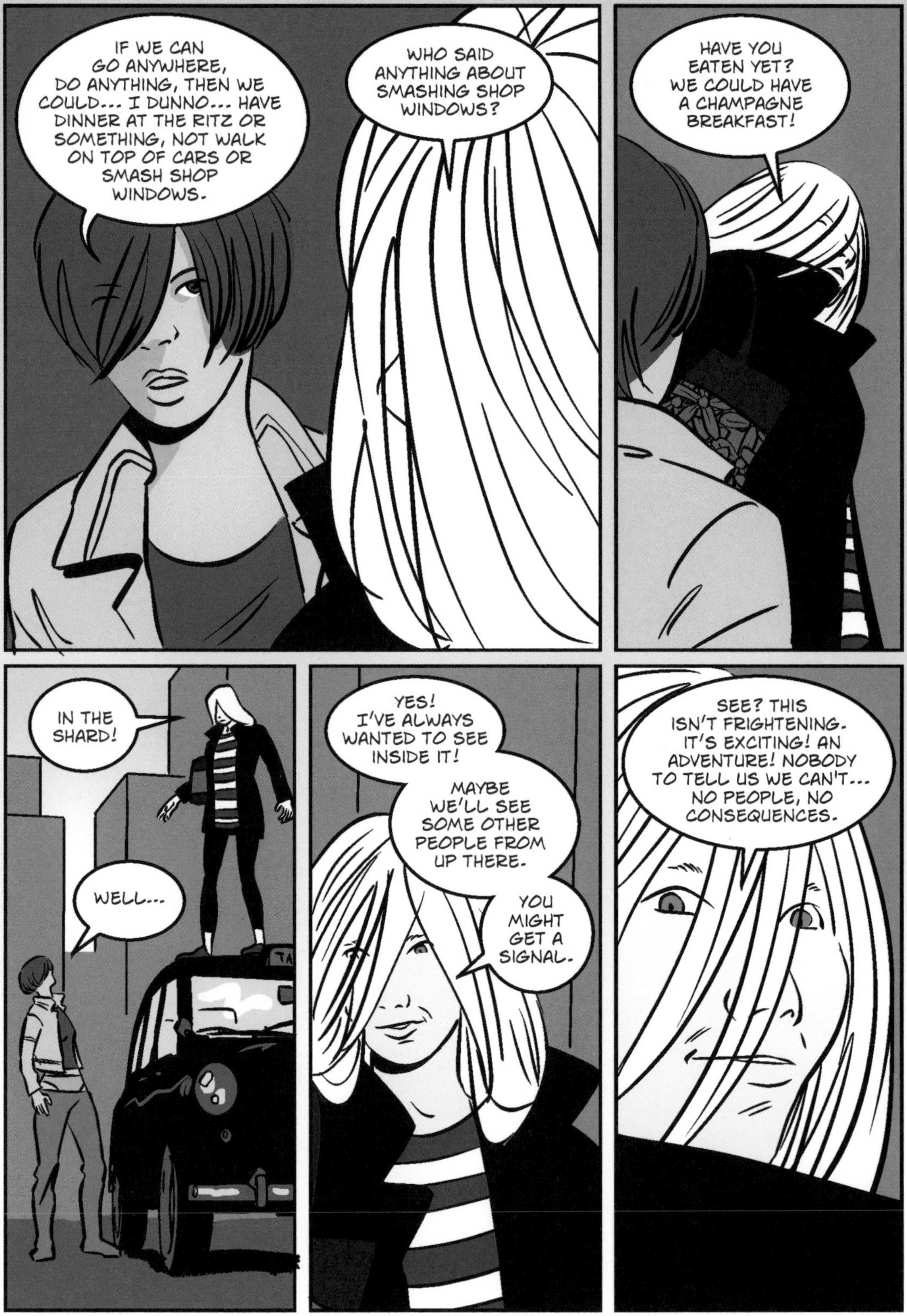
IF WE CAN GO ANYWHERE, DO ANYTHING, THEN WE COULD... I DUNNO... HAVE DINNER AT THE RITZ OR SOMETHING, NOT WALK ON TOP OF CARS OR SMASH SHOP WINDOWS.
WHO SAID ANYTHING ABOUT SMASHING SHOP WINDOWS?
HAVE YOU EATEN YET? WE COULD HAVE A CHAMPAGNE BREAKFAST!
IN THE SHARD!
WELL...
YES! I'VE ALWAYS WANTED TO SEE INSIDE IT!
MAYBE WE'LL SEE SOME OTHER PEOPLE FROM UP THERE.
YOU MIGHT GET A SIGNAL.
SEE? THIS ISN'T FRIGHTENING. IT'S EXCITING! AN ADVENTURE! NOBODY TO TELL US WE CAN'T... NO PEOPLE, NO CONSEQUENCES.

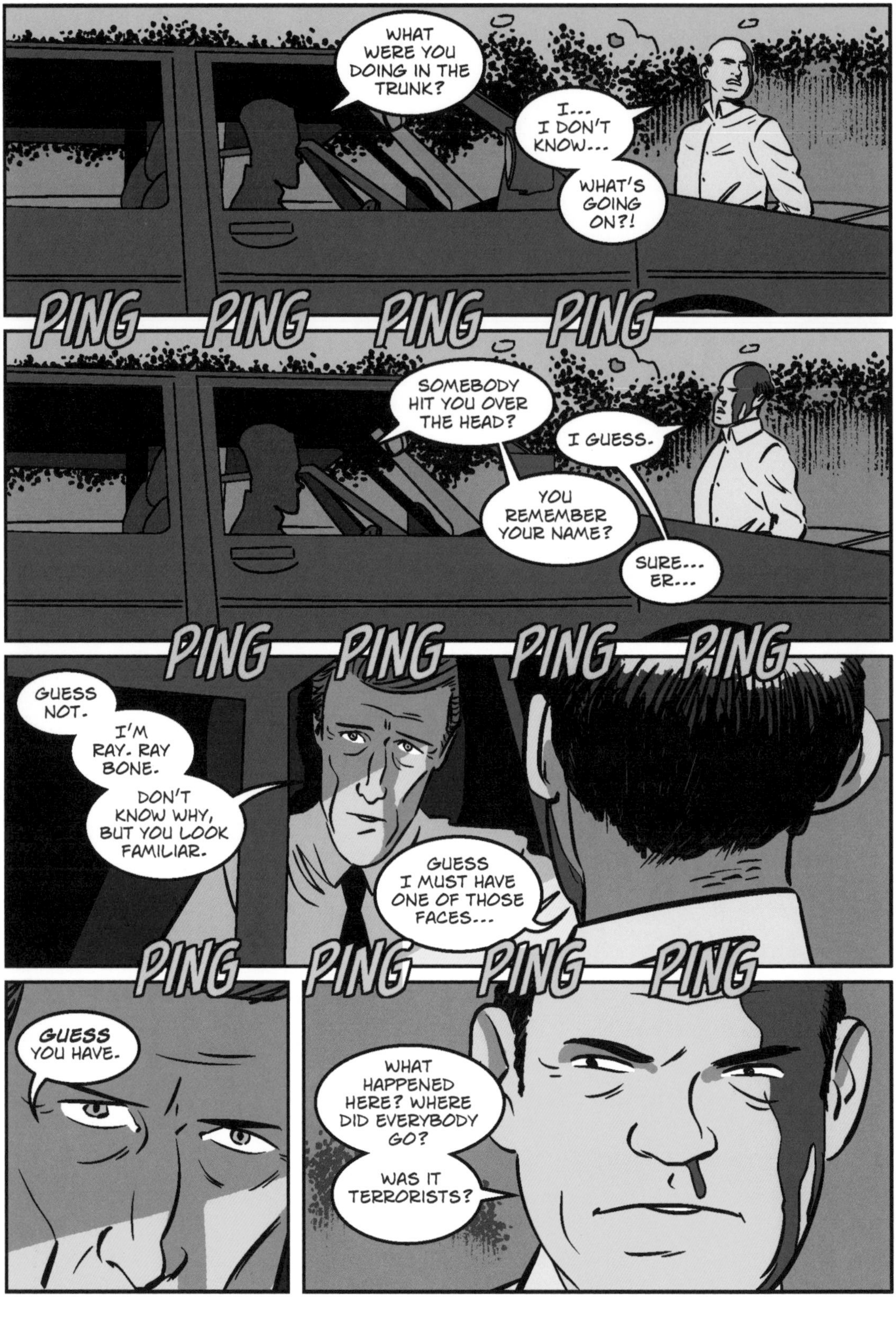
WHAT WERE YOU DOING IN THE TRUNK?
I... I DON'T KNOW...
WHAT'S GOING ON?!
PING PING PING PING
SOMEBODY HIT YOU OVER THE HEAD?
I GUESS.
YOU REMEMBER YOUR NAME?
SURE... ER...
PING PING PING PING
GUESS NOT.
I'M RAY. RAY BONE.
DON'T KNOW WHY, BUT YOU LOOK FAMILIAR.
GUESS I MUST HAVE ONE OF THOSE FACES...
PING PING PING PING
GUESS YOU HAVE.
WHAT HAPPENED HERE? WHERE DID EVERYBODY GO?
WAS IT TERRORISTS?

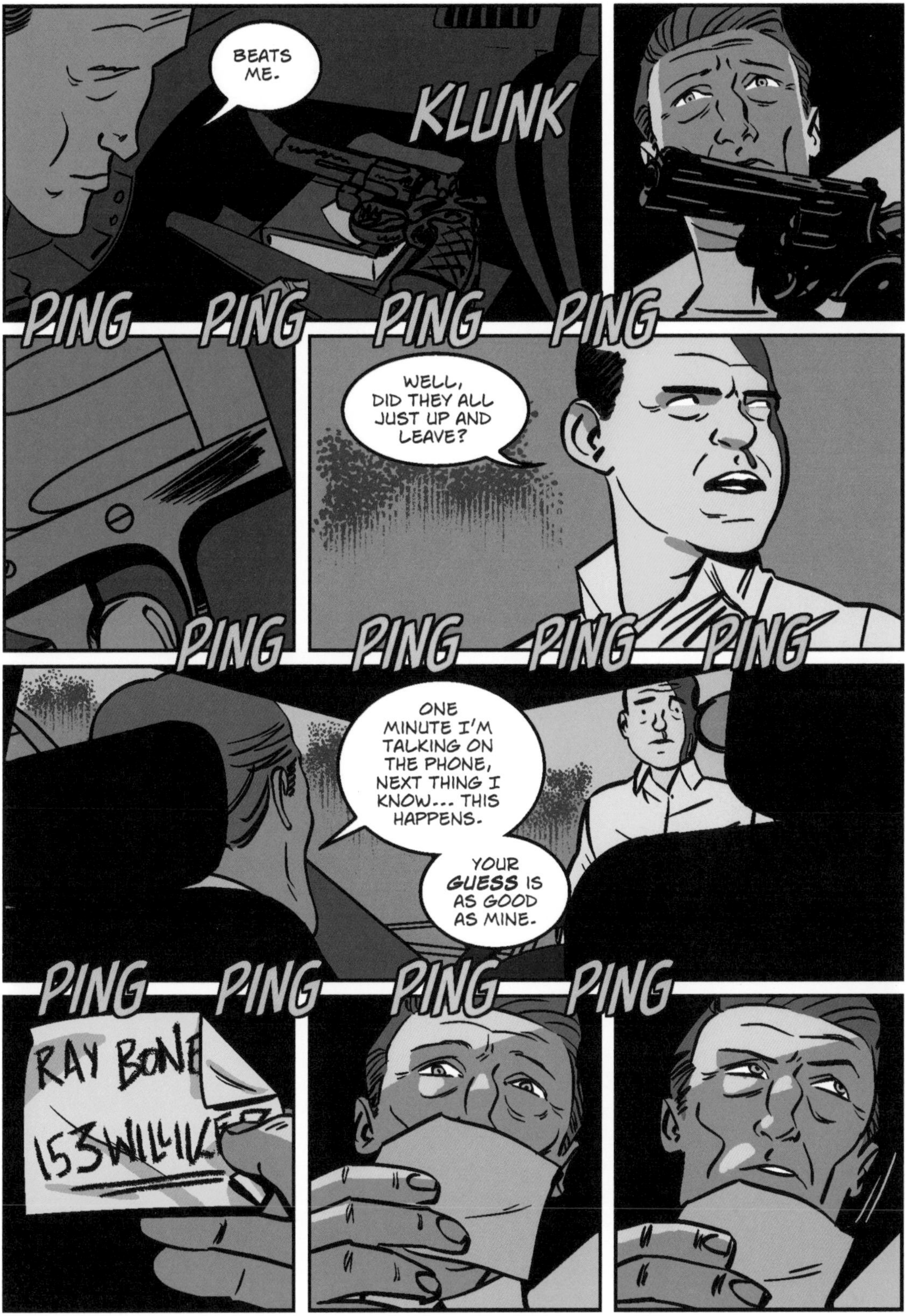
BEATS ME.
KLUNK
PING PING PING PING
WELL, DID THEY ALL JUST UP AND LEAVE?
PING PING PING PING
ONE MINUTE I'M TALKING ON THE PHONE, NEXT THING I KNOW... THIS HAPPENS.
YOUR **GUESS** IS AS GOOD AS MINE.
PING PING PING PING
RAY BONE

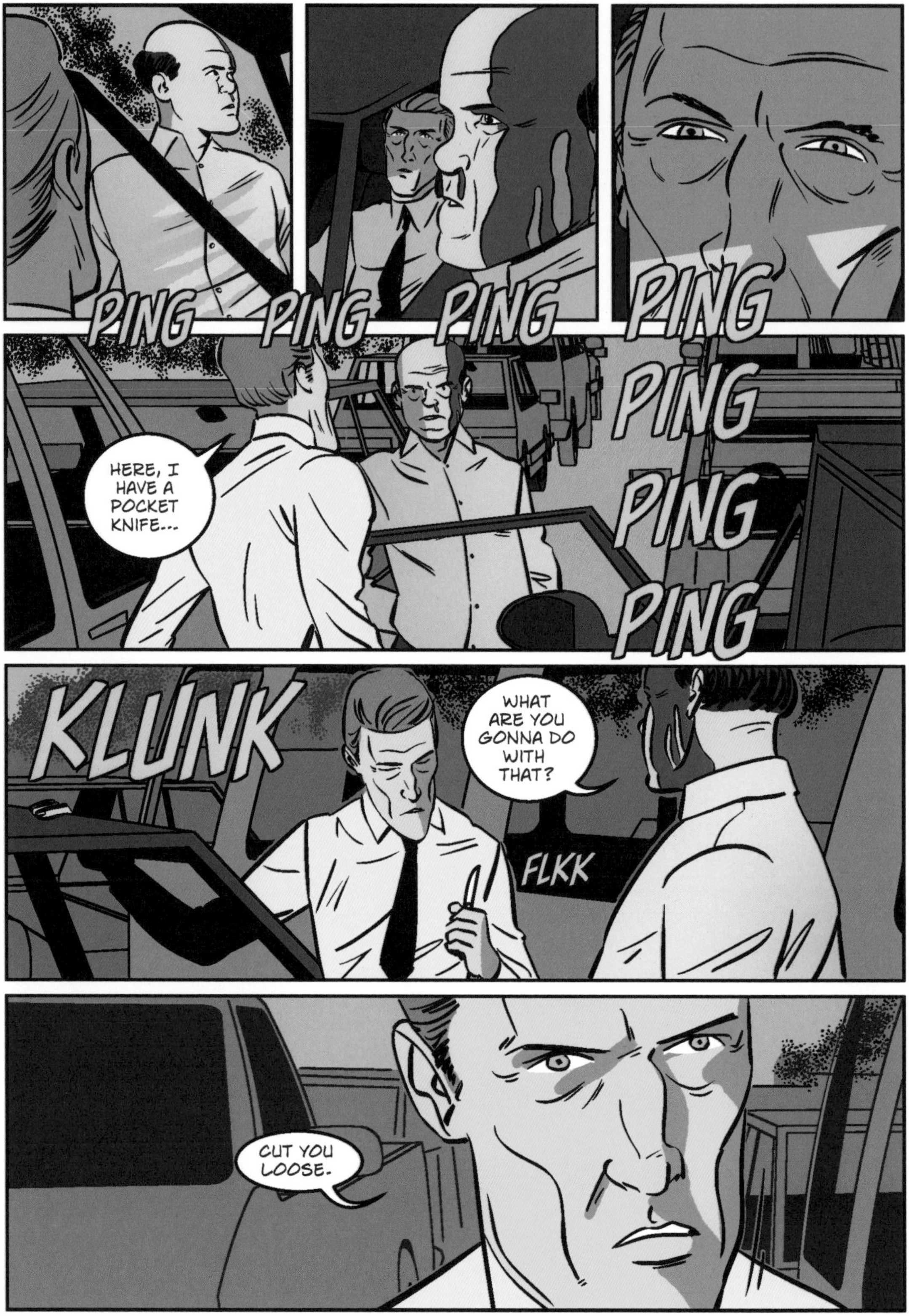
PING PING PING PING
PING
PING
PING
HERE, I HAVE A POCKET KNIFE...
KLUNK
WHAT ARE YOU GONNA DO WITH THAT?
FLKK
CUT YOU LOOSE.

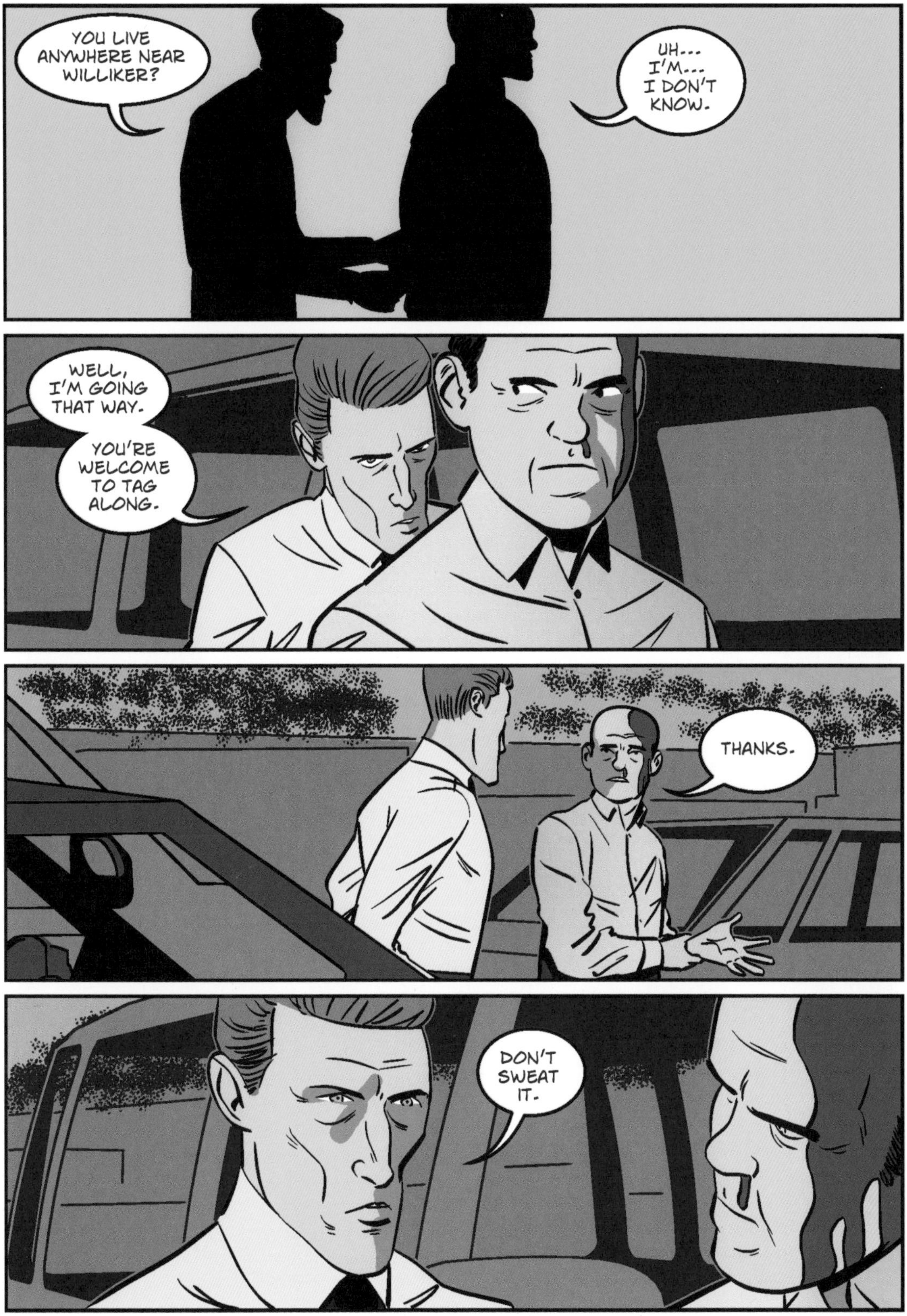
YOU LIVE ANYWHERE NEAR WILLIKER?
UH... I'M... I DON'T KNOW.
WELL, I'M GOING THAT WAY.
YOU'RE WELCOME TO TAG ALONG.
THANKS.
DON'T SWEAT IT.

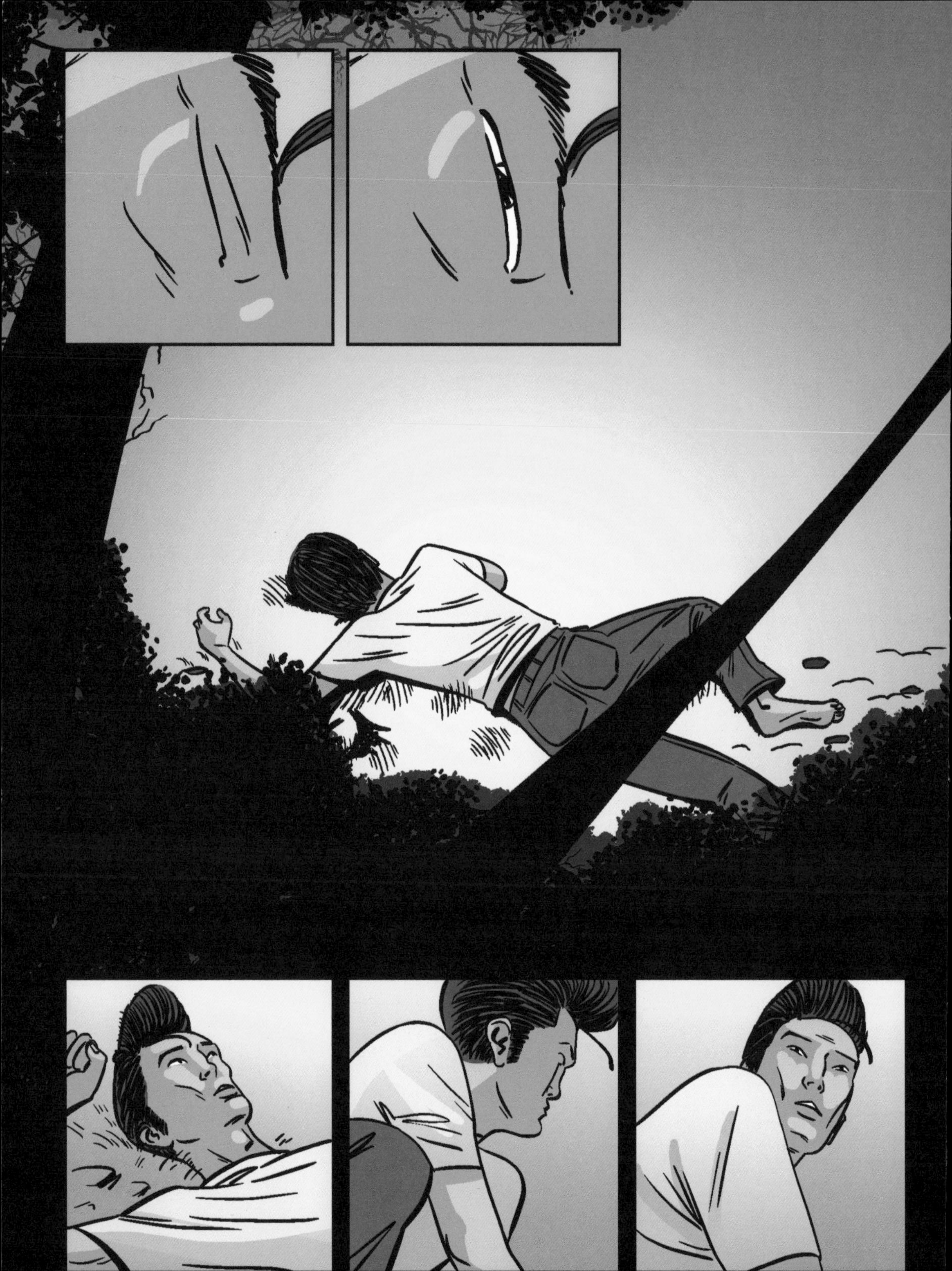

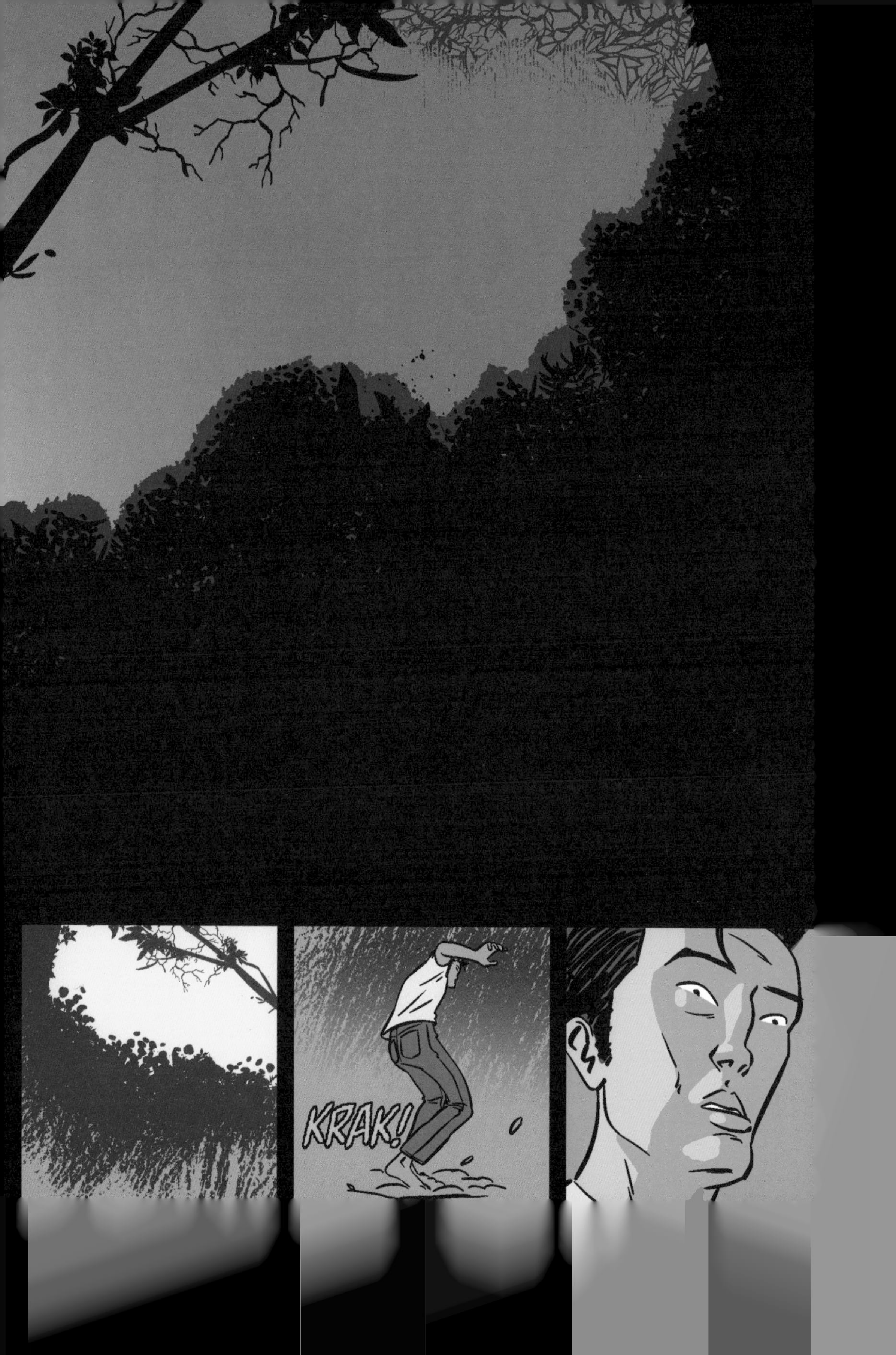
KRAK!

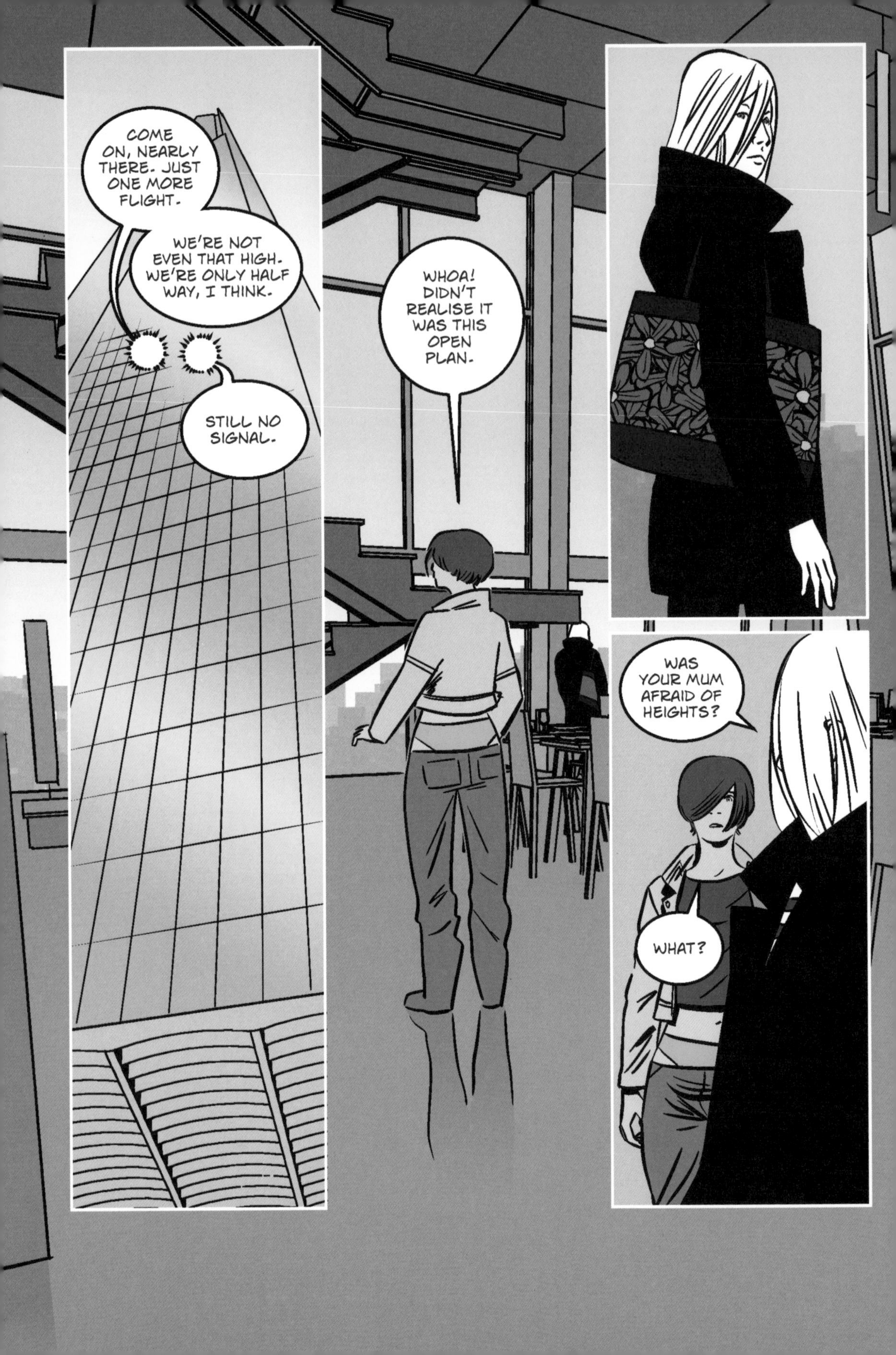
COME ON, NEARLY THERE. JUST ONE MORE FLIGHT.
WE'RE NOT EVEN THAT HIGH. WE'RE ONLY HALF WAY, I THINK.
STILL NO SIGNAL.
WHOA! DIDN'T REALISE IT WAS THIS OPEN PLAN.
WAS YOUR MUM AFRAID OF HEIGHTS?
WHAT?

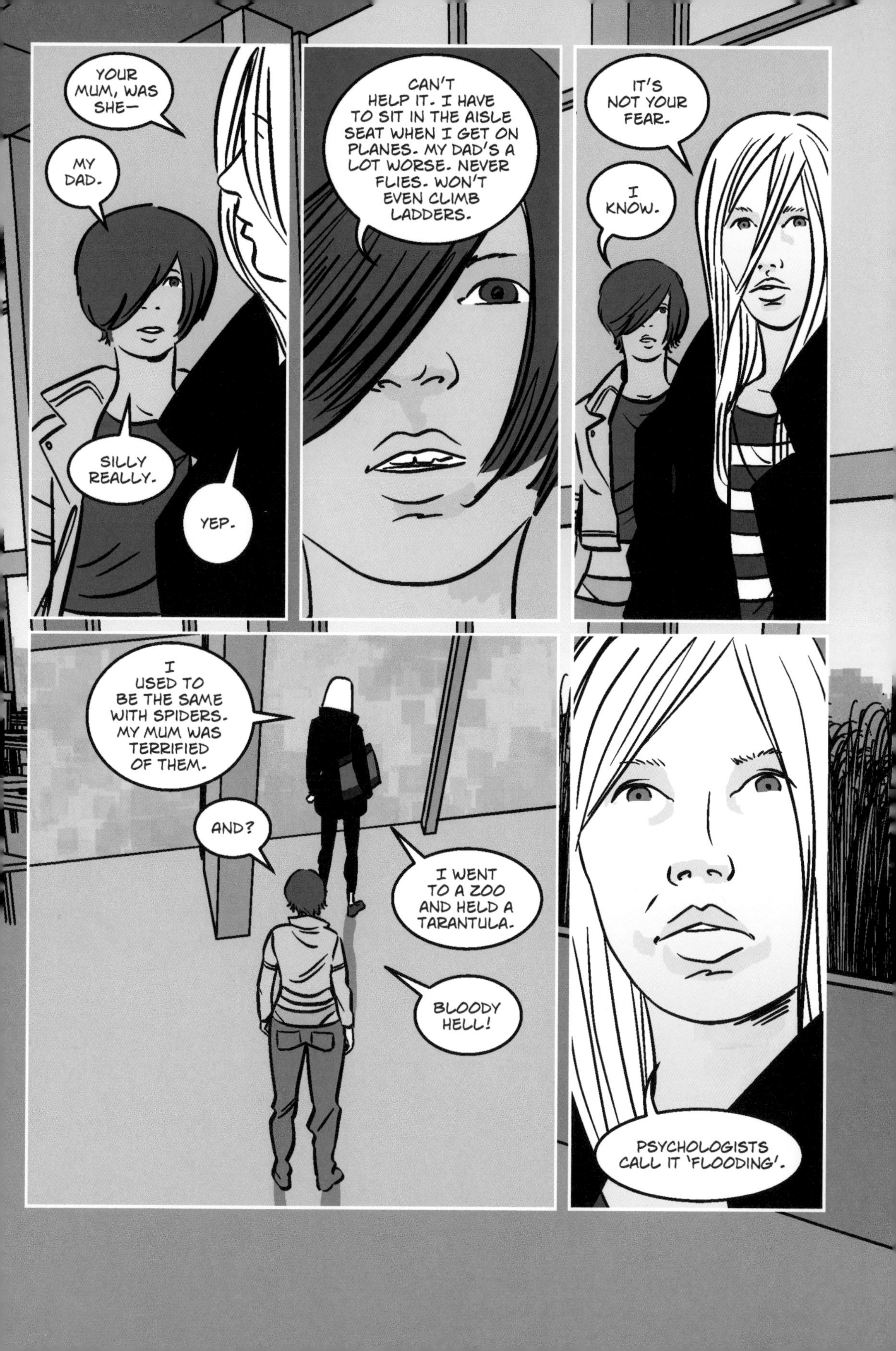
YOUR MUM, WAS SHE—
MY DAD.
SILLY REALLY.
YEP.
CAN'T HELP IT. I HAVE TO SIT IN THE AISLE SEAT WHEN I GET ON PLANES. MY DAD'S A LOT WORSE. NEVER FLIES. WON'T EVEN CLIMB LADDERS.
IT'S NOT YOUR FEAR.
I KNOW.
I USED TO BE THE SAME WITH SPIDERS. MY MUM WAS TERRIFIED OF THEM.
AND?
I WENT TO A ZOO AND HELD A TARANTULA.
BLOODY HELL!
PSYCHOLOGISTS CALL IT 'FLOODING'.

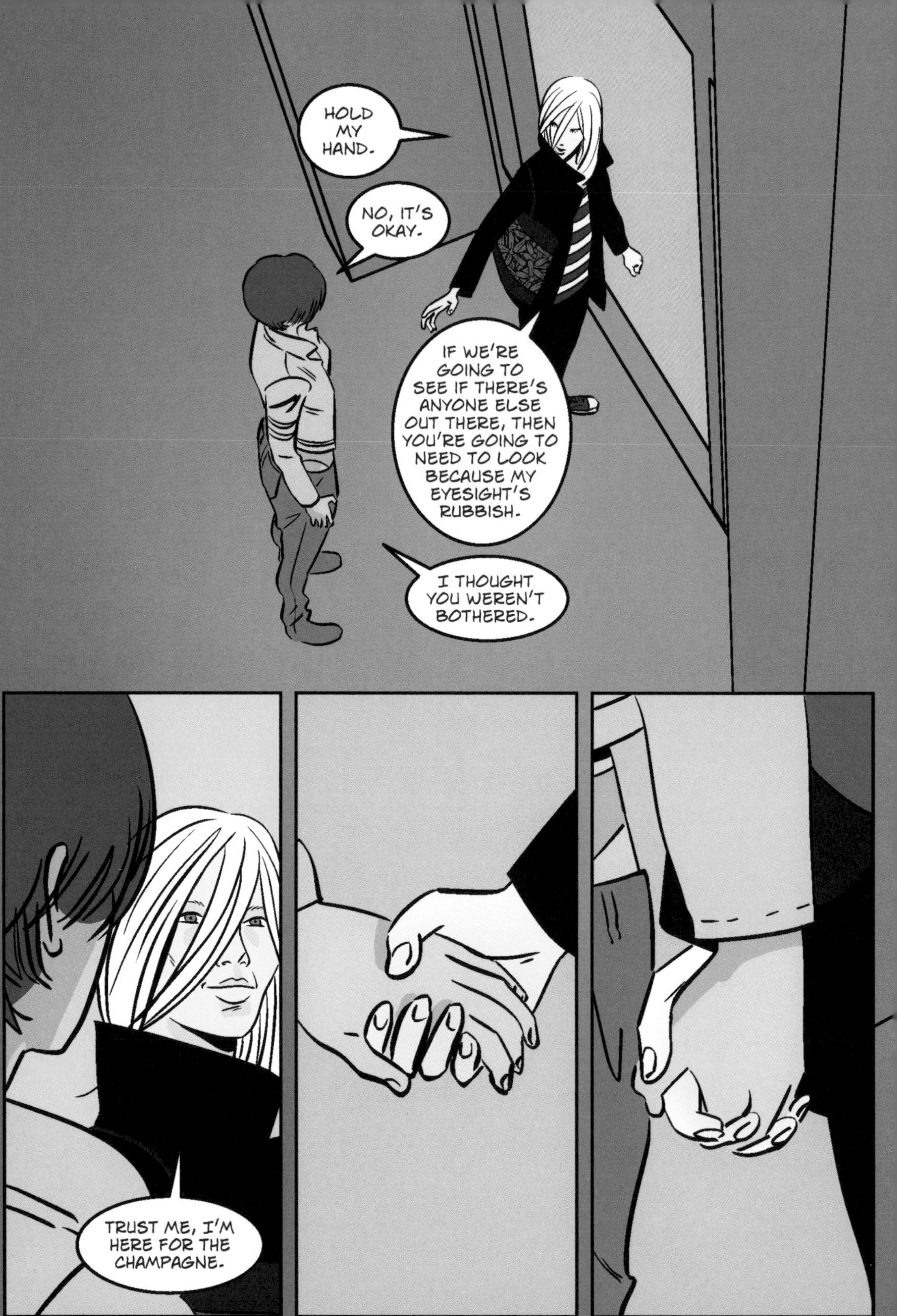
HOLD MY HAND.
NO, IT'S OKAY.
IF WE'RE GOING TO SEE IF THERE'S ANYONE ELSE OUT THERE, THEN YOU'RE GOING TO NEED TO LOOK BECAUSE MY EYESIGHT'S RUBBISH.
I THOUGHT YOU WEREN'T BOTHERED.
TRUST ME, I'M HERE FOR THE CHAMPAGNE.

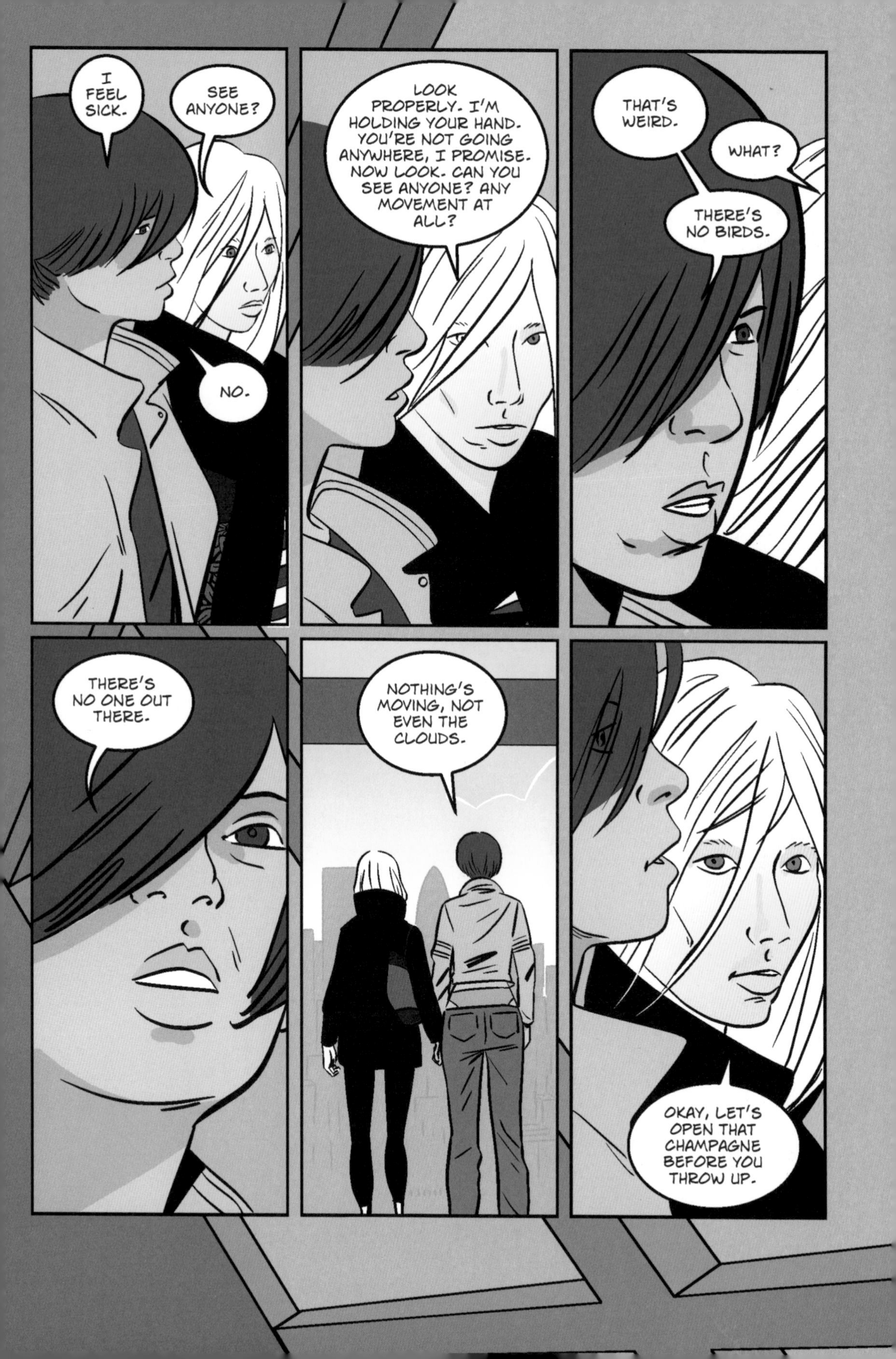
I FEEL SICK.
SEE ANYONE?
NO.
LOOK PROPERLY. I'M HOLDING YOUR HAND. YOU'RE NOT GOING ANYWHERE, I PROMISE. NOW LOOK. CAN YOU SEE ANYONE? ANY MOVEMENT AT ALL?
THAT'S WEIRD.
WHAT?
THERE'S NO BIRDS.
THERE'S NO ONE OUT THERE.
NOTHING'S MOVING, NOT EVEN THE CLOUDS.
OKAY, LET'S OPEN THAT CHAMPAGNE BEFORE YOU THROW UP.

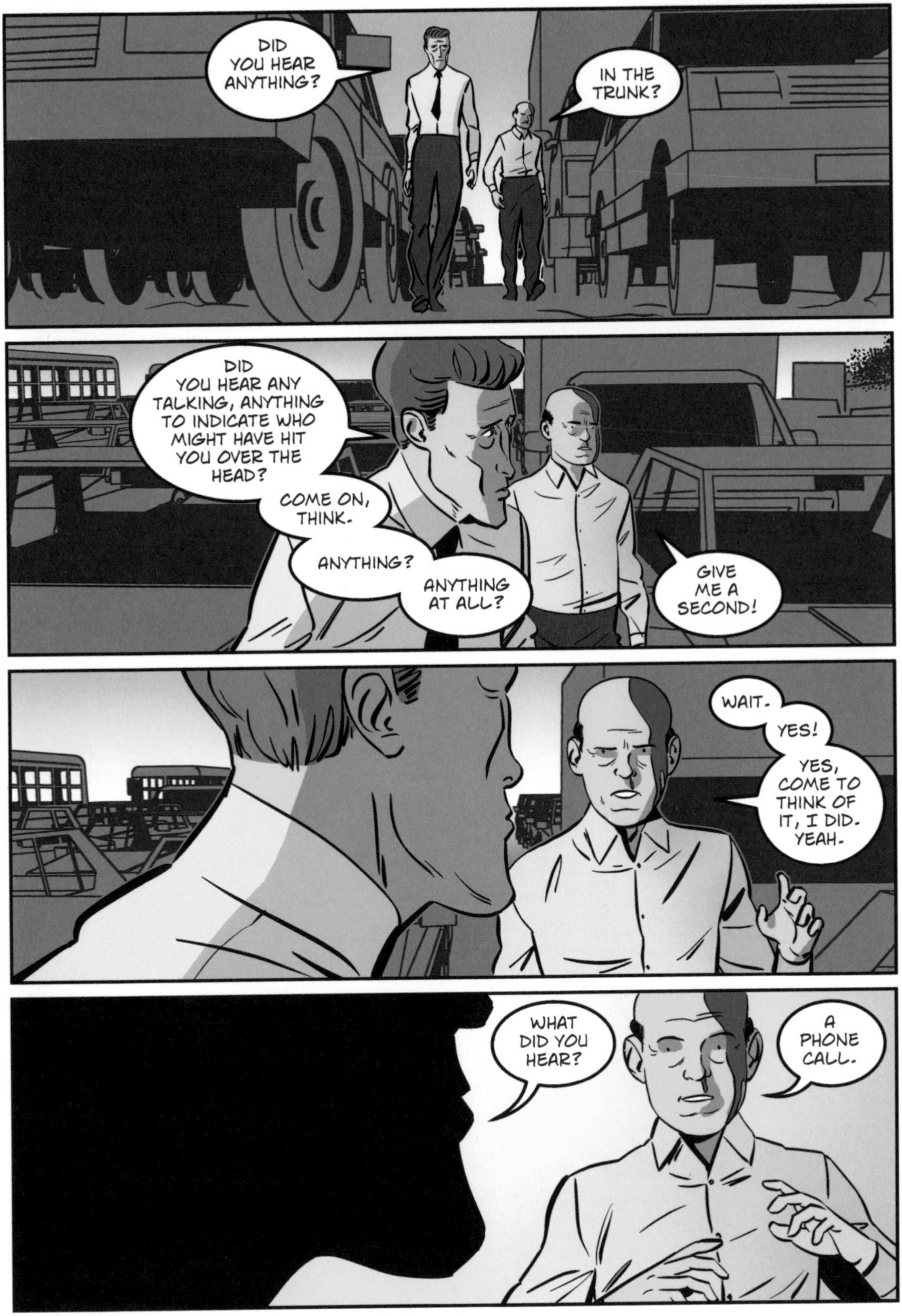
DID YOU HEAR ANYTHING?
IN THE TRUNK?
DID YOU HEAR ANY TALKING, ANYTHING TO INDICATE WHO MIGHT HAVE HIT YOU OVER THE HEAD?
COME ON, THINK.
ANYTHING?
ANYTHING AT ALL?
GIVE ME A SECOND!
WAIT.
YES!
YES, COME TO THINK OF IT, I DID. YEAH.
WHAT DID YOU HEAR?
A PHONE CALL.

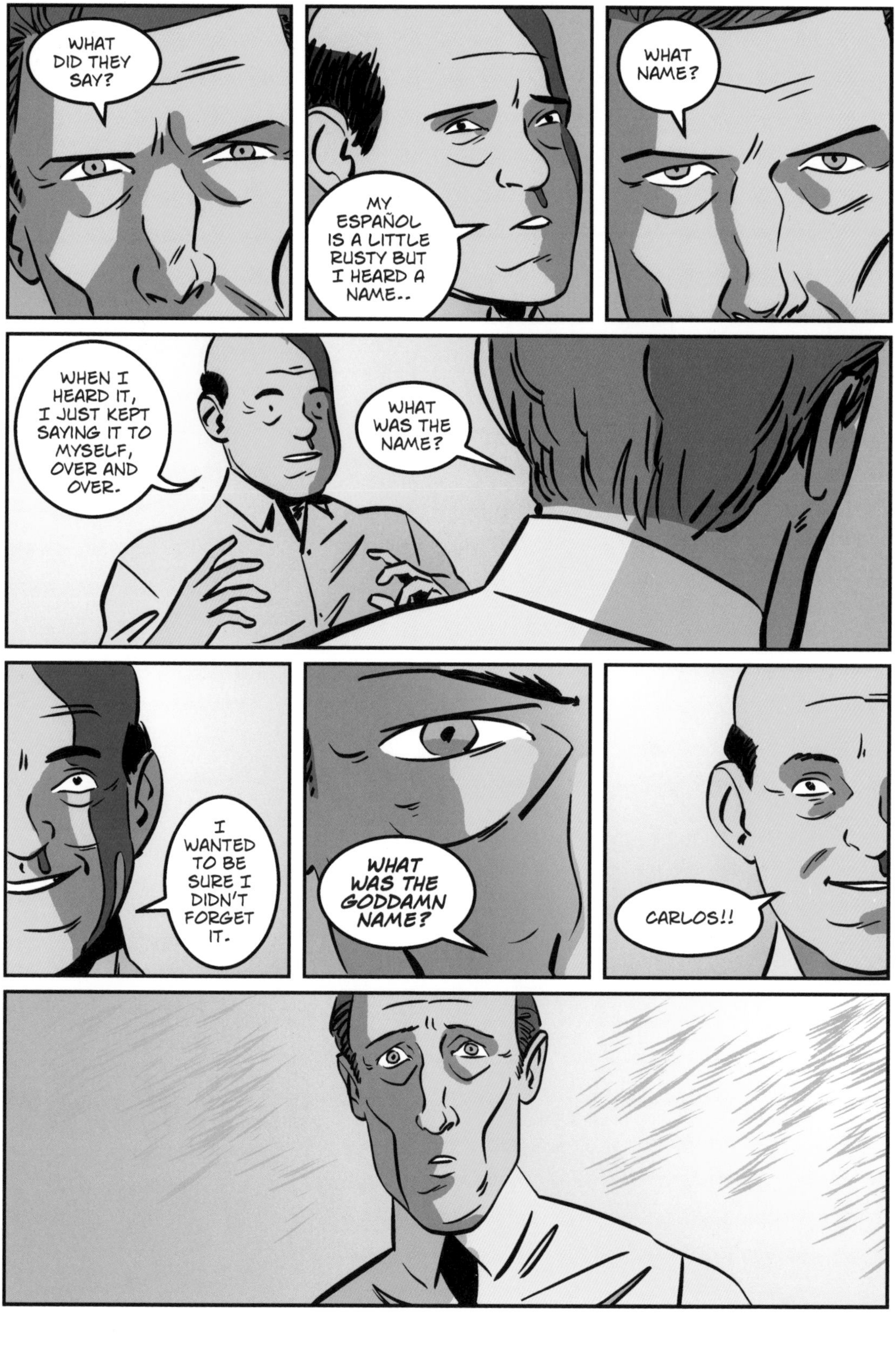
WHAT DID THEY SAY?
MY ESPAÑOL IS A LITTLE RUSTY BUT I HEARD A NAME..
WHAT NAME?
WHEN I HEARD IT, I JUST KEPT SAYING IT TO MYSELF, OVER AND OVER.
WHAT WAS THE NAME?
I WANTED TO BE SURE I DIDN'T FORGET IT.
WHAT WAS THE GODDAMN NAME?
CARLOS!!

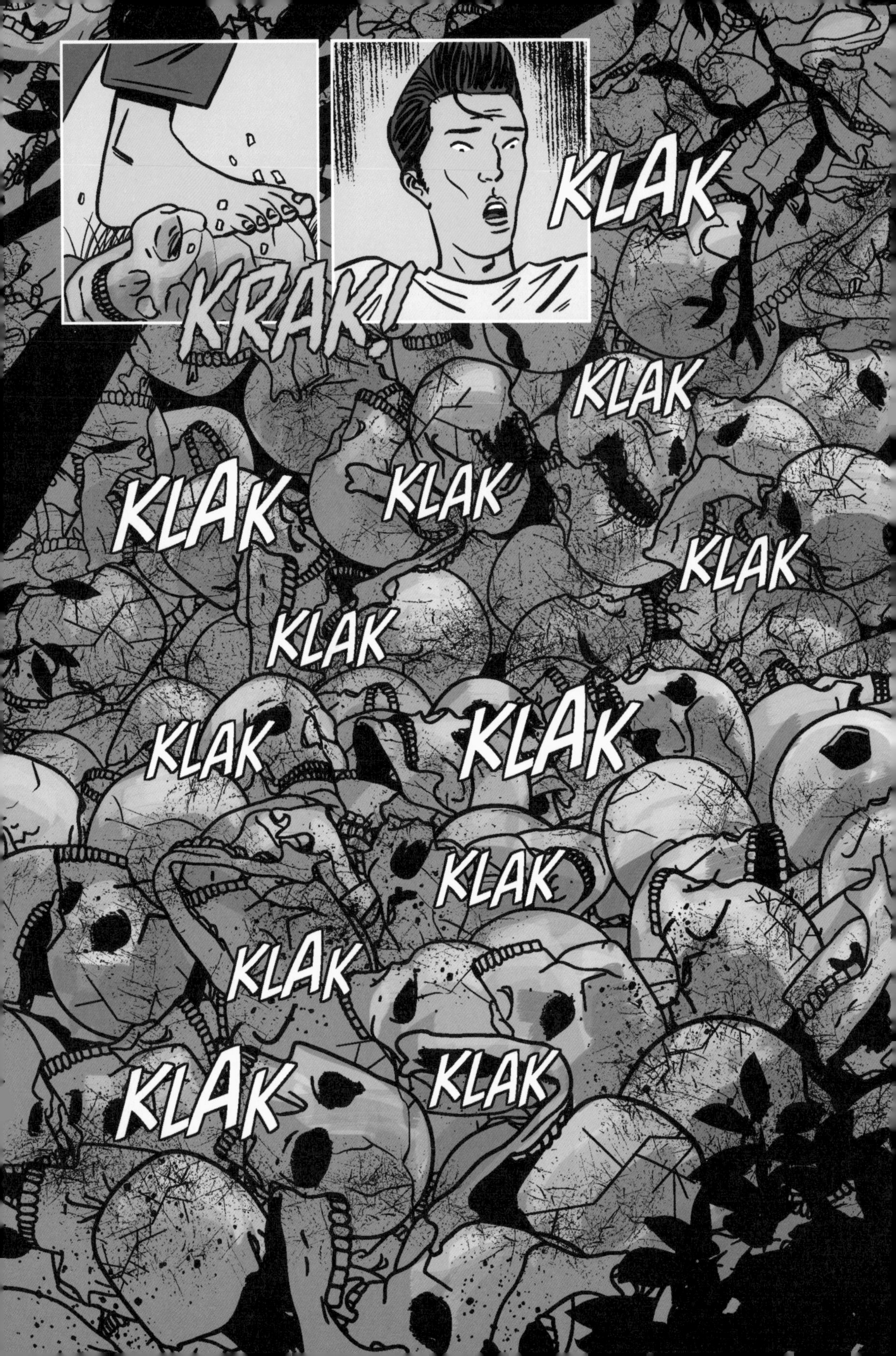
KRAK!
KLAK
KLAK
KLAK
KLAK
KLAK
KLAK
KLAK
KLAK
KLAK
KLAK
KLAK
KLAK

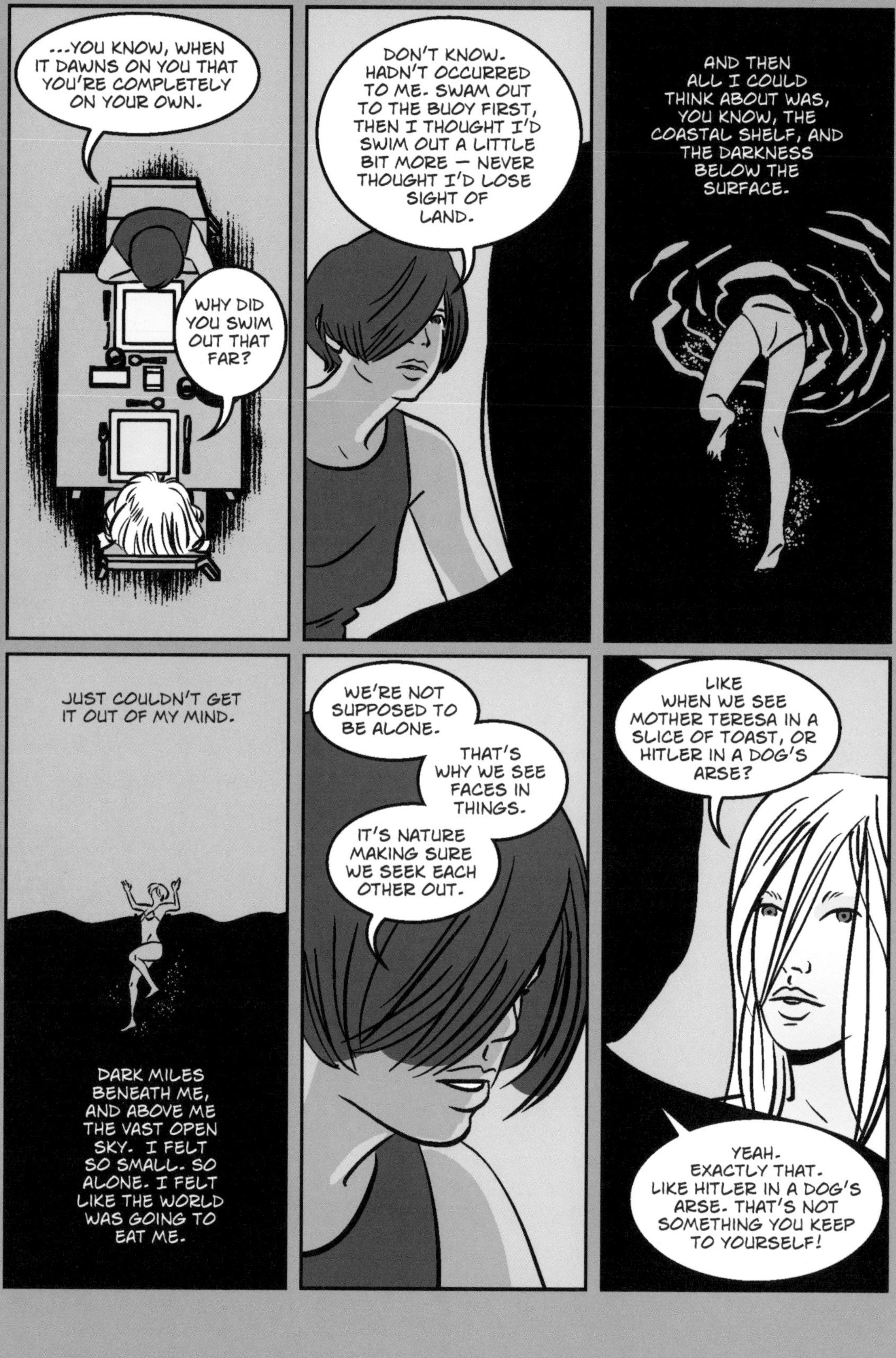
...YOU KNOW, WHEN IT DAWNS ON YOU THAT YOU'RE COMPLETELY ON YOUR OWN.
WHY DID YOU SWIM OUT THAT FAR?
DON'T KNOW. HADN'T OCCURRED TO ME. SWAM OUT TO THE BUOY FIRST, THEN I THOUGHT I'D SWIM OUT A LITTLE BIT MORE — NEVER THOUGHT I'D LOSE SIGHT OF LAND.
AND THEN ALL I COULD THINK ABOUT WAS, YOU KNOW, THE COASTAL SHELF, AND THE DARKNESS BELOW THE SURFACE.
JUST COULDN'T GET IT OUT OF MY MIND.
DARK MILES BENEATH ME, AND ABOVE ME THE VAST OPEN SKY. I FELT SO SMALL. SO ALONE. I FELT LIKE THE WORLD WAS GOING TO EAT ME.
WE'RE NOT SUPPOSED TO BE ALONE.
THAT'S WHY WE SEE FACES IN THINGS.
IT'S NATURE MAKING SURE WE SEEK EACH OTHER OUT.
LIKE WHEN WE SEE MOTHER TERESA IN A SLICE OF TOAST, OR HITLER IN A DOG'S ARSE?
YEAH. EXACTLY THAT. LIKE HITLER IN A DOG'S ARSE. THAT'S NOT SOMETHING YOU KEEP TO YOURSELF!

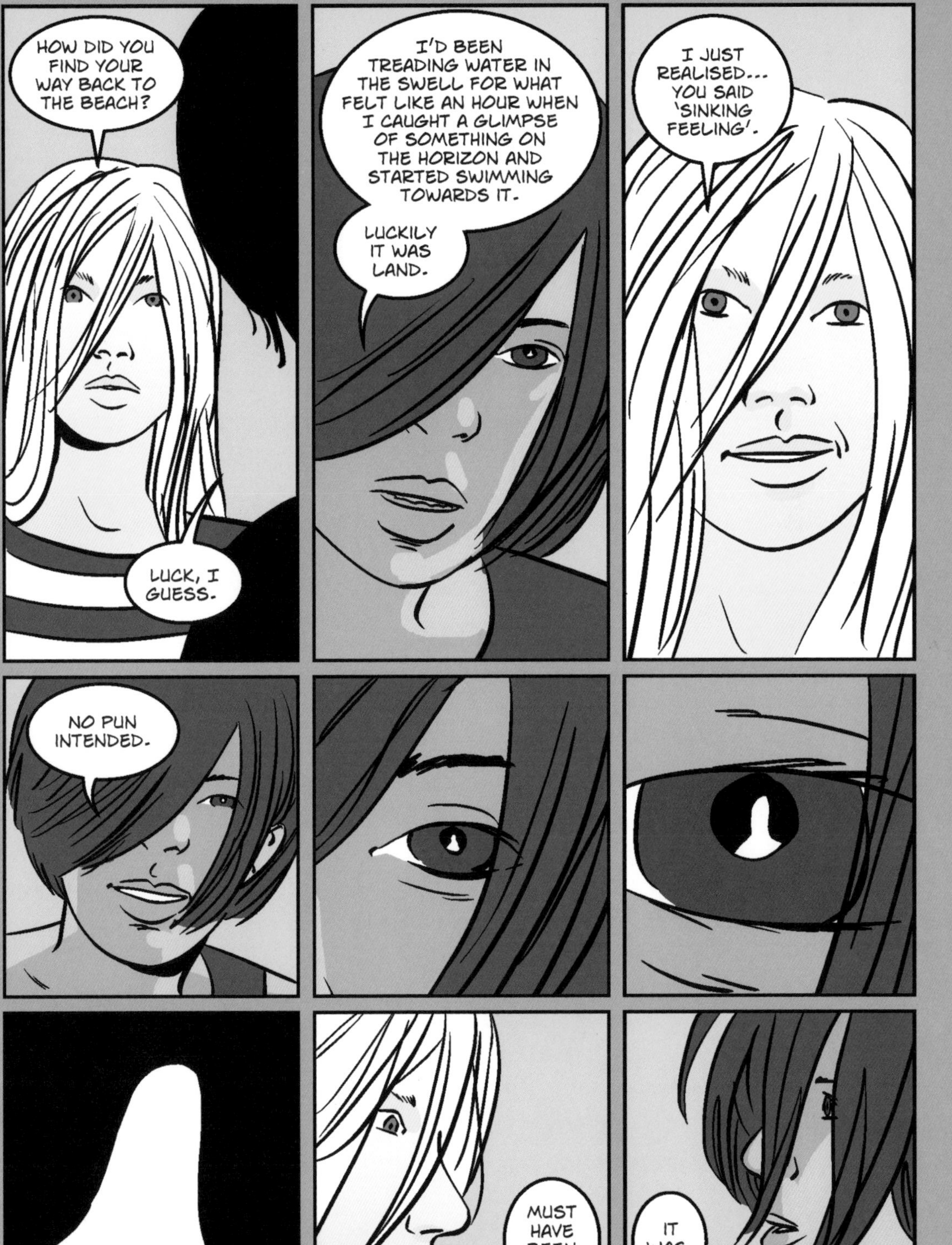
HOW DID YOU FIND YOUR WAY BACK TO THE BEACH?
LUCK, I GUESS.
I'D BEEN TREADING WATER IN THE SWELL FOR WHAT FELT LIKE AN HOUR WHEN I CAUGHT A GLIMPSE OF SOMETHING ON THE HORIZON AND STARTED SWIMMING TOWARDS IT.
LUCKILY IT WAS LAND.
I JUST REALISED... YOU SAID 'SINKING FEELING'.
NO PUN INTENDED.
MUST HAVE BEEN SCARY.
IT WAS.

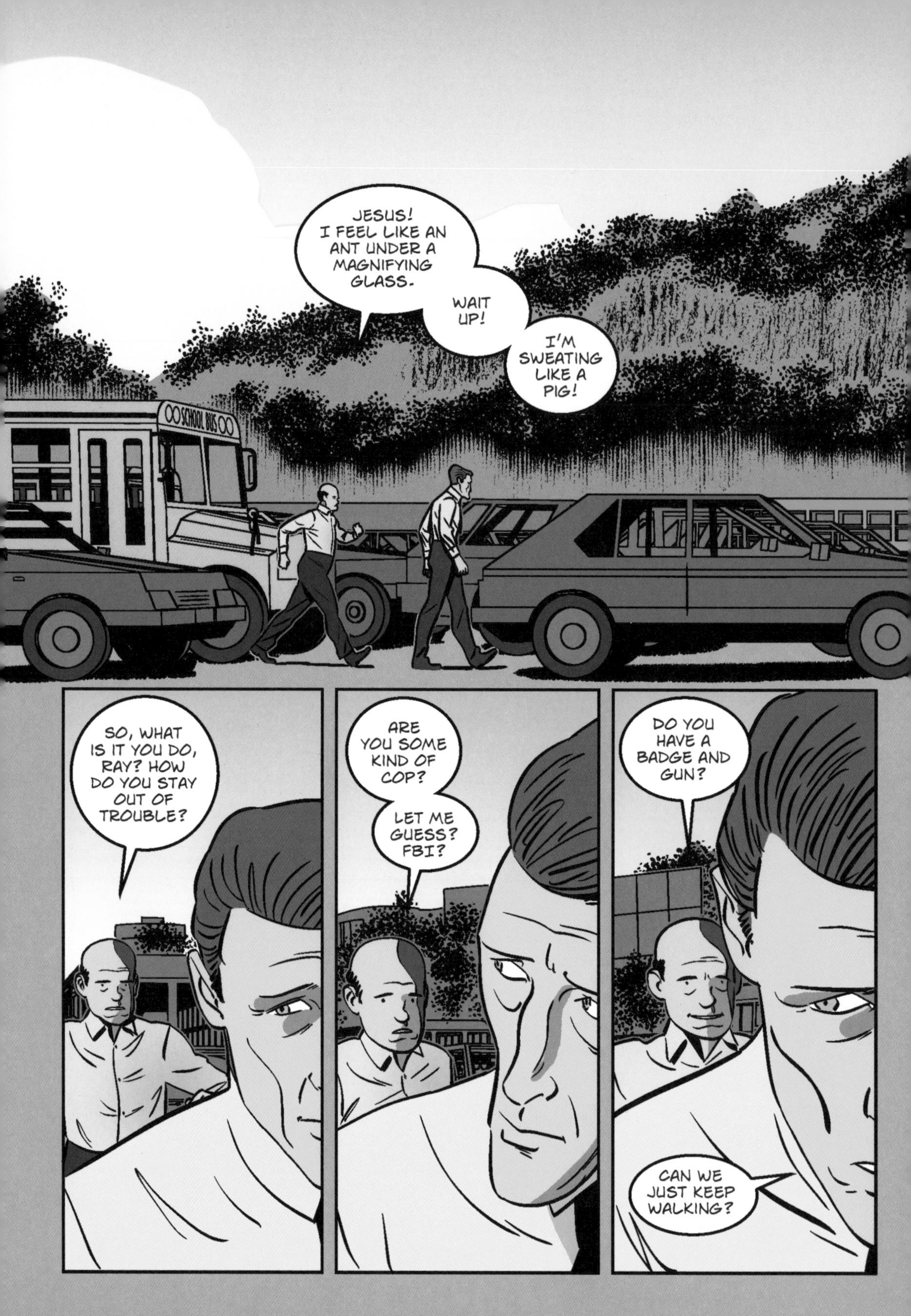
JESUS! I FEEL LIKE AN ANT UNDER A MAGNIFYING GLASS.
WAIT UP!
I'M SWEATING LIKE A PIG!
SO, WHAT IS IT YOU DO, RAY? HOW DO YOU STAY OUT OF TROUBLE?
ARE YOU SOME KIND OF COP?
LET ME GUESS? FBI?
DO YOU HAVE A BADGE AND GUN?
CAN WE JUST KEEP WALKING?

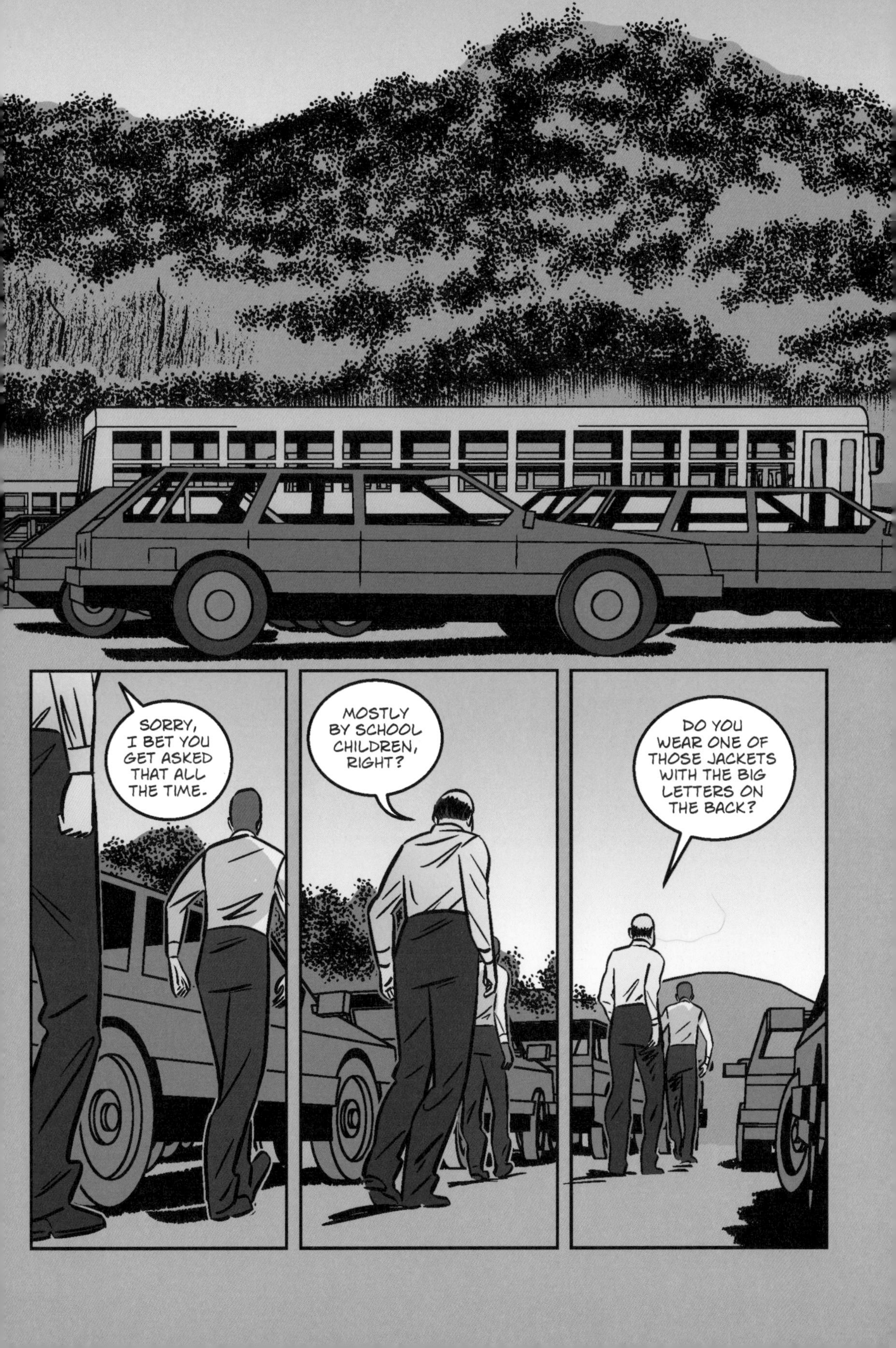
SORRY, I BET YOU GET ASKED THAT ALL THE TIME.
MOSTLY BY SCHOOL CHILDREN, RIGHT?
DO YOU WEAR ONE OF THOSE JACKETS WITH THE BIG LETTERS ON THE BACK?

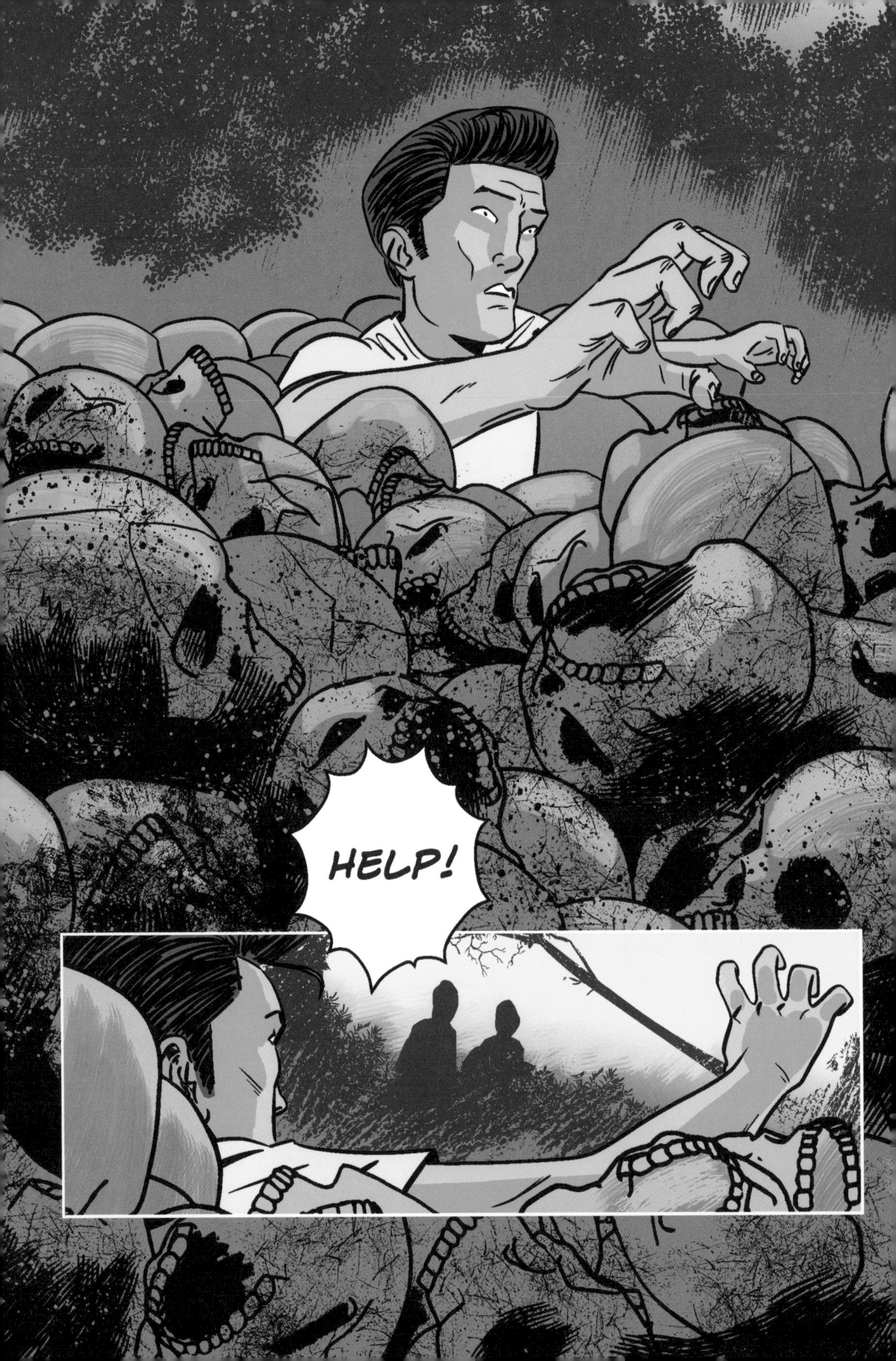
HELP!

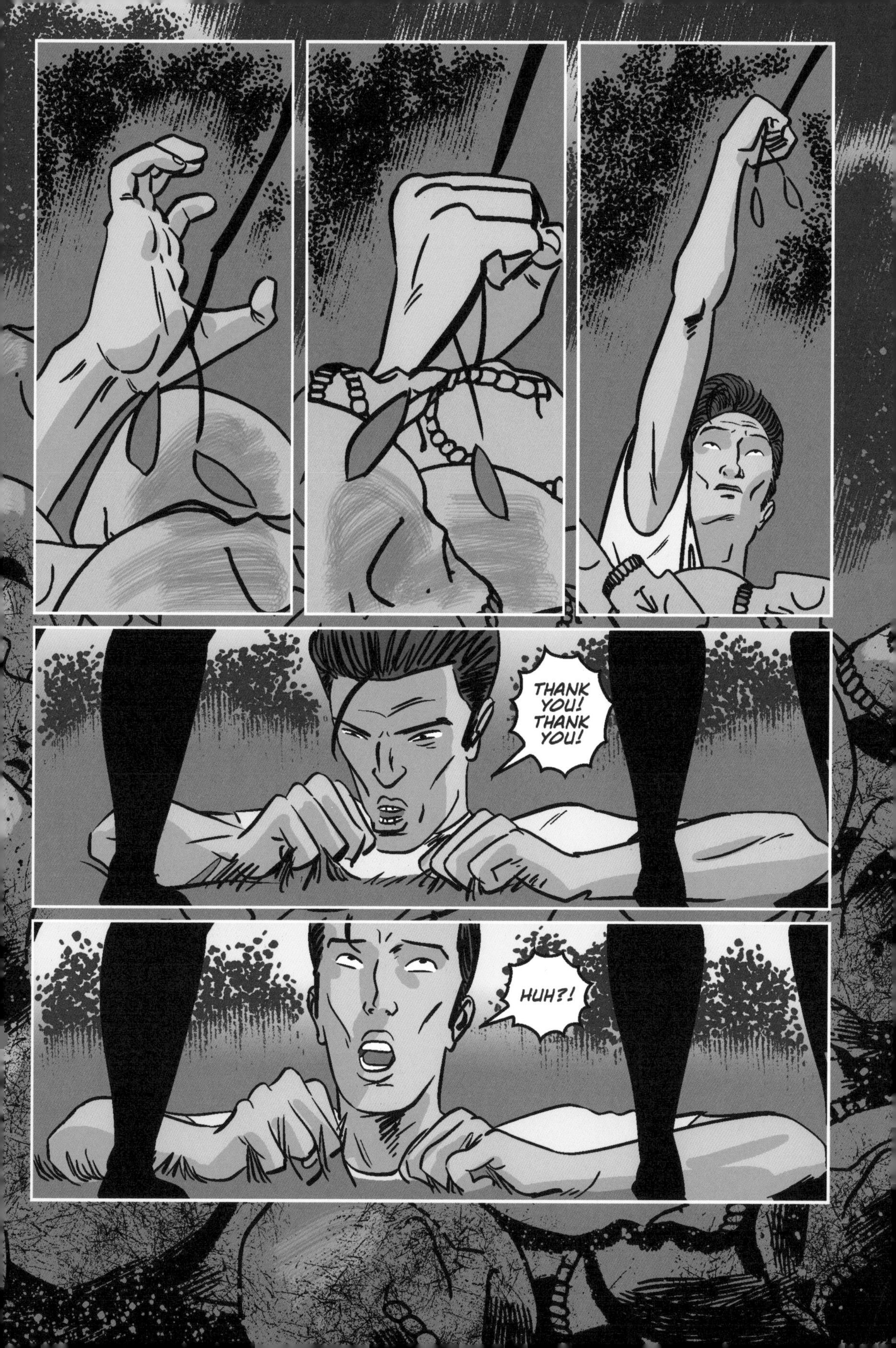
THANK YOU! THANK YOU!
HUH?!

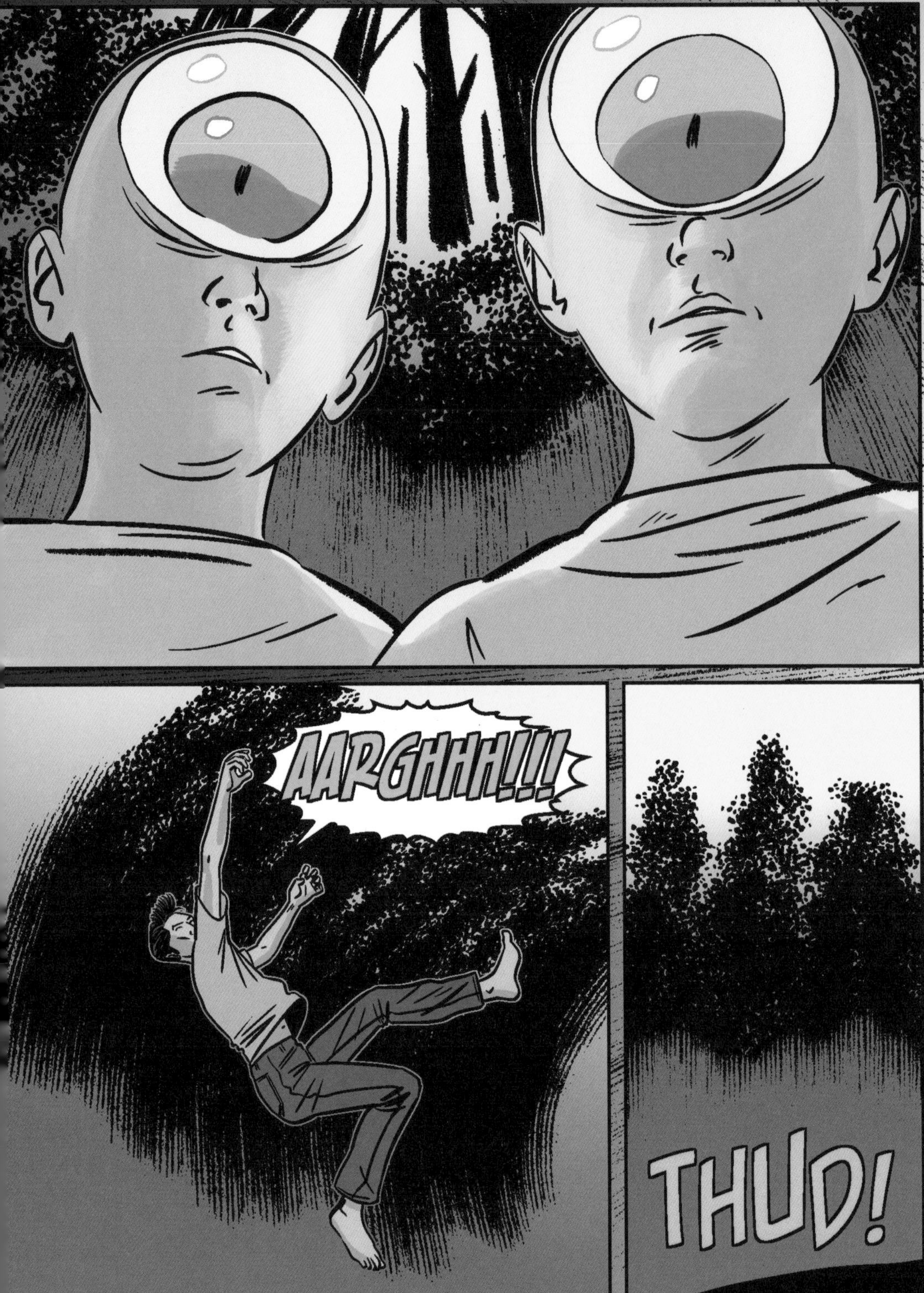
AARGHHH!!!
THUD!

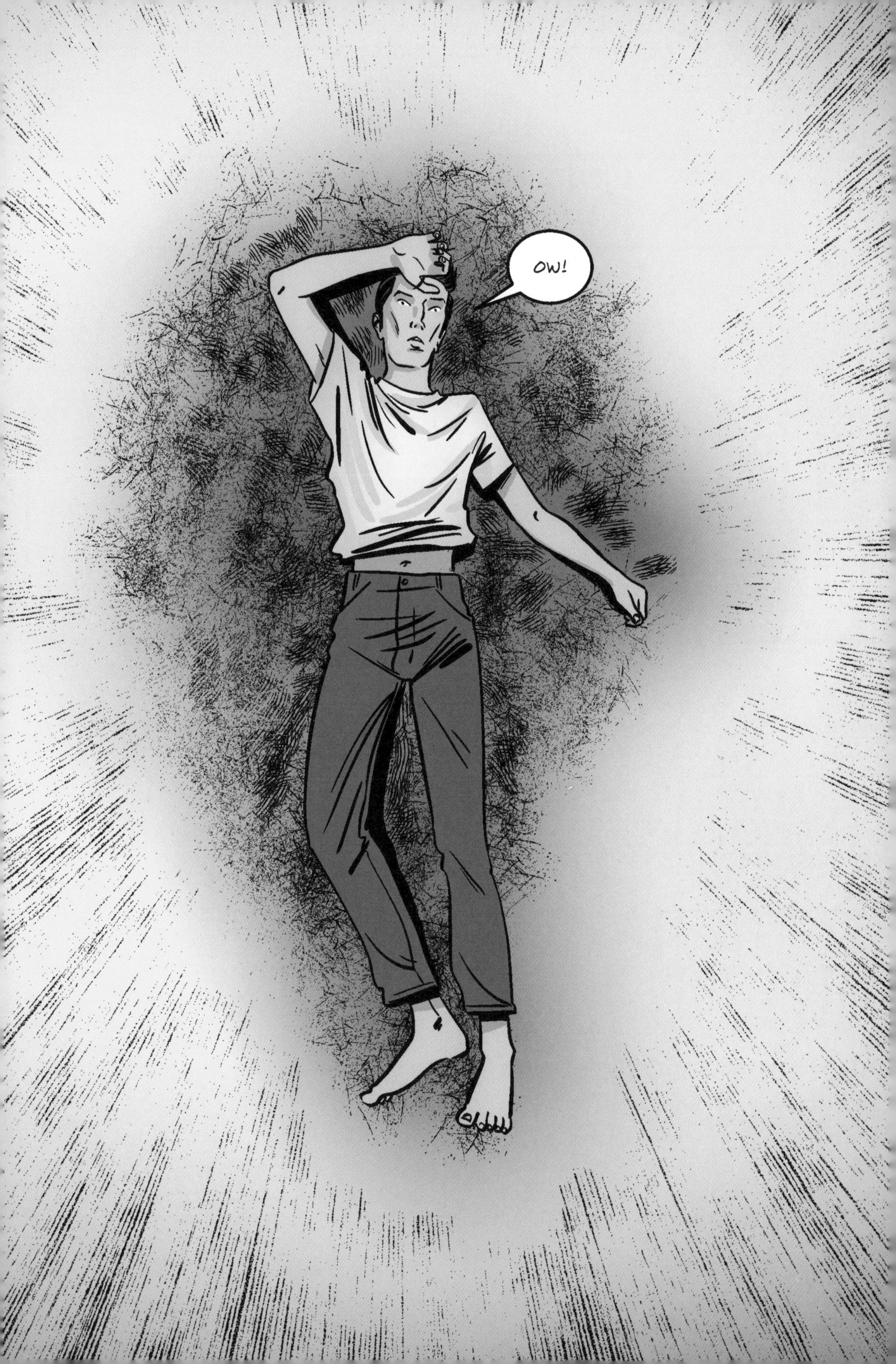
OW!

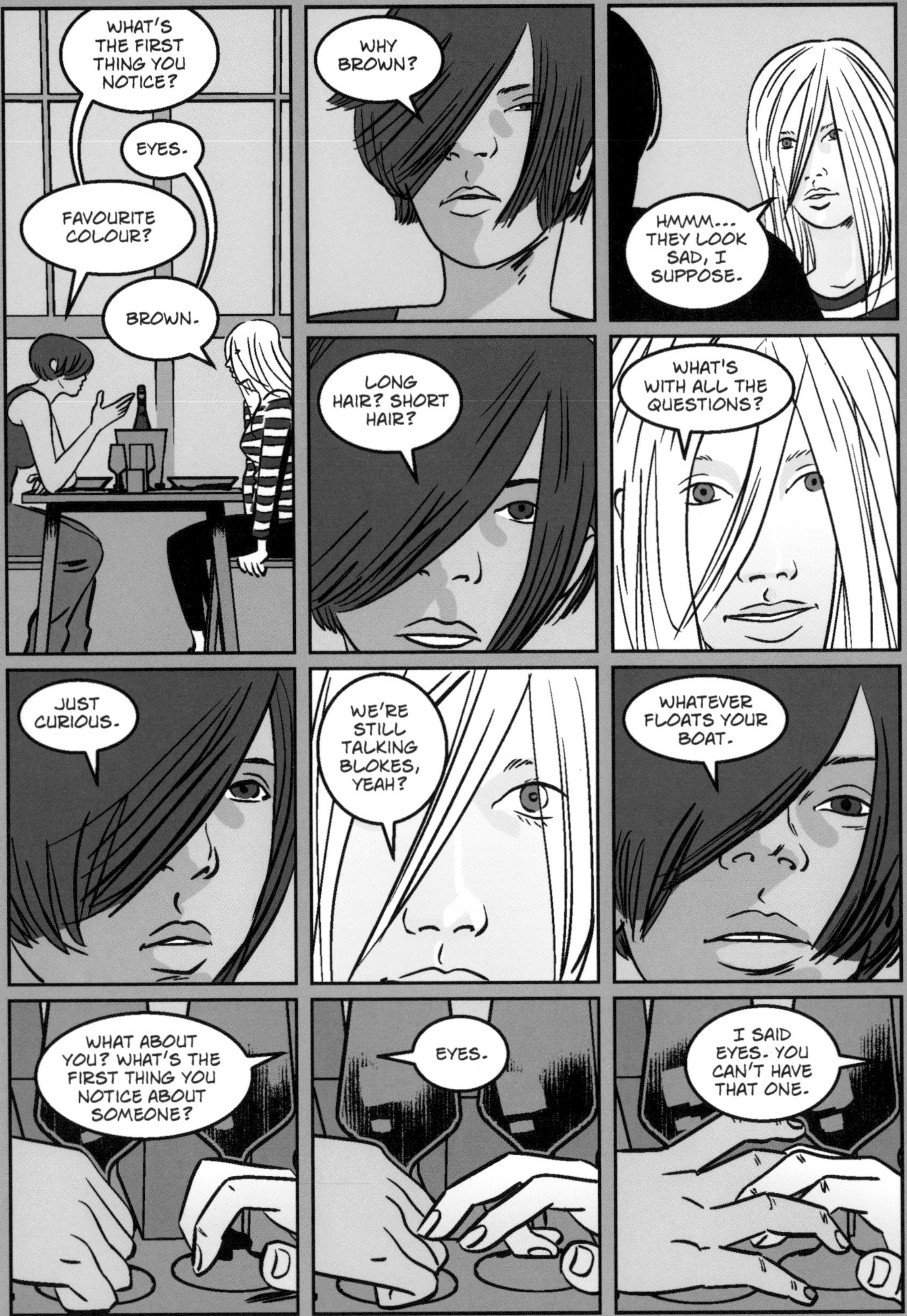
WHAT'S THE FIRST THING YOU NOTICE?
EYES.
FAVOURITE COLOUR?
BROWN.
WHY BROWN?
HMMM... THEY LOOK SAD, I SUPPOSE.
LONG HAIR? SHORT HAIR?
WHAT'S WITH ALL THE QUESTIONS?
JUST CURIOUS.
WE'RE STILL TALKING BLOKES, YEAH?
WHATEVER FLOATS YOUR BOAT.
WHAT ABOUT YOU? WHAT'S THE FIRST THING YOU NOTICE ABOUT SOMEONE?
EYES.
I SAID EYES. YOU CAN'T HAVE THAT ONE.

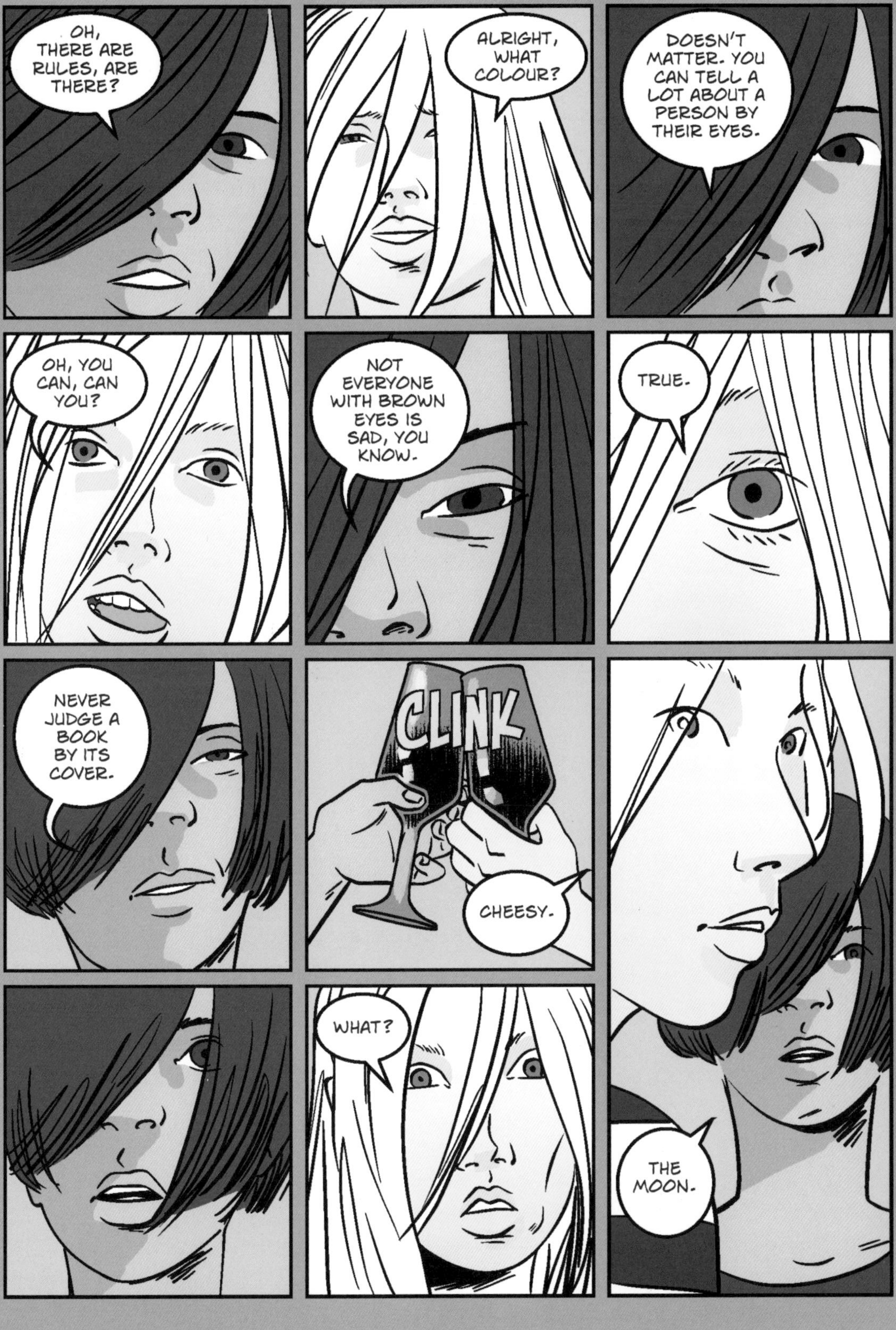
OH, THERE ARE RULES, ARE THERE?
ALRIGHT, WHAT COLOUR?
DOESN'T MATTER. YOU CAN TELL A LOT ABOUT A PERSON BY THEIR EYES.
OH, YOU CAN, CAN YOU?
NOT EVERYONE WITH BROWN EYES IS SAD, YOU KNOW.
TRUE.
NEVER JUDGE A BOOK BY ITS COVER.
CLINK
CHEESY.
WHAT?
THE MOON.

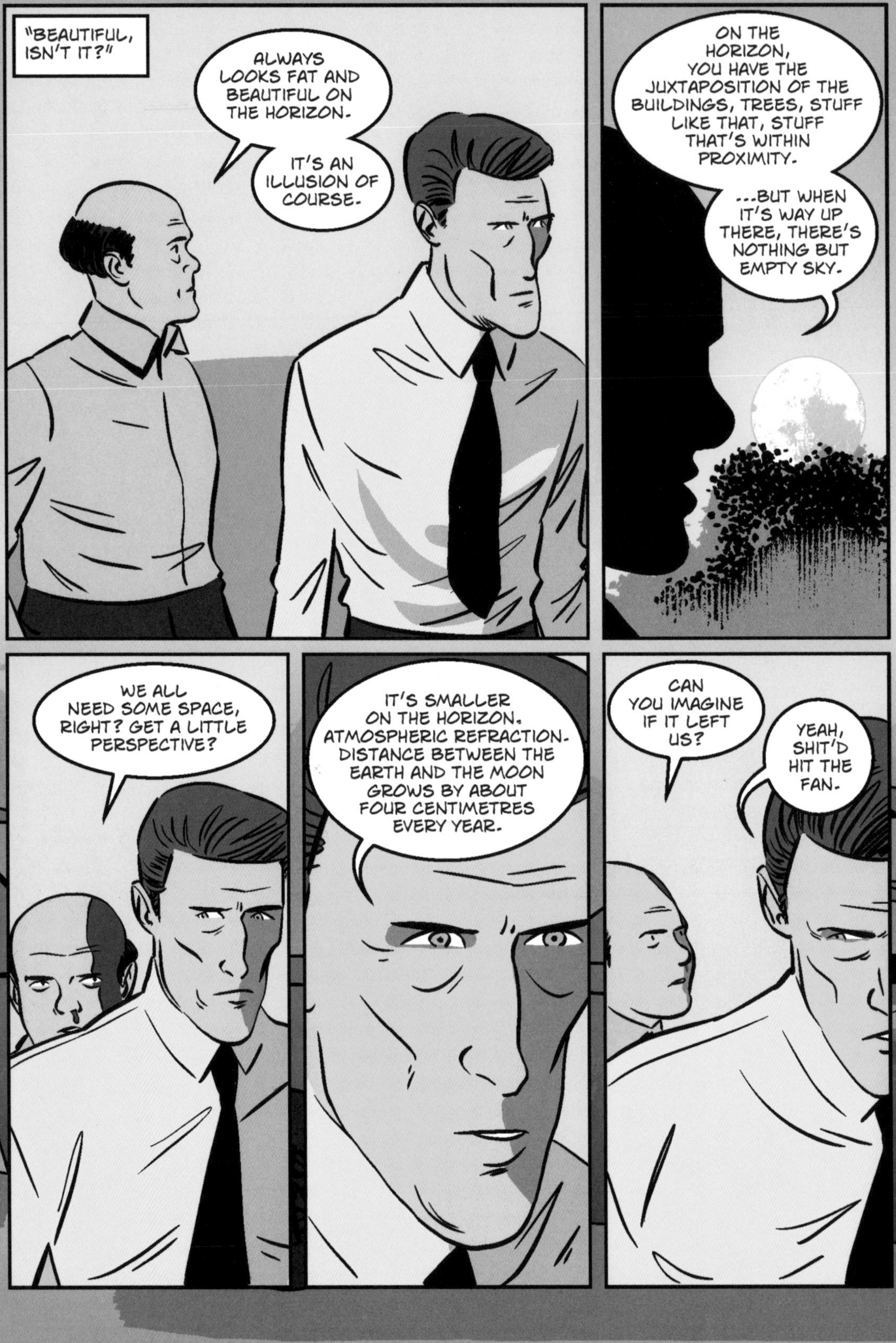
"BEAUTIFUL, ISN'T IT?"
ALWAYS LOOKS FAT AND BEAUTIFUL ON THE HORIZON.
IT'S AN ILLUSION OF COURSE.
ON THE HORIZON, YOU HAVE THE JUXTAPOSITION OF THE BUILDINGS, TREES, STUFF LIKE THAT, STUFF THAT'S WITHIN PROXIMITY.
...BUT WHEN IT'S WAY UP THERE, THERE'S NOTHING BUT EMPTY SKY.
WE ALL NEED SOME SPACE, RIGHT? GET A LITTLE PERSPECTIVE?
IT'S SMALLER ON THE HORIZON. ATMOSPHERIC REFRACTION. DISTANCE BETWEEN THE EARTH AND THE MOON GROWS BY ABOUT FOUR CENTIMETRES EVERY YEAR.
CAN YOU IMAGINE IF IT LEFT US?
YEAH, SHIT'D HIT THE FAN.

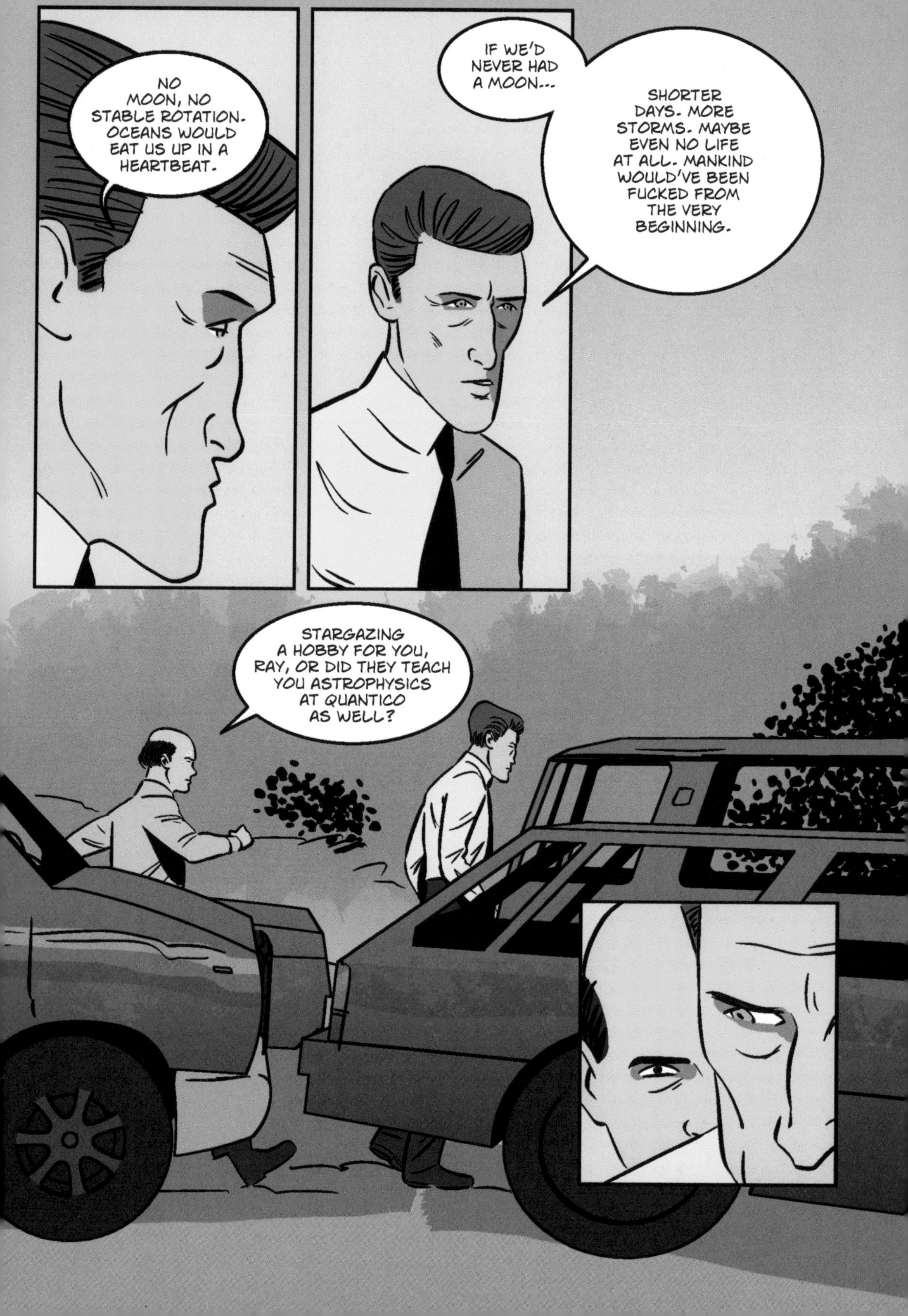
NO MOON, NO STABLE ROTATION. OCEANS WOULD EAT US UP IN A HEARTBEAT.
IF WE'D NEVER HAD A MOON...
SHORTER DAYS. MORE STORMS. MAYBE EVEN NO LIFE AT ALL. MANKIND WOULD'VE BEEN FUCKED FROM THE VERY BEGINNING.
STARGAZING A HOBBY FOR YOU, RAY, OR DID THEY TEACH YOU ASTROPHYSICS AT QUANTICO AS WELL?

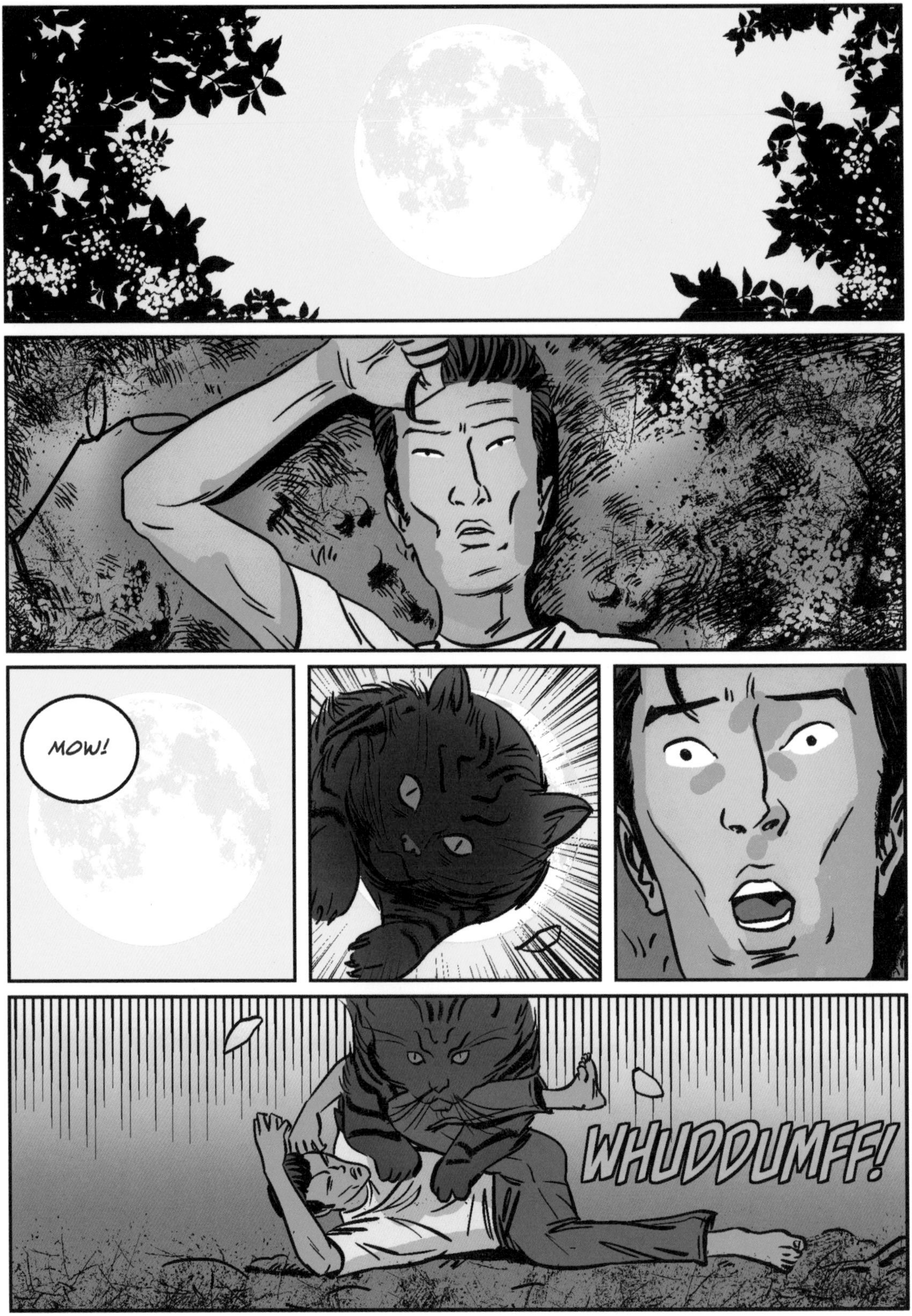
MOW!
WHUDDUMFF!

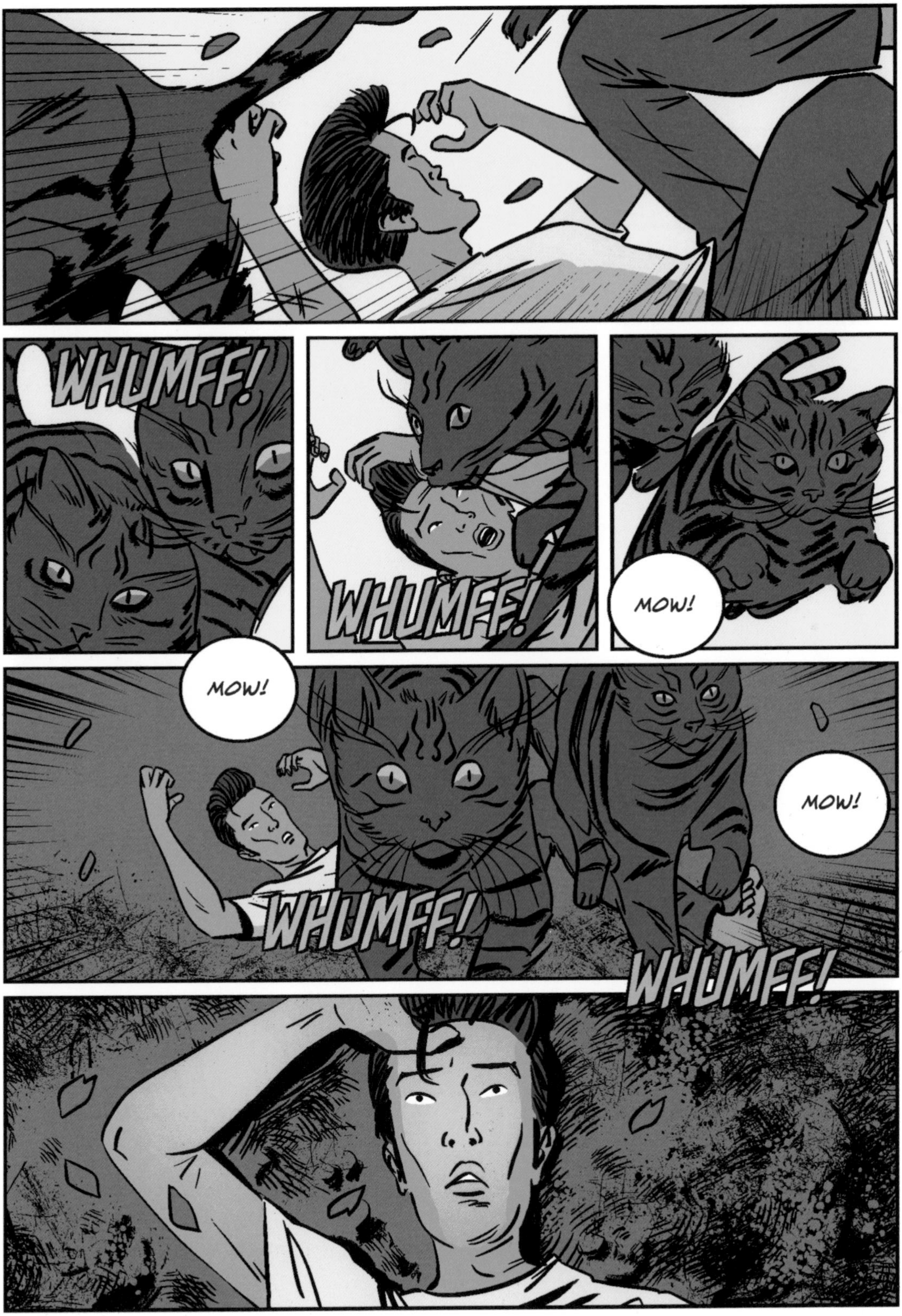
WHUMFF!
WHUMFF!
MOW!
MOW!
MOW!
WHUMFF!
WHUMFF!

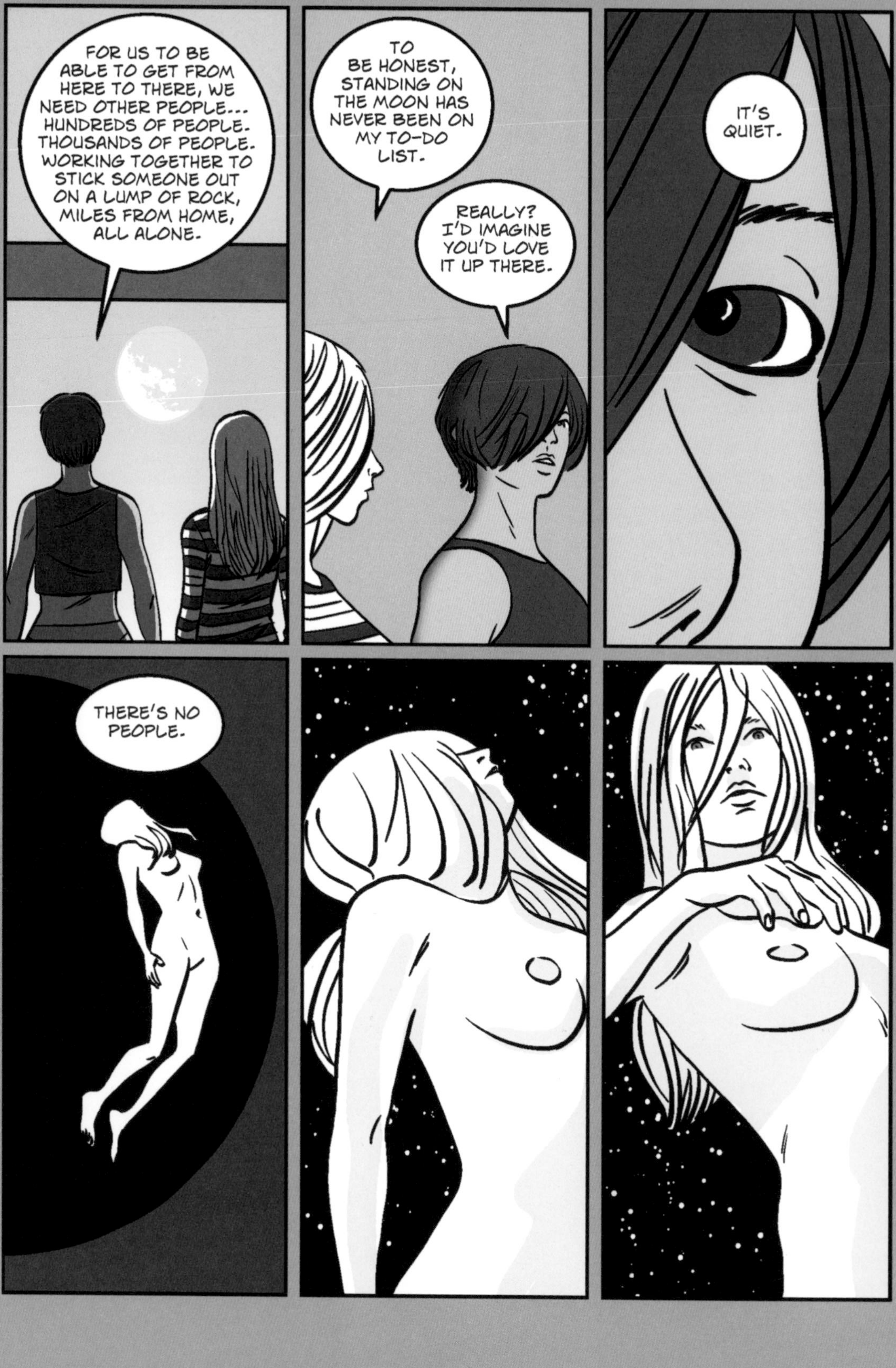
FOR US TO BE ABLE TO GET FROM HERE TO THERE, WE NEED OTHER PEOPLE... HUNDREDS OF PEOPLE. THOUSANDS OF PEOPLE. WORKING TOGETHER TO STICK SOMEONE OUT ON A LUMP OF ROCK, MILES FROM HOME, ALL ALONE.
TO BE HONEST, STANDING ON THE MOON HAS NEVER BEEN ON MY TO-DO LIST.
REALLY? I'D IMAGINE YOU'D LOVE IT UP THERE.
IT'S QUIET.
THERE'S NO PEOPLE.

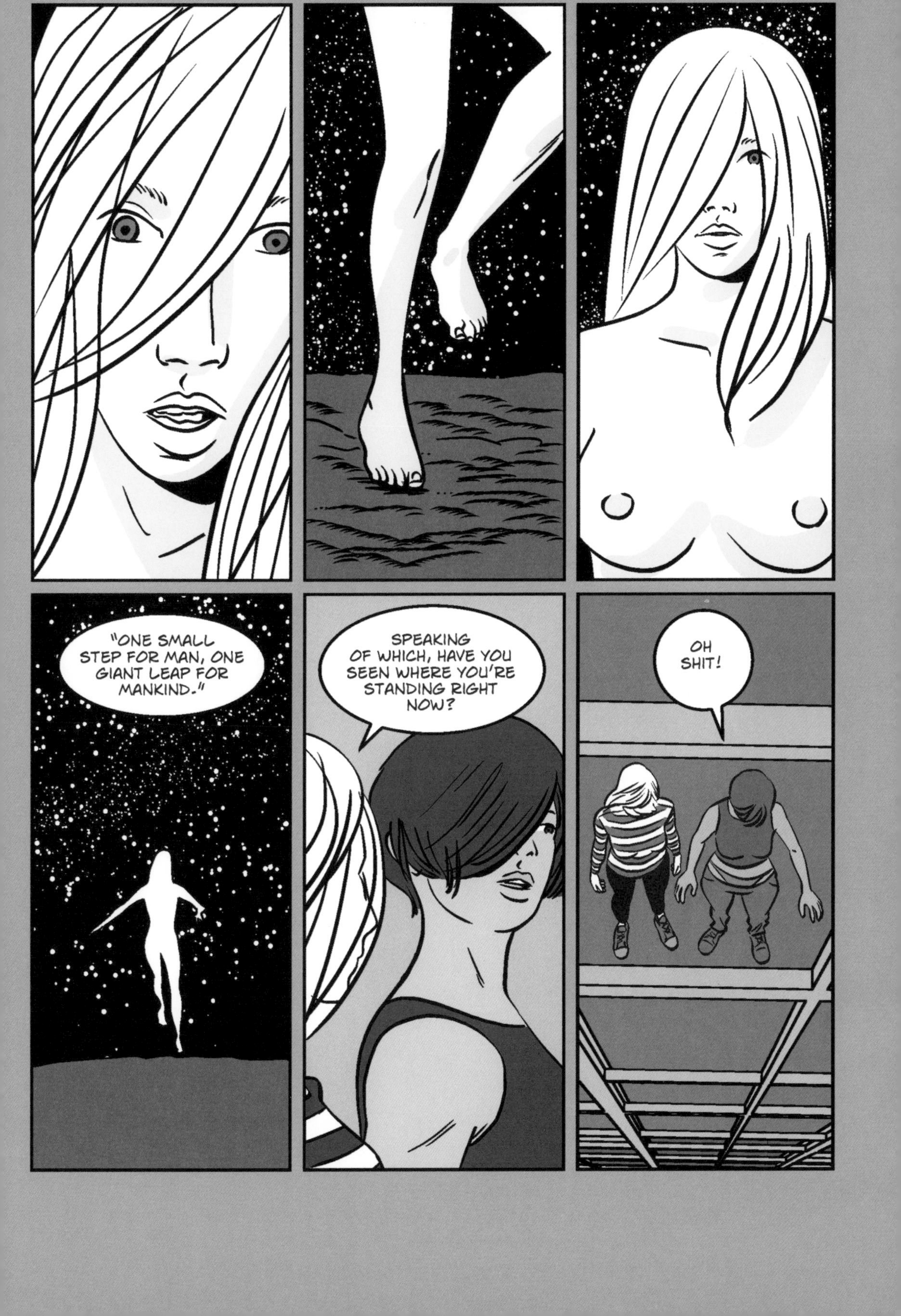
"ONE SMALL STEP FOR MAN, ONE GIANT LEAP FOR MANKIND."
SPEAKING OF WHICH, HAVE YOU SEEN WHERE YOU'RE STANDING RIGHT NOW?
OH SHIT!

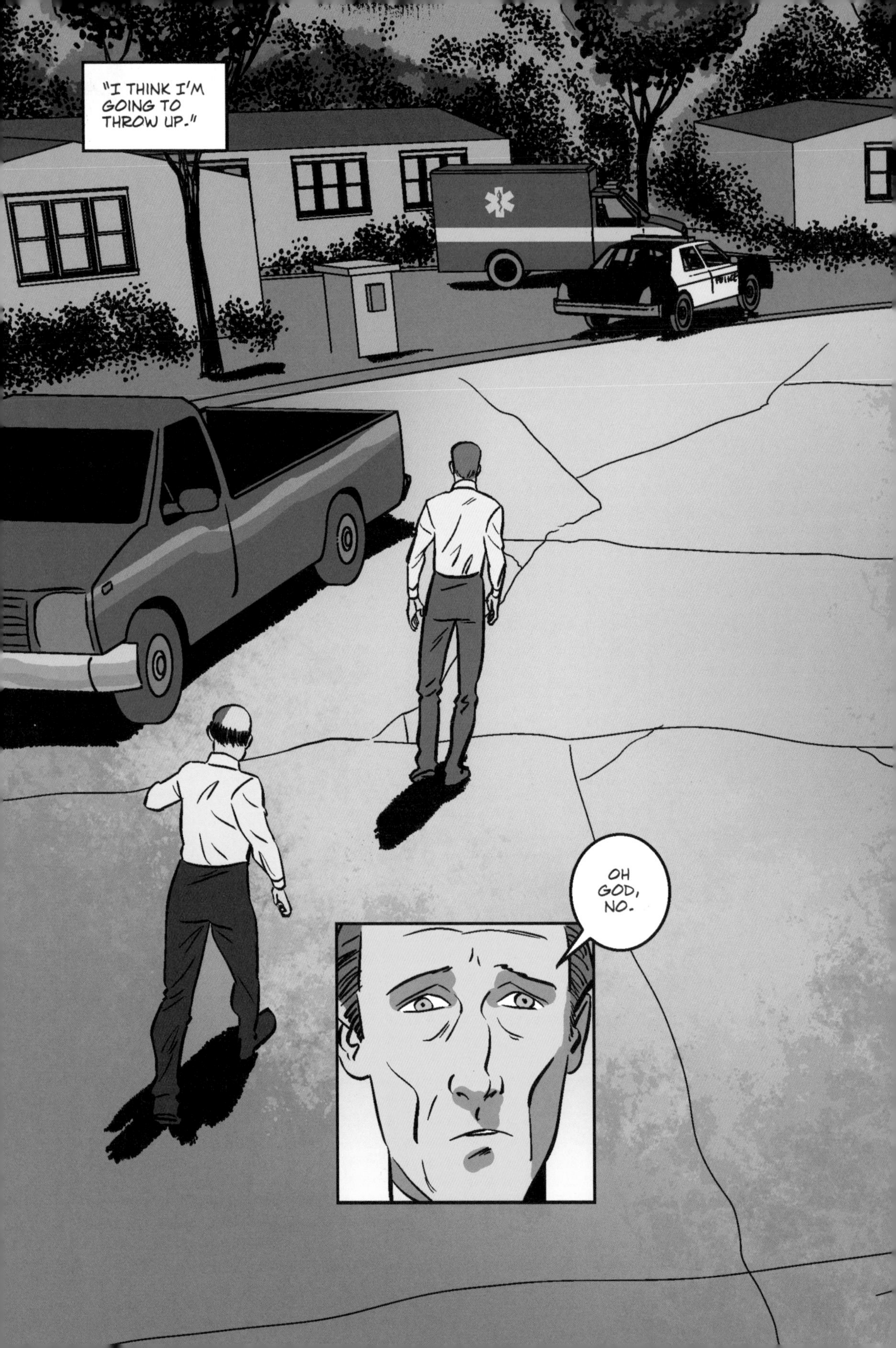
"I THINK I'M GOING TO THROW UP."
POLICE
OH GOD, NO.

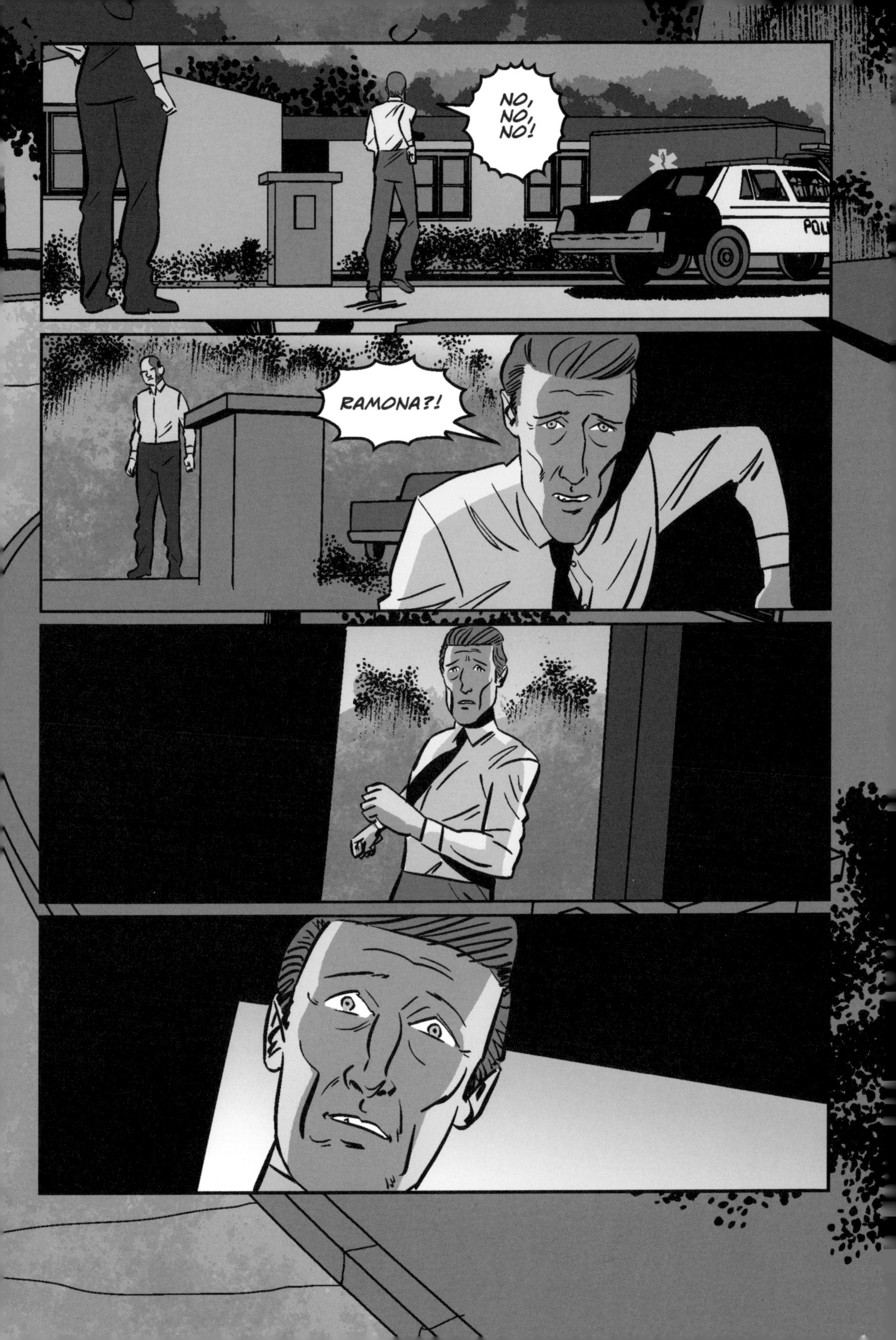
NO, NO, NO!
POLI
RAMONA?!

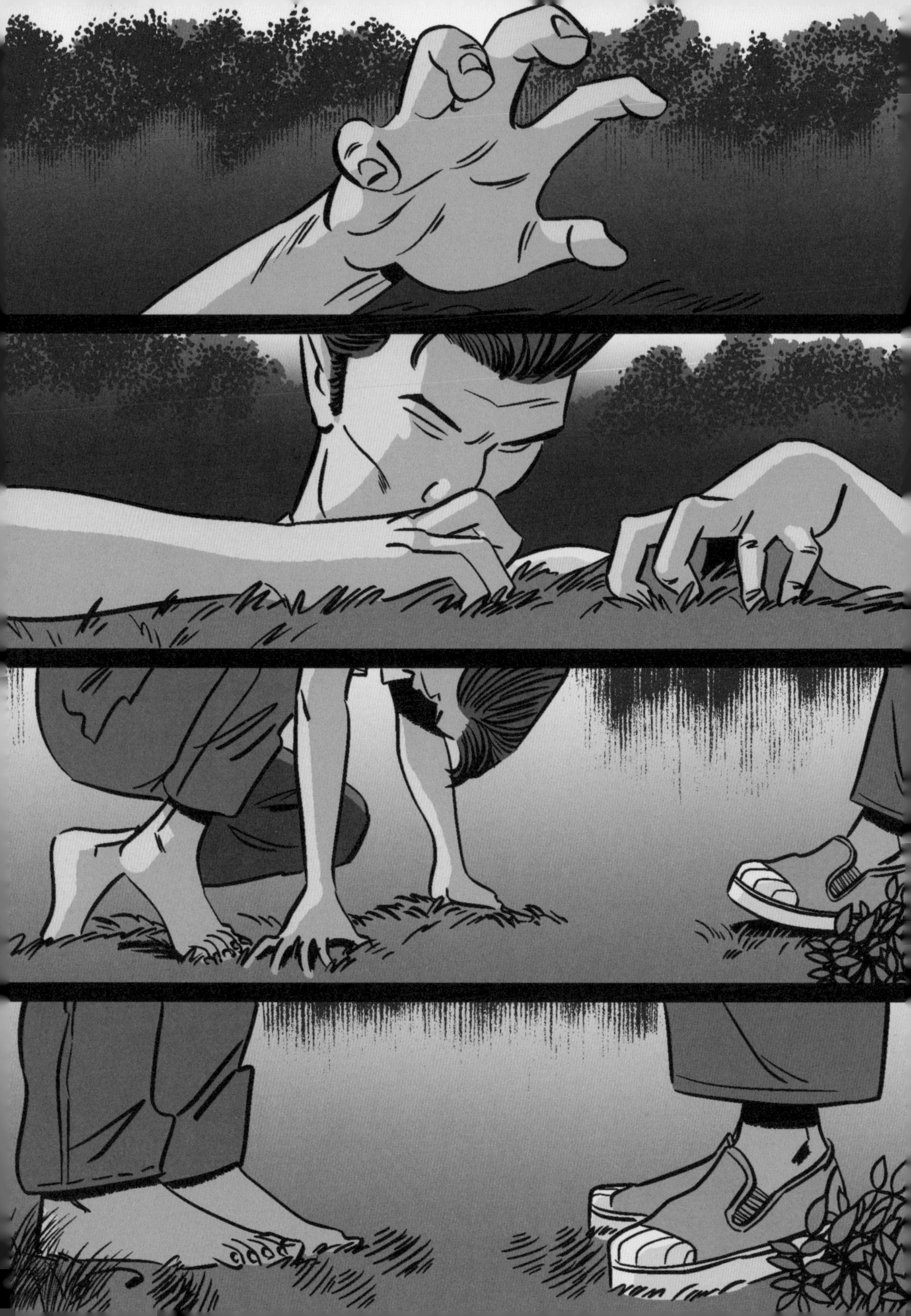

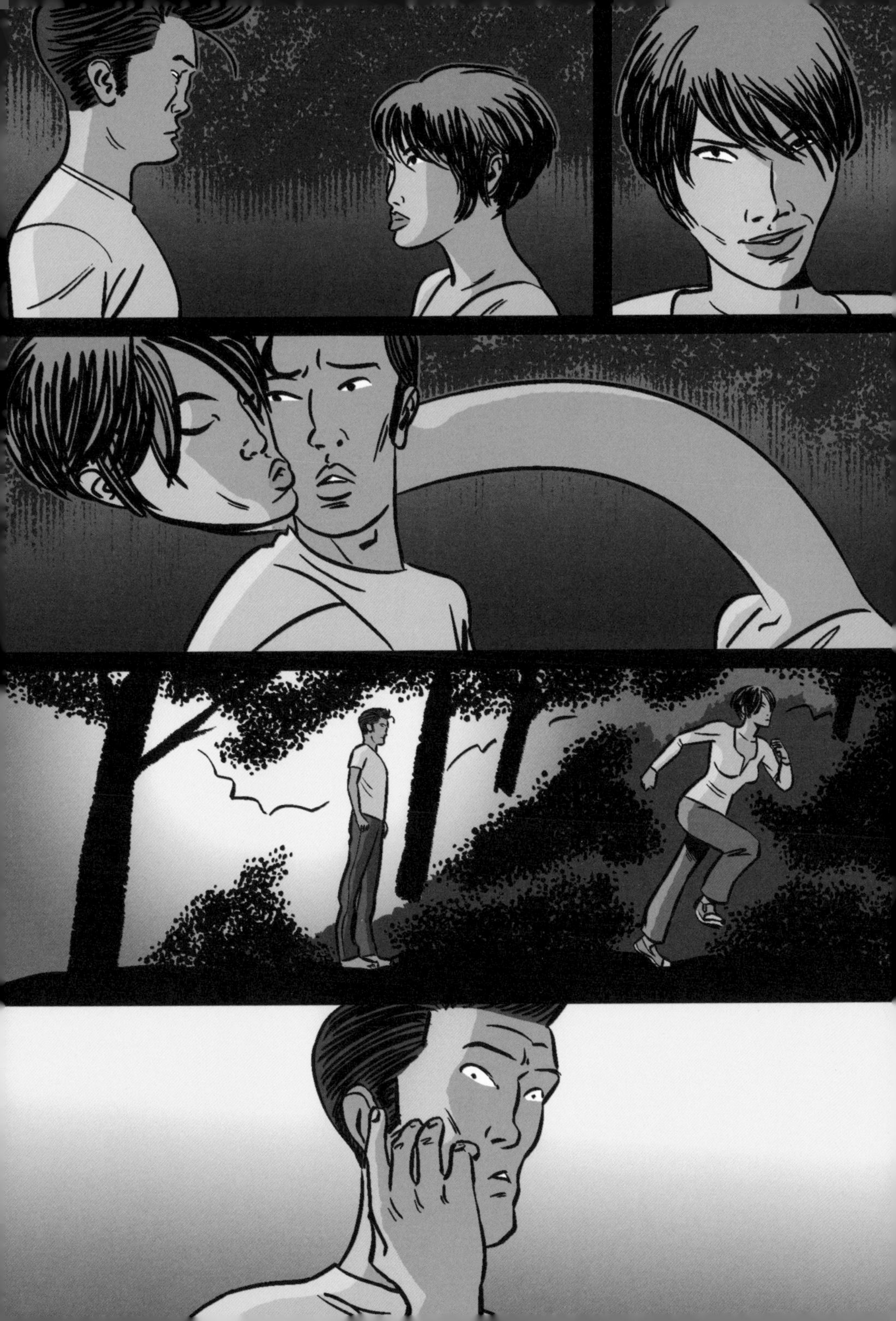

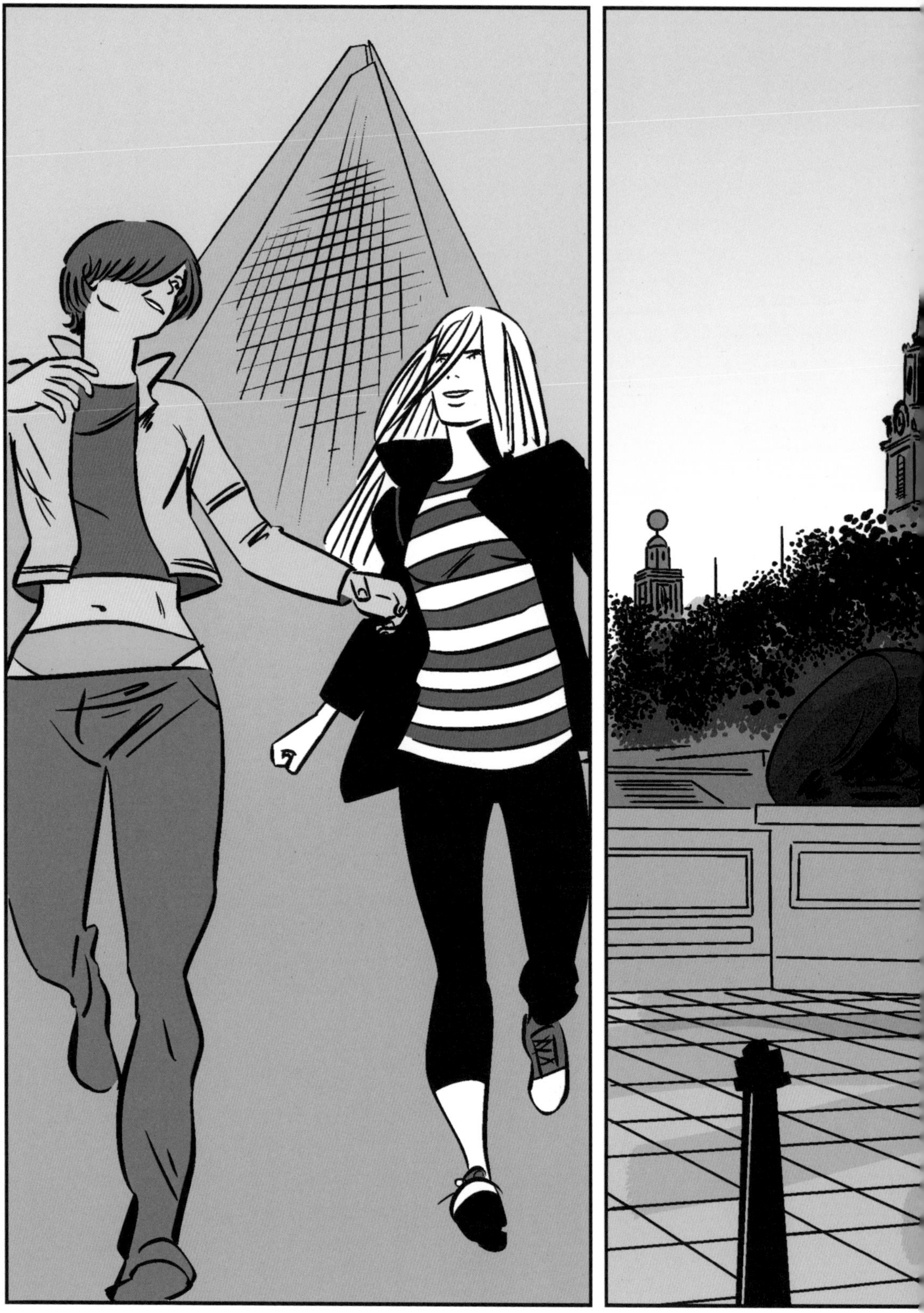

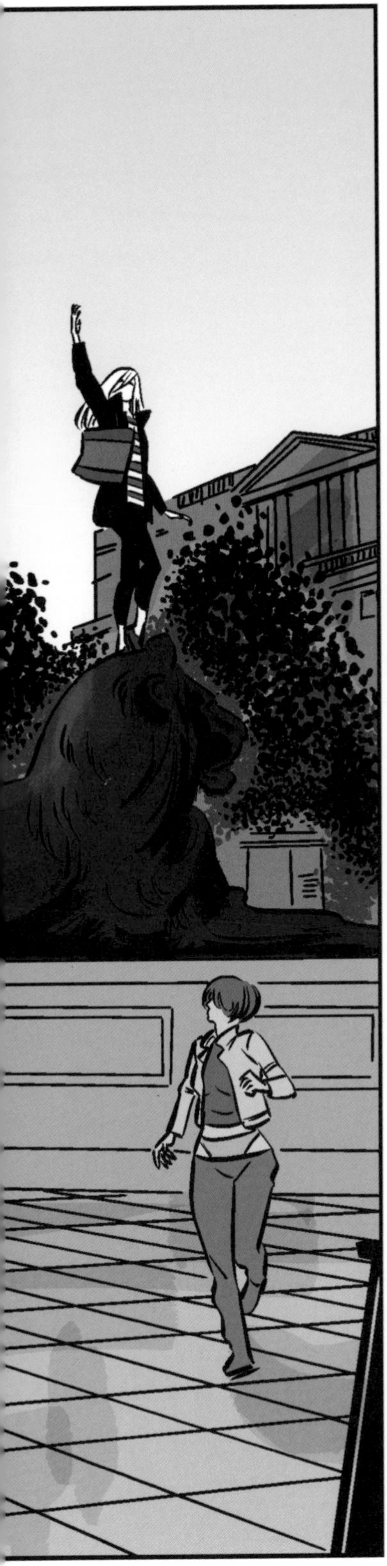
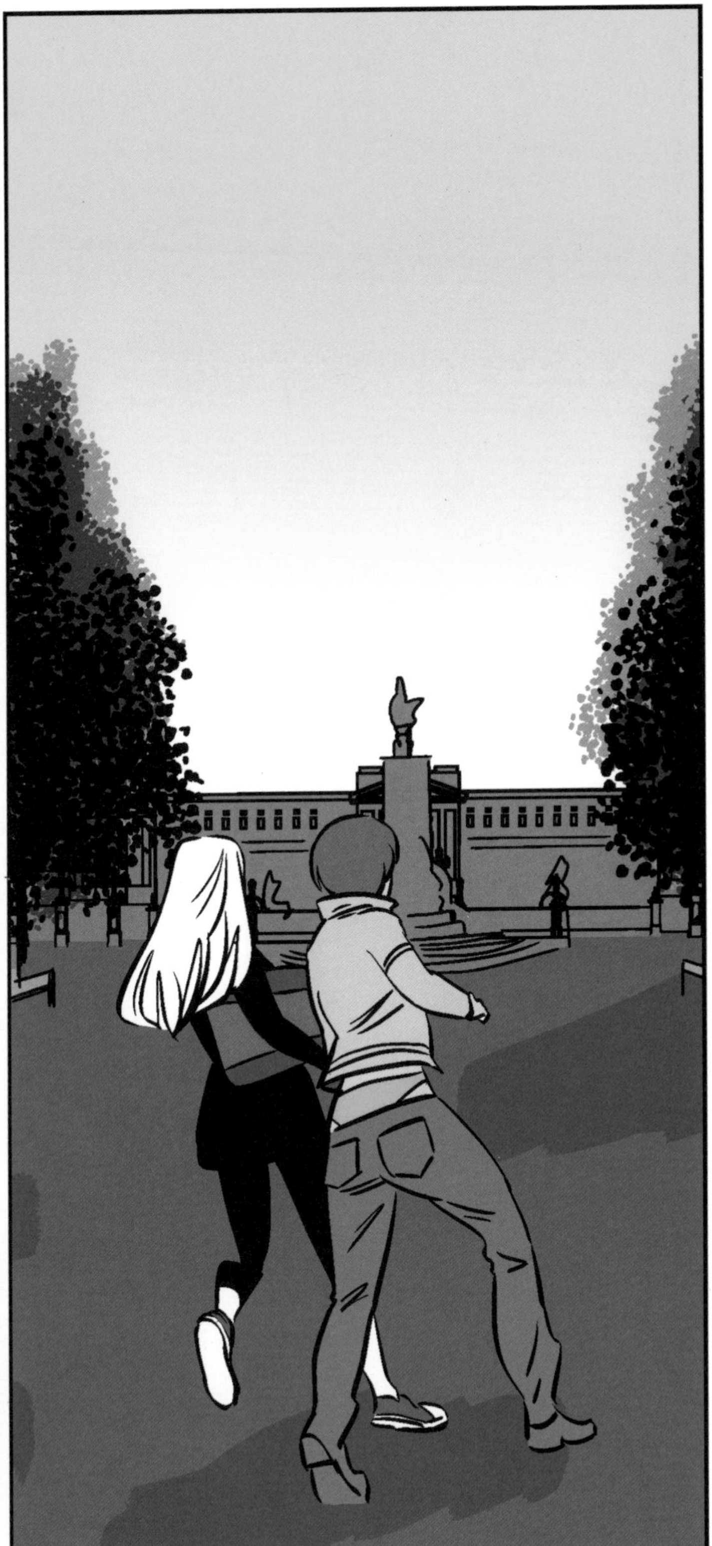

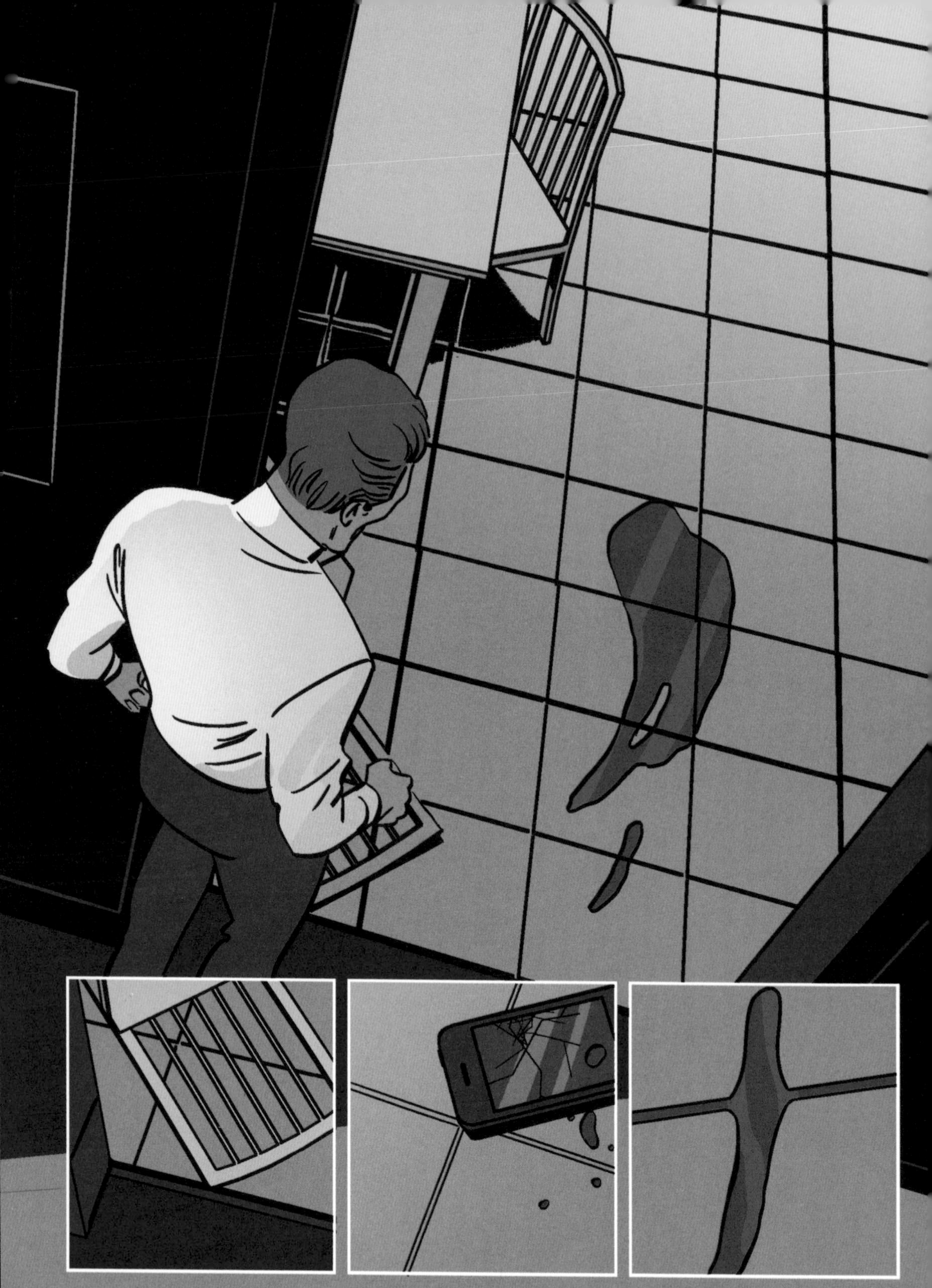

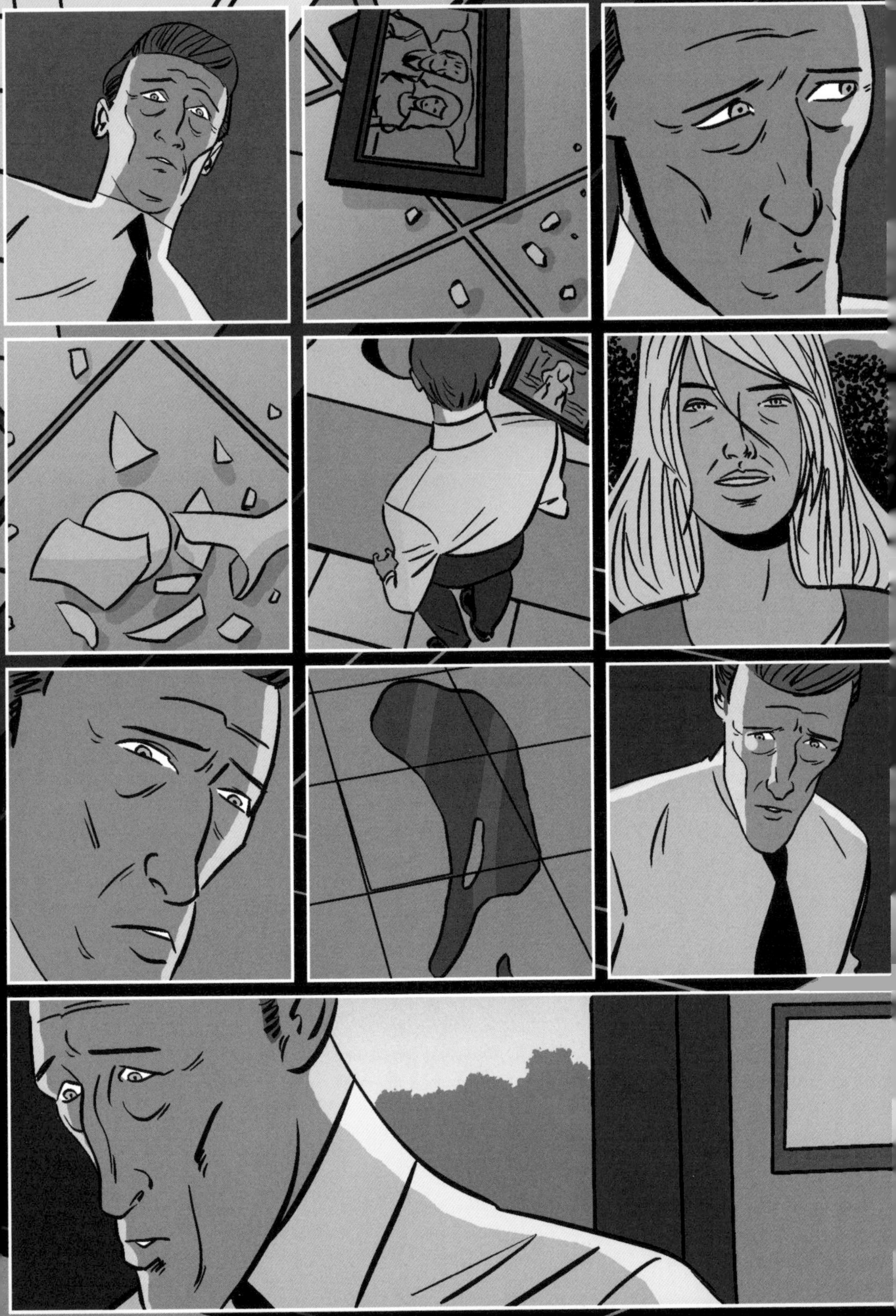

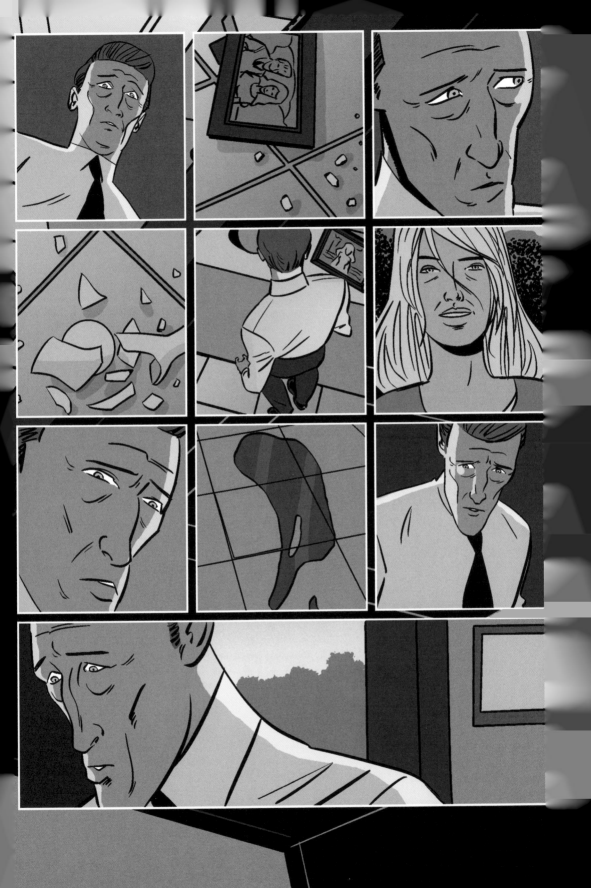

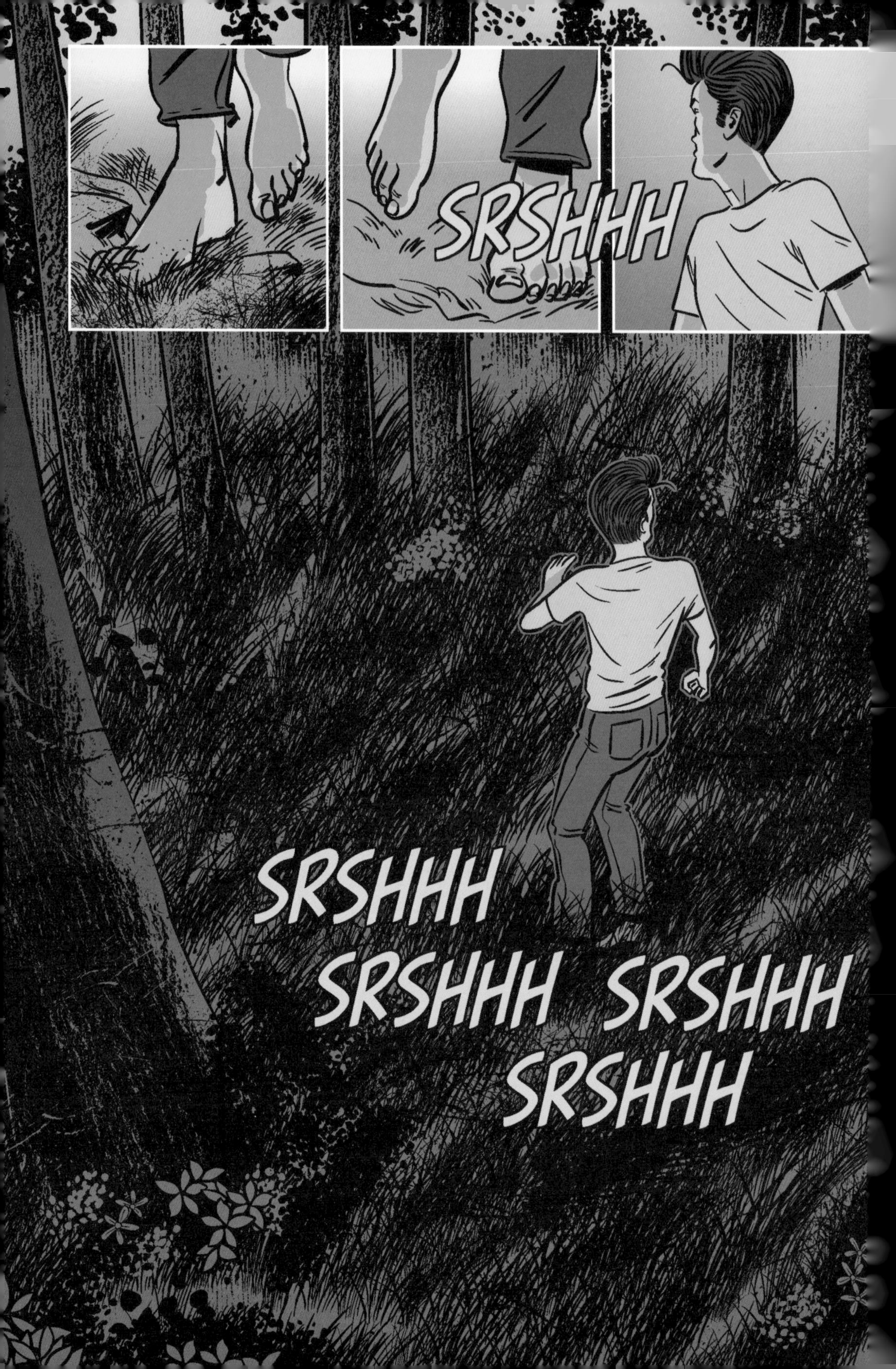
SRSHHH
SRSHHH
SRSHHH SRSHHH
SRSHHH

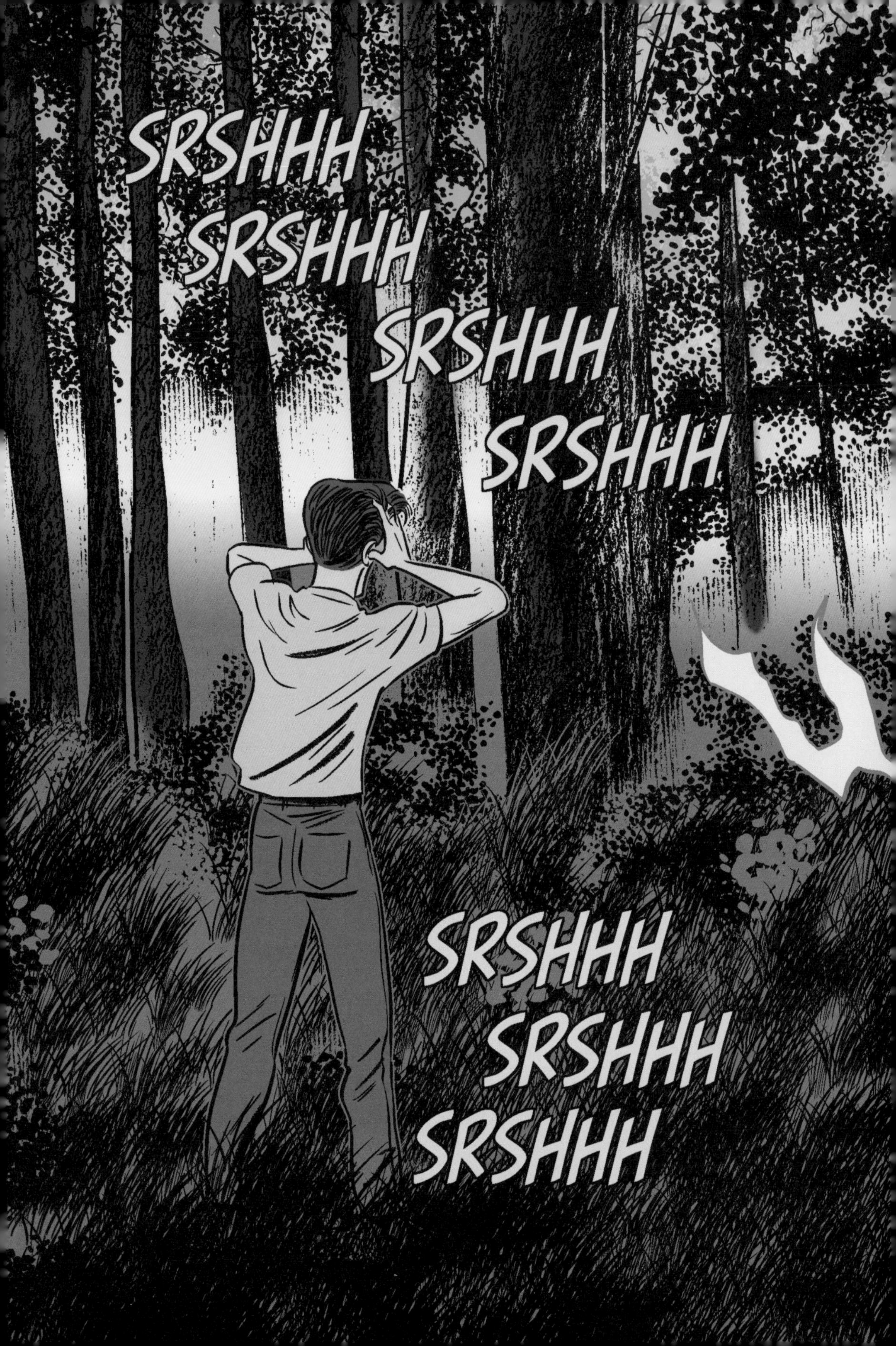
SRSHHH
SRSHHH
SRSHHH
SRSHHH
SRSHHH
SRSHHH
SRSHHH

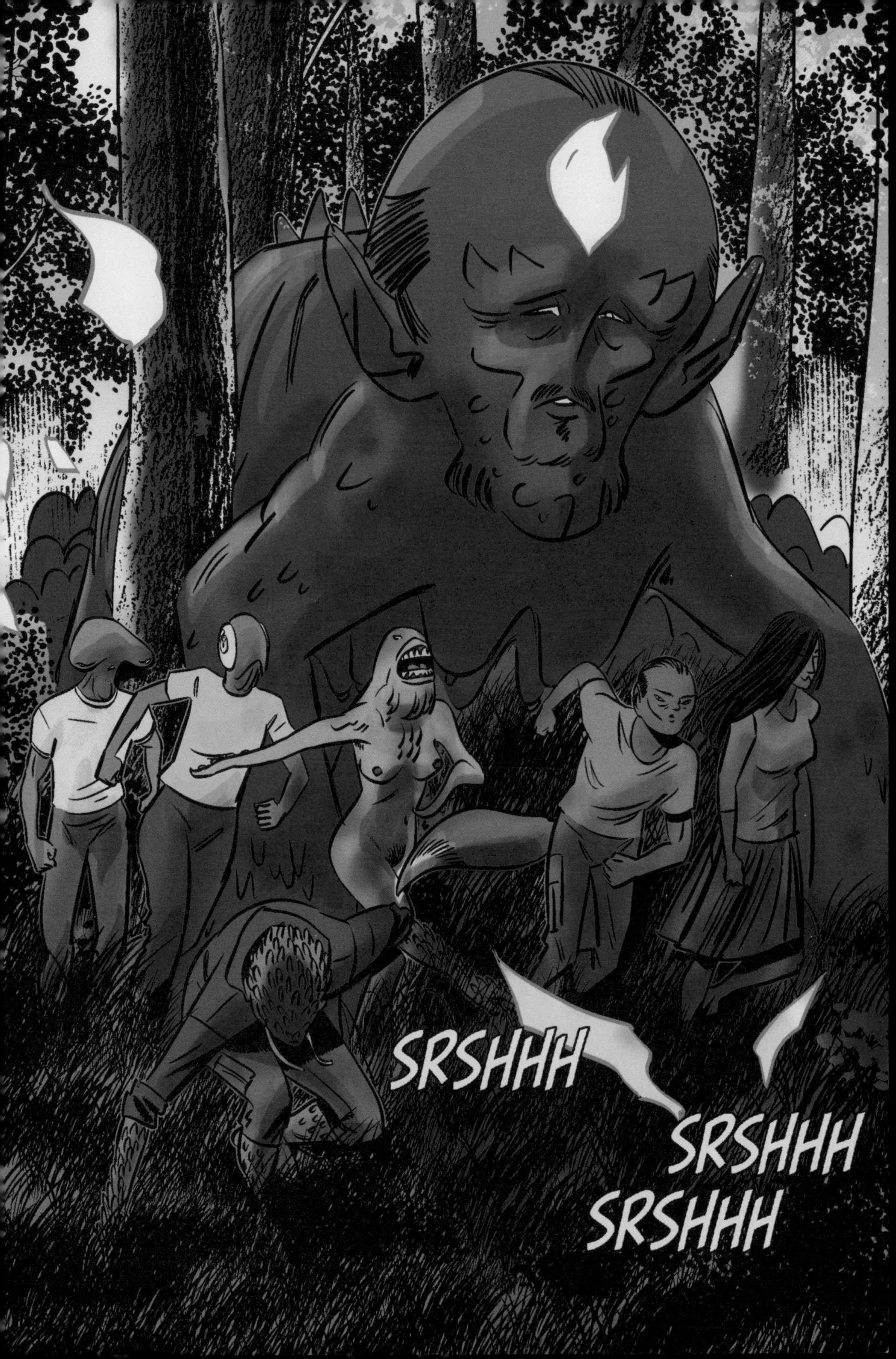
SRSHHH
SRSHHH
SRSHHH

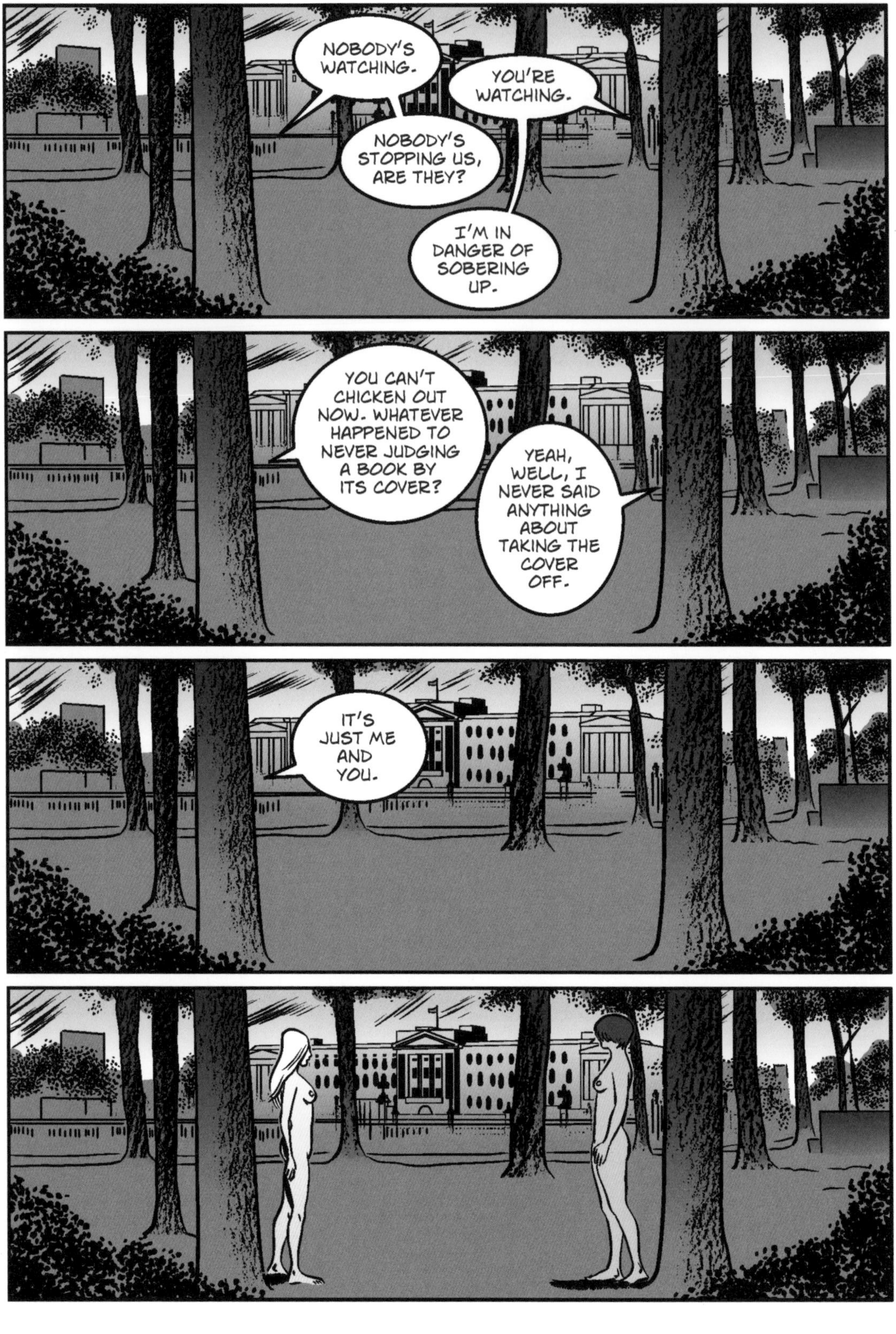
NOBODY'S WATCHING.
YOU'RE WATCHING.
NOBODY'S STOPPING US, ARE THEY?
I'M IN DANGER OF SOBERING UP.
YOU CAN'T CHICKEN OUT NOW. WHATEVER HAPPENED TO NEVER JUDGING A BOOK BY ITS COVER?
YEAH, WELL, I NEVER SAID ANYTHING ABOUT TAKING THE COVER OFF.
IT'S JUST ME AND YOU.

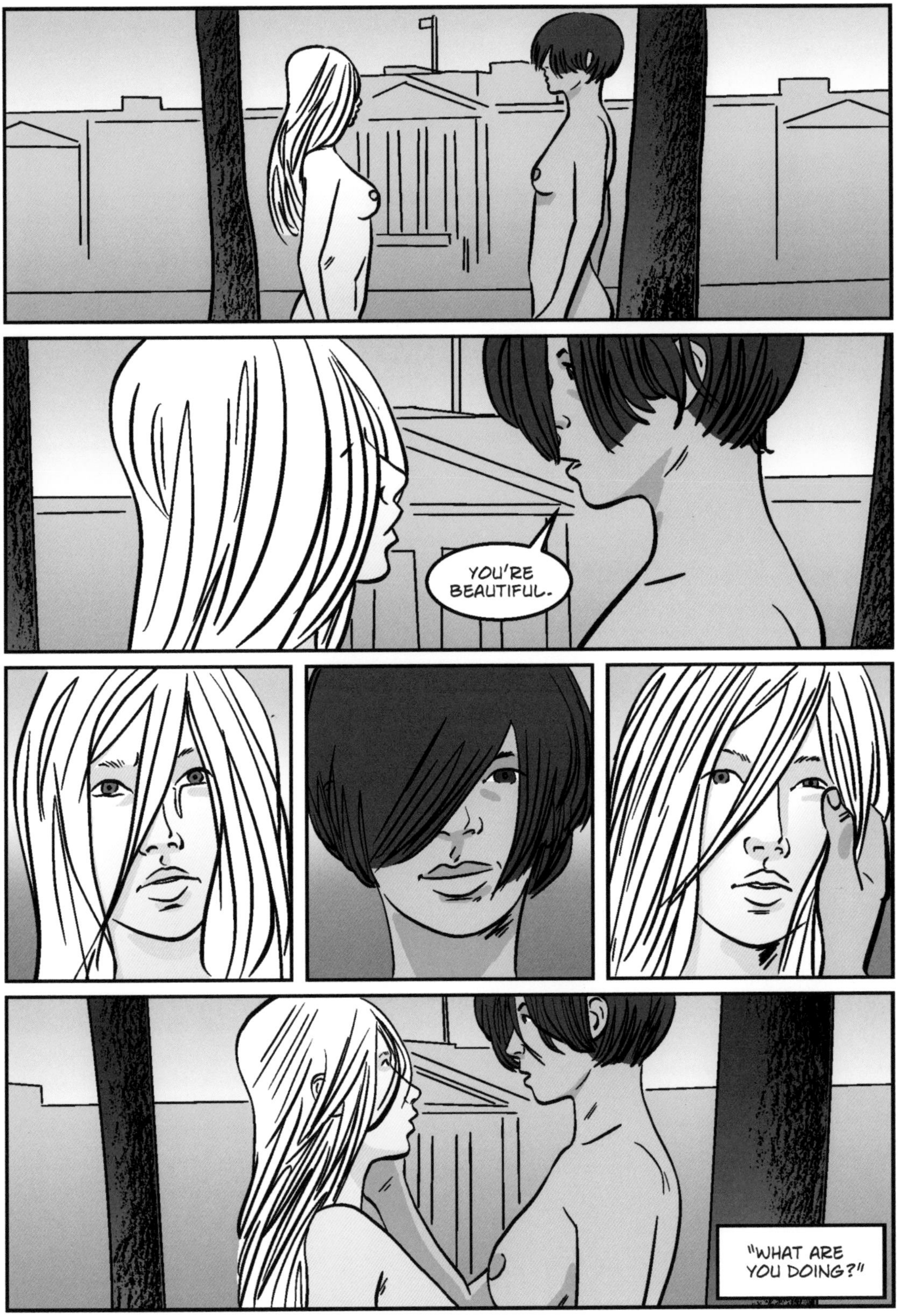
YOU'RE BEAUTIFUL.
"WHAT ARE YOU DOING?"

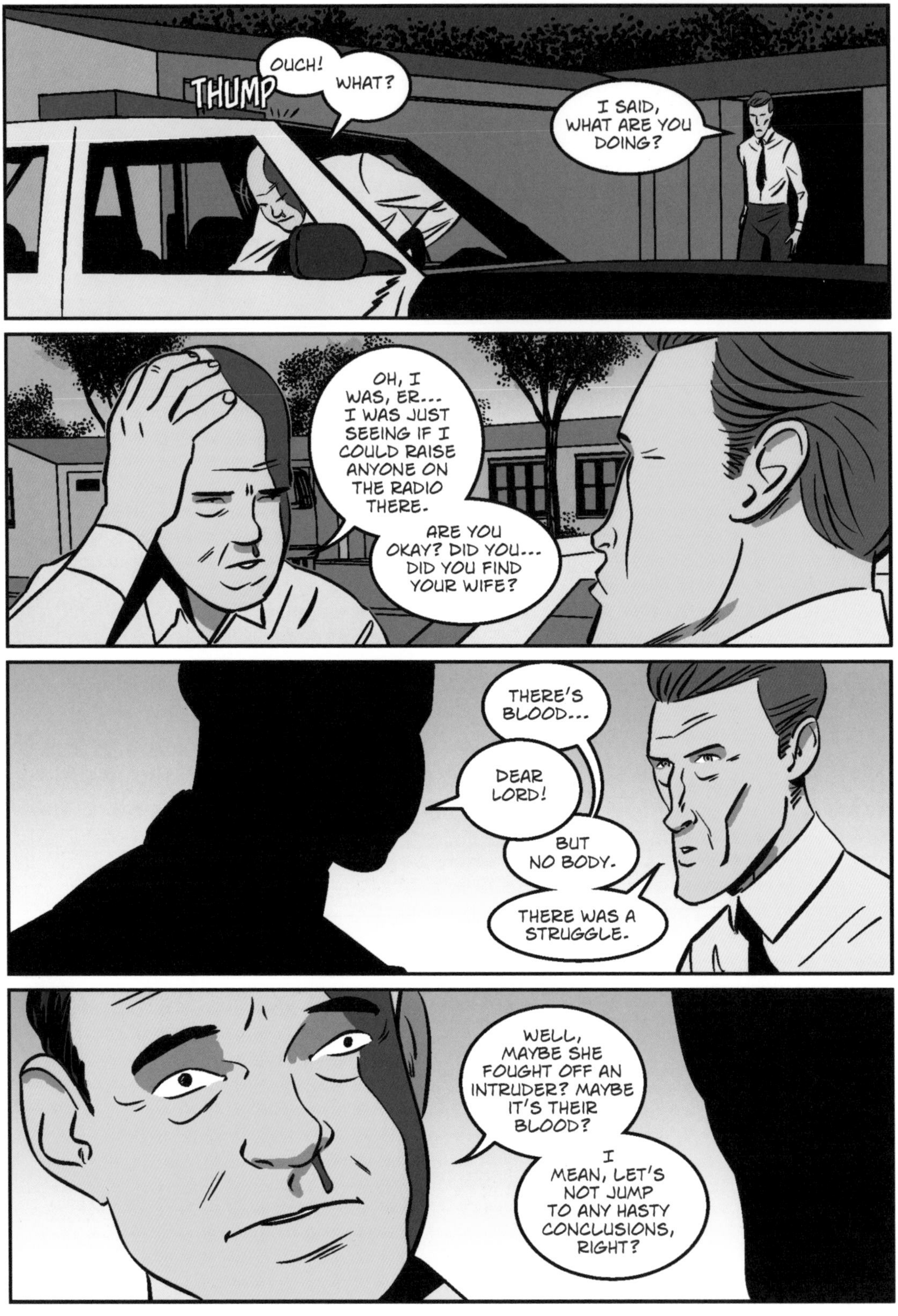
THUMP
OUCH!
WHAT?
I SAID, WHAT ARE YOU DOING?
OH, I WAS, ER... I WAS JUST SEEING IF I COULD RAISE ANYONE ON THE RADIO THERE.
ARE YOU OKAY? DID YOU... DID YOU FIND YOUR WIFE?
THERE'S BLOOD...
DEAR LORD!
BUT NO BODY.
THERE WAS A STRUGGLE.
WELL, MAYBE SHE FOUGHT OFF AN INTRUDER? MAYBE IT'S THEIR BLOOD?
I MEAN, LET'S NOT JUMP TO ANY HASTY CONCLUSIONS, RIGHT?

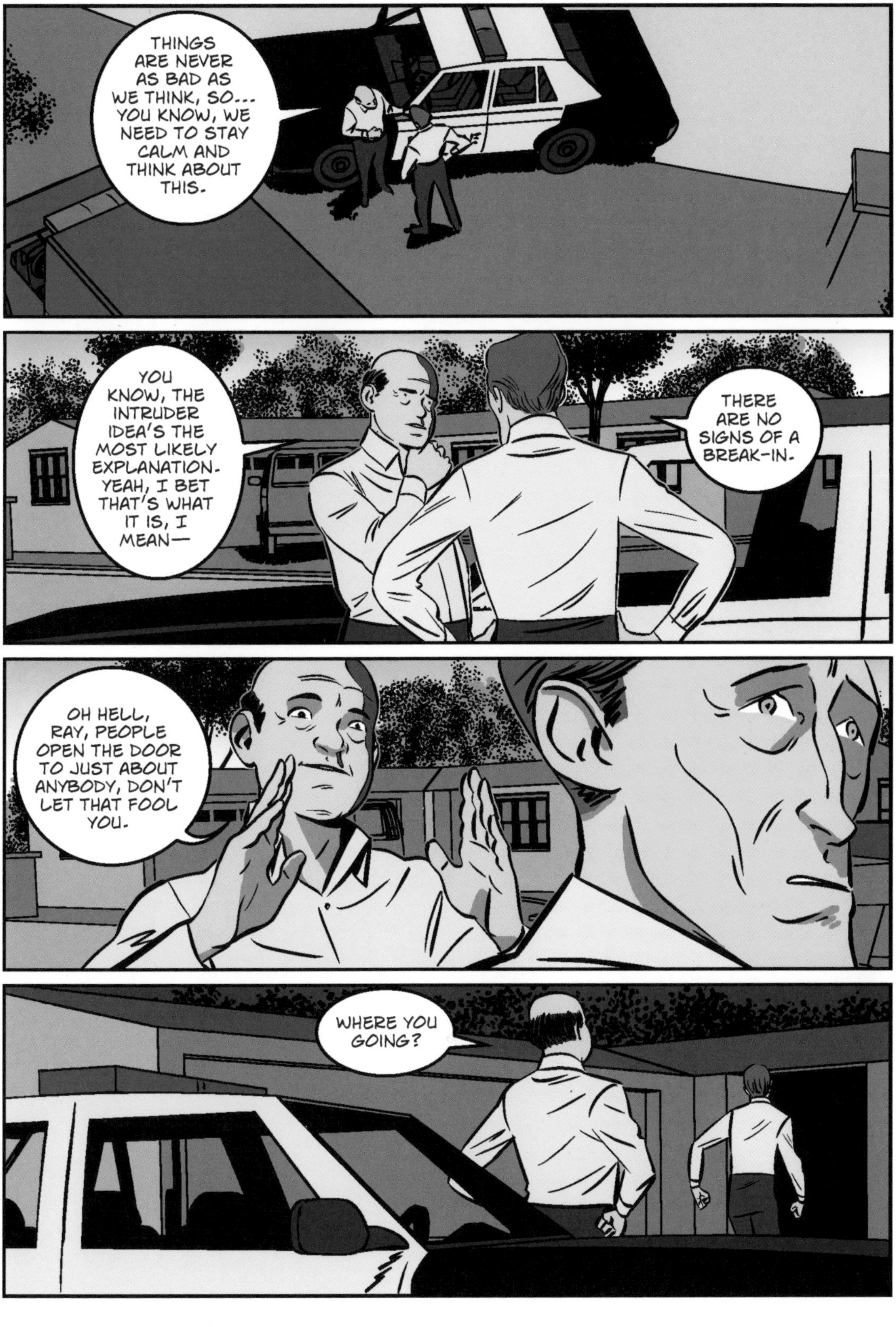
THINGS ARE NEVER AS BAD AS WE THINK, SO... YOU KNOW, WE NEED TO STAY CALM AND THINK ABOUT THIS.
YOU KNOW, THE INTRUDER IDEA'S THE MOST LIKELY EXPLANATION. YEAH, I BET THAT'S WHAT IT IS, I MEAN—
THERE ARE NO SIGNS OF A BREAK-IN.
OH HELL, RAY, PEOPLE OPEN THE DOOR TO JUST ABOUT ANYBODY, DON'T LET THAT FOOL YOU.
WHERE YOU GOING?

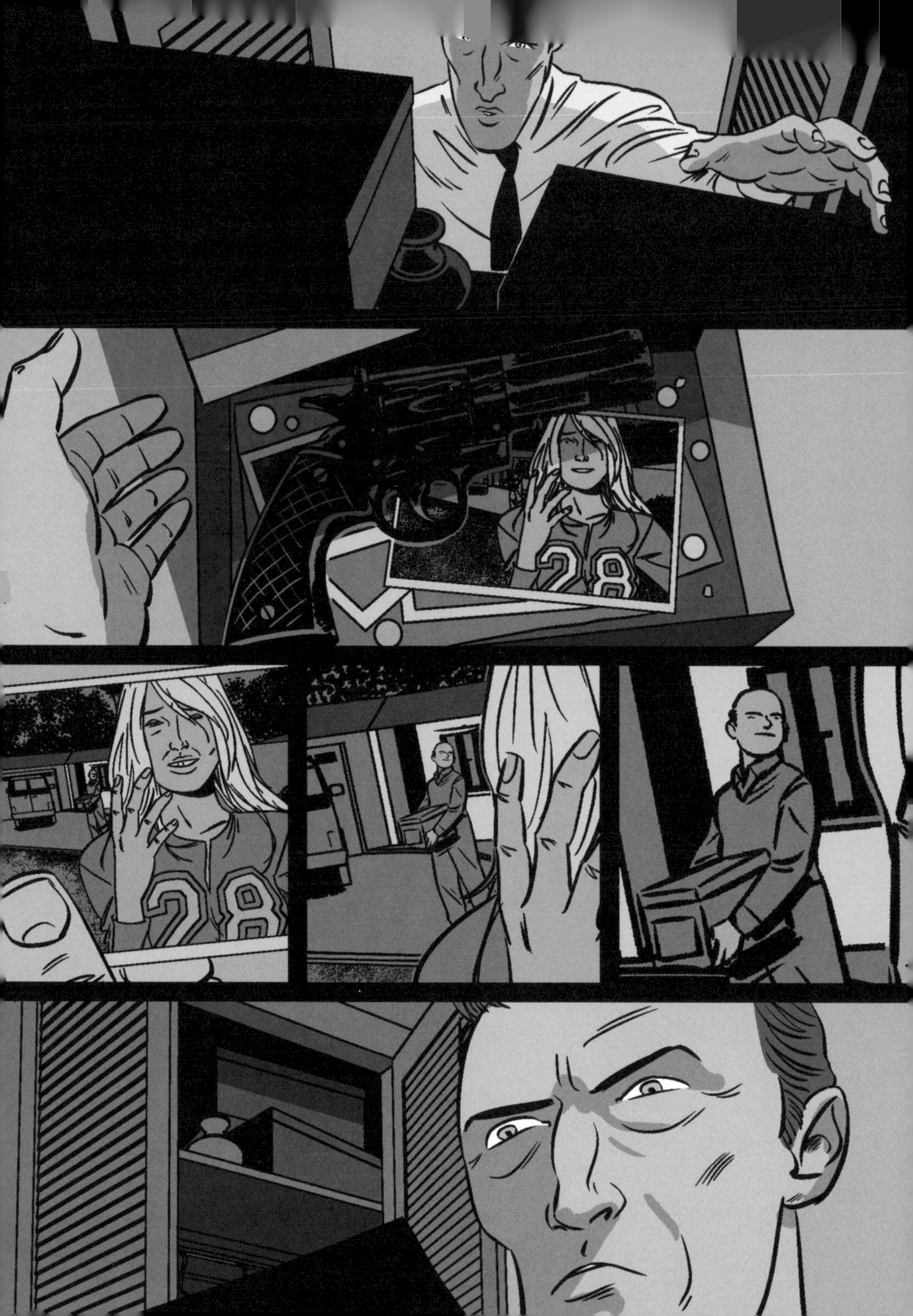

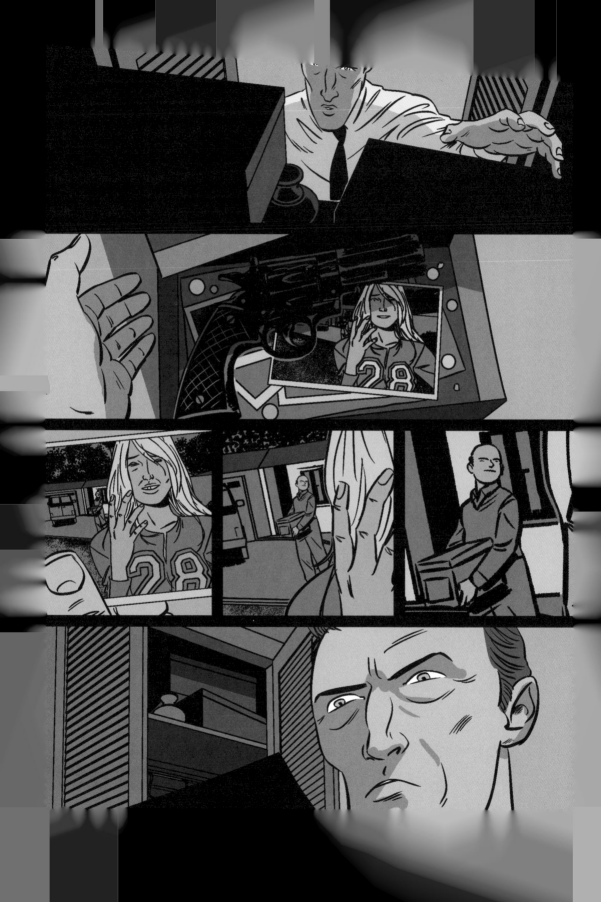

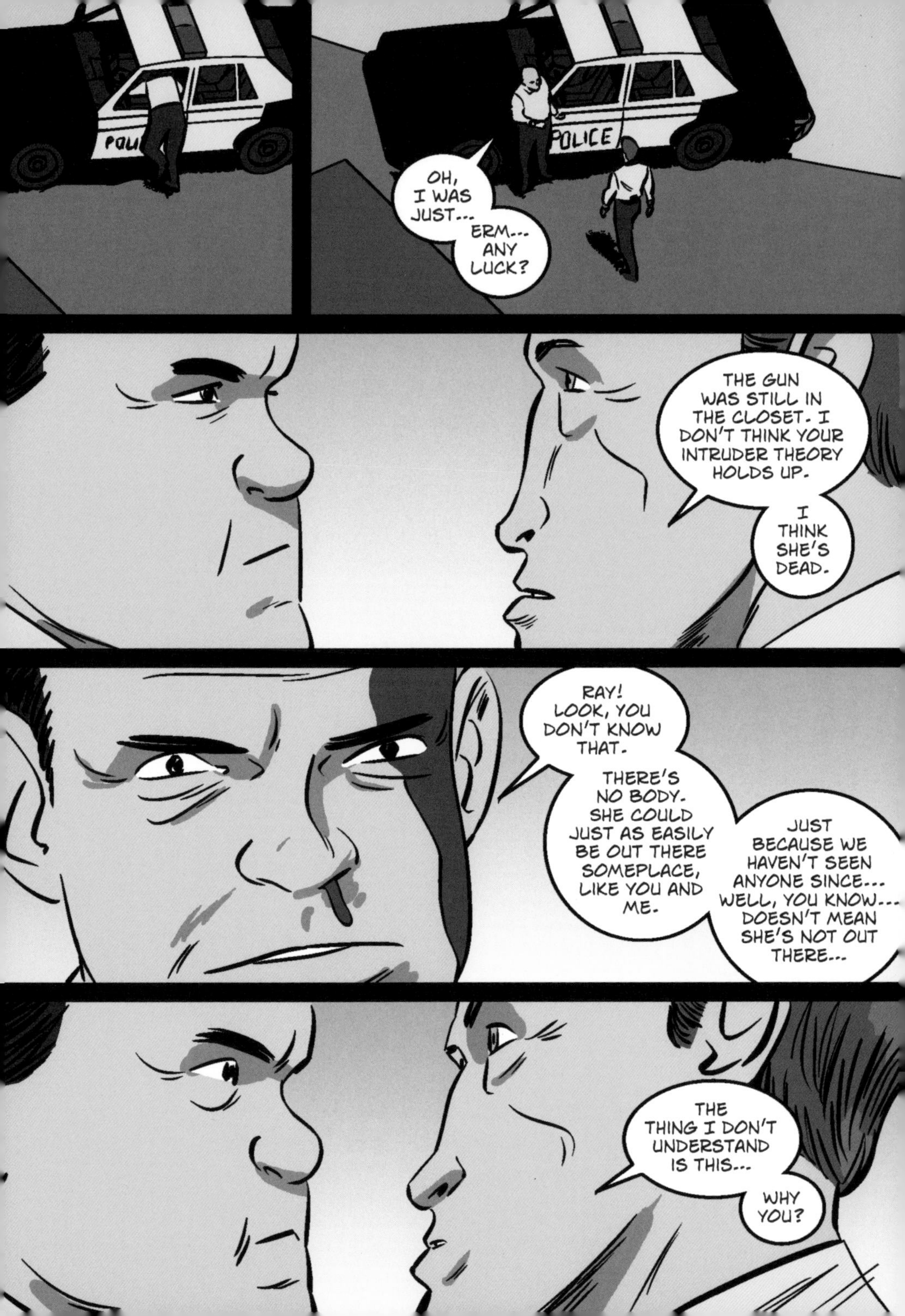
POLICE
POLICE
OH, I WAS JUST... ERM... ANY LUCK?
THE GUN WAS STILL IN THE CLOSET. I DON'T THINK YOUR INTRUDER THEORY HOLDS UP.
I THINK SHE'S DEAD.
RAY! LOOK, YOU DON'T KNOW THAT.
THERE'S NO BODY. SHE COULD JUST AS EASILY BE OUT THERE SOMEPLACE, LIKE YOU AND ME.
JUST BECAUSE WE HAVEN'T SEEN ANYONE SINCE... WELL, YOU KNOW... DOESN'T MEAN SHE'S NOT OUT THERE...
THE THING I DON'T UNDERSTAND IS THIS...
WHY YOU?

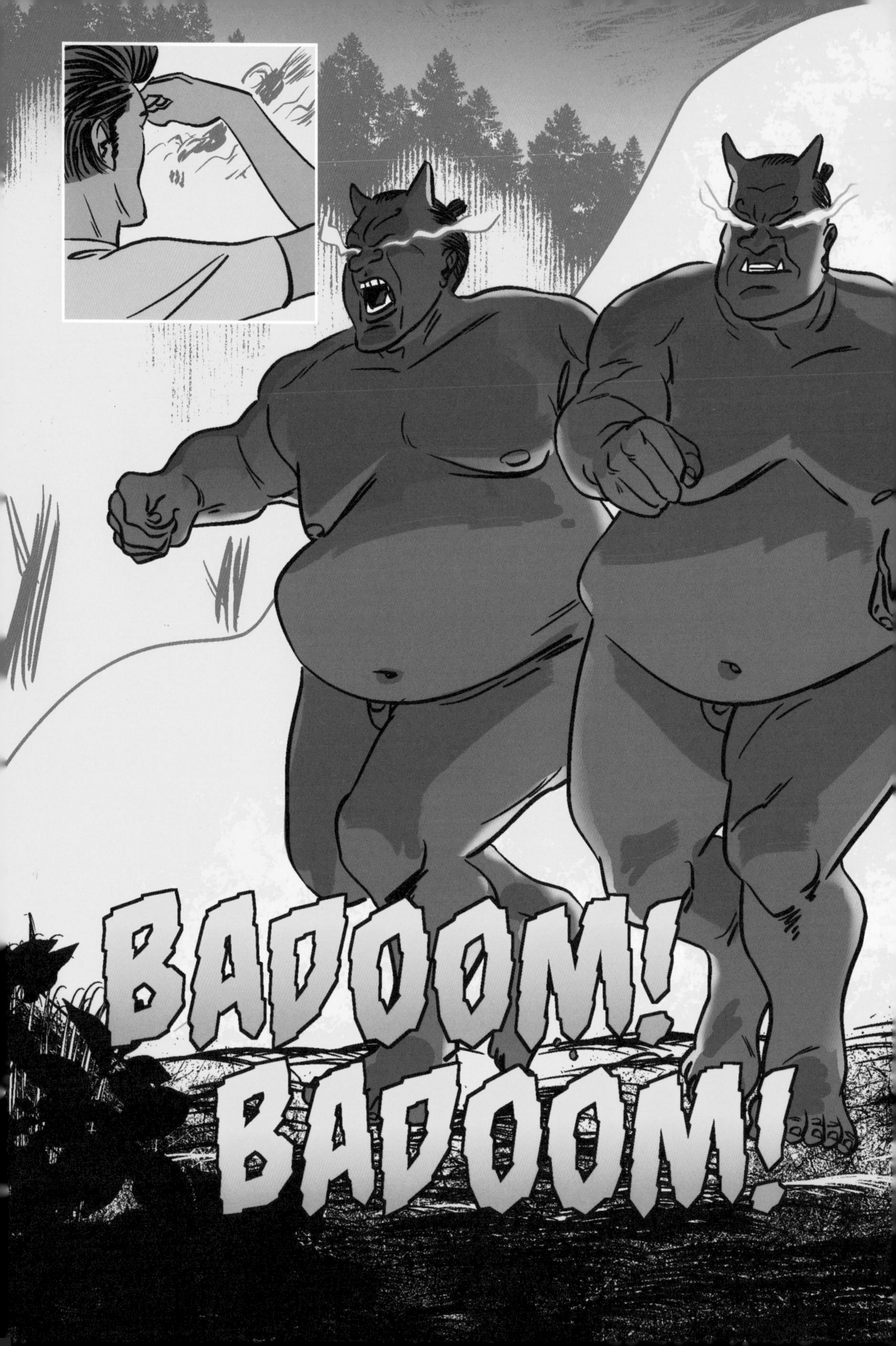
BADOOM!
BADOOM!

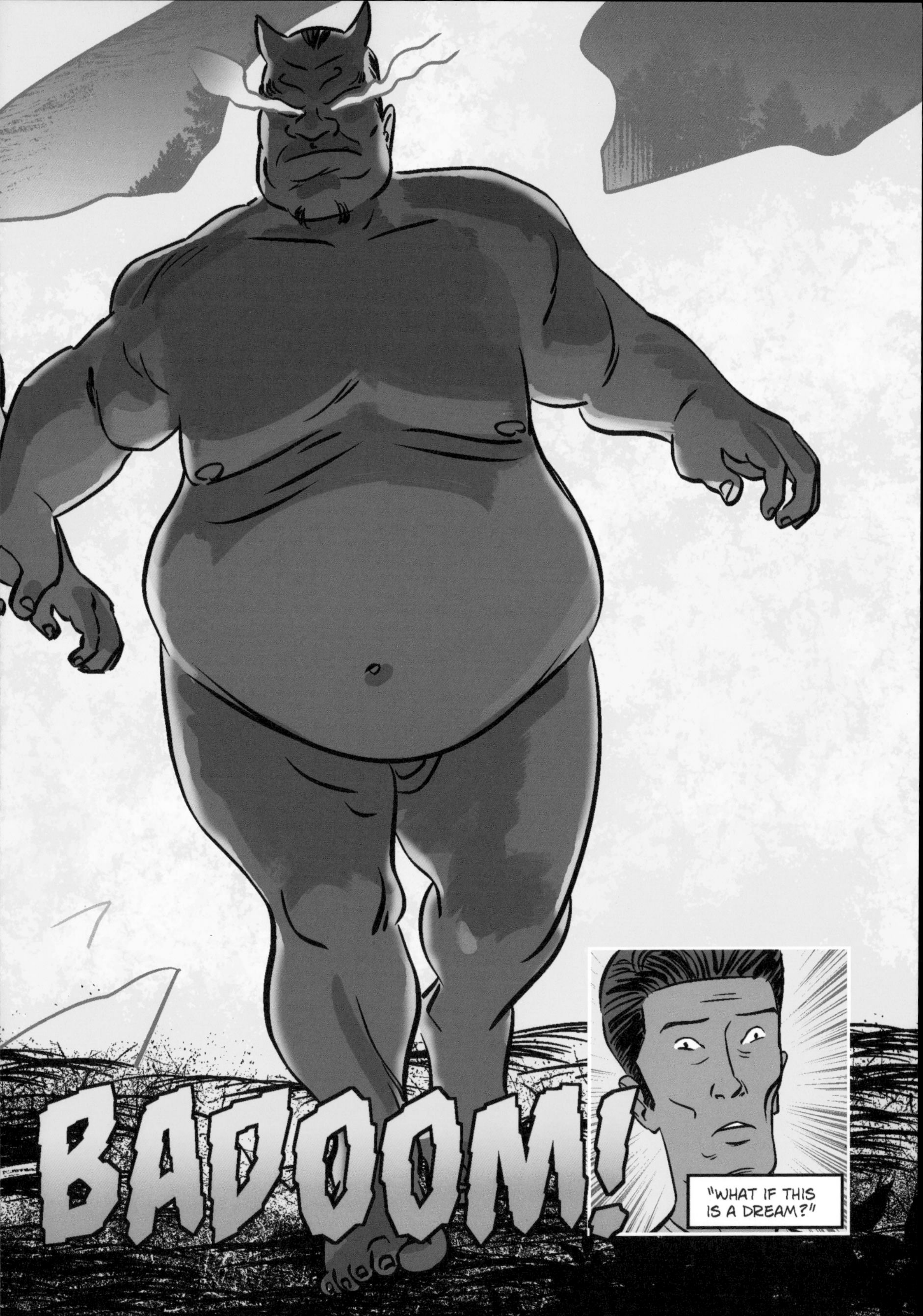
BADOOM!
"WHAT IF THIS IS A DREAM?"

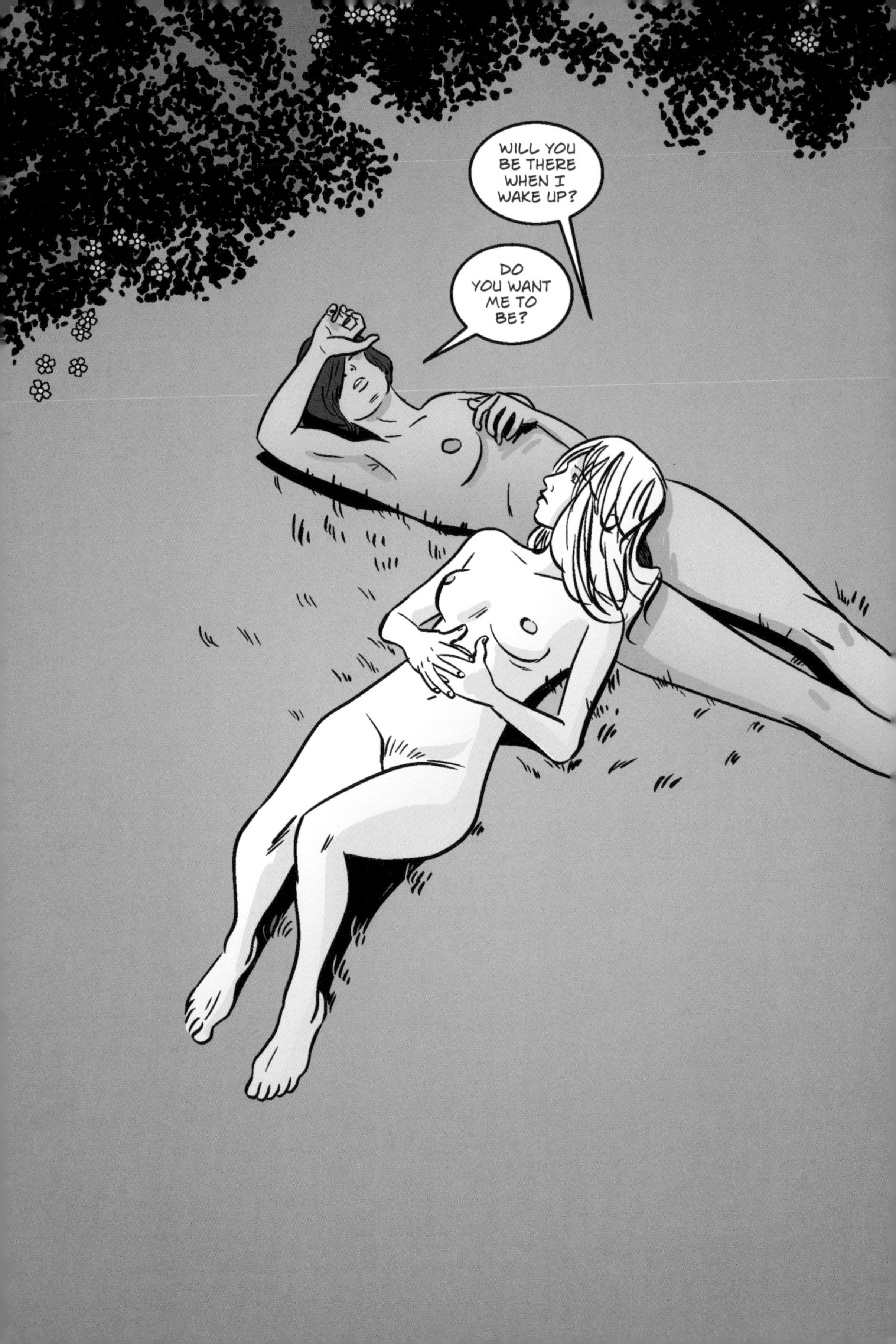
WILL YOU BE THERE WHEN I WAKE UP?
DO YOU WANT ME TO BE?

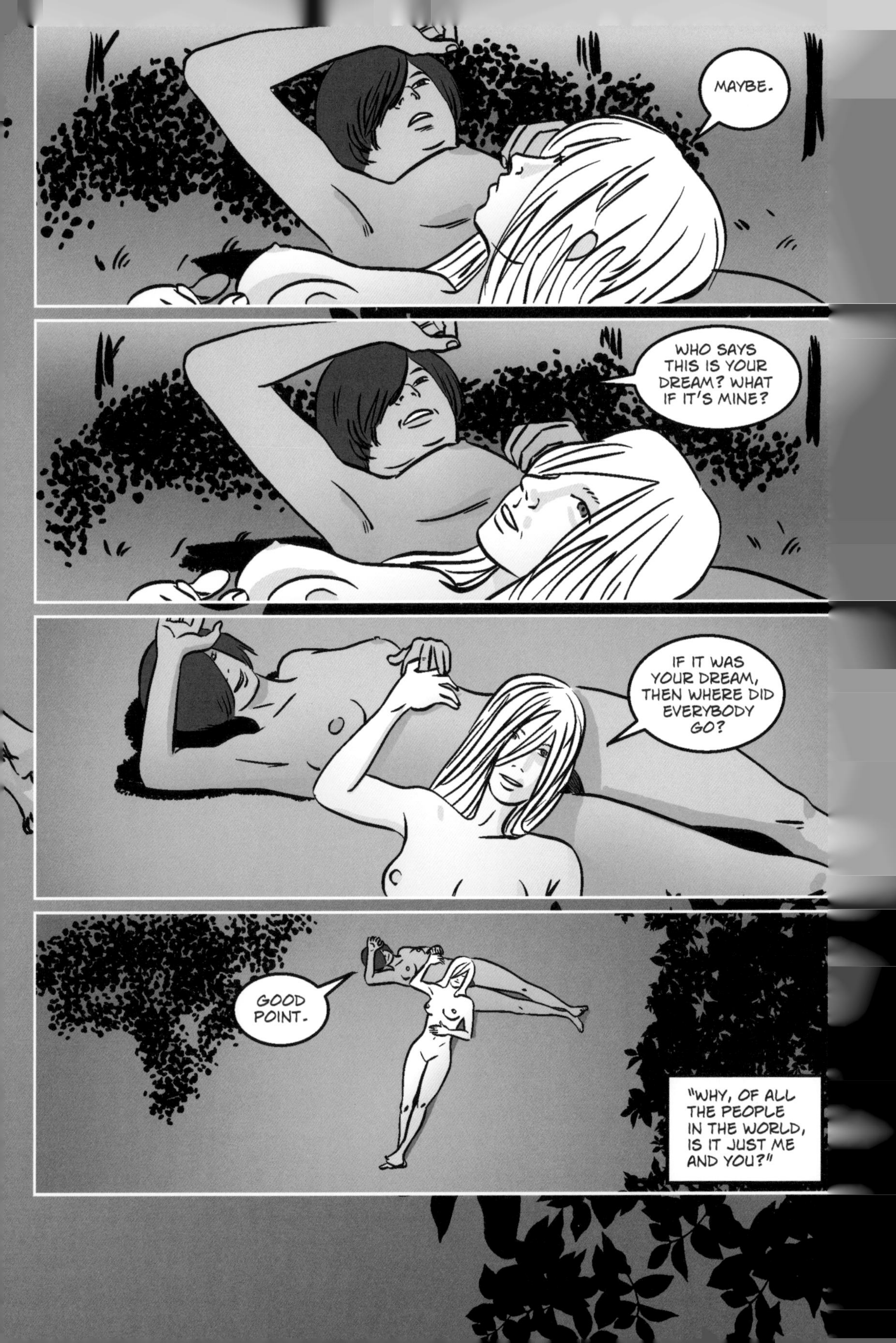
MAYBE.
WHO SAYS THIS IS YOUR DREAM? WHAT IF IT'S MINE?
IF IT WAS YOUR DREAM, THEN WHERE DID EVERYBODY GO?
GOOD POINT.
"WHY, OF ALL THE PEOPLE IN THE WORLD, IS IT JUST ME AND YOU?"

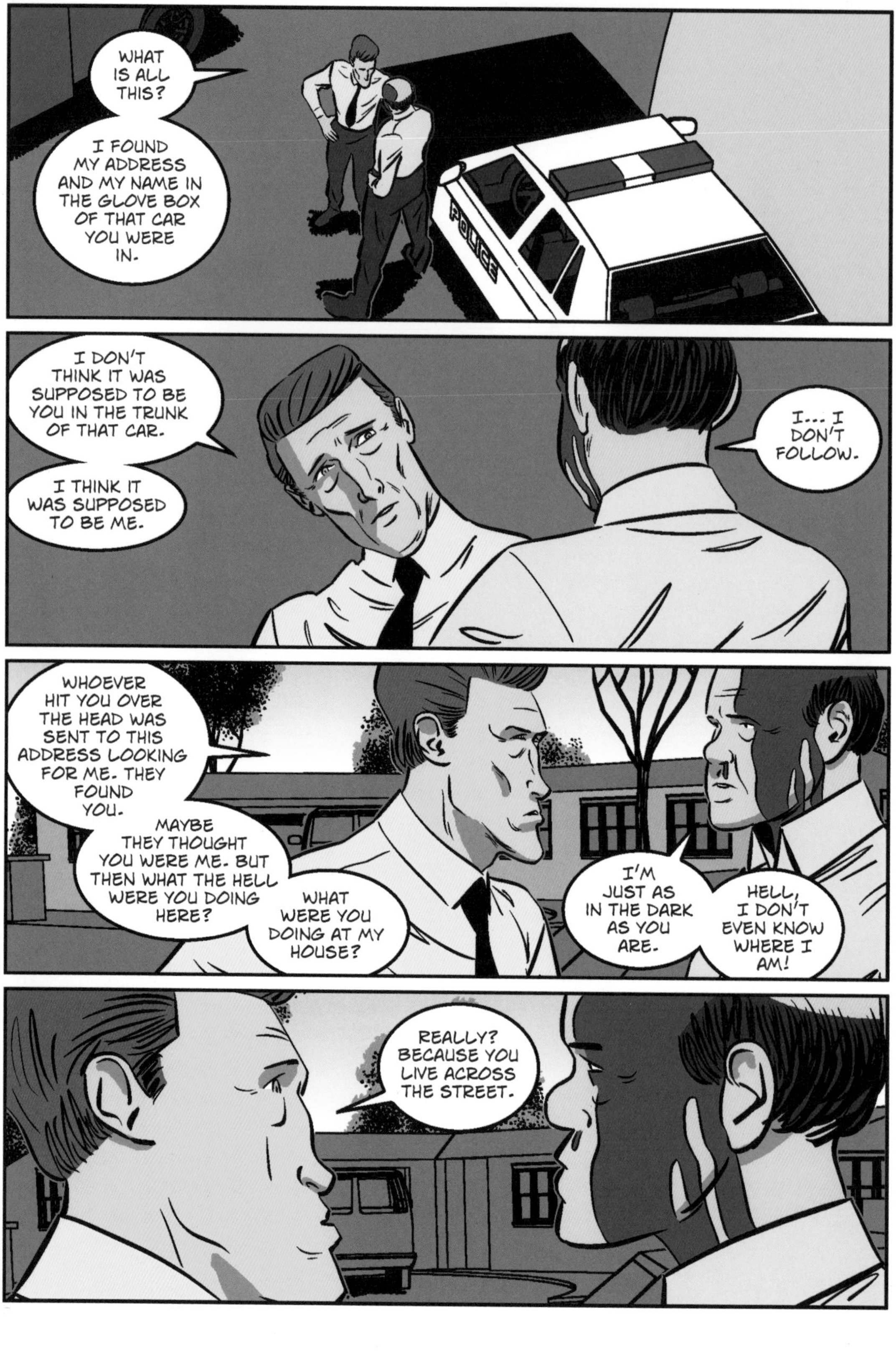
WHAT IS ALL THIS?
I FOUND MY ADDRESS AND MY NAME IN THE GLOVE BOX OF THAT CAR YOU WERE IN.
POLICE
I DON'T THINK IT WAS SUPPOSED TO BE YOU IN THE TRUNK OF THAT CAR.
I THINK IT WAS SUPPOSED TO BE ME.
I... I DON'T FOLLOW.
WHOEVER HIT YOU OVER THE HEAD WAS SENT TO THIS ADDRESS LOOKING FOR ME. THEY FOUND YOU.
MAYBE THEY THOUGHT YOU WERE ME. BUT THEN WHAT THE HELL WERE YOU DOING HERE?
WHAT WERE YOU DOING AT MY HOUSE?
I'M JUST AS IN THE DARK AS YOU ARE.
HELL, I DON'T EVEN KNOW WHERE I AM!
REALLY? BECAUSE YOU LIVE ACROSS THE STREET.

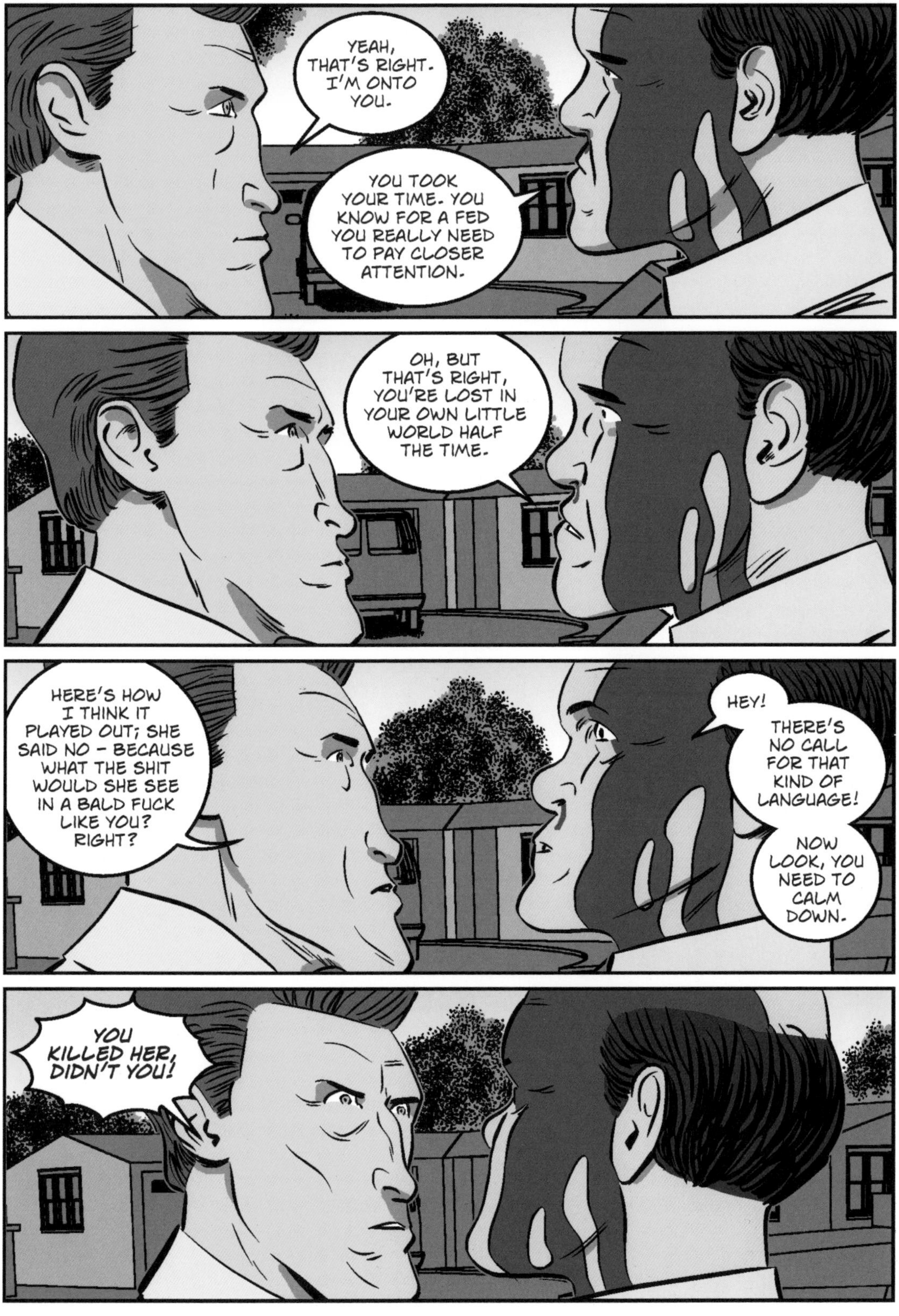
YEAH, THAT'S RIGHT. I'M ONTO YOU.
YOU TOOK YOUR TIME. YOU KNOW FOR A FED YOU REALLY NEED TO PAY CLOSER ATTENTION.
OH, BUT THAT'S RIGHT, YOU'RE LOST IN YOUR OWN LITTLE WORLD HALF THE TIME.
HERE'S HOW I THINK IT PLAYED OUT; SHE SAID NO – BECAUSE WHAT THE SHIT WOULD SHE SEE IN A BALD FUCK LIKE YOU? RIGHT?
HEY!
THERE'S NO CALL FOR THAT KIND OF LANGUAGE!
NOW LOOK, YOU NEED TO CALM DOWN.
YOU KILLED HER, DIDN'T YOU!

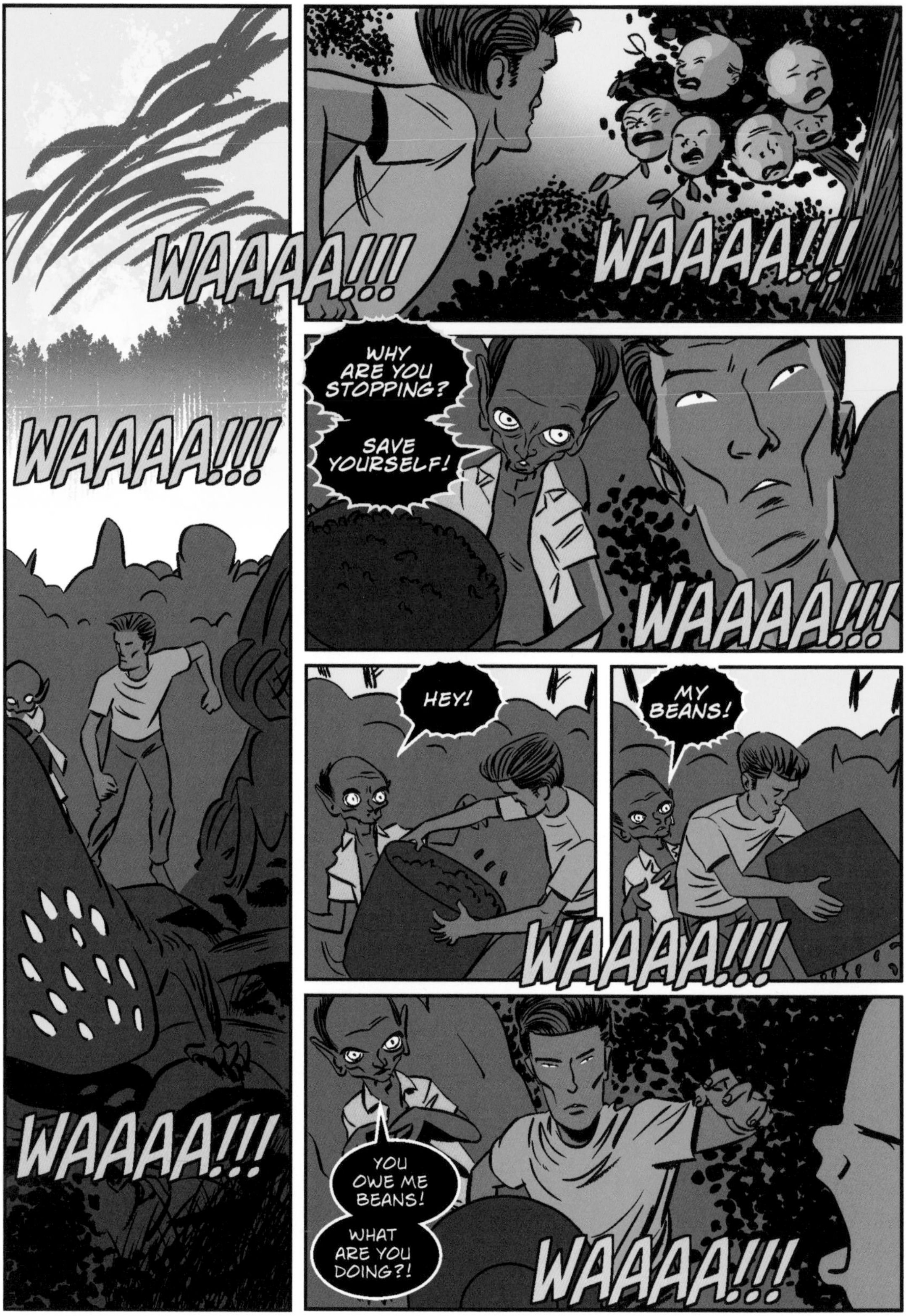
WAAAA!!!
WAAAA!!!
WAAAA!!!
WAAAA!!!
WHY ARE YOU STOPPING?
SAVE YOURSELF!
WAAAA!!!
HEY!
MY BEANS!
WAAAA!!!
WAAAA!!!
YOU OWE ME BEANS!
WHAT ARE YOU DOING?!
WAAAA!!!

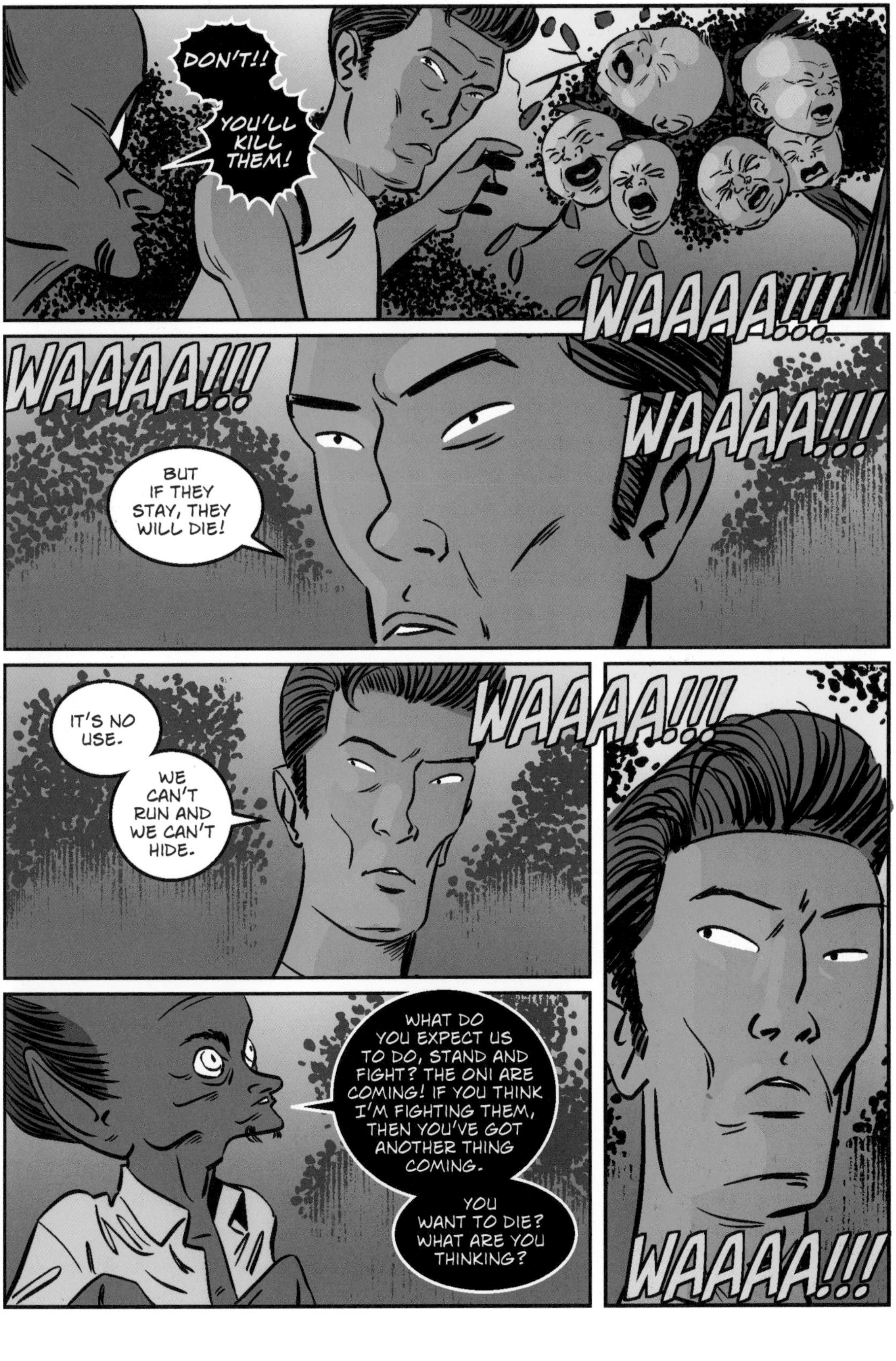
DON'T!!
YOU'LL KILL THEM!
WAAAA!!!
WAAAA!!!
WAAAA!!!
BUT IF THEY STAY, THEY WILL DIE!
WAAAA!!!
IT'S NO USE.
WE CAN'T RUN AND WE CAN'T HIDE.
WHAT DO YOU EXPECT US TO DO, STAND AND FIGHT? THE ONI ARE COMING! IF YOU THINK I'M FIGHTING THEM, THEN YOU'VE GOT ANOTHER THING COMING.
YOU WANT TO DIE? WHAT ARE YOU THINKING?
WAAAA!!!

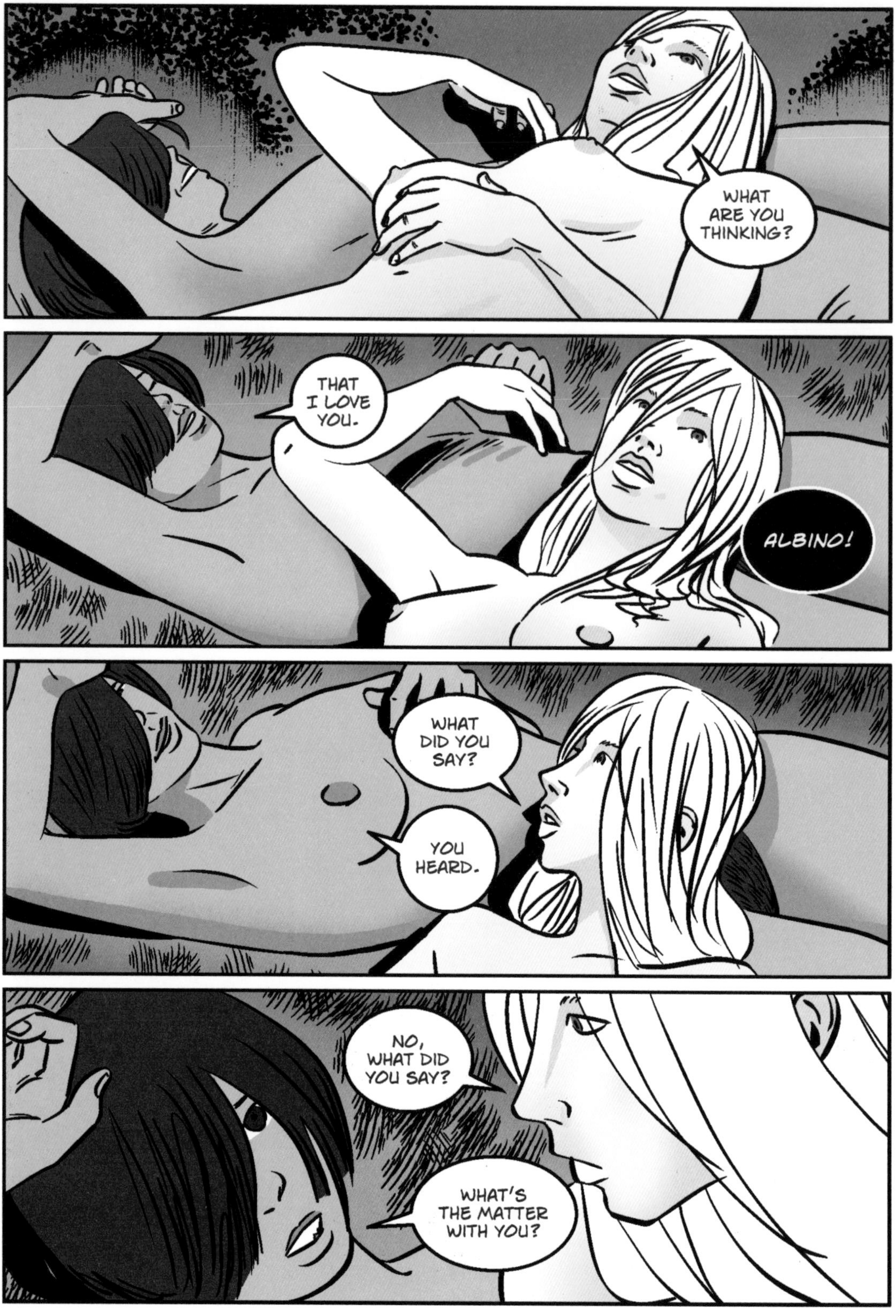
WHAT ARE YOU THINKING?
THAT I LOVE YOU.
ALBINO!
WHAT DID YOU SAY?
YOU HEARD.
NO, WHAT DID YOU SAY?
WHAT'S THE MATTER WITH YOU?

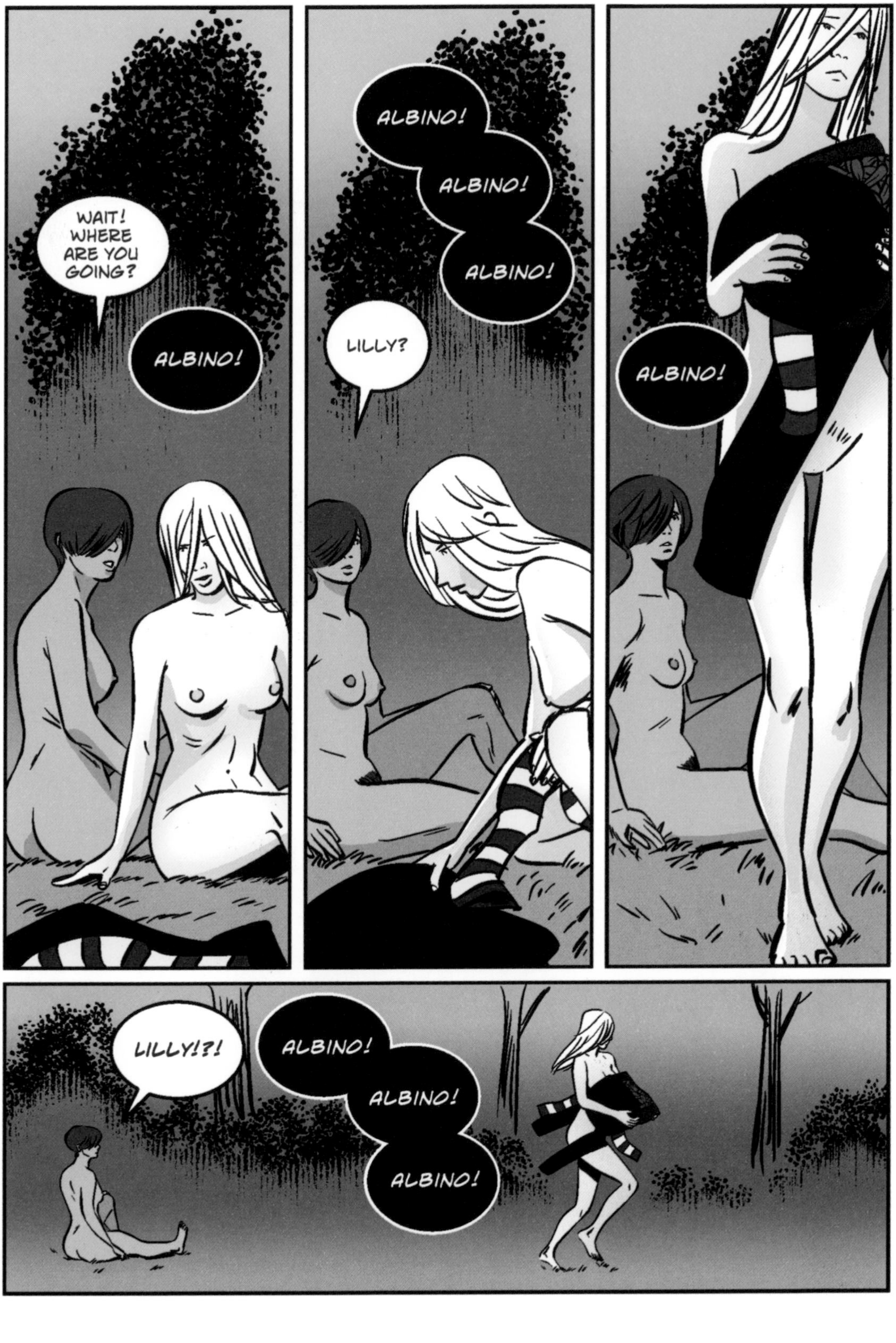
WAIT! WHERE ARE YOU GOING?
ALBINO!
ALBINO!
ALBINO!
ALBINO!
LILLY?
ALBINO!
LILLY!?!
ALBINO!
ALBINO!
ALBINO!

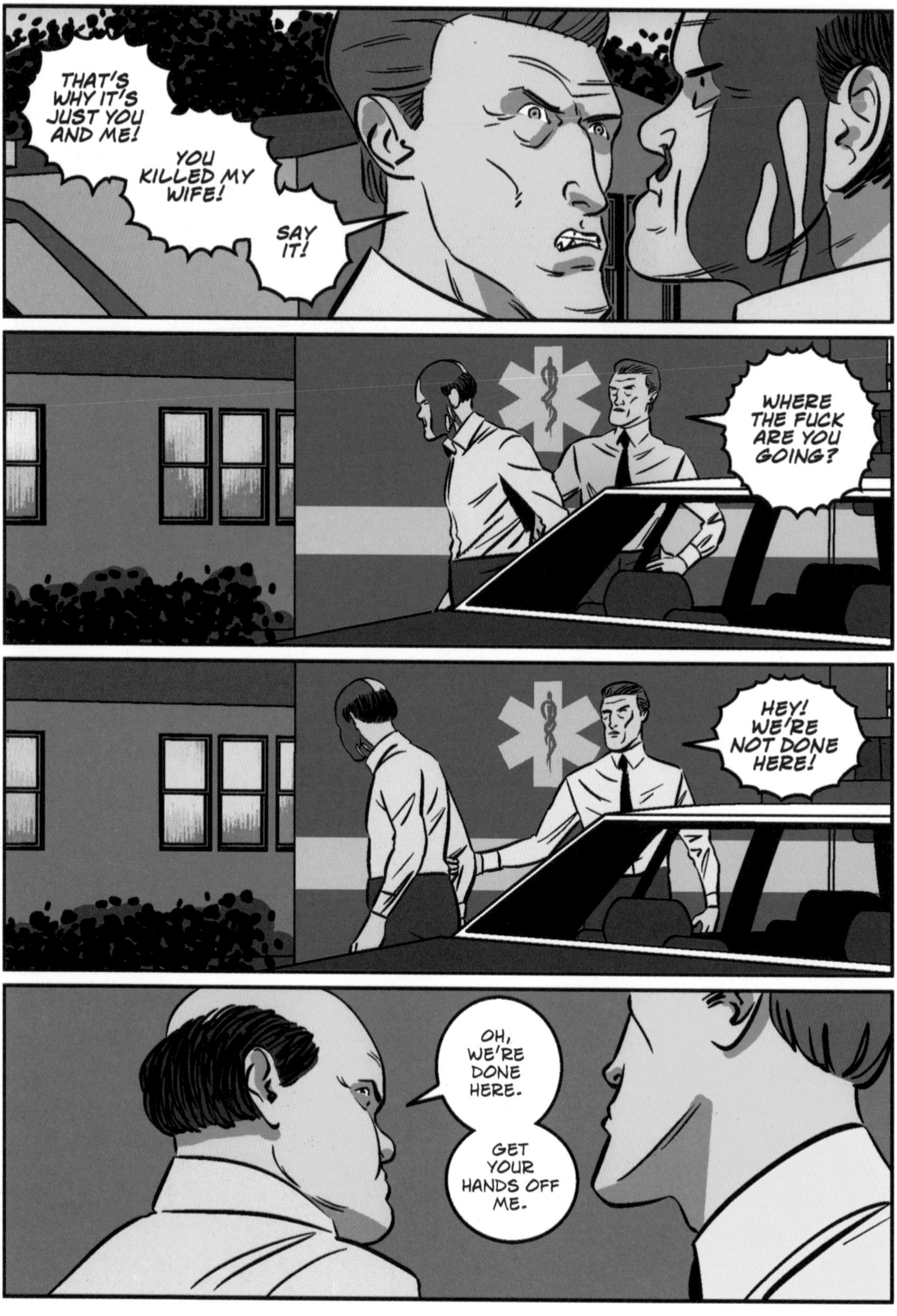
THAT'S WHY IT'S JUST YOU AND ME!
YOU KILLED MY WIFE!
SAY IT!
WHERE THE FUCK ARE YOU GOING?
HEY! WE'RE NOT DONE HERE!
OH, WE'RE DONE HERE.
GET YOUR HANDS OFF ME.

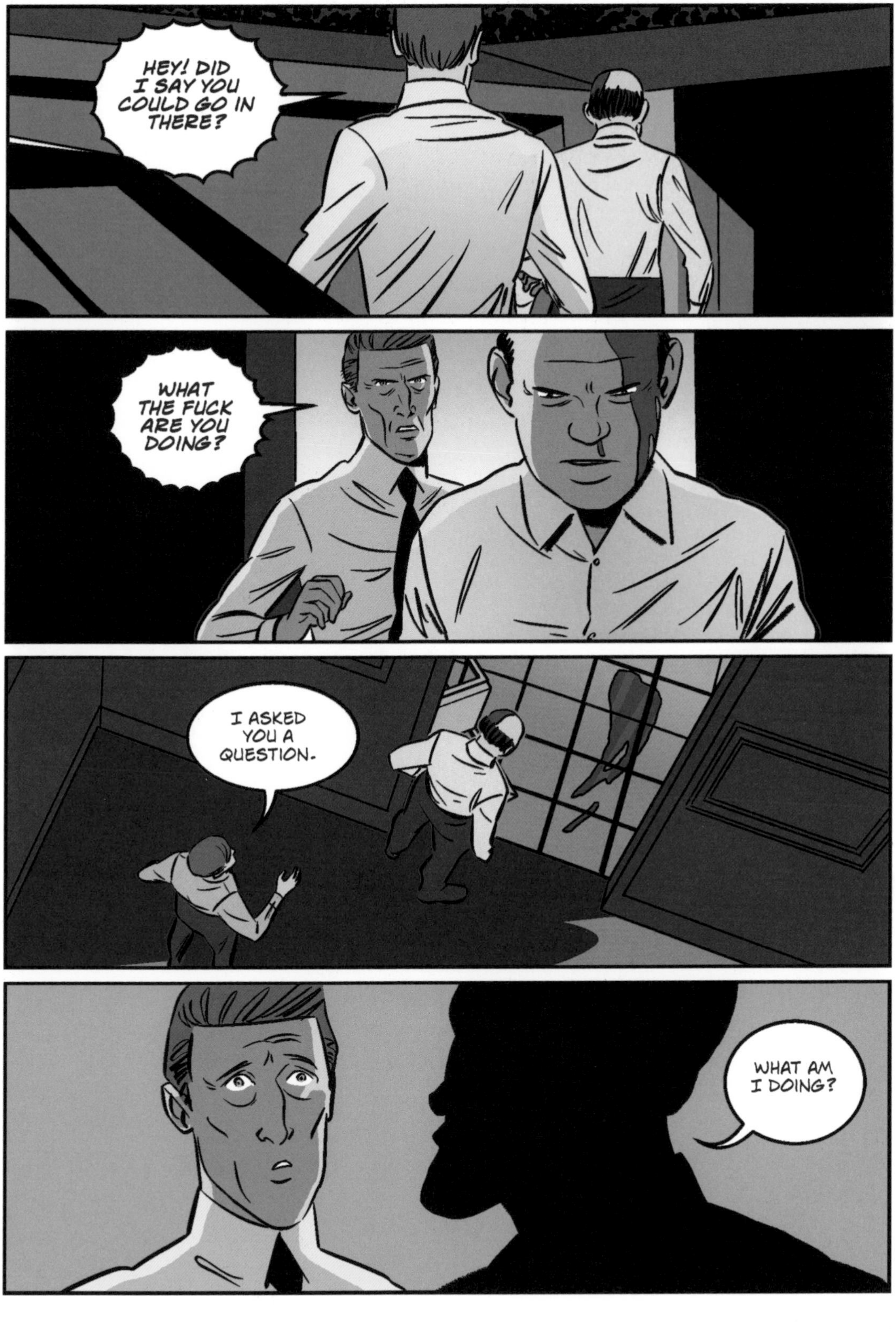
HEY! DID I SAY YOU COULD GO IN THERE?
WHAT THE FUCK ARE YOU DOING?
I ASKED YOU A QUESTION.
WHAT AM I DOING?

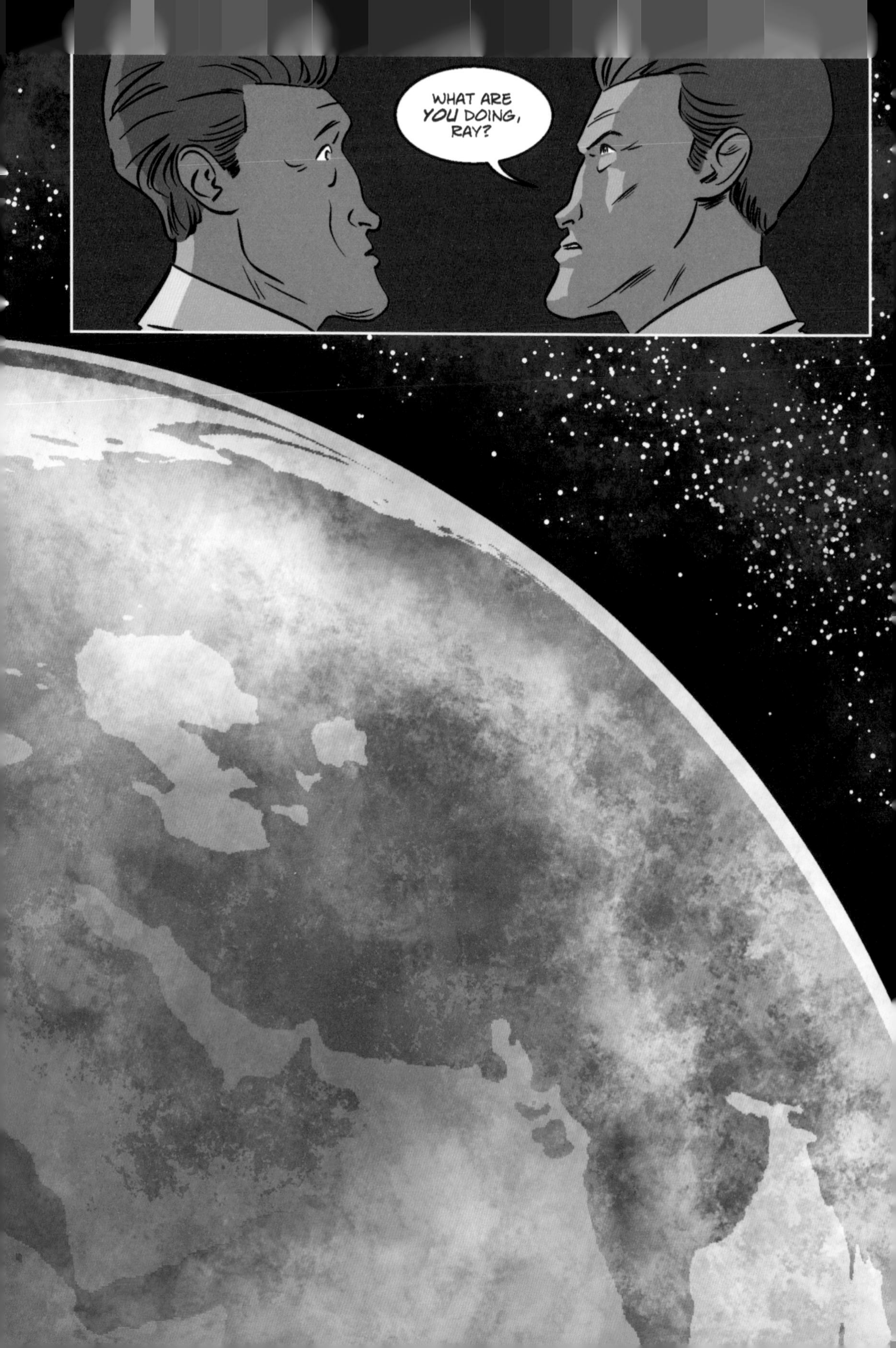
WHAT ARE YOU DOING, RAY?

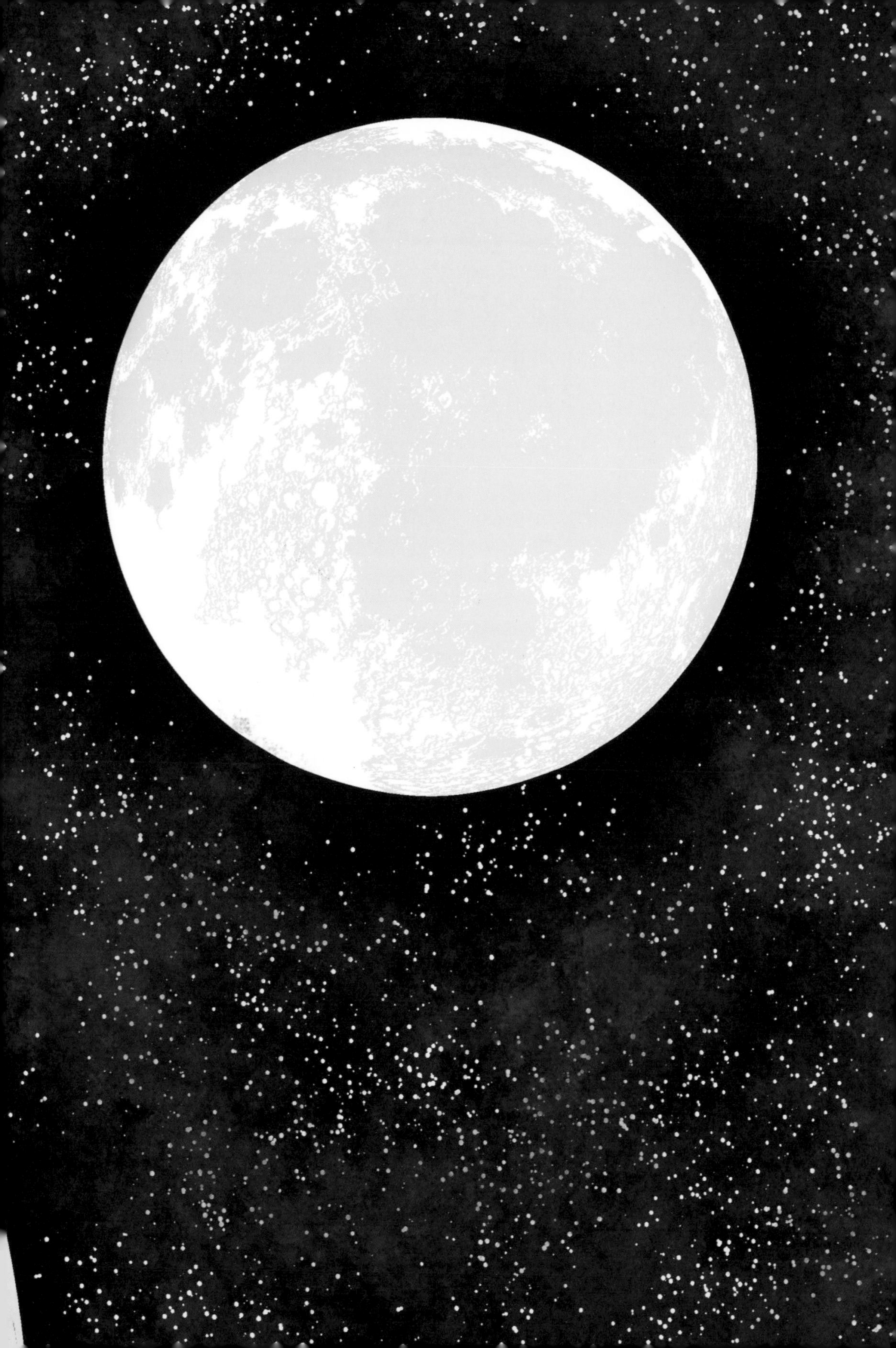

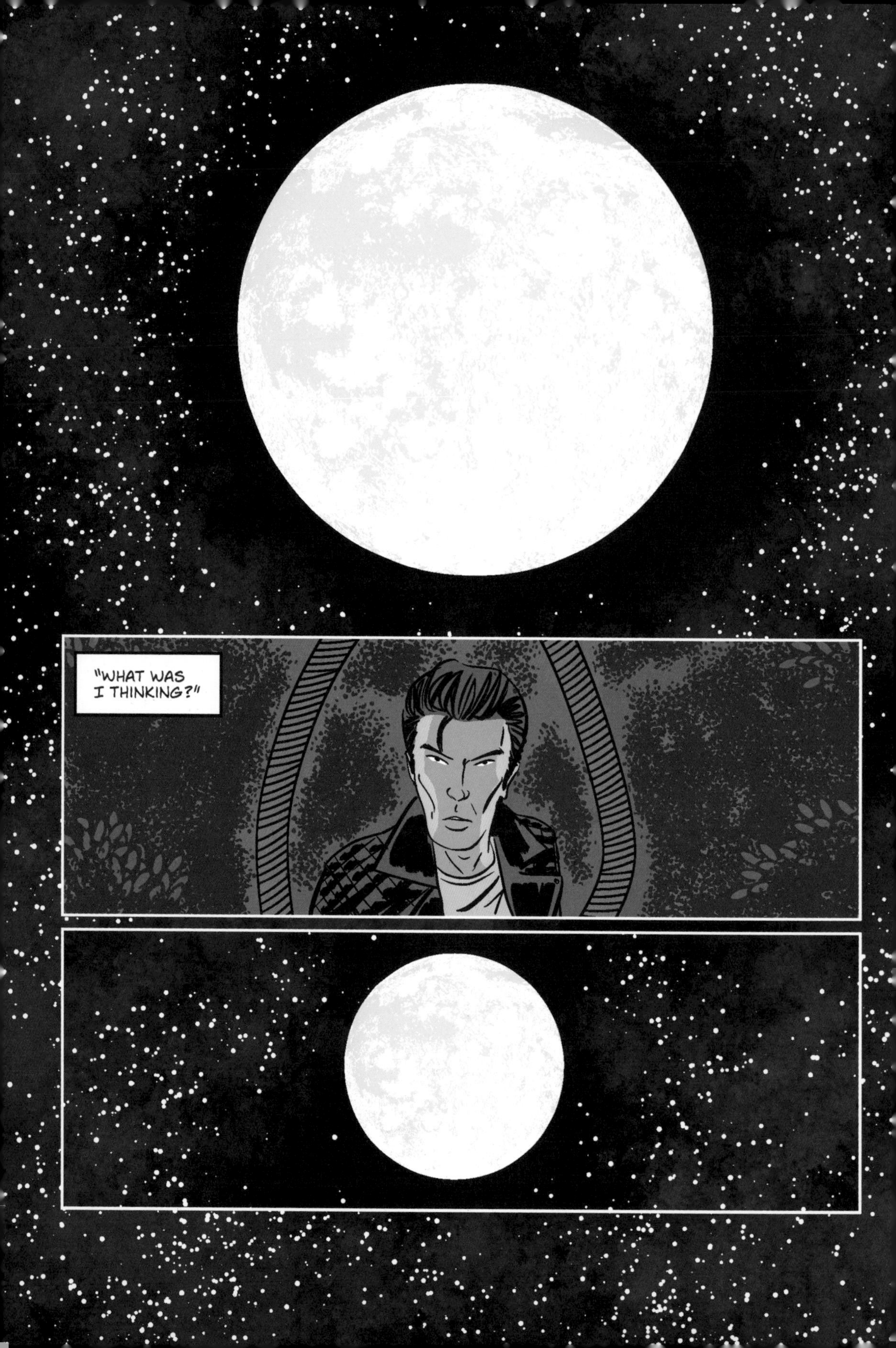
"WHAT WAS I THINKING?"

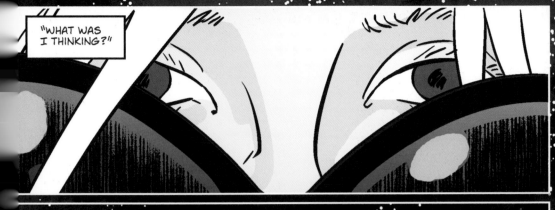

"WHAT WAS I THINKING?"

"WHAT WAS I THINKING?"

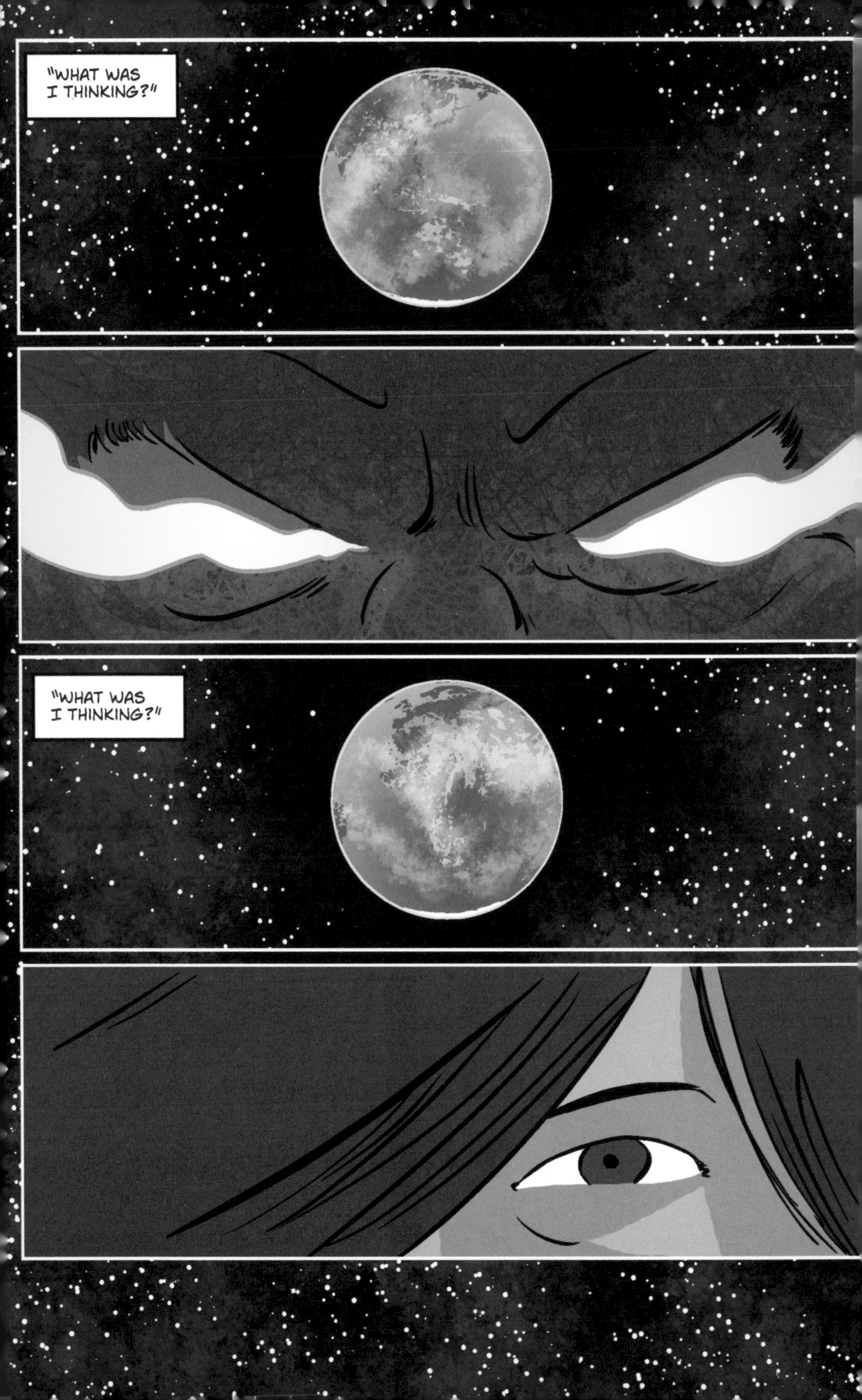
"WHAT WAS I THINKING?"
"WHAT WAS I THINKING?"

"WHAT WAS
I THINKING?"

"WHAT WAS
I THINKING?"

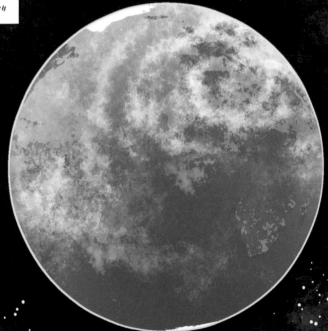

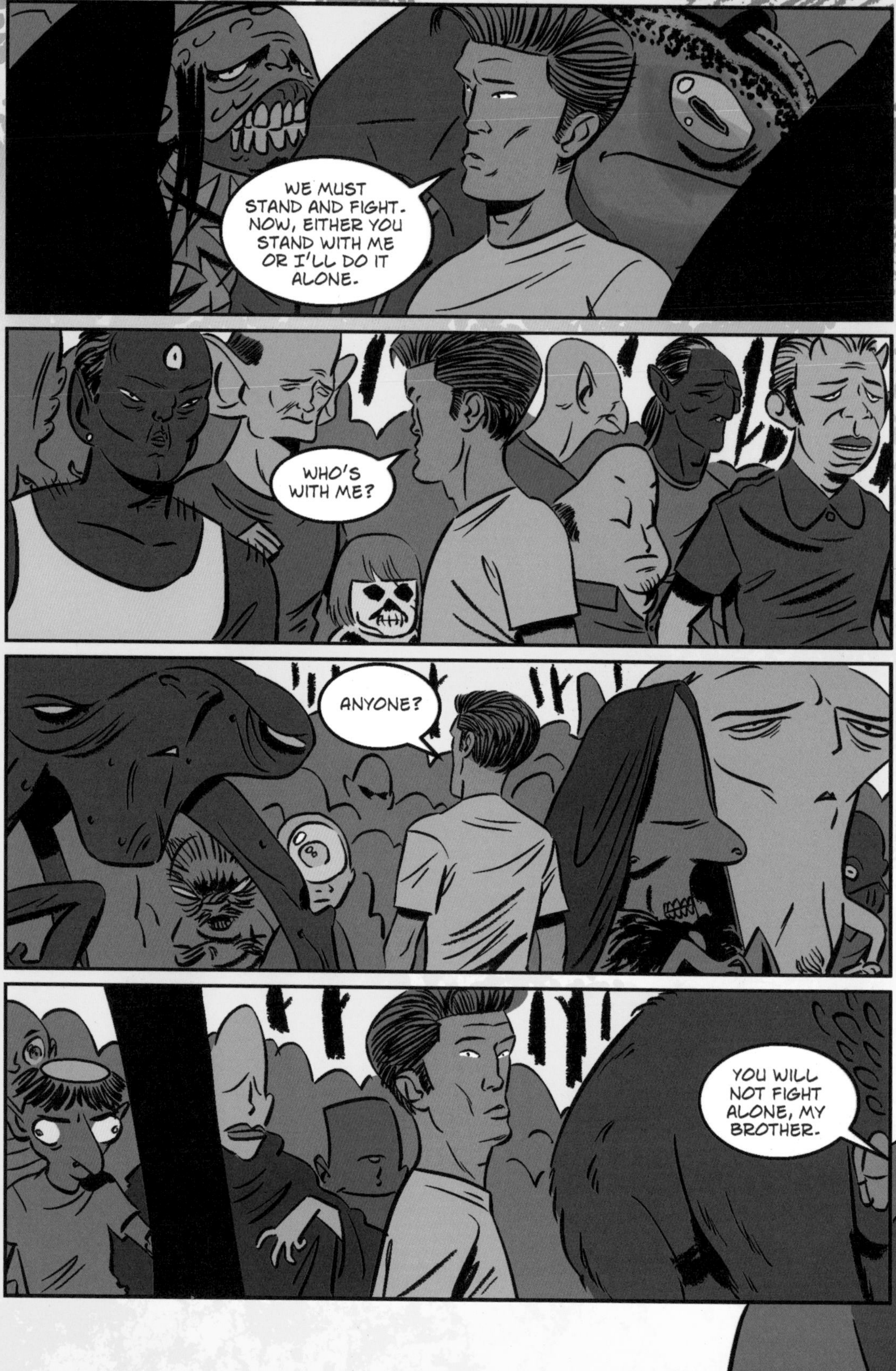
WE MUST STAND AND FIGHT. NOW, EITHER YOU STAND WITH ME OR I'LL DO IT ALONE.
WHO'S WITH ME?
ANYONE?
YOU WILL NOT FIGHT ALONE, MY BROTHER.

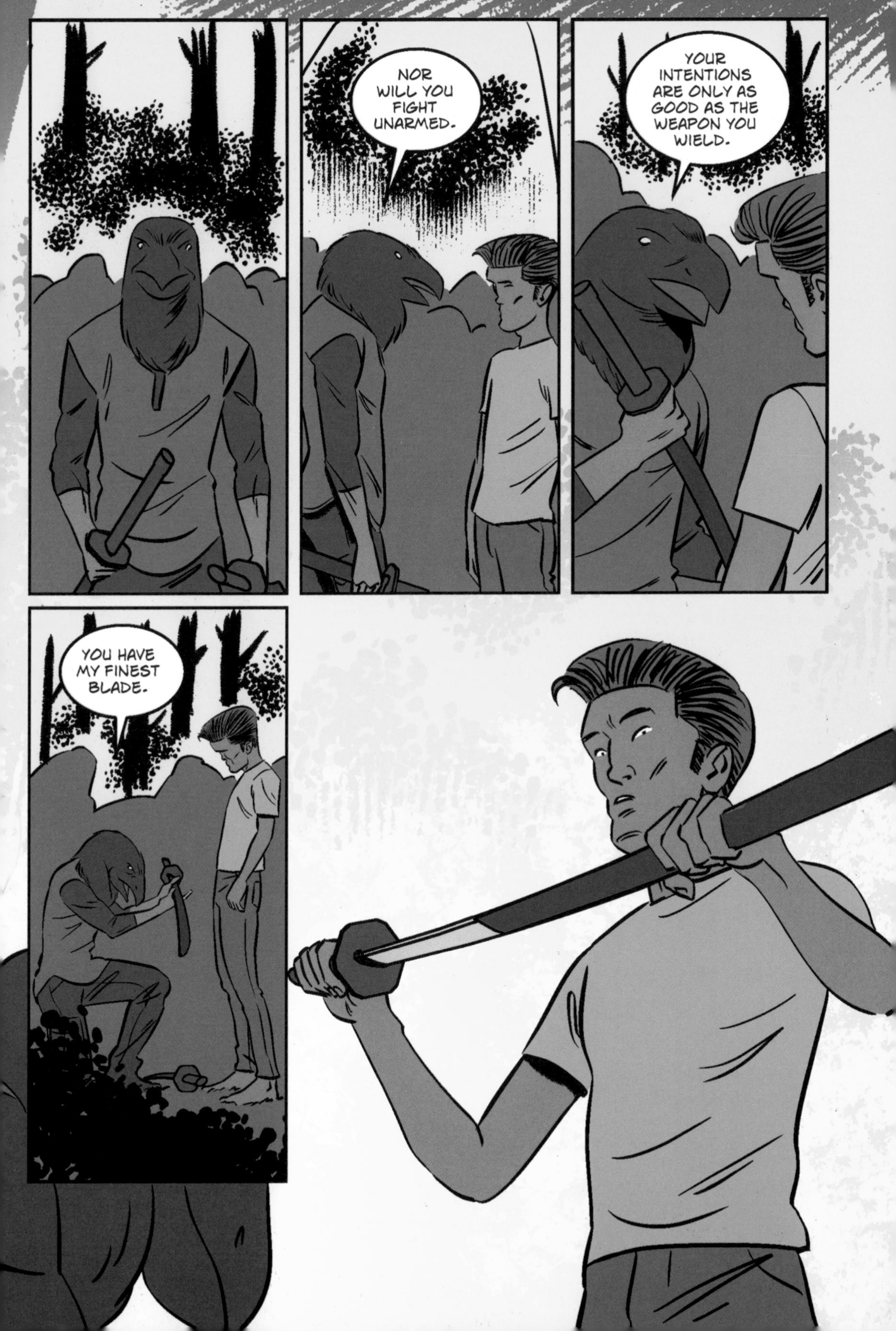
NOR WILL YOU FIGHT UNARMED.
YOUR INTENTIONS ARE ONLY AS GOOD AS THE WEAPON YOU WIELD.
YOU HAVE MY FINEST BLADE.

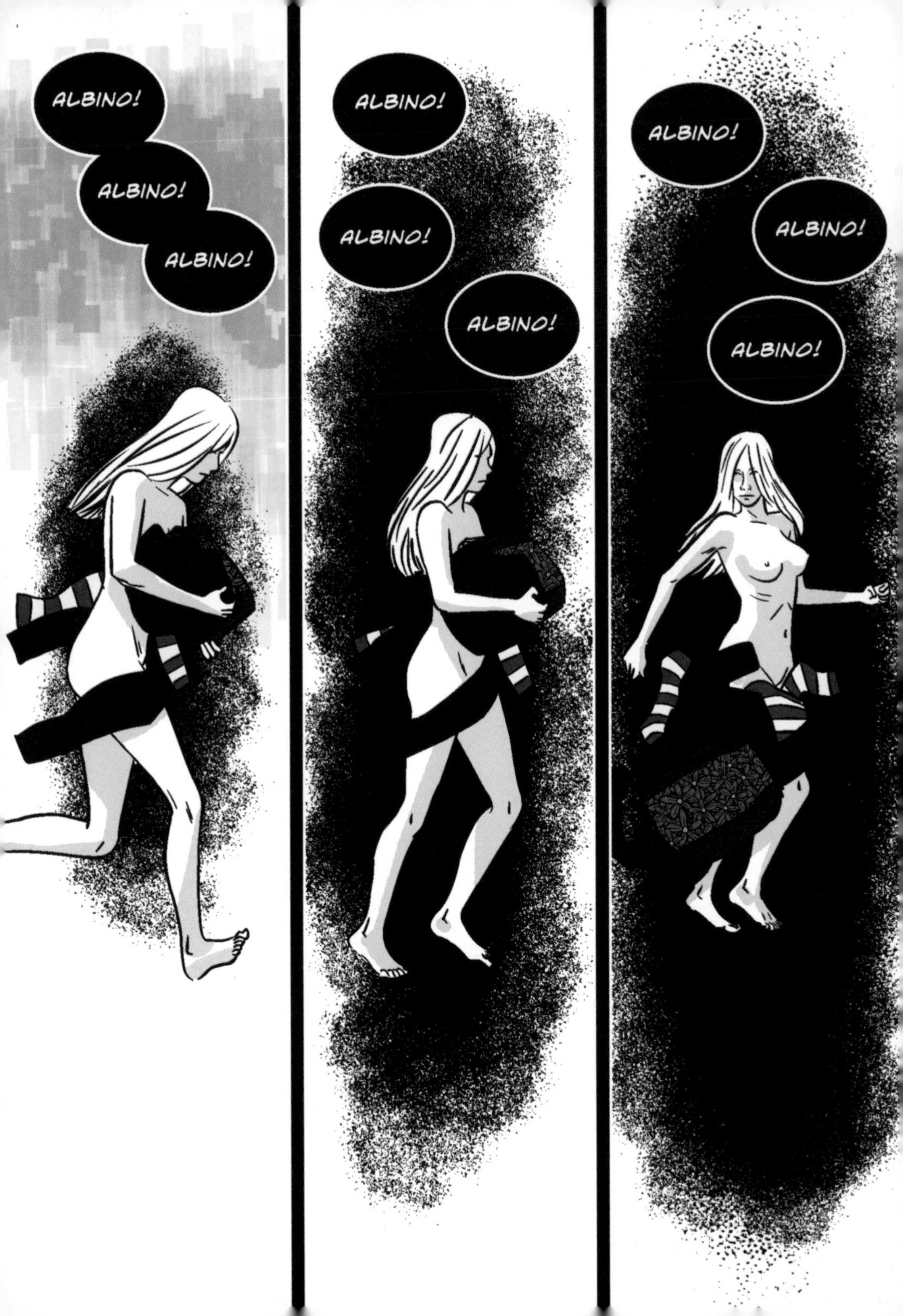
ALBINO!
ALBINO!
ALBINO!
ALBINO!
ALBINO!
ALBINO!
ALBINO!
ALBINO!
ALBINO!

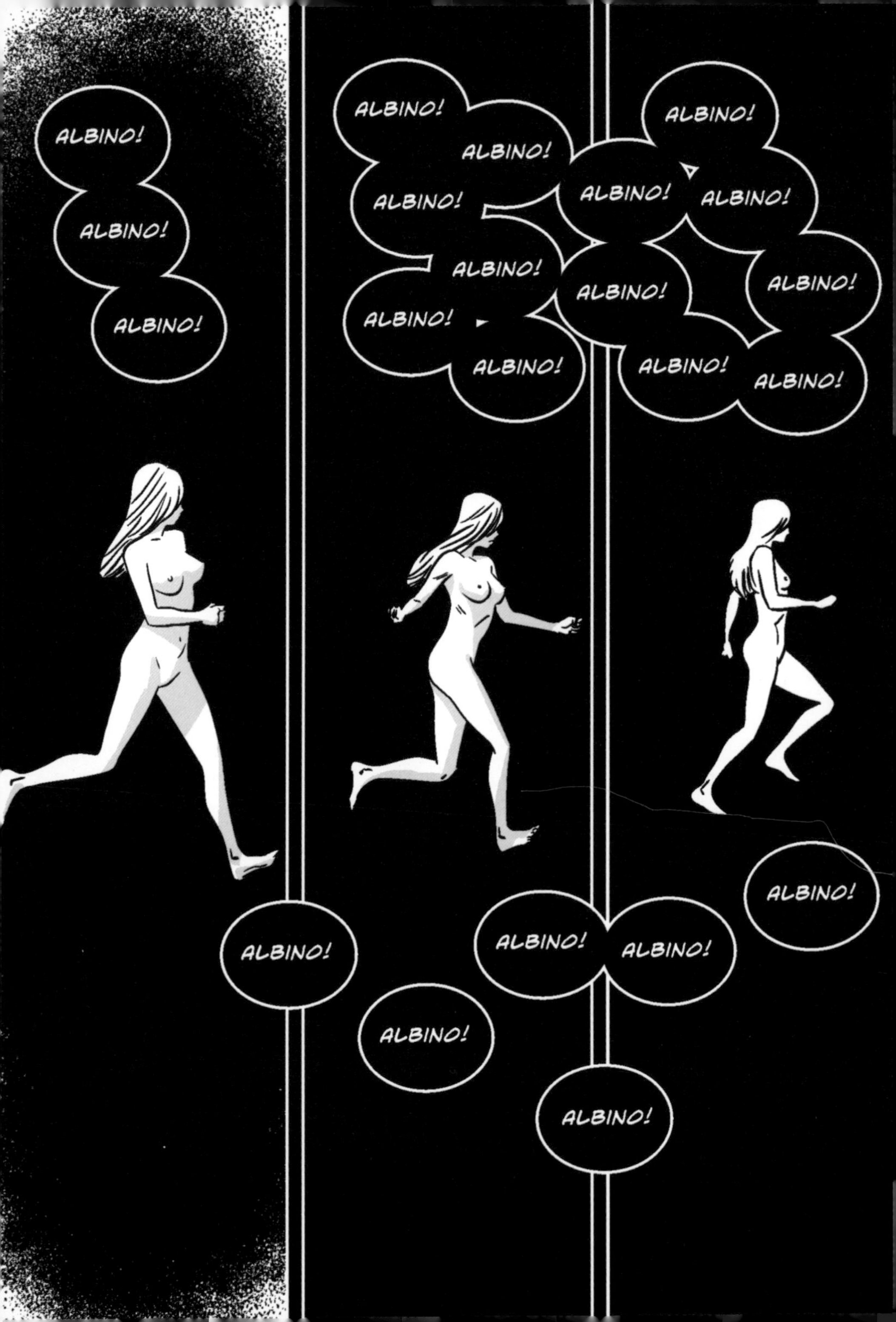

ALBINO!
ALBINO!
ALBINO!
ALBINO!
ALBINO!
ALBINO!
ALBINO!
ALBINO!
ALBINO!
ALBINO!
ALBINO!
ALBINO!
ALBINO!
ALBINO!
ALBINO!
ALBINO!
ALBINO!
ALBINO!
ALBINO!
ALBINO!
ALBINO!
ALBINO!

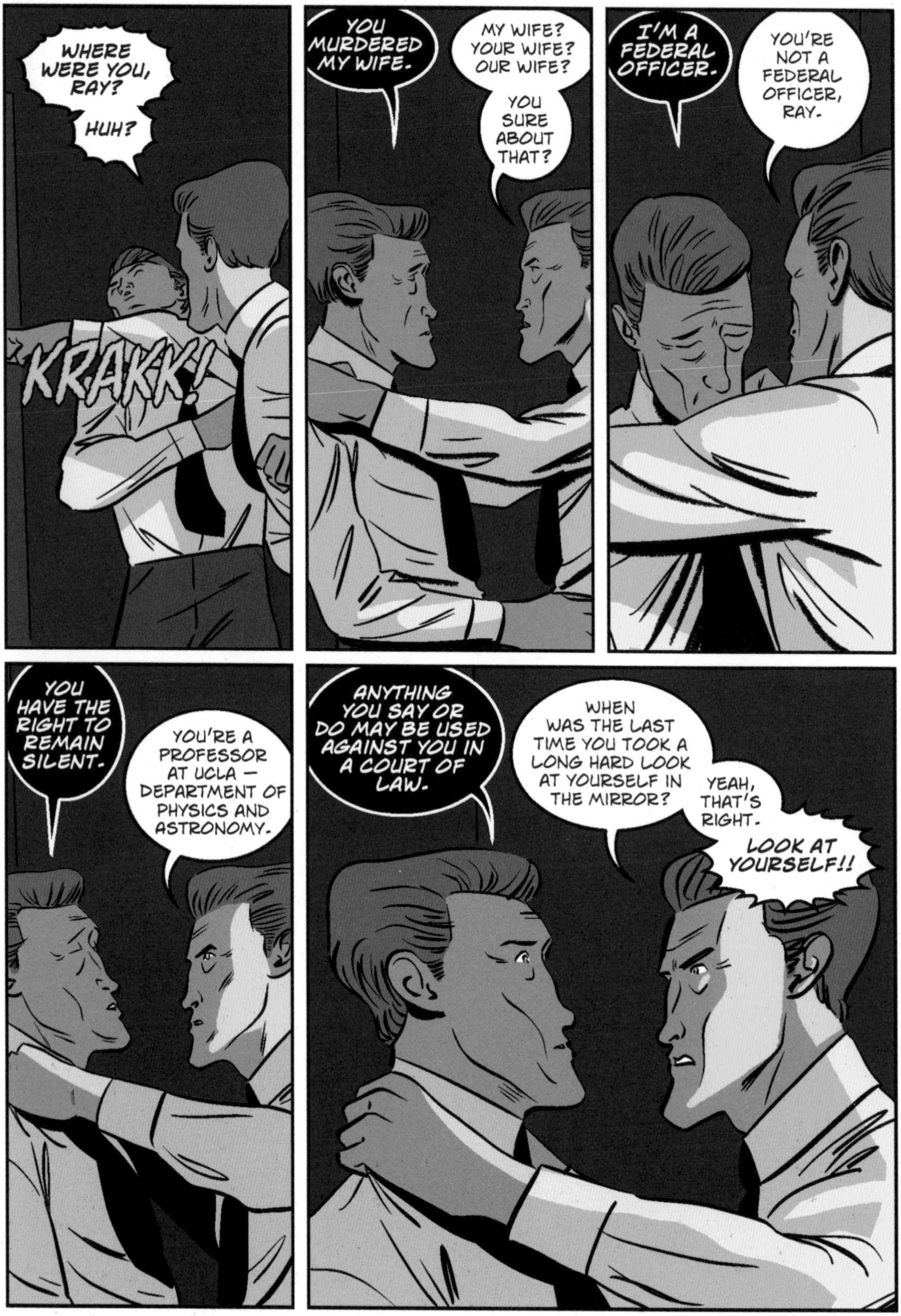
WHERE WERE YOU, RAY?
HUH?
KRAKK!
YOU MURDERED MY WIFE.
MY WIFE? YOUR WIFE? OUR WIFE?
YOU SURE ABOUT THAT?
I'M A FEDERAL OFFICER.
YOU'RE NOT A FEDERAL OFFICER, RAY.
YOU HAVE THE RIGHT TO REMAIN SILENT.
YOU'RE A PROFESSOR AT UCLA — DEPARTMENT OF PHYSICS AND ASTRONOMY.
ANYTHING YOU SAY OR DO MAY BE USED AGAINST YOU IN A COURT OF LAW.
WHEN WAS THE LAST TIME YOU TOOK A LONG HARD LOOK AT YOURSELF IN THE MIRROR?
YEAH, THAT'S RIGHT.
LOOK AT YOURSELF!!

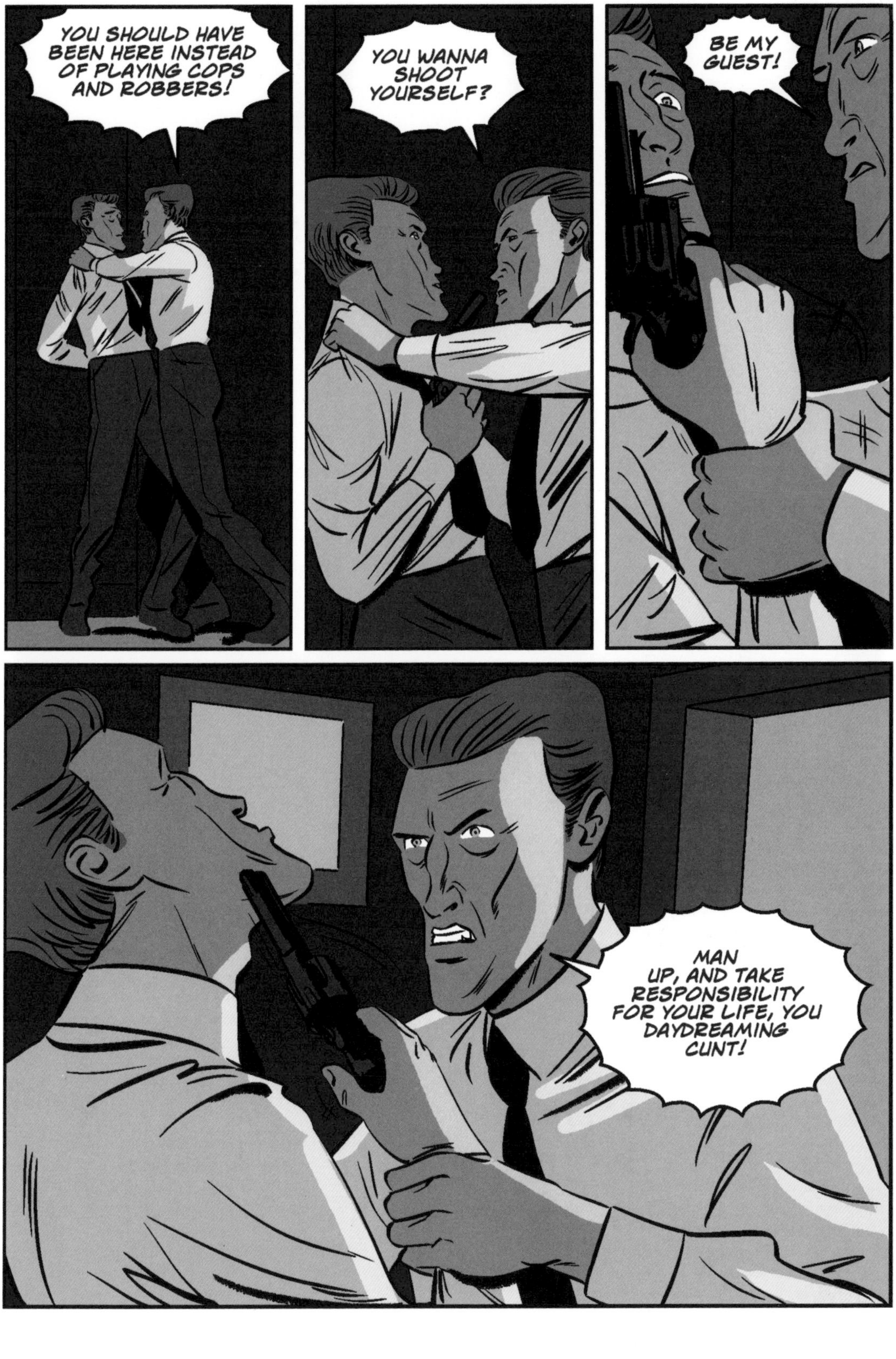
YOU SHOULD HAVE BEEN HERE INSTEAD OF PLAYING COPS AND ROBBERS!
YOU WANNA SHOOT YOURSELF?
BE MY GUEST!
MAN UP, AND TAKE RESPONSIBILITY FOR YOUR LIFE, YOU DAYDREAMING CUNT!

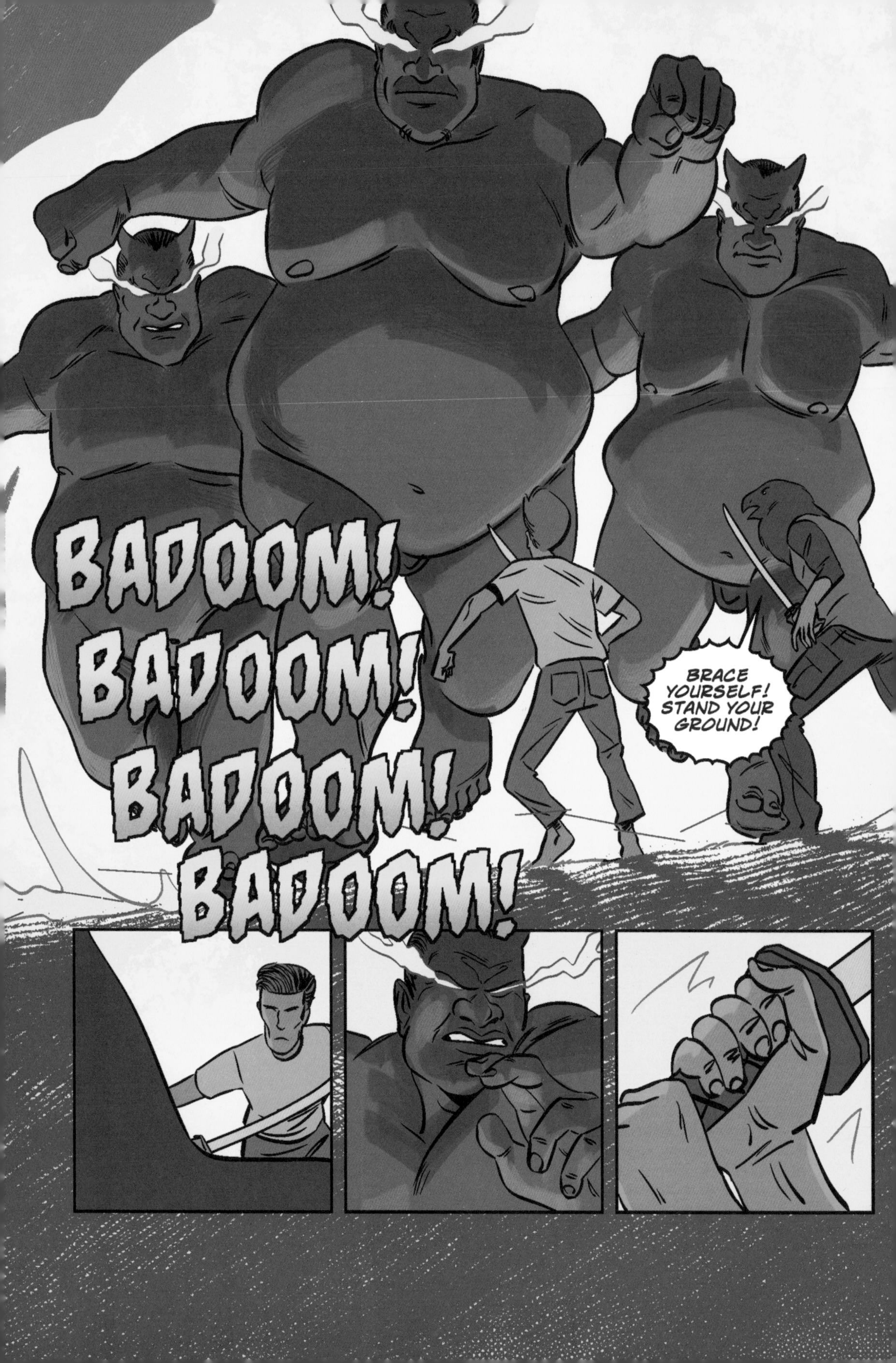
BADOOM!
BADOOM!
BADOOM!
BADOOM!
BRACE YOURSELF! STAND YOUR GROUND!

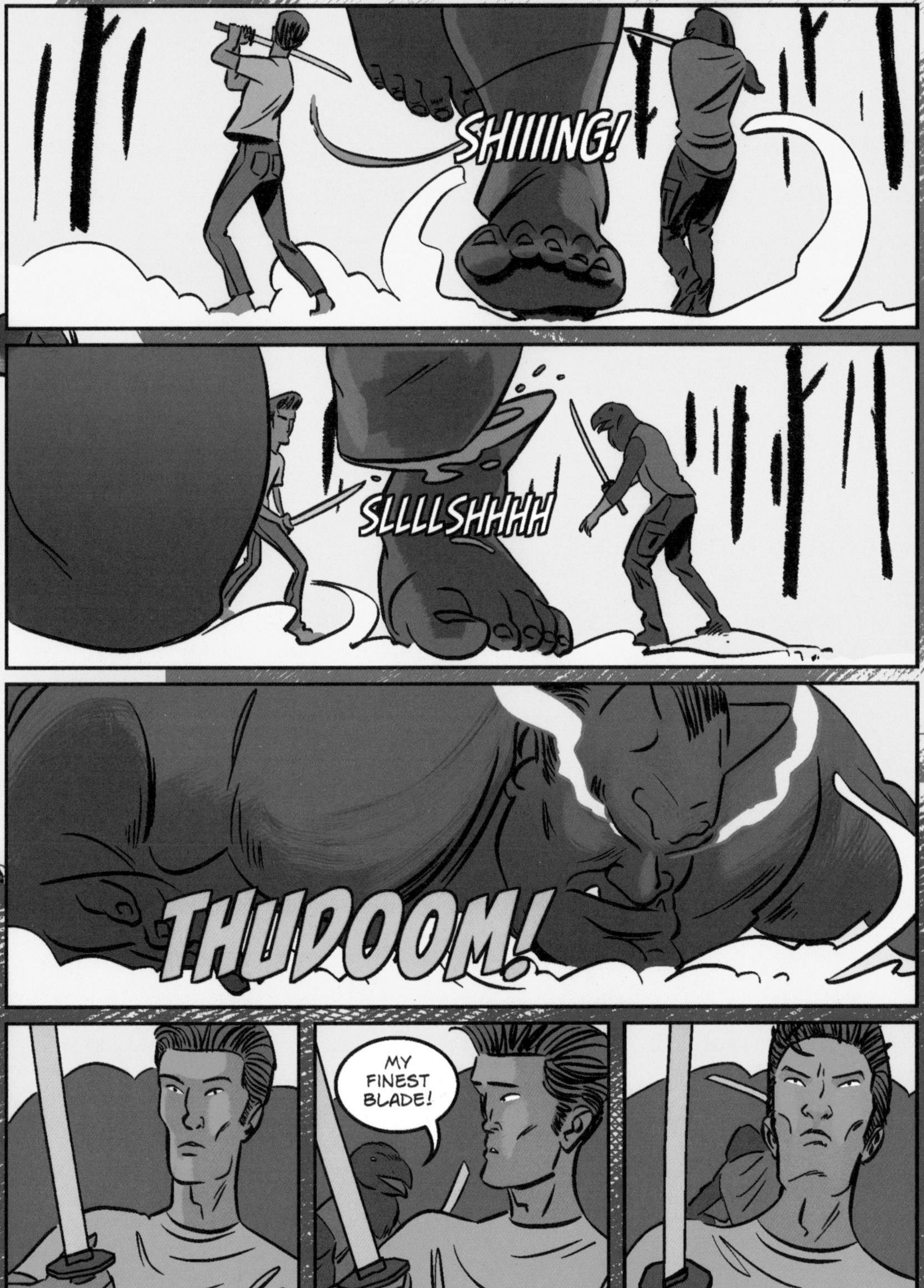
SHIIIING!
SLLLLSHHHH
THUDOOM!
MY FINEST BLADE!

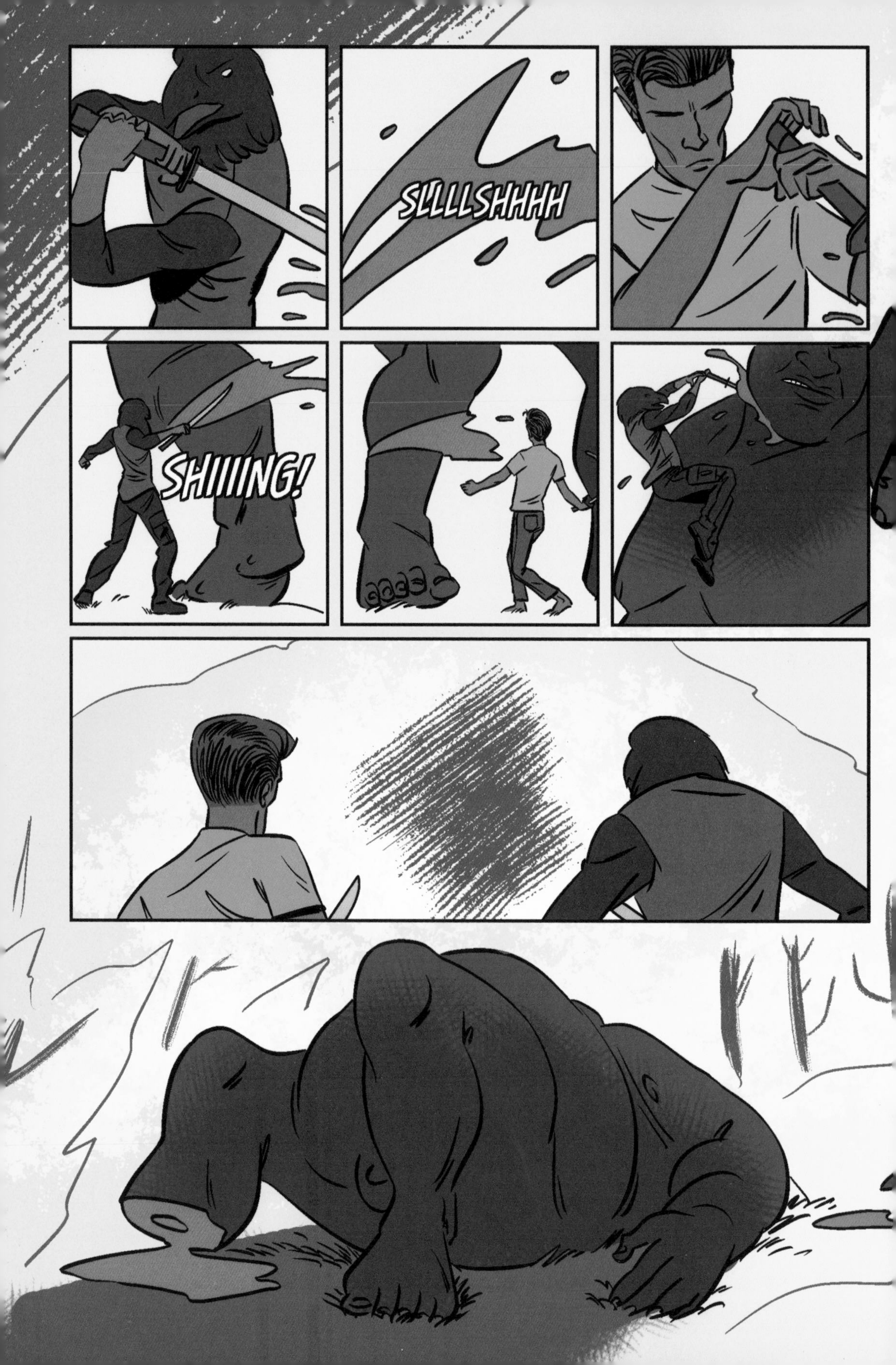
SLLLLSHHHH
SHIIIING!

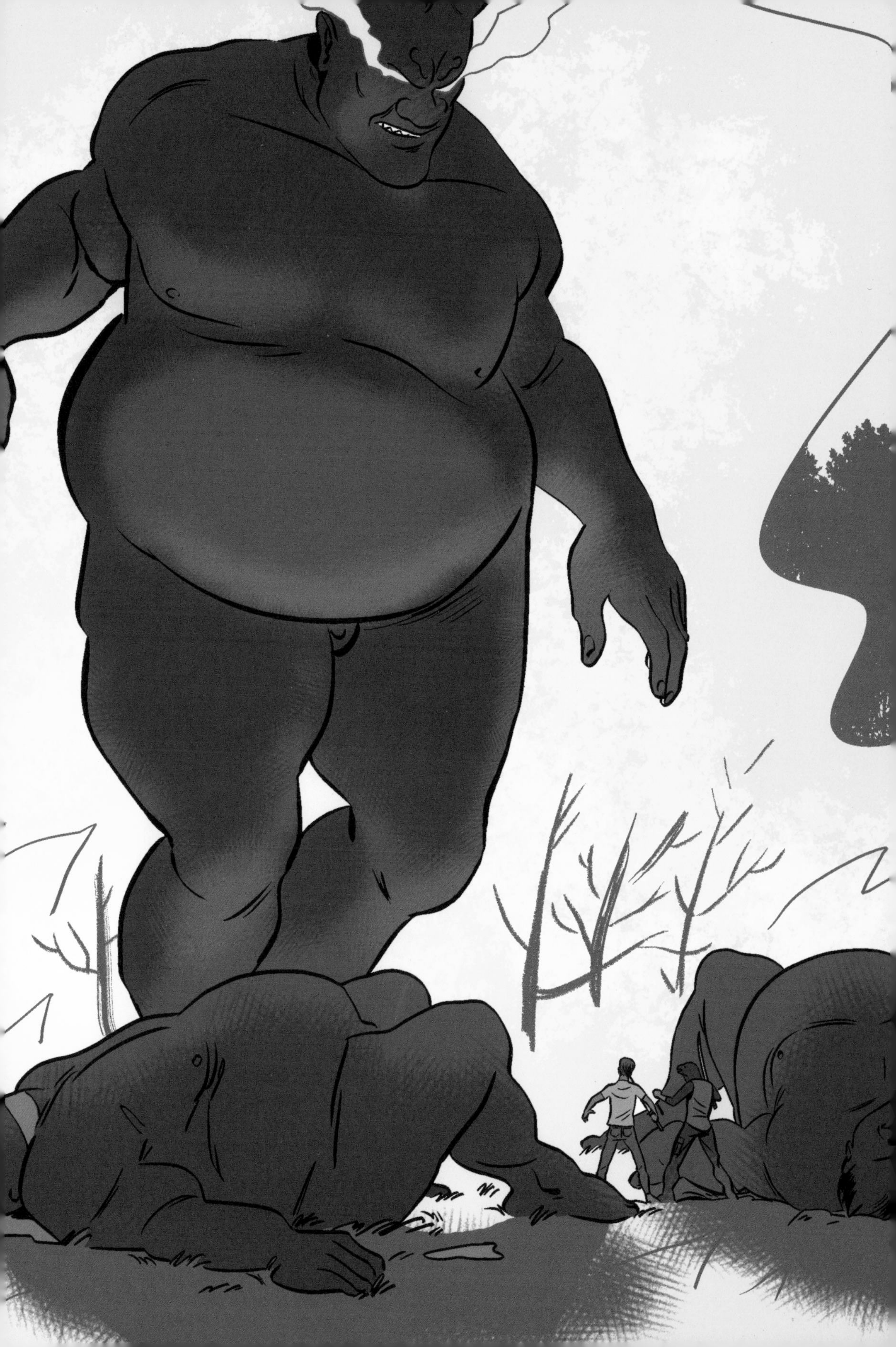

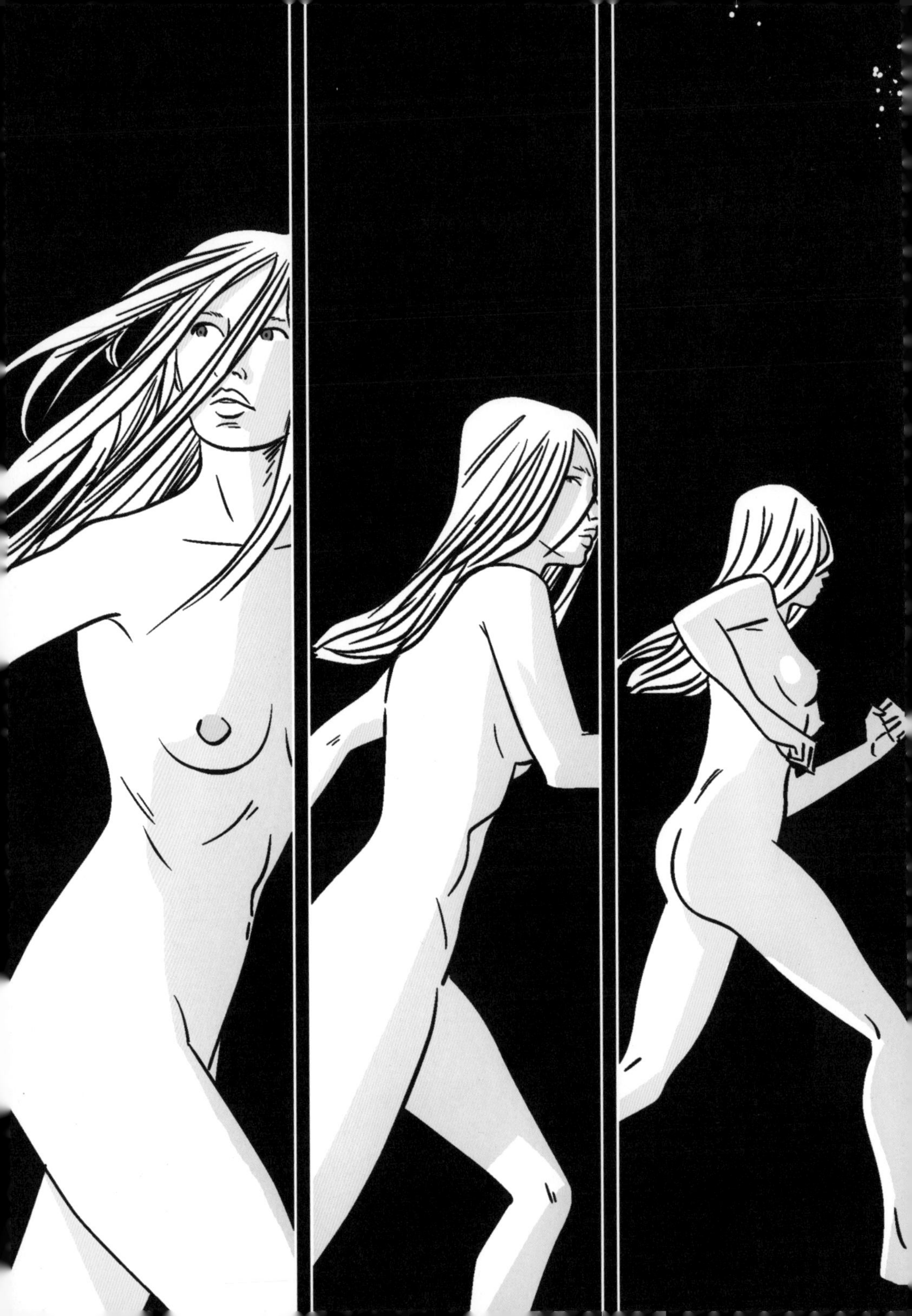

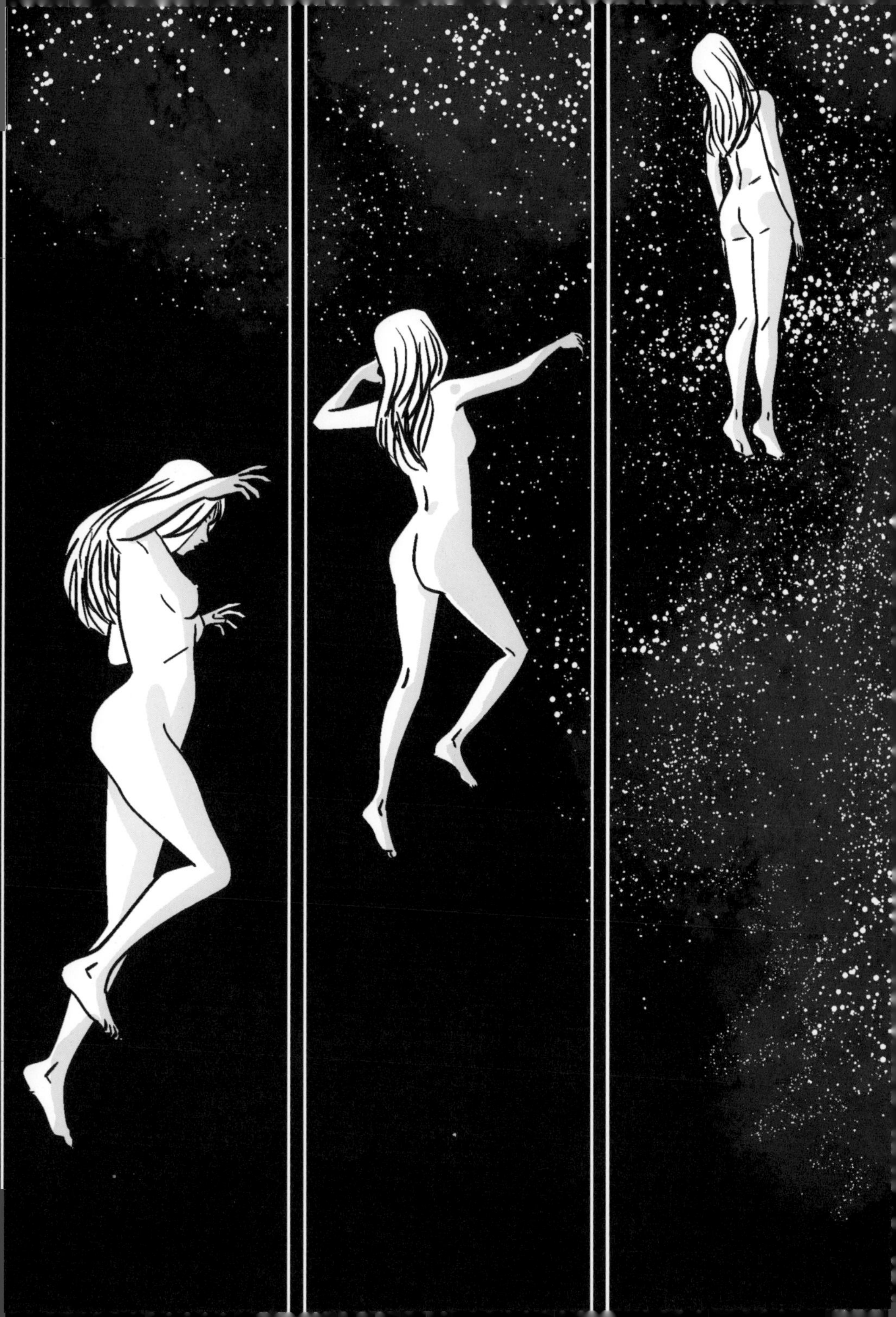

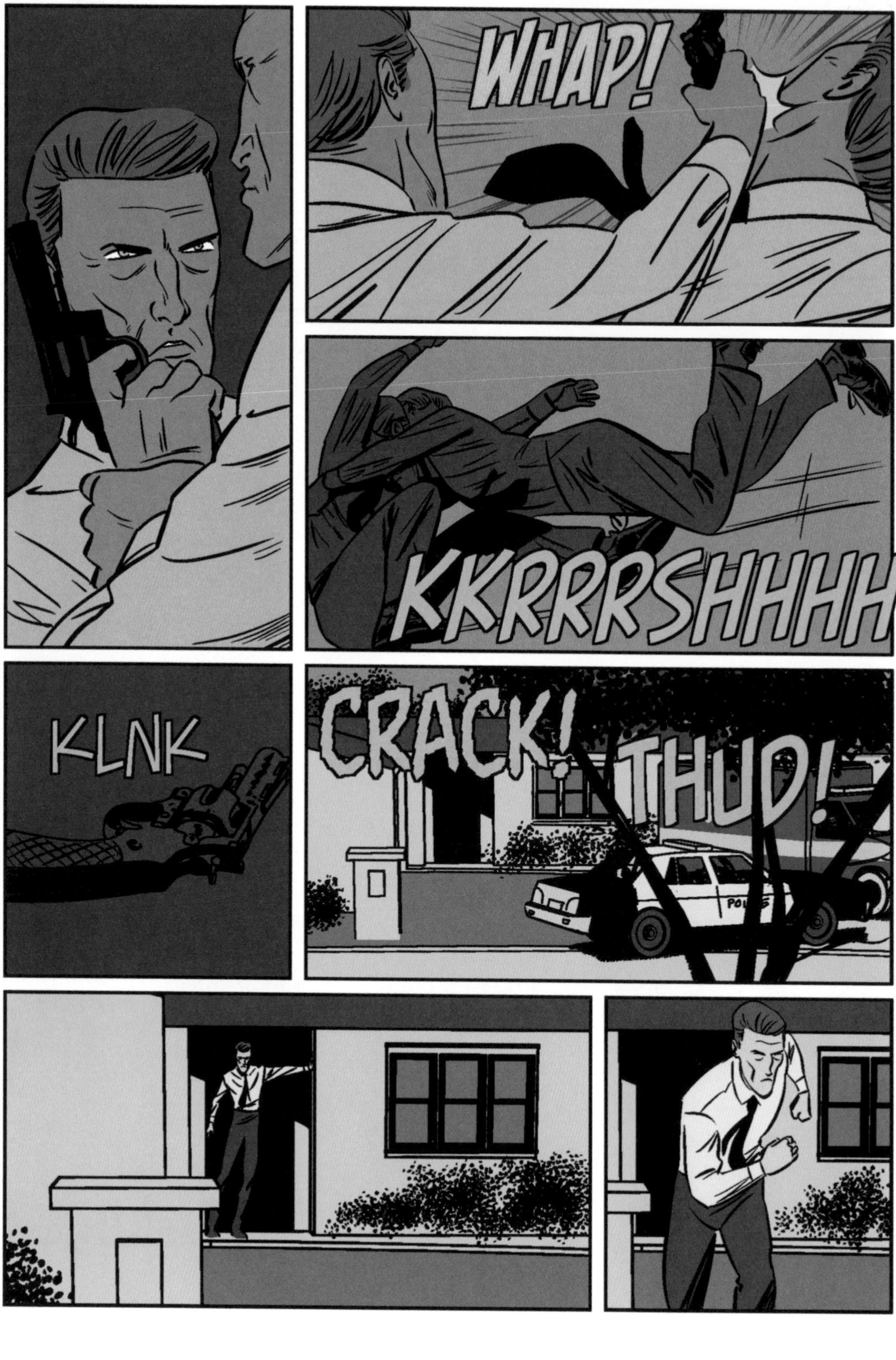
WHAP!
KKRRRSHHHH
KLNK
CRACK!
THUD!

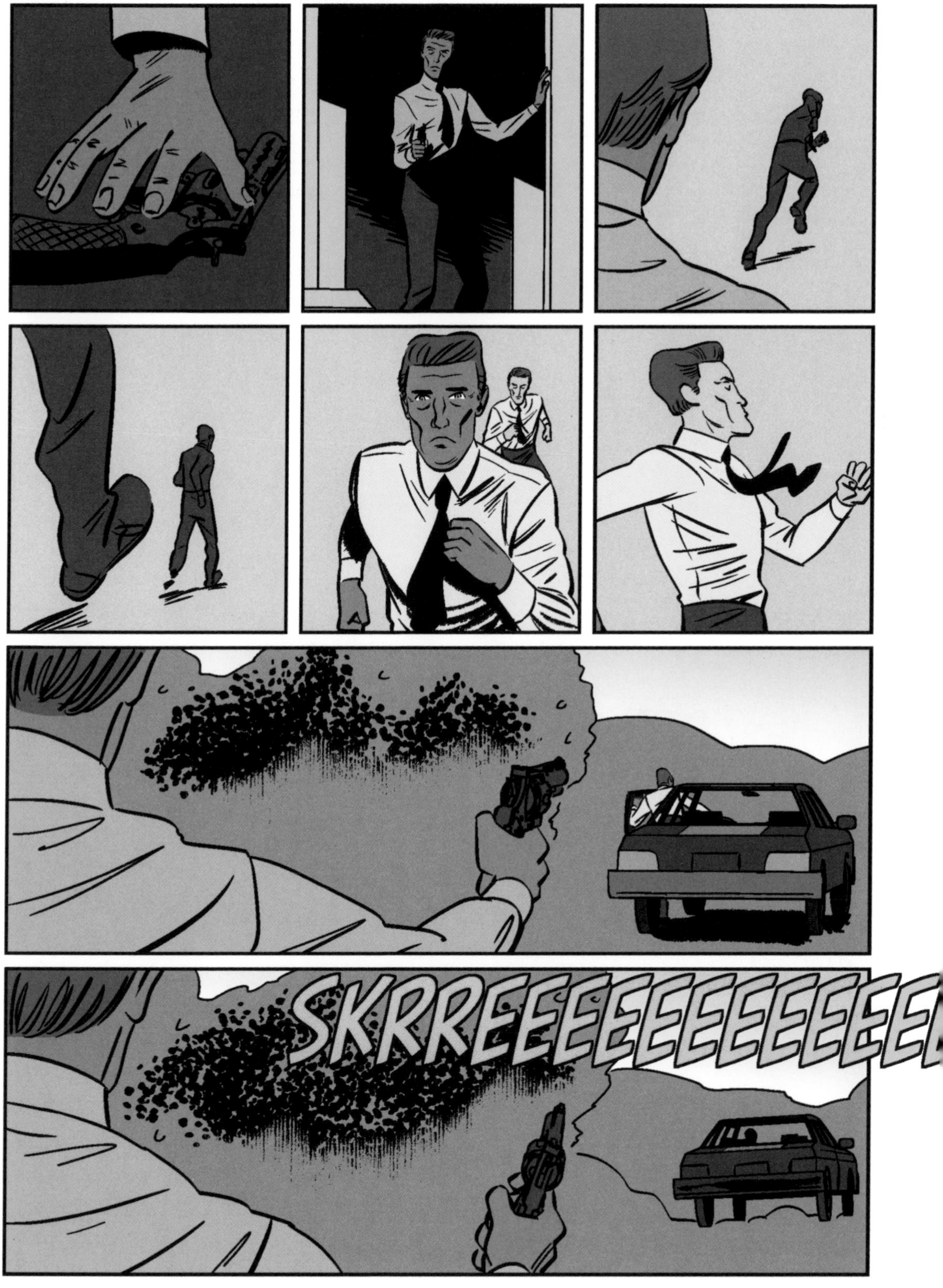
SKRREEEEEEEEEEEEEE

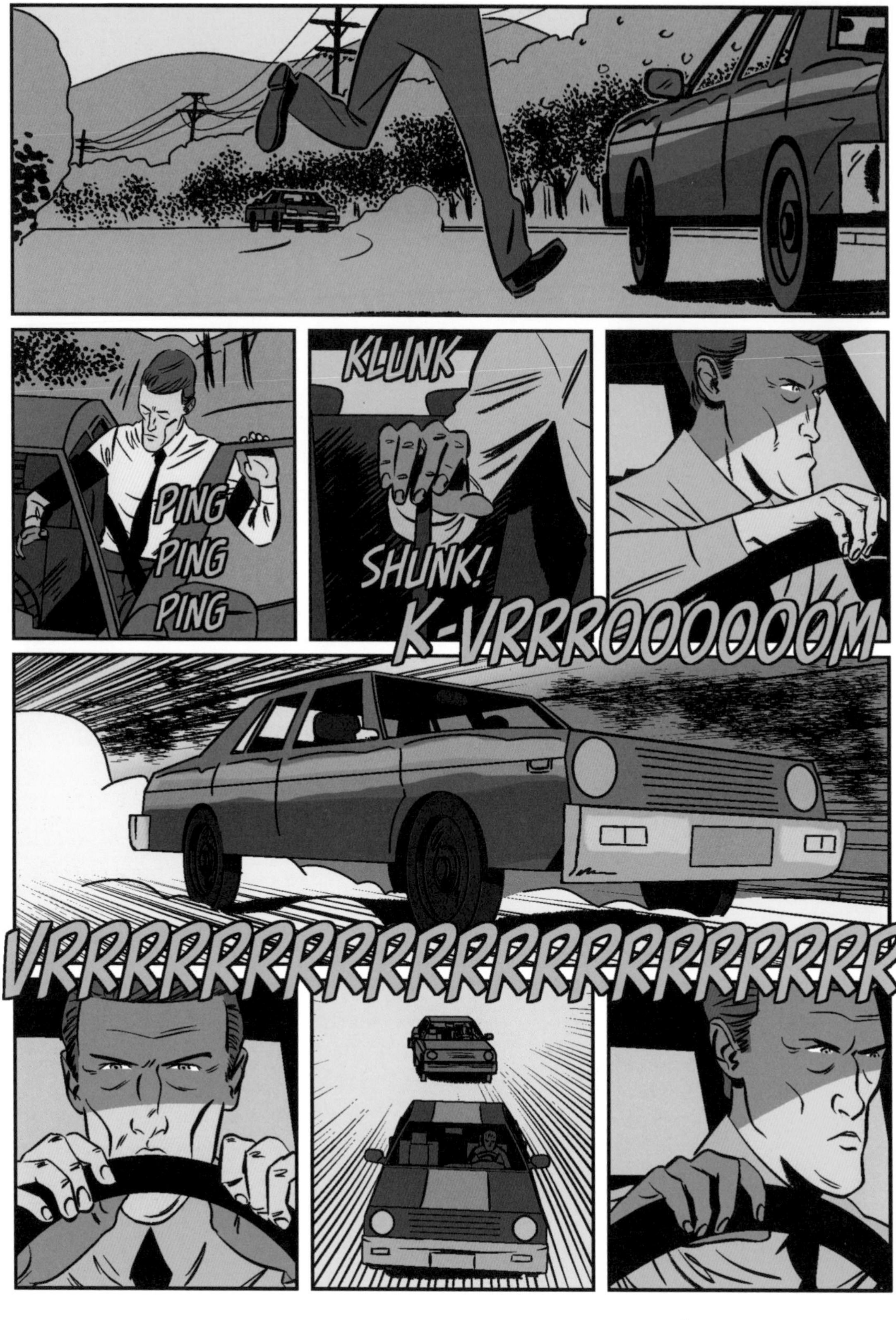
PING
PING
PING
KLUNK
SHUNK!
K-VRRROOOOOOM
VRRRRRRRRRRRRRRRRRRRRRR

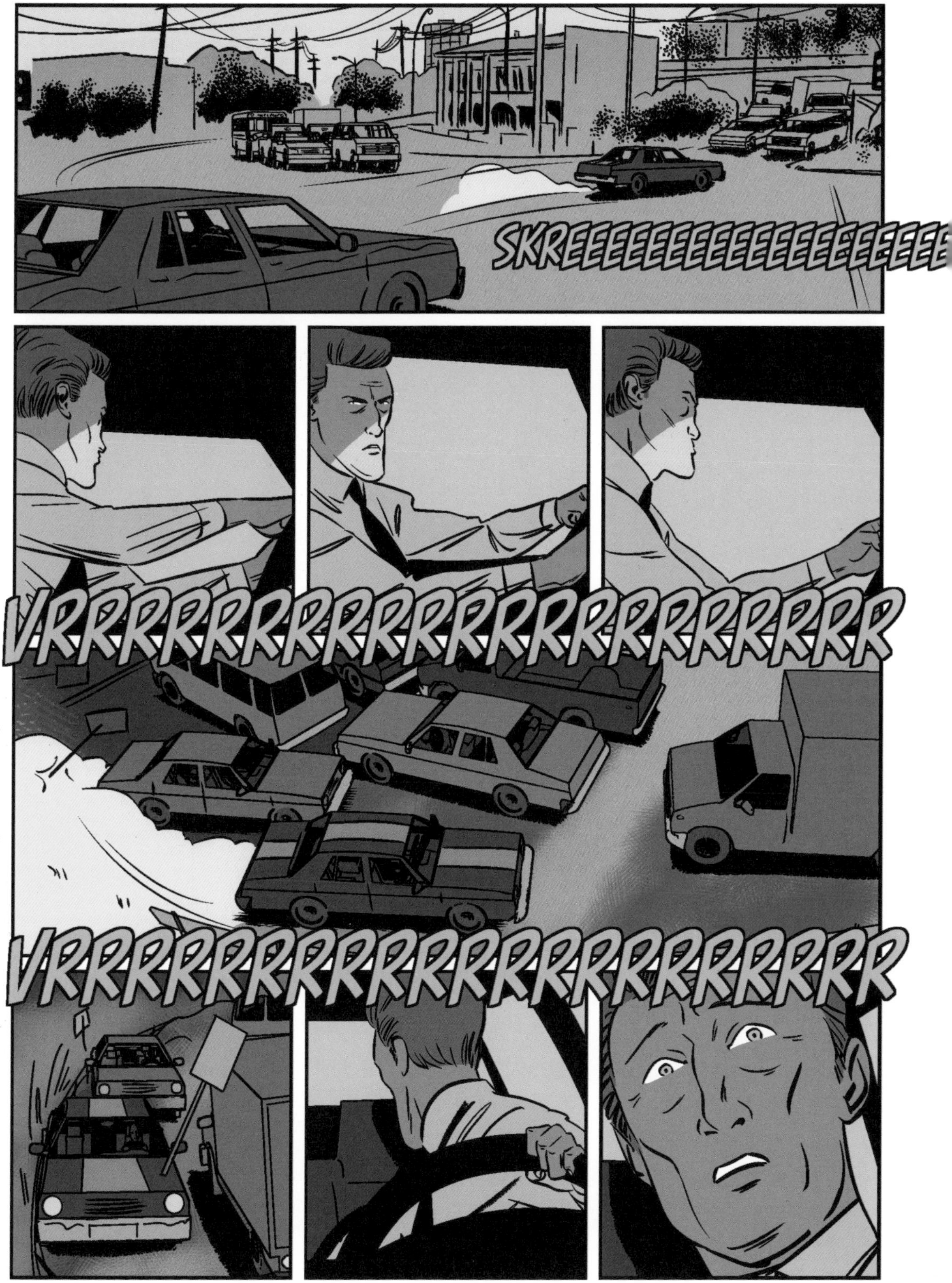
SKREEEEEEEEEEEEEEEEEE
VRRRRRRRRRRRRRRRRRRRRR
VRRRRRRRRRRRRRRRRRRRRRR

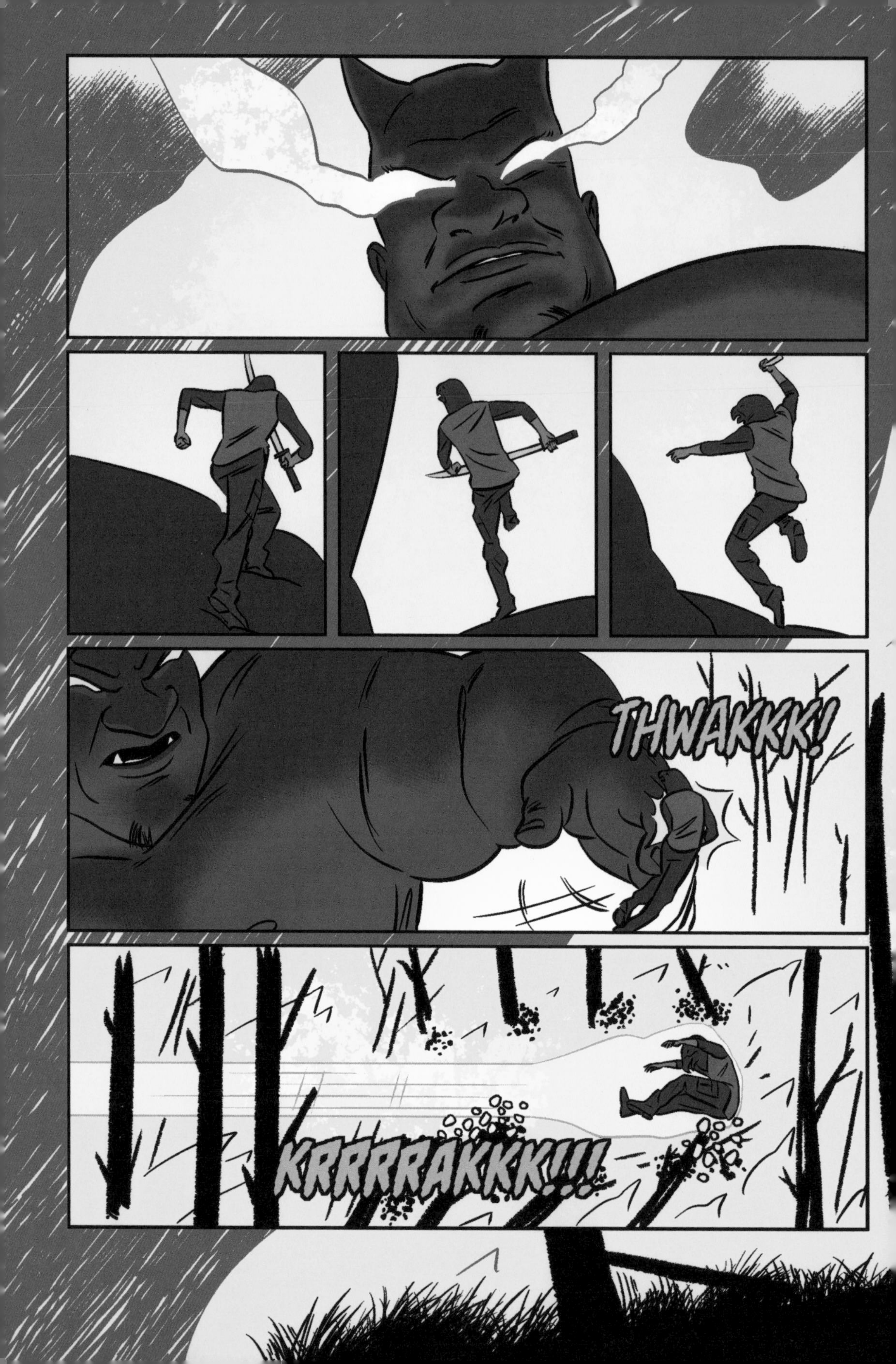
THWAKKK!
KRRRRAKKK!!!

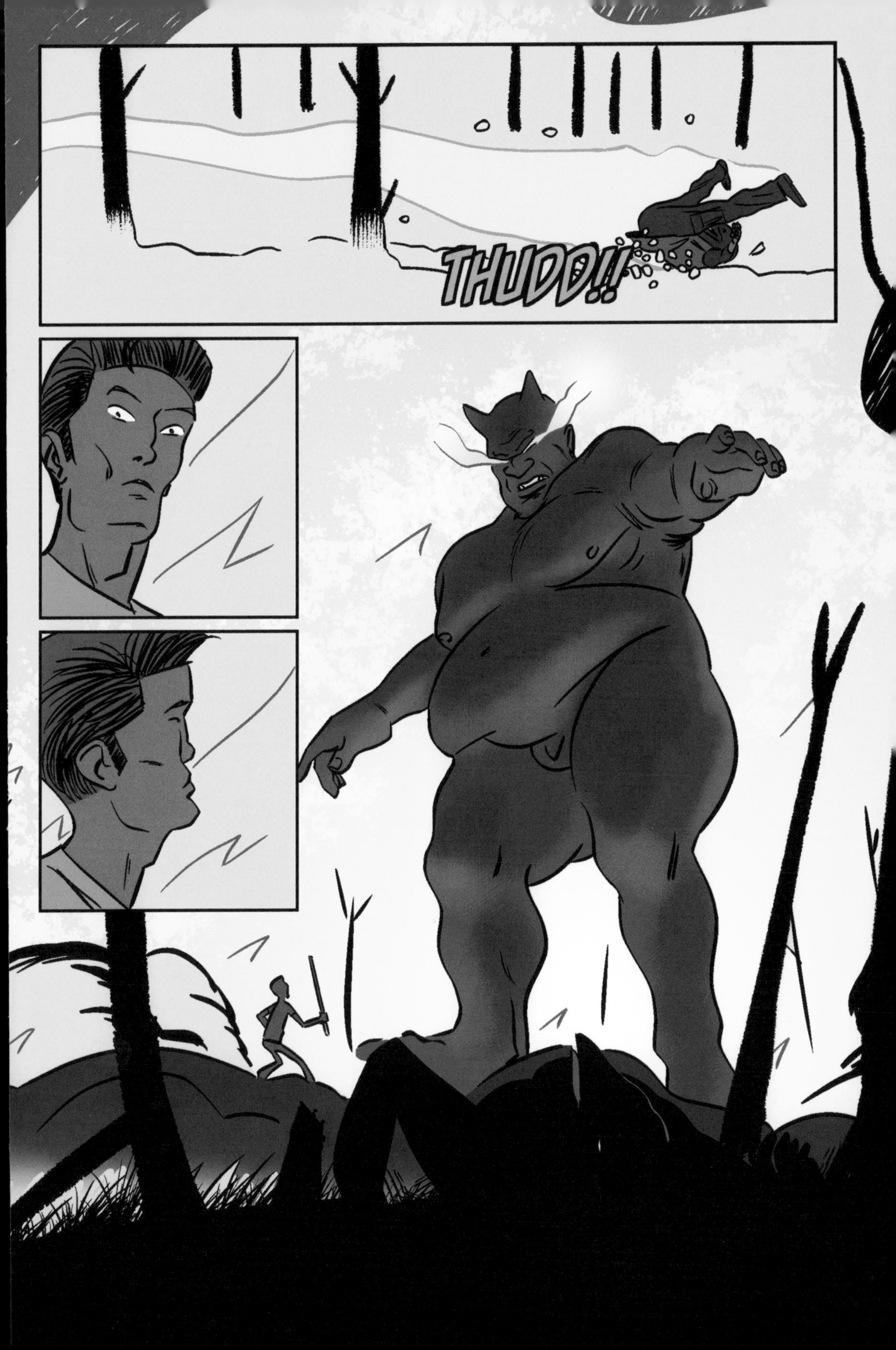
THUDD!!

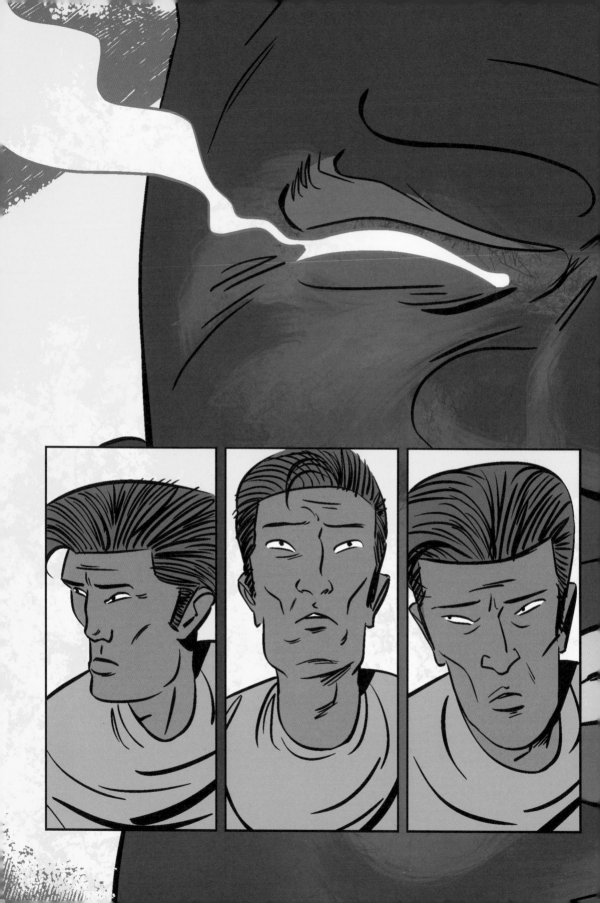

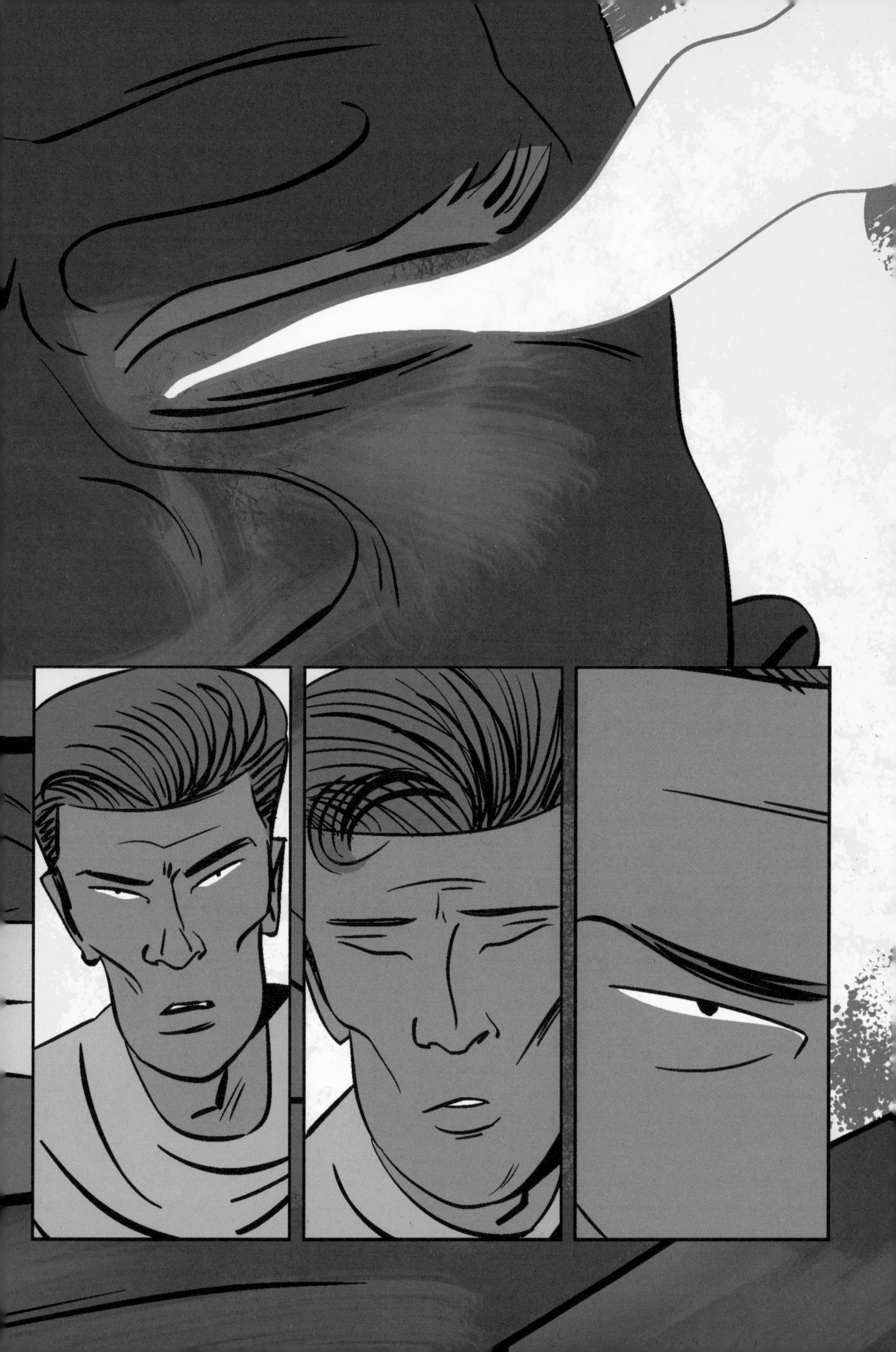

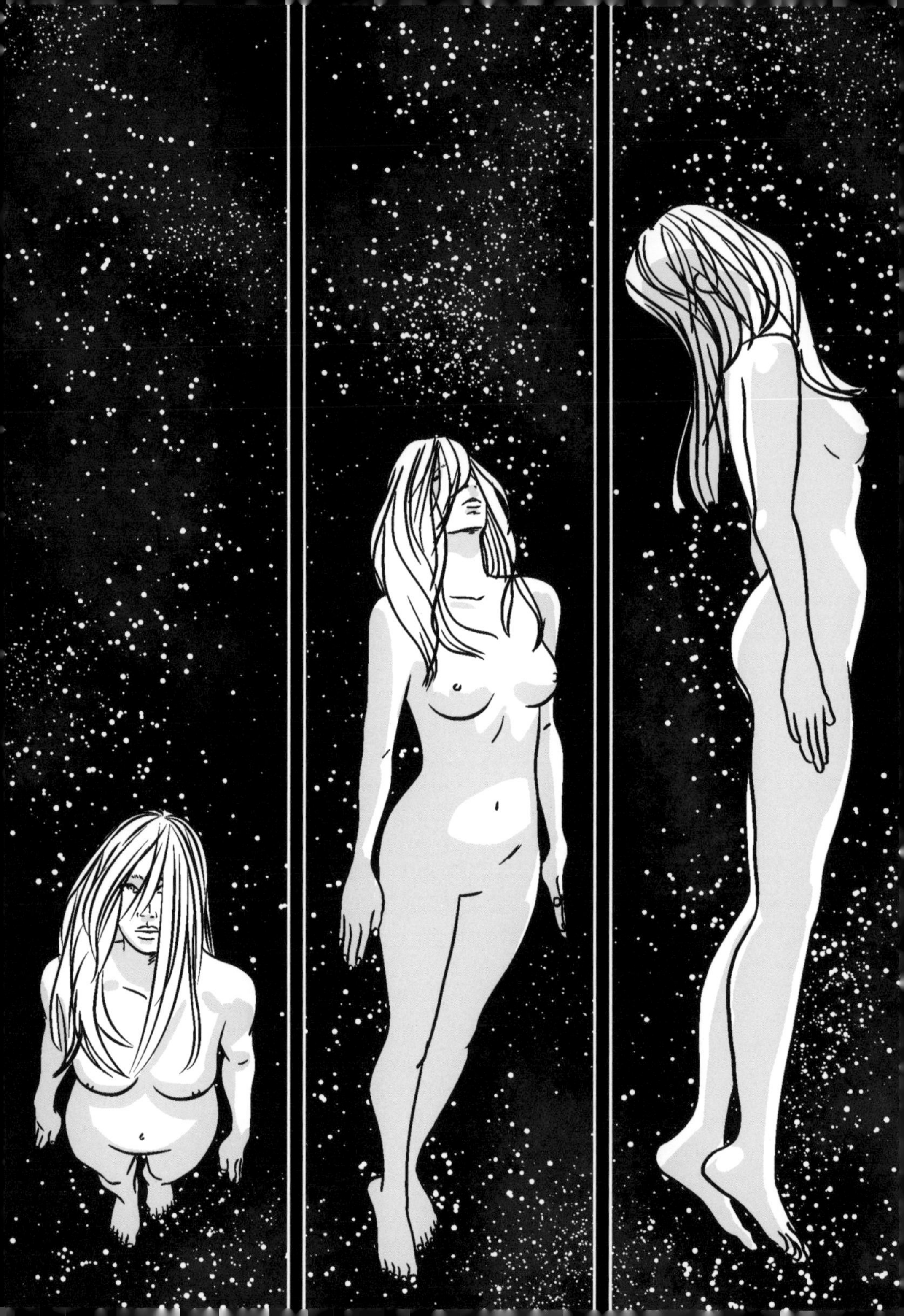

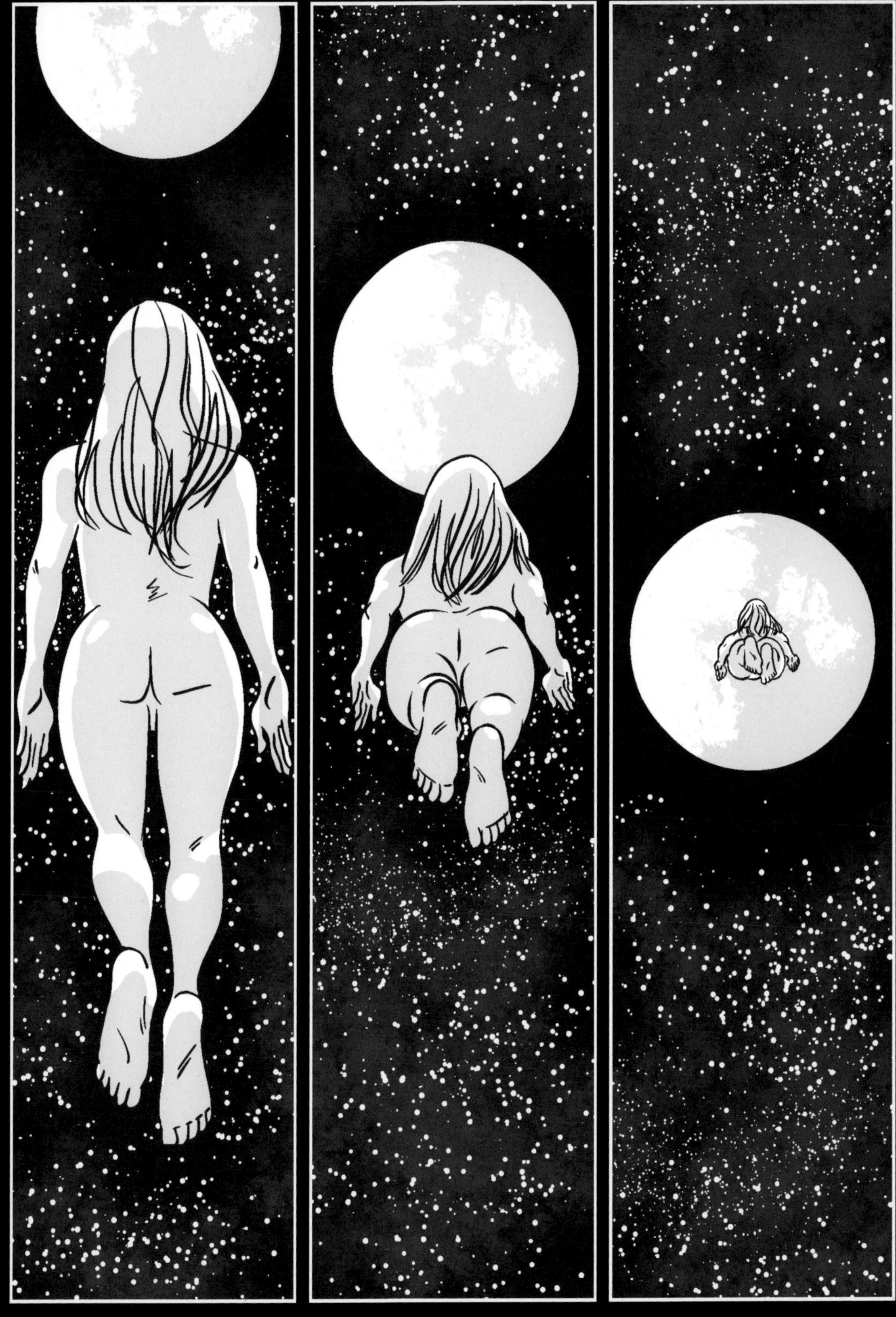

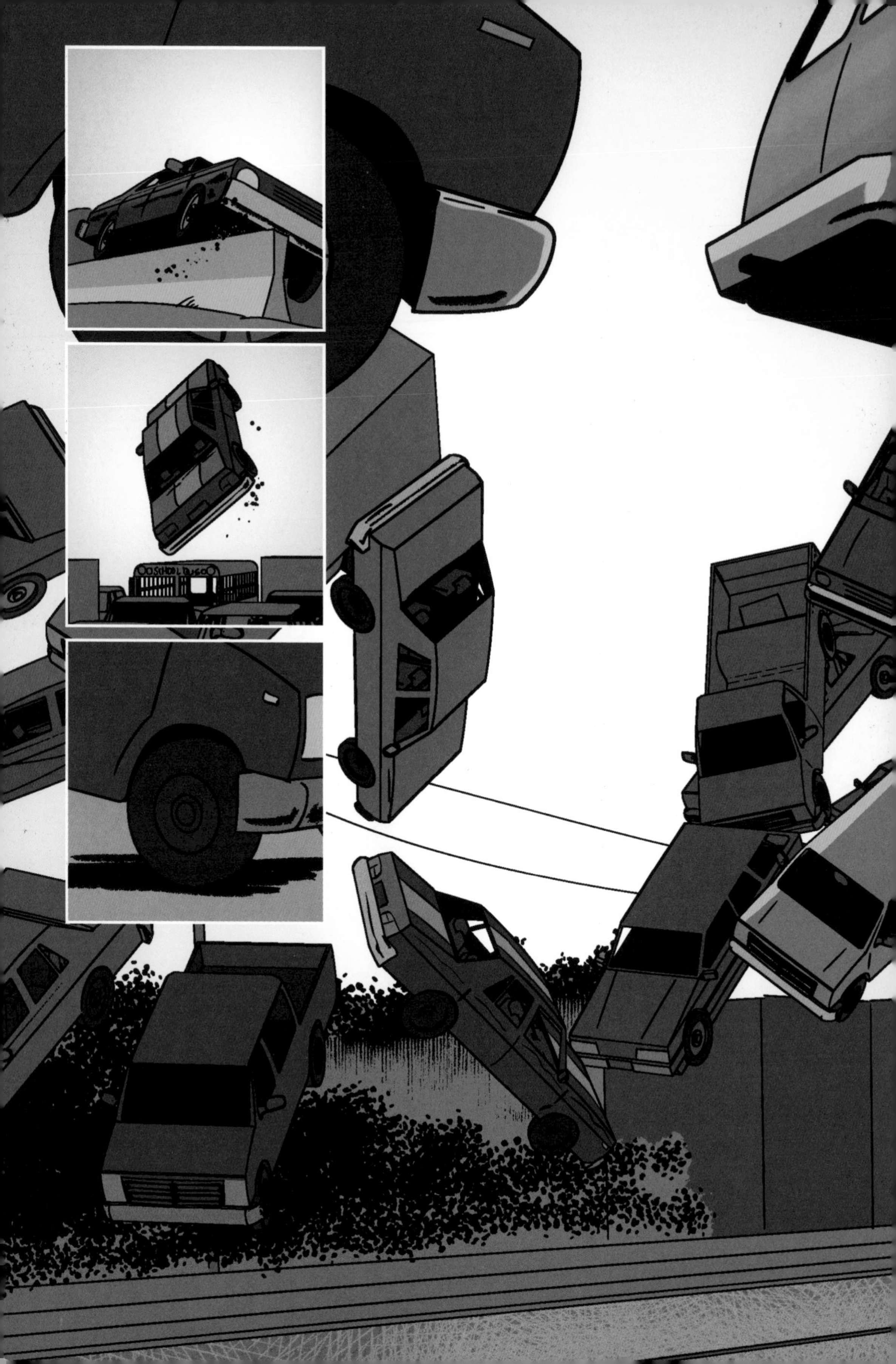
SCHOOL BUS

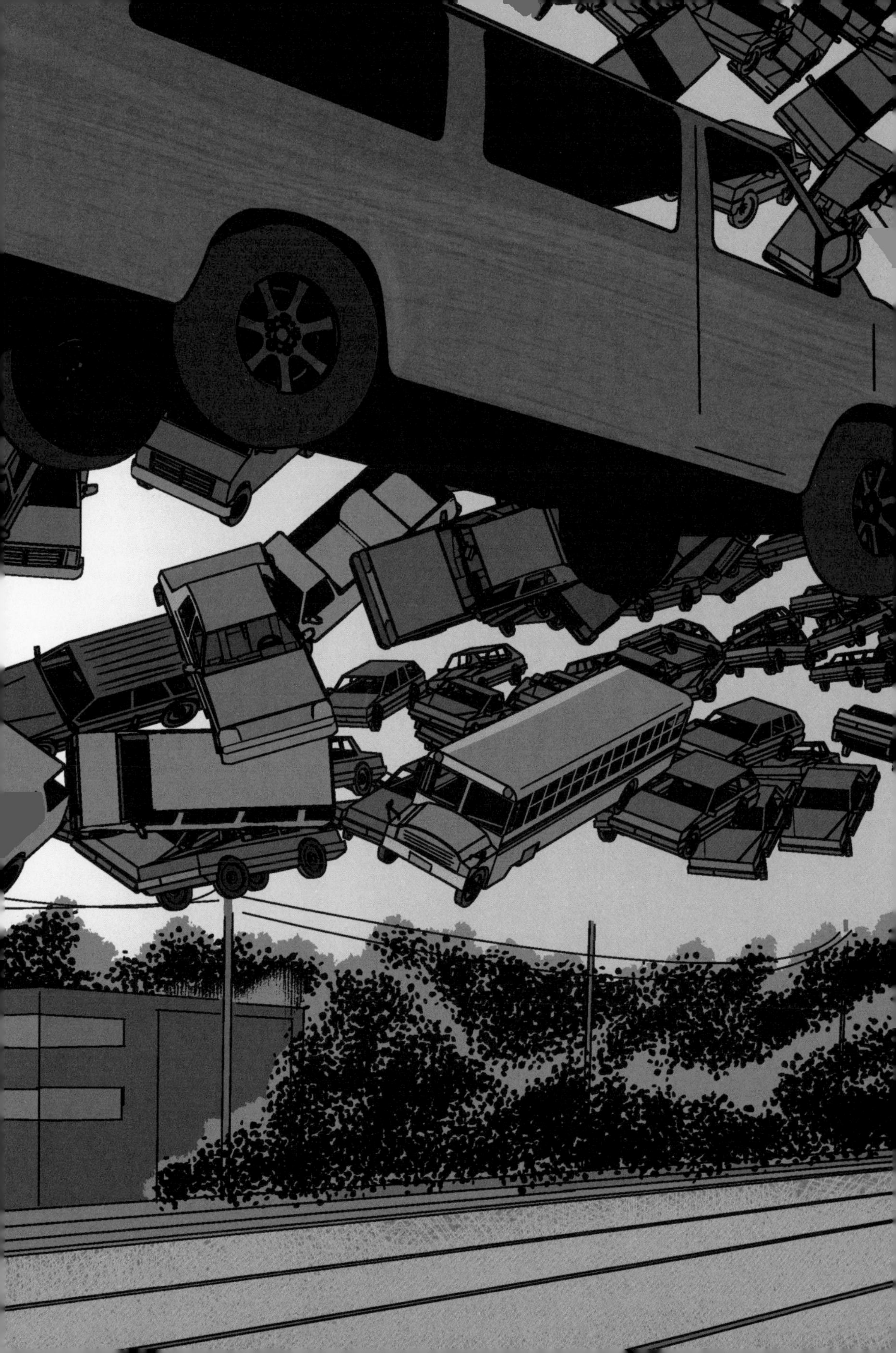

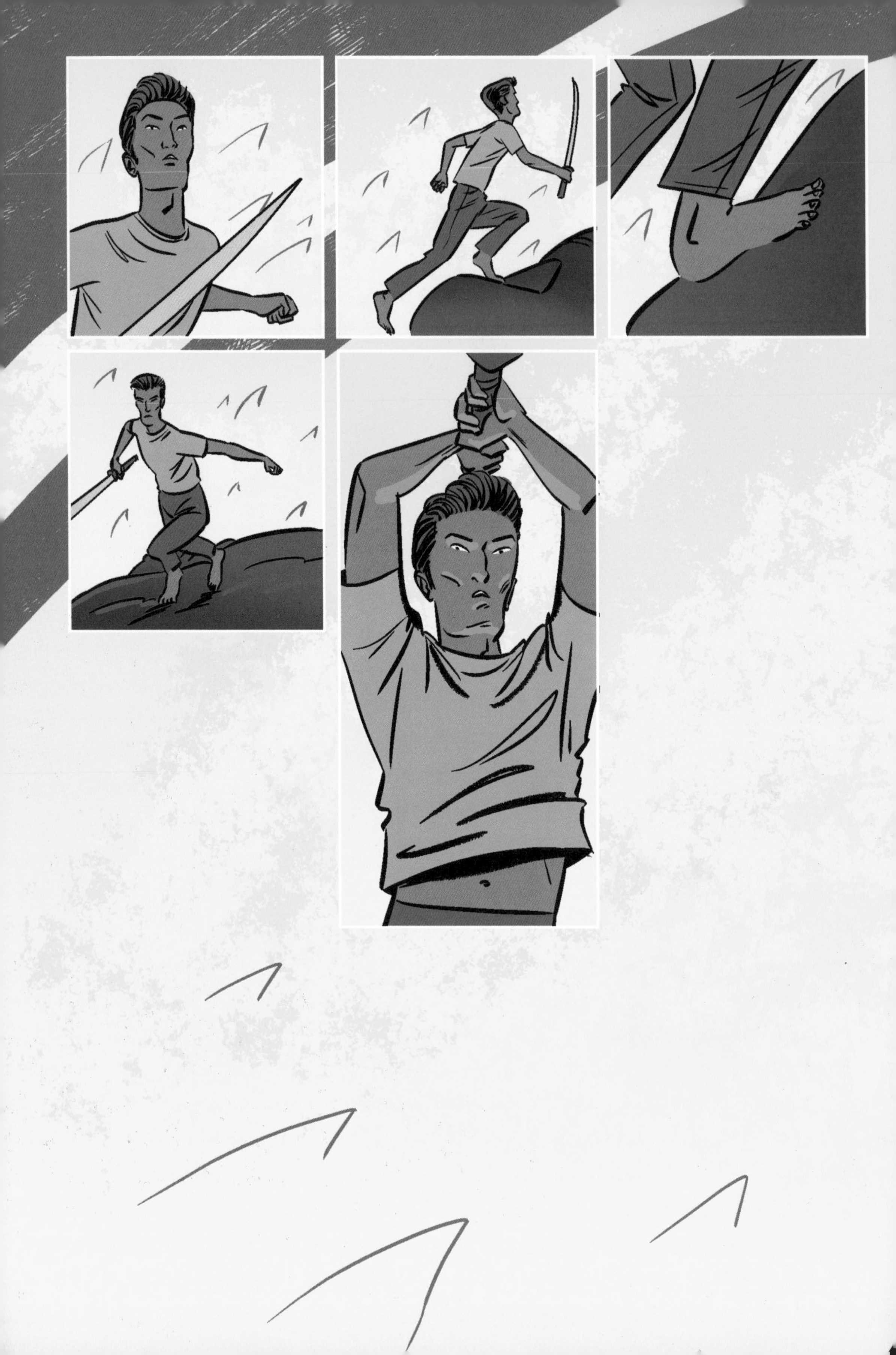

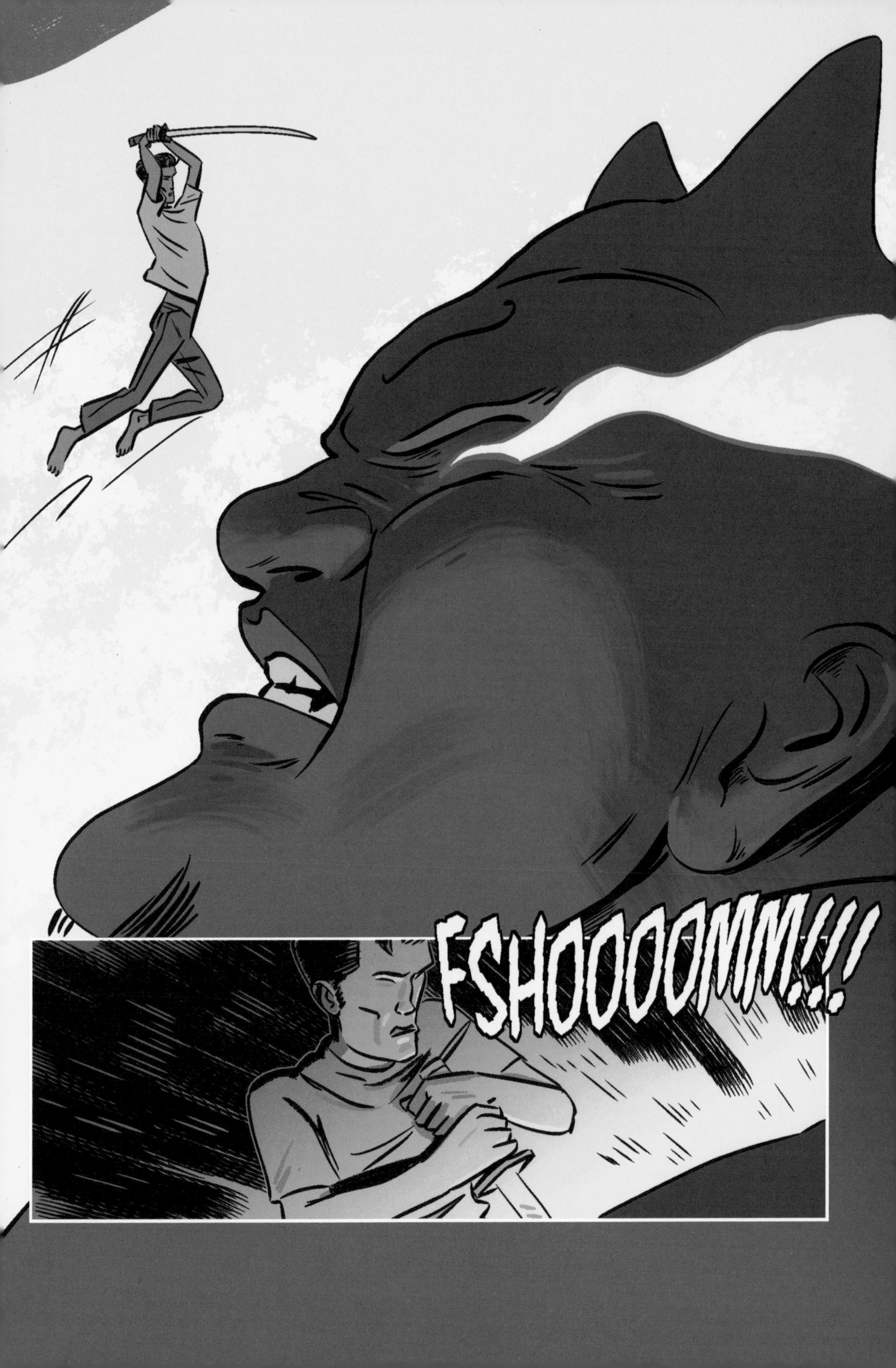
FSHOOOOMM!!!

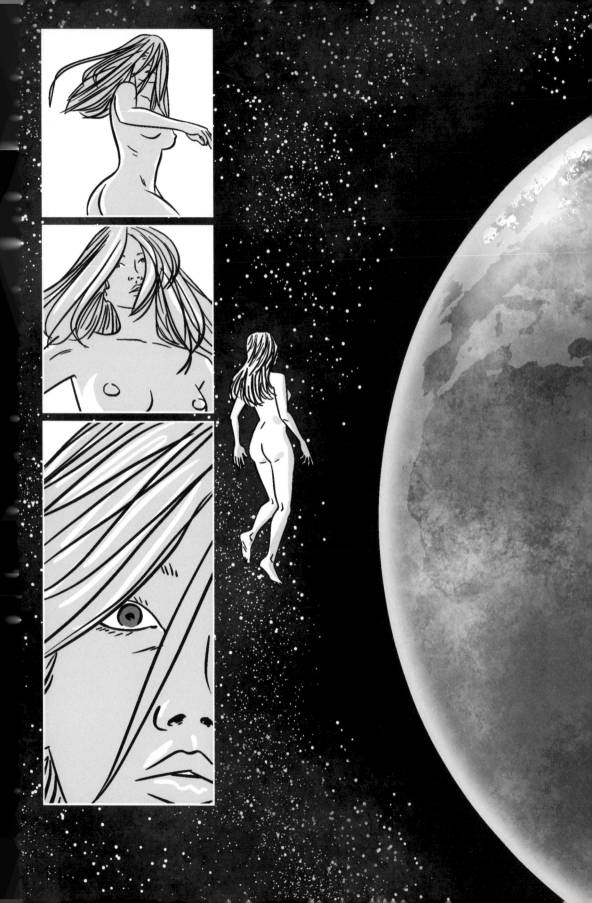

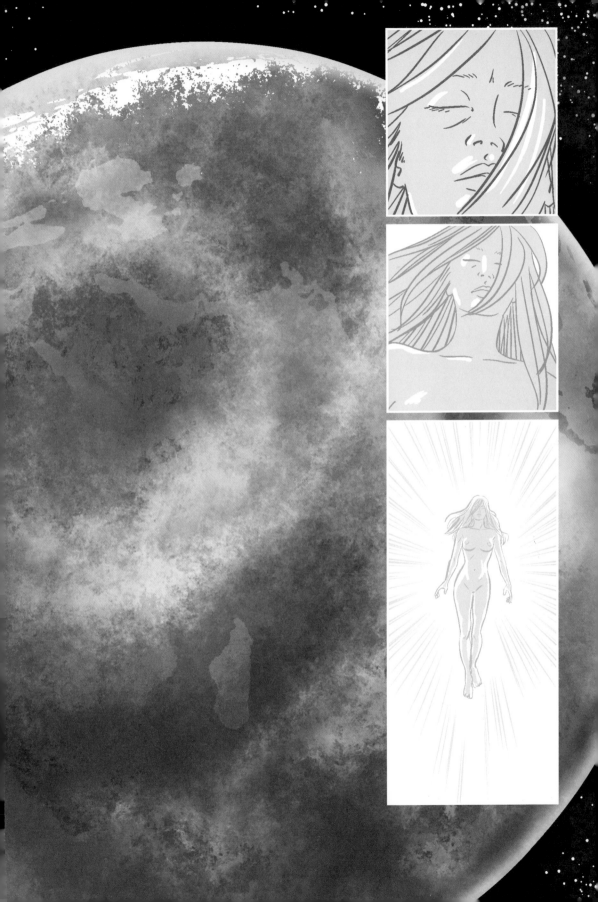

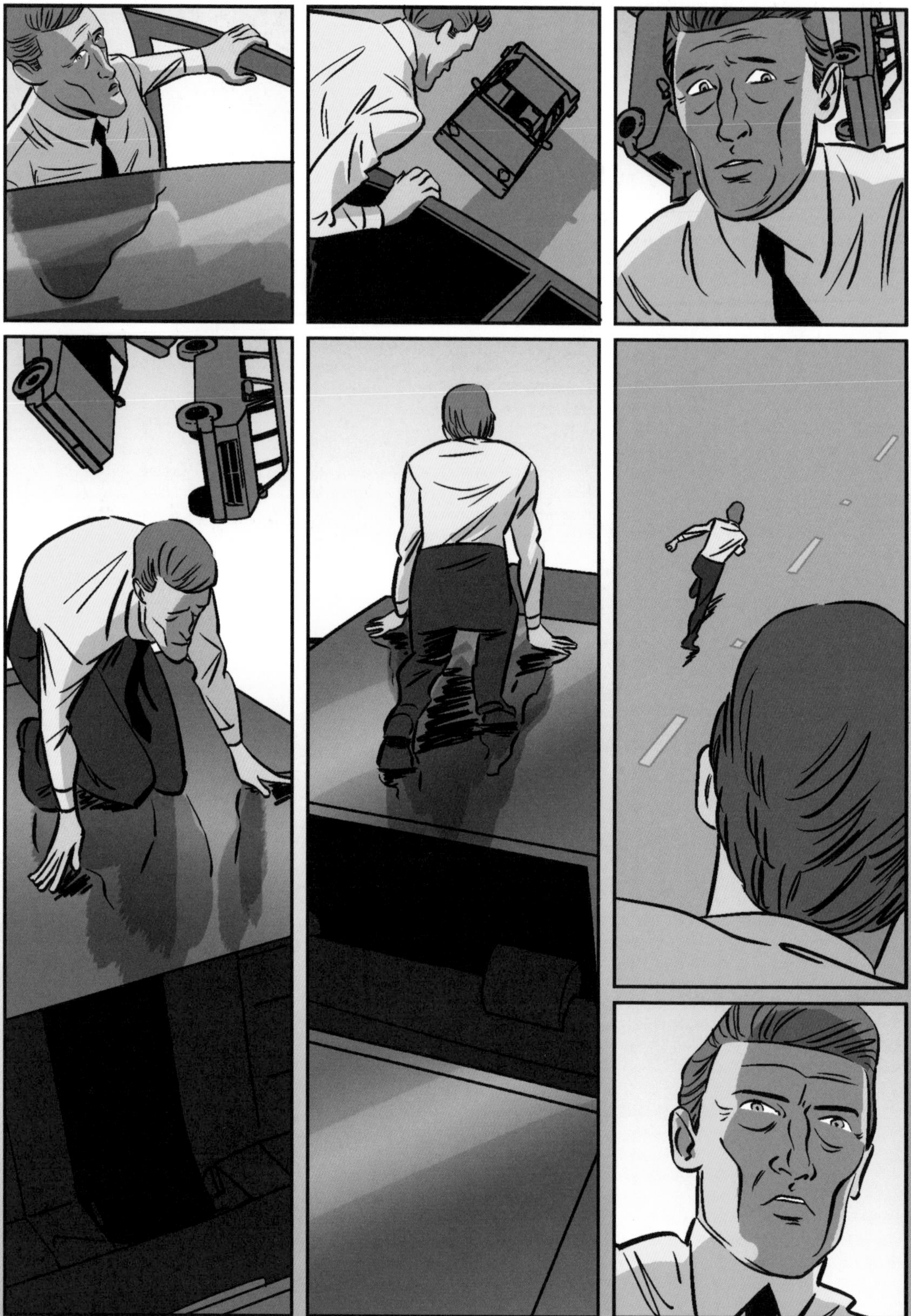

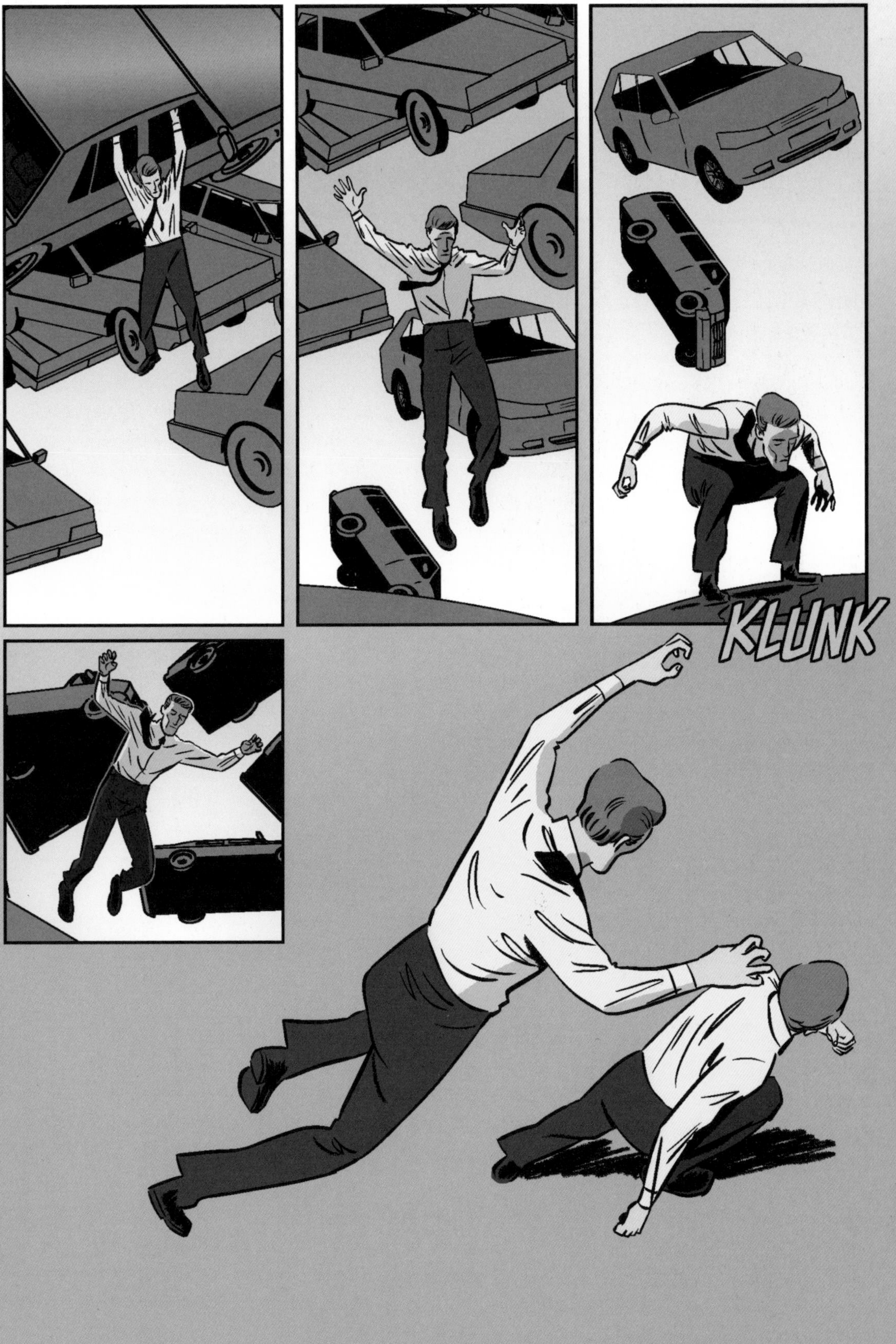
KLUNK

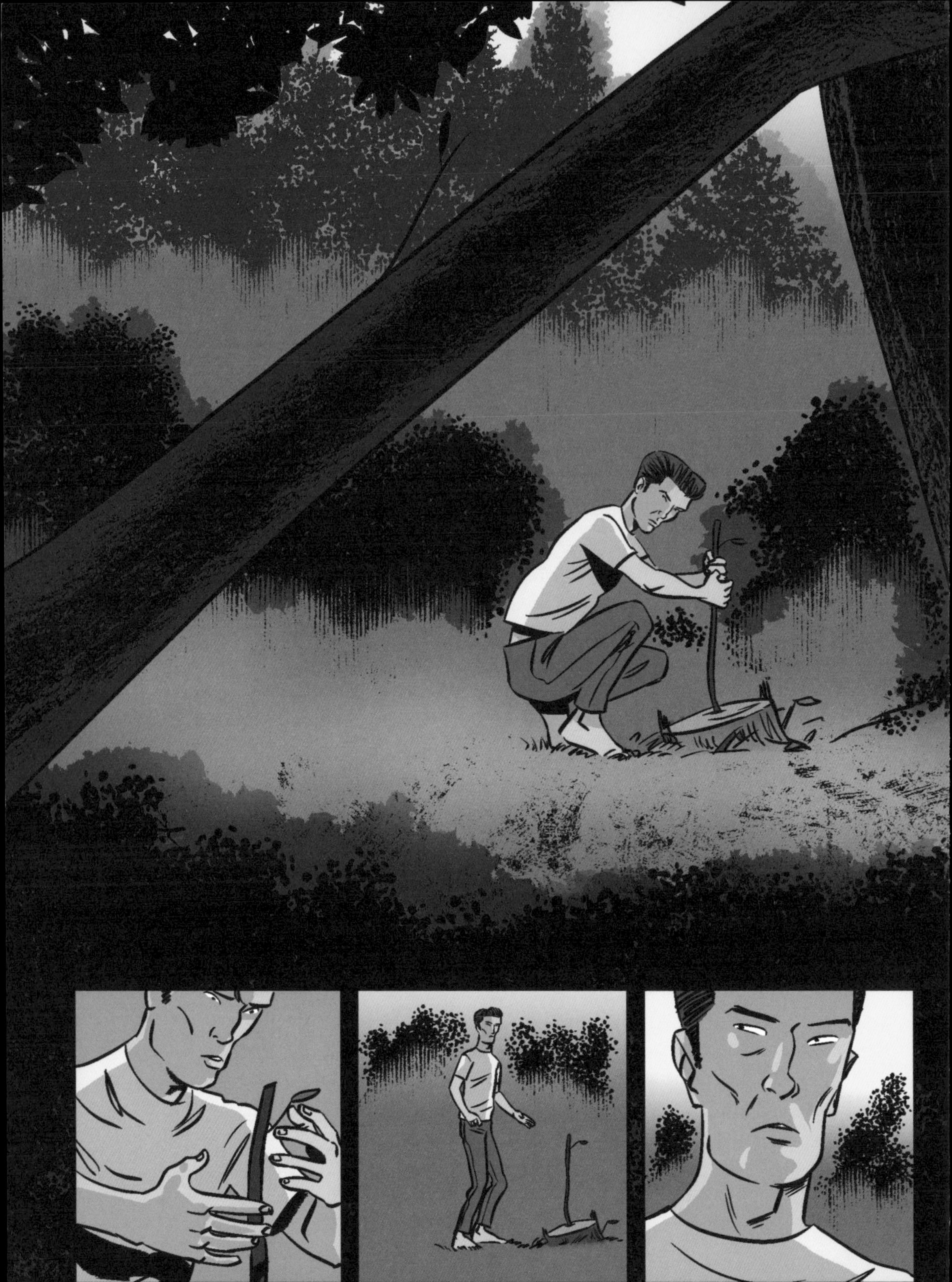

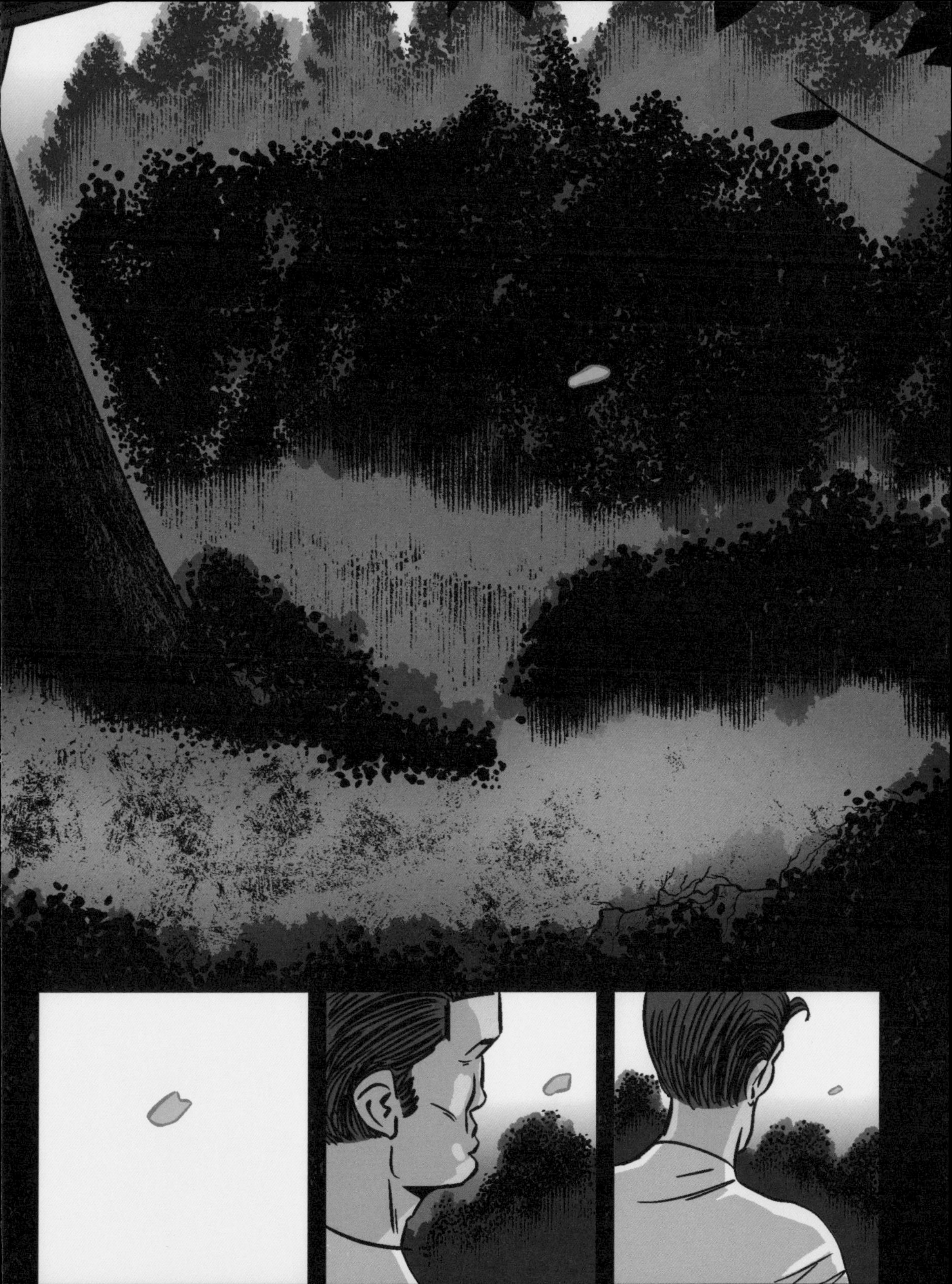

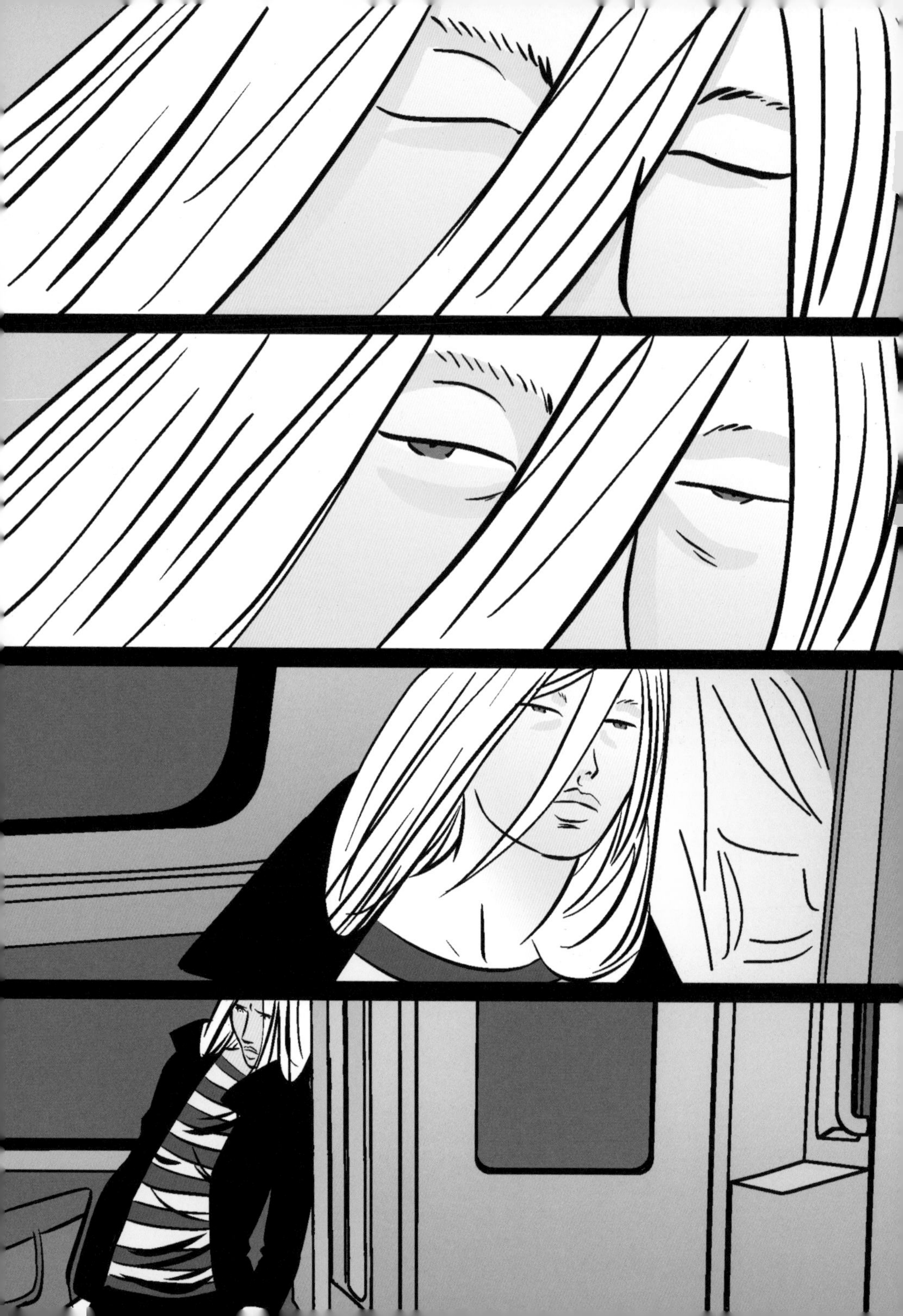

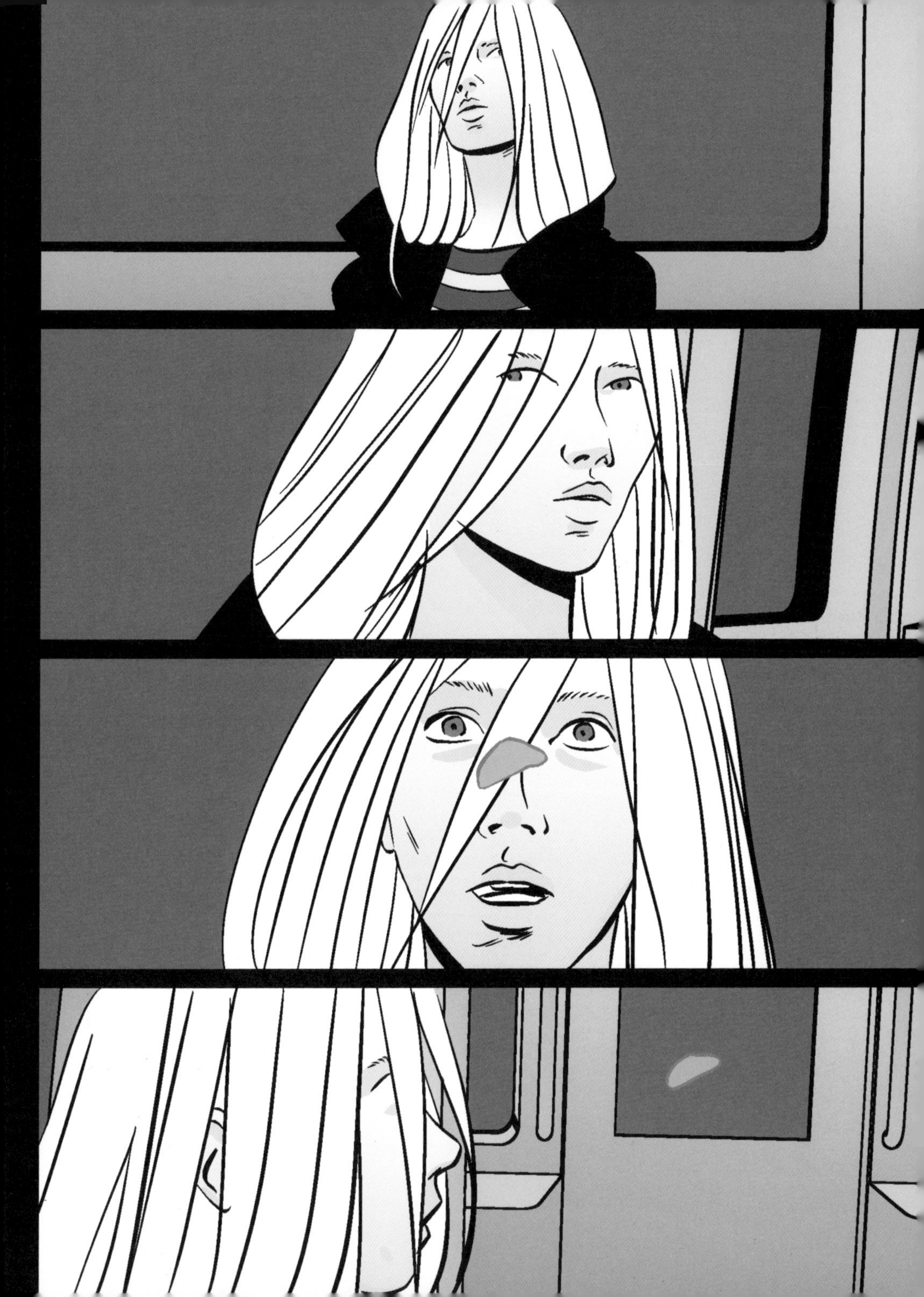

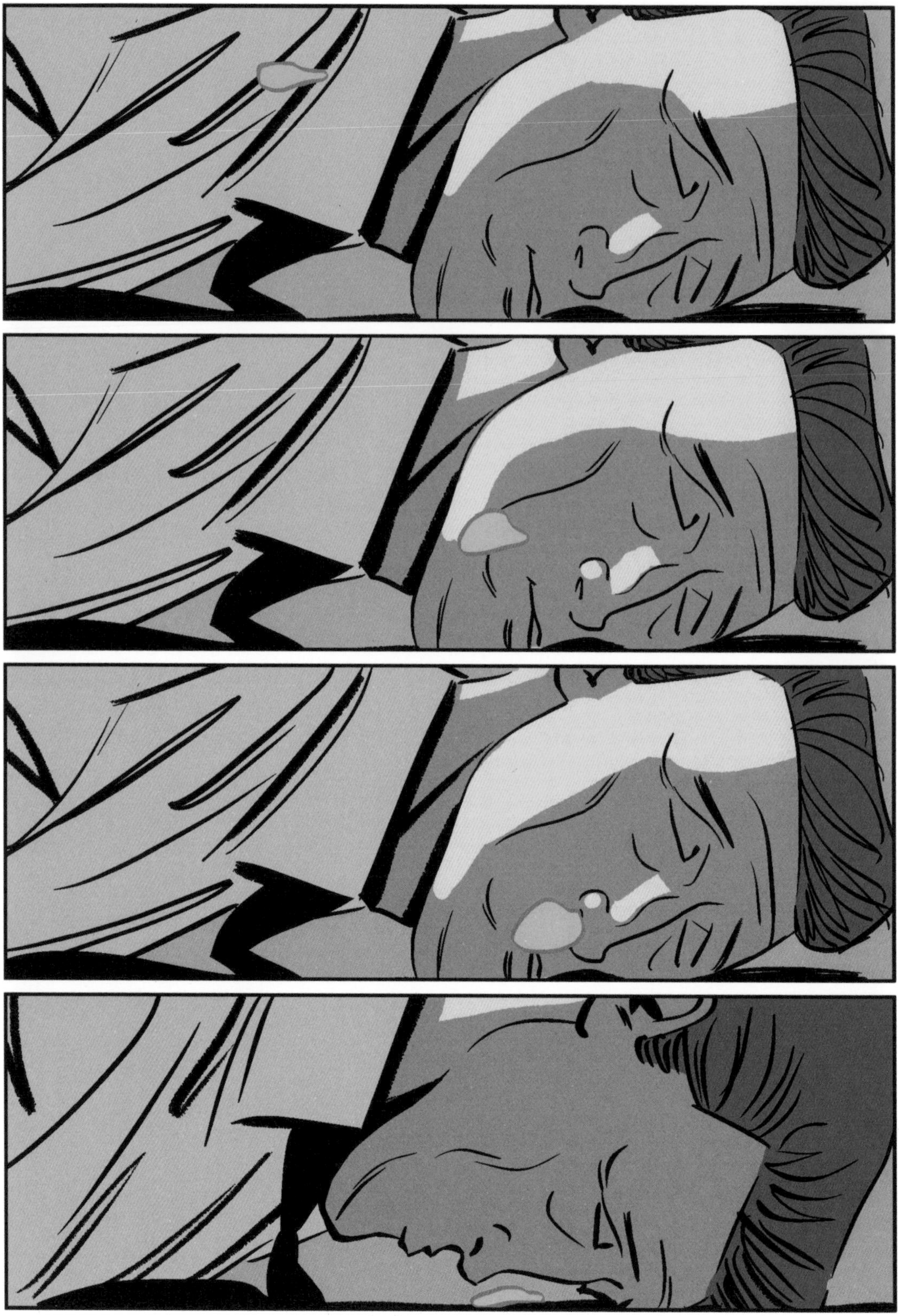

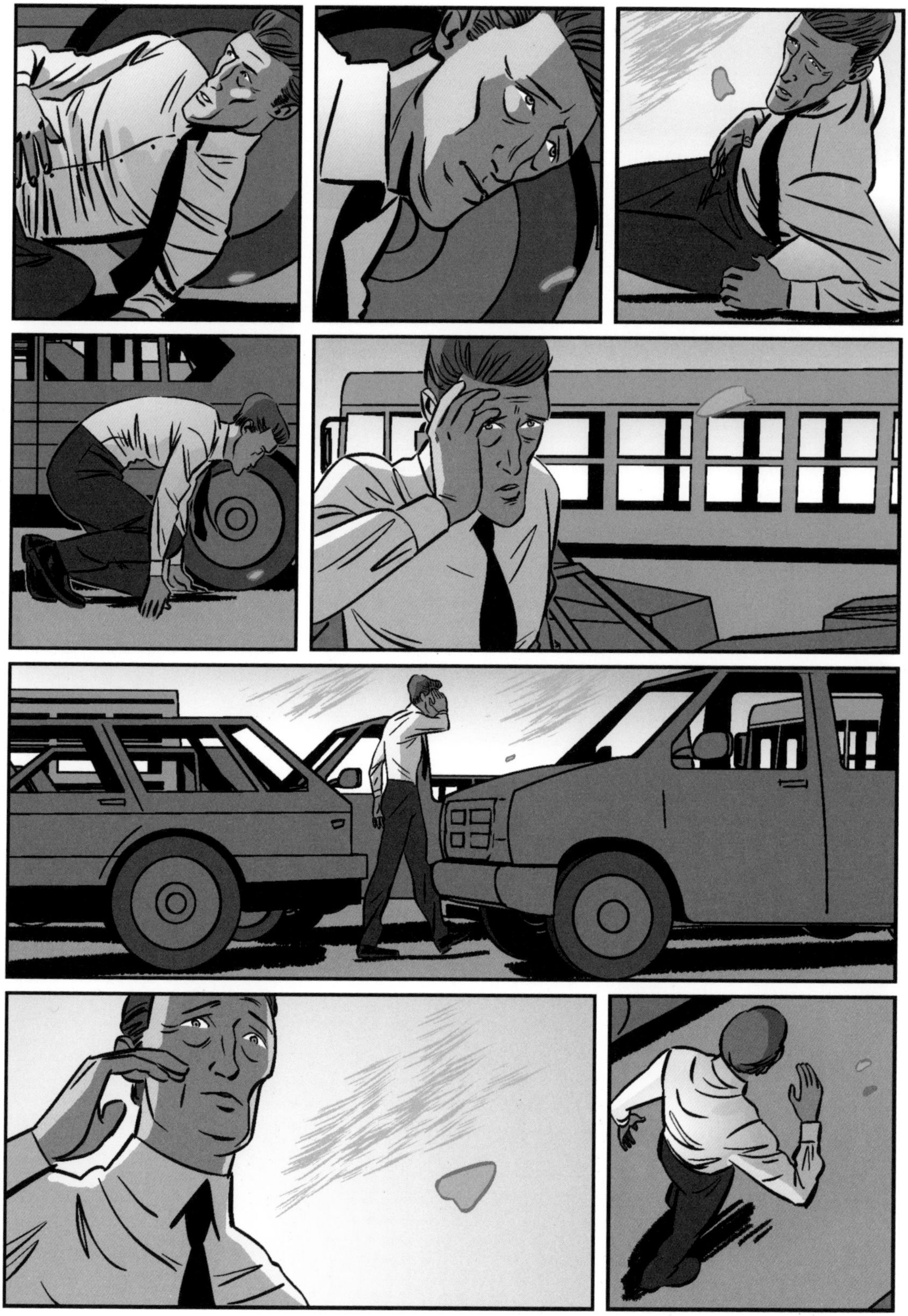

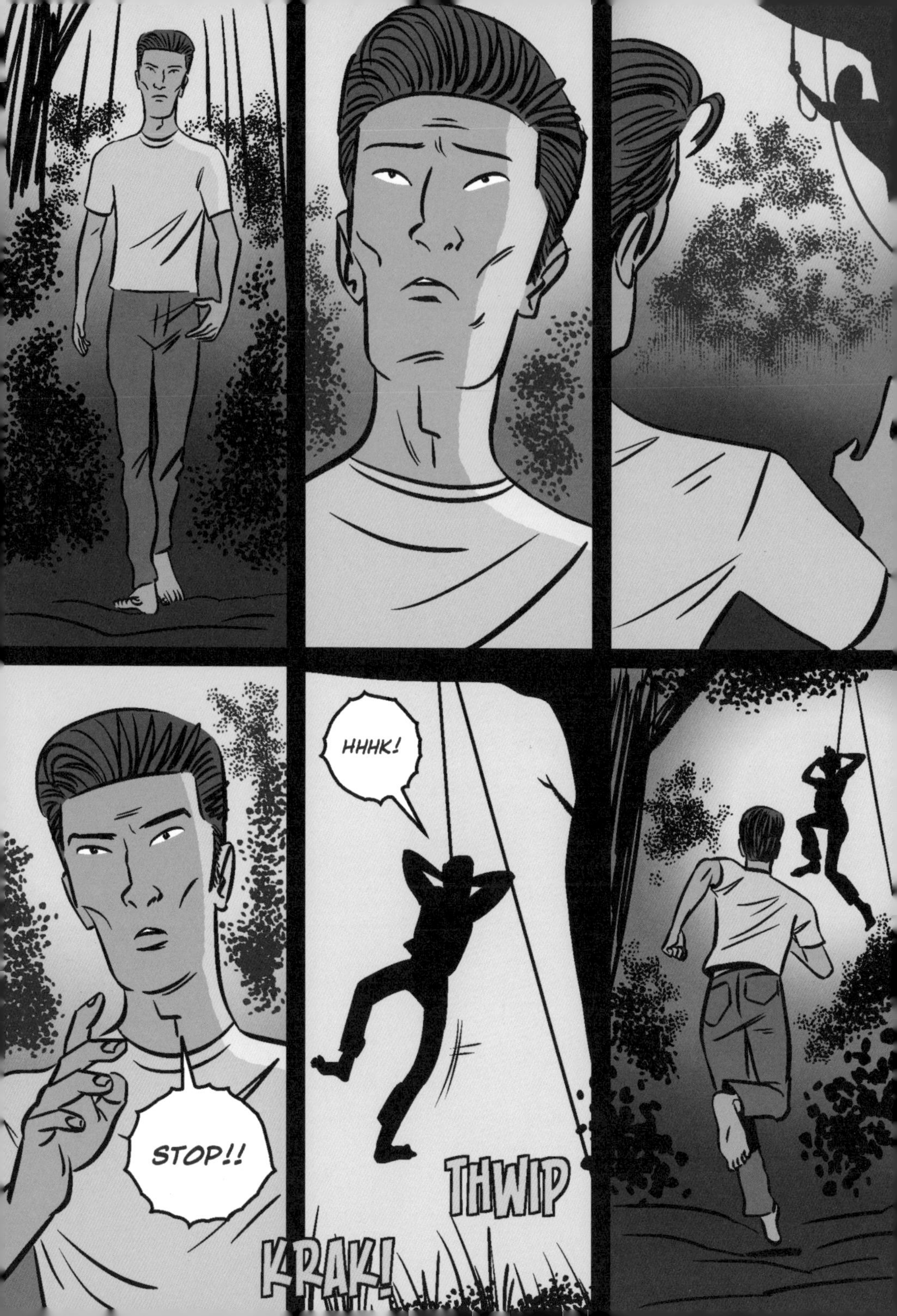
STOP!!
HHHK!
THWIP
KRAK!

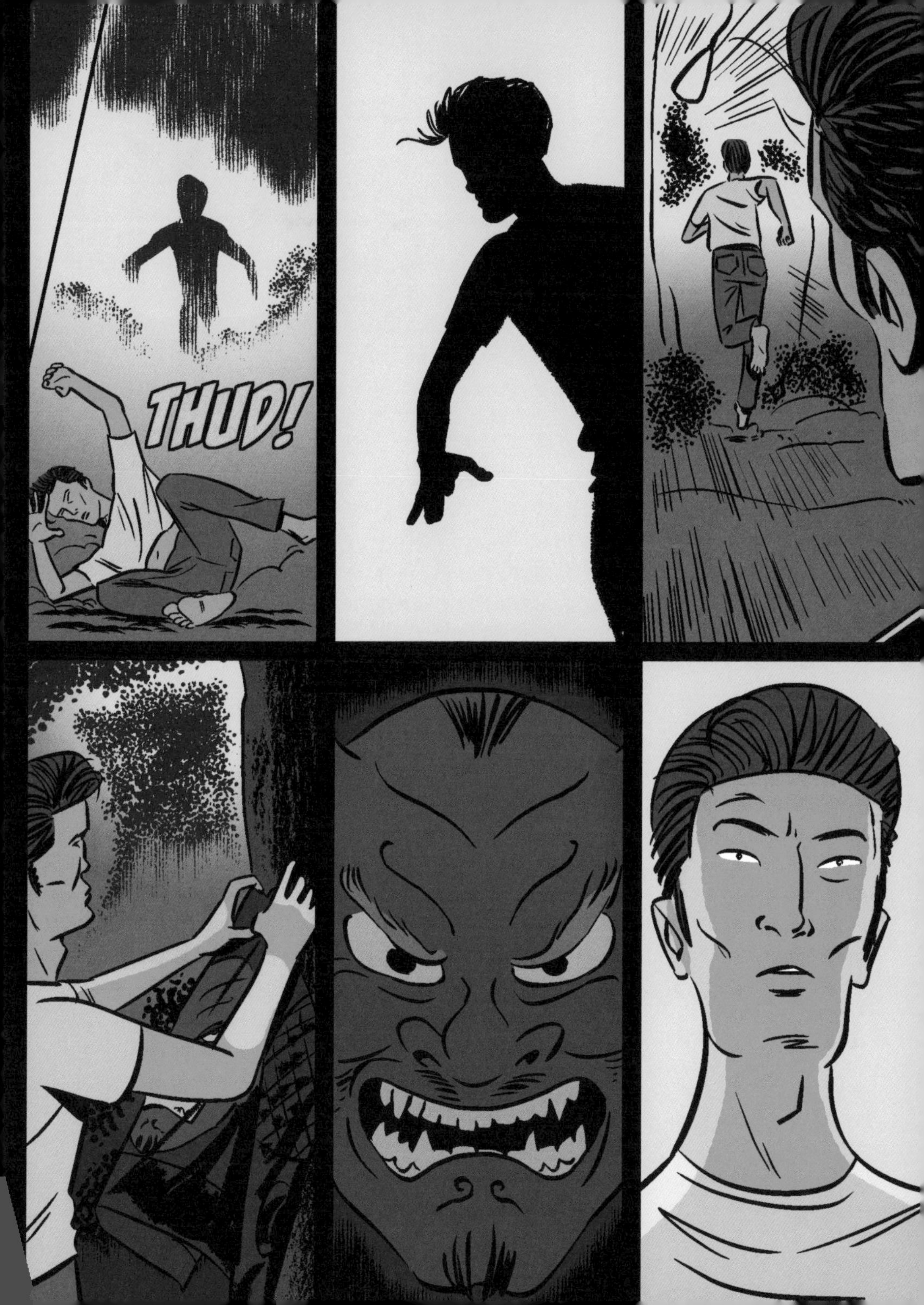
THUD!

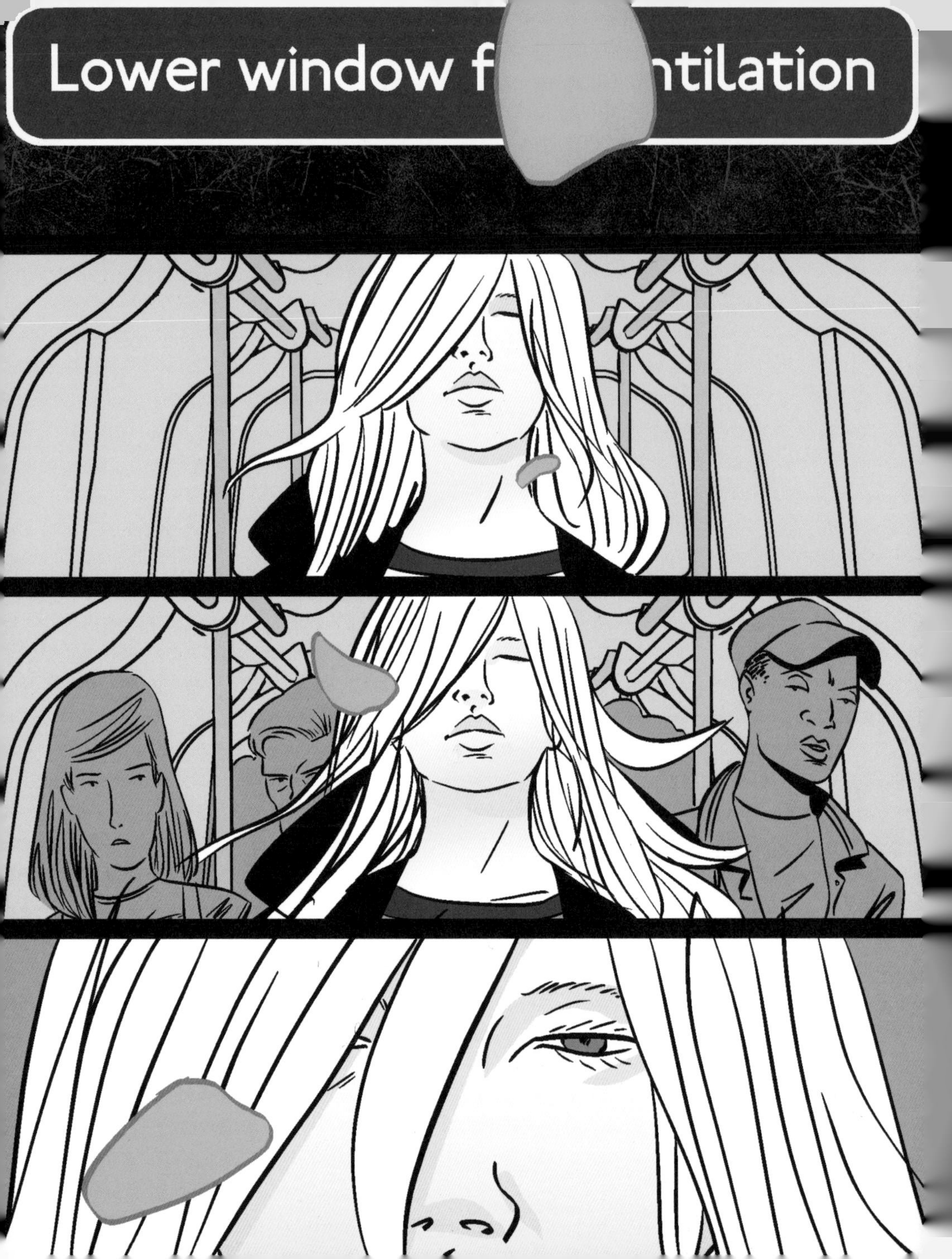

Lower window f ntilation

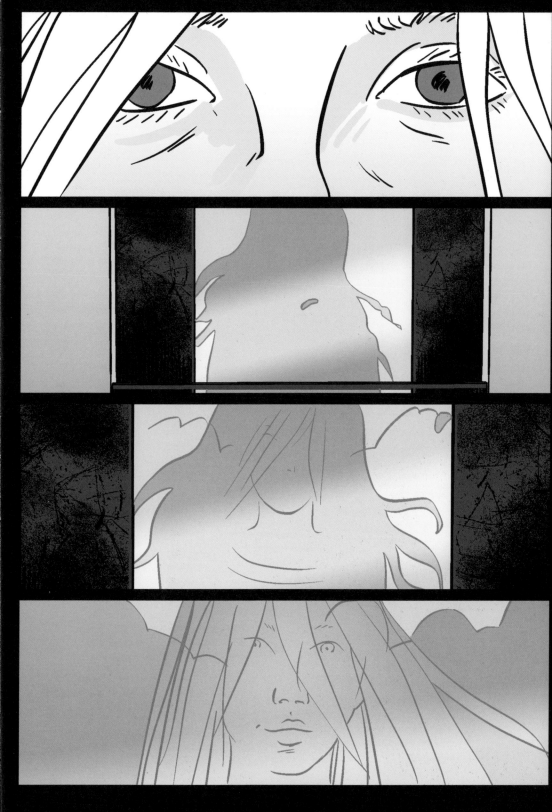

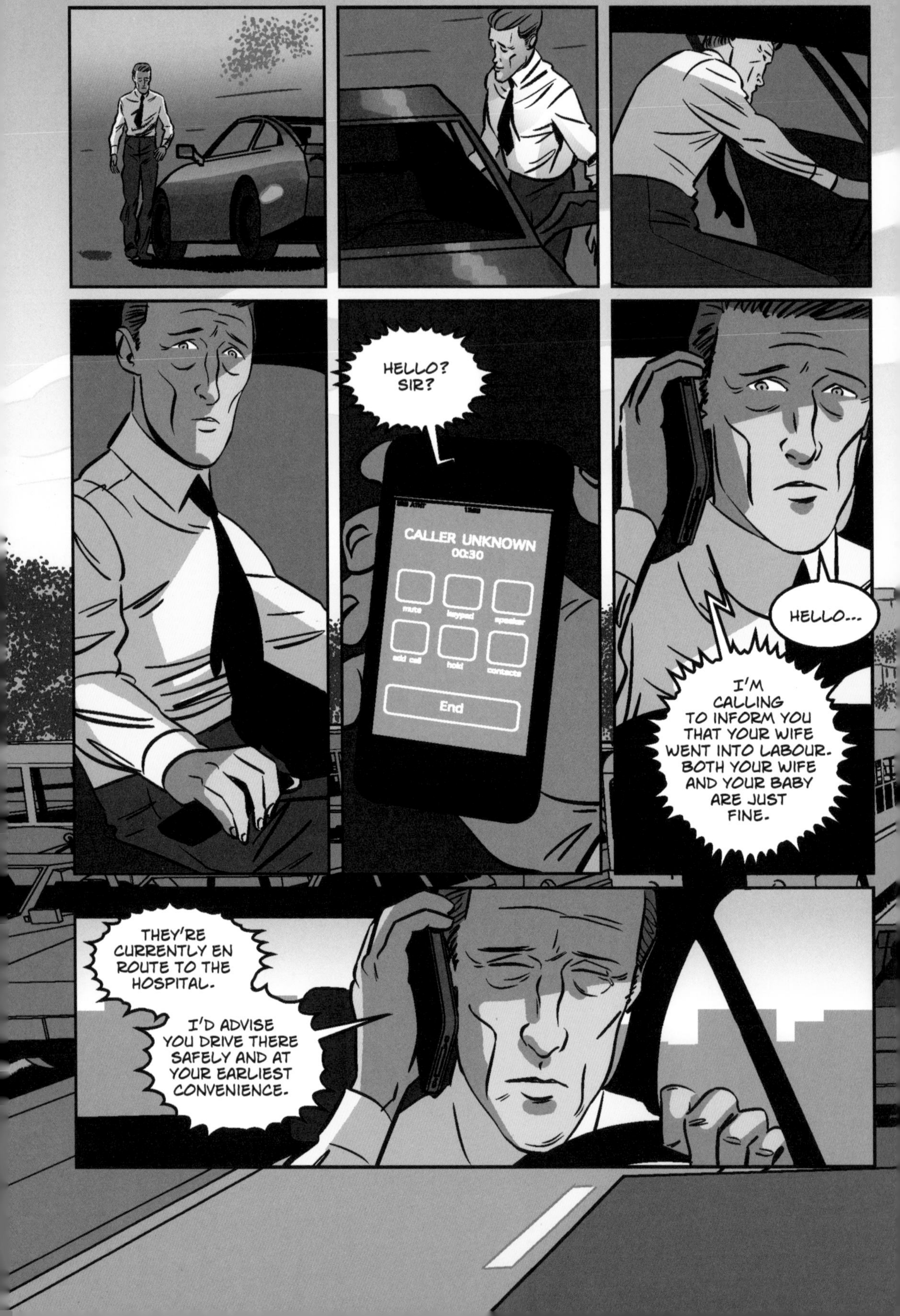
HELLO? SIR?
CALLER UNKNOWN
00:30
mute
keypad
speaker
add call
hold
contacts
End
HELLO...
I'M CALLING TO INFORM YOU THAT YOUR WIFE WENT INTO LABOUR. BOTH YOUR WIFE AND YOUR BABY ARE JUST FINE.
THEY'RE CURRENTLY EN ROUTE TO THE HOSPITAL.
I'D ADVISE YOU DRIVE THERE SAFELY AND AT YOUR EARLIEST CONVENIENCE.

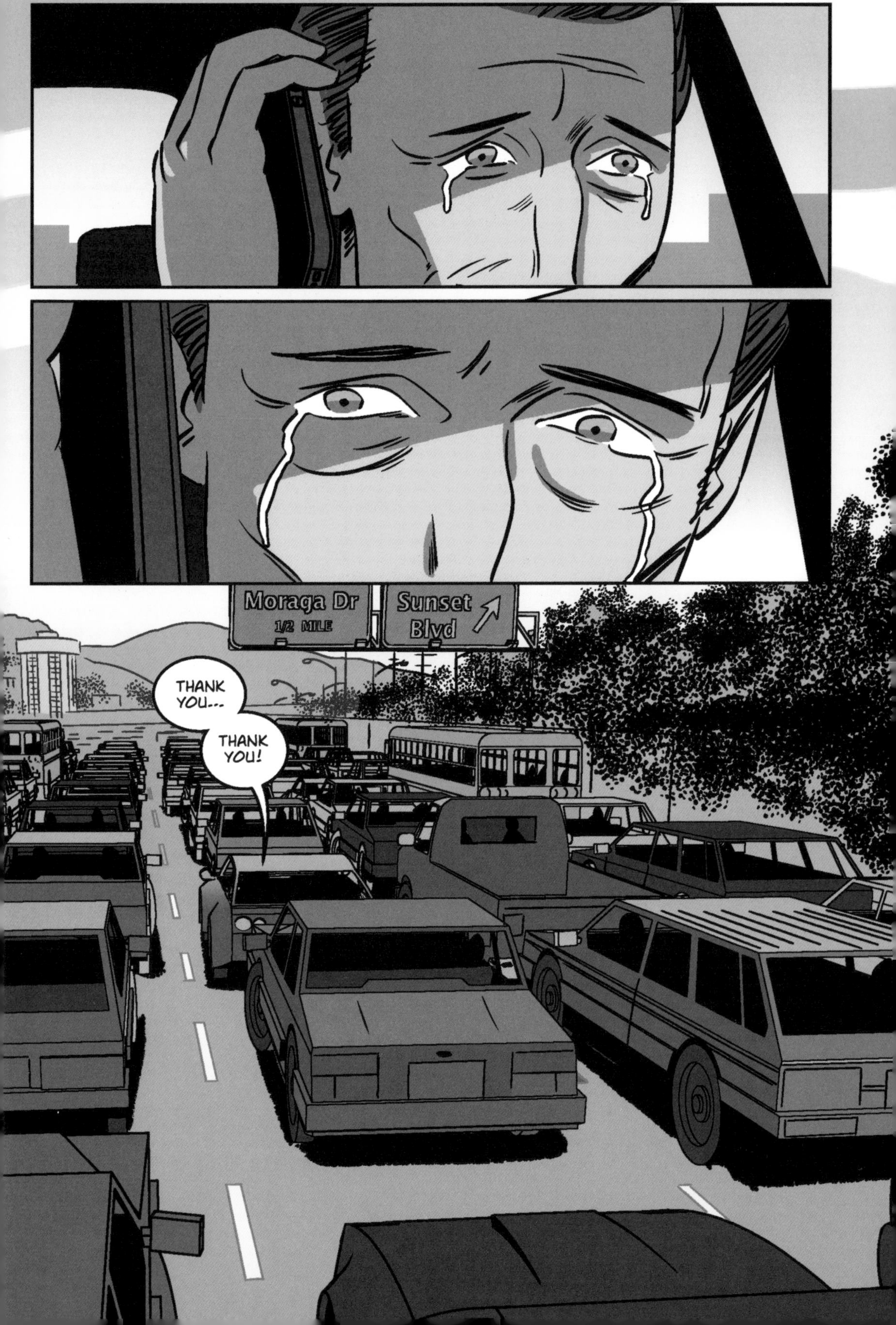
Moraga Dr
1/2 MILE
Sunset
Blvd
THANK YOU...
THANK YOU!

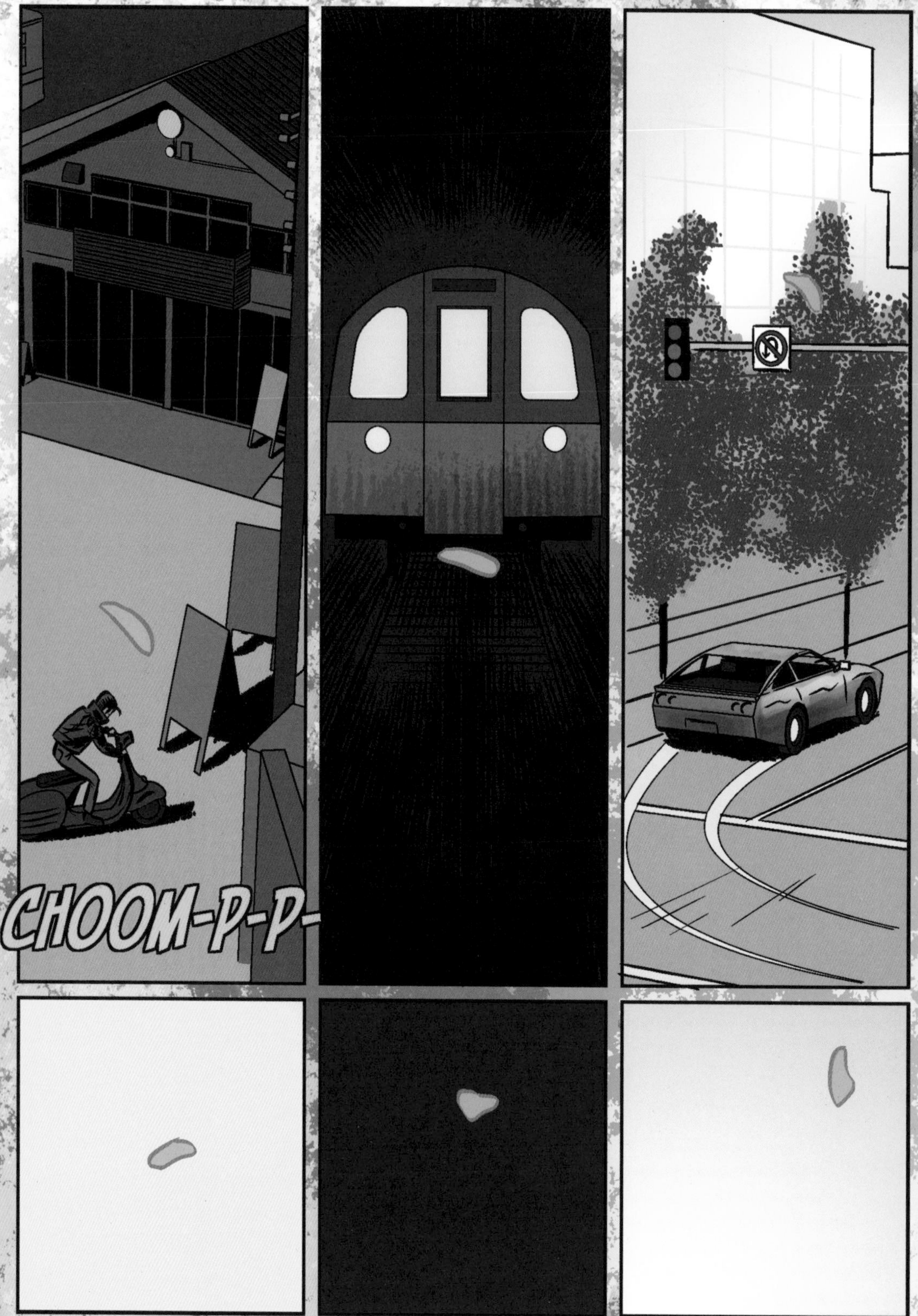
CHOOM-P-P-

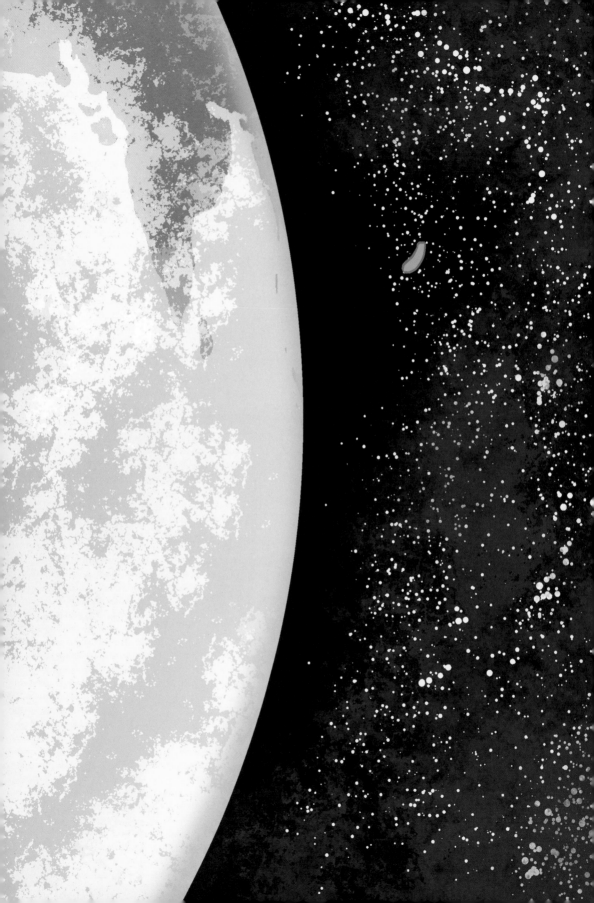

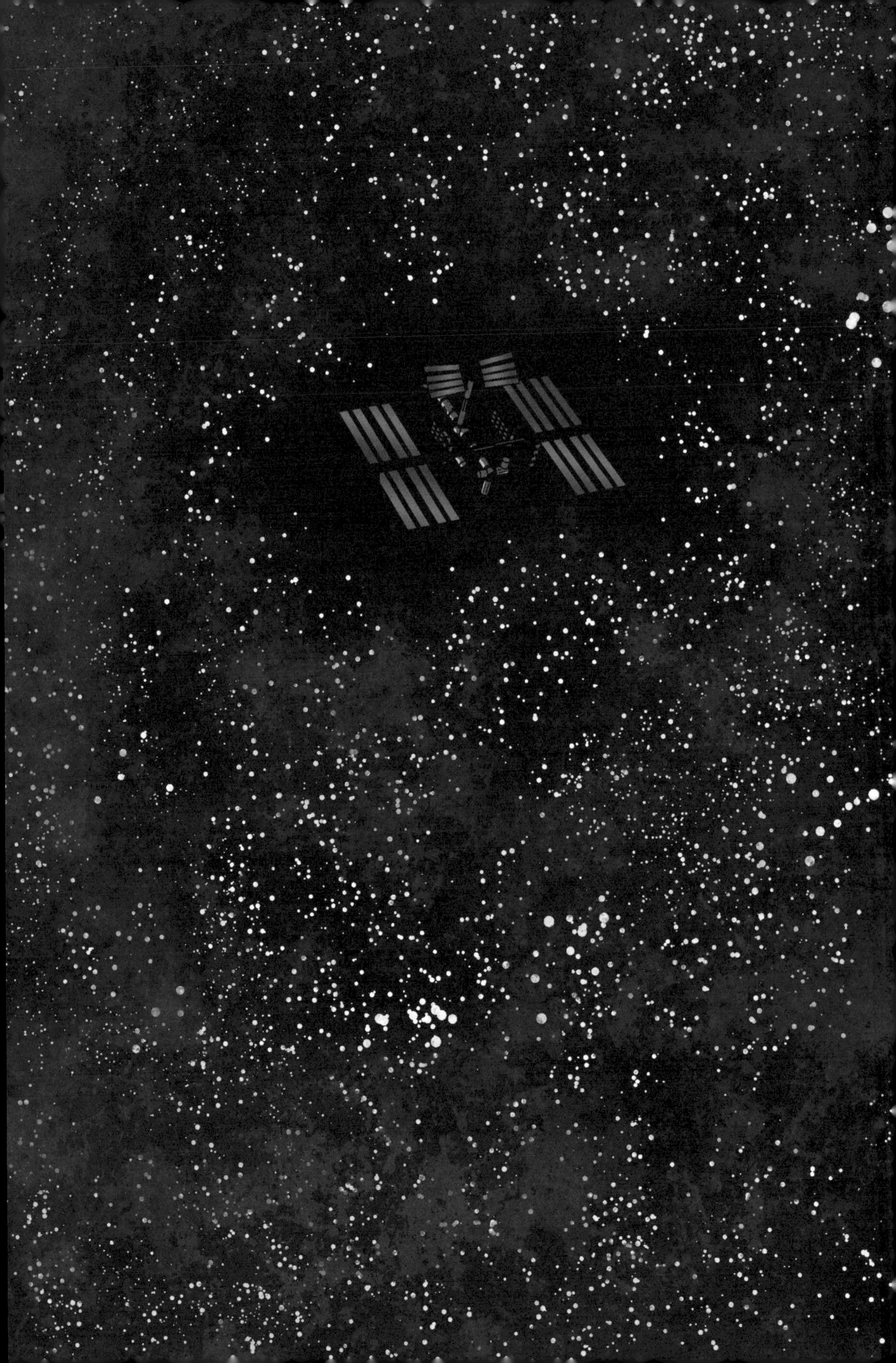

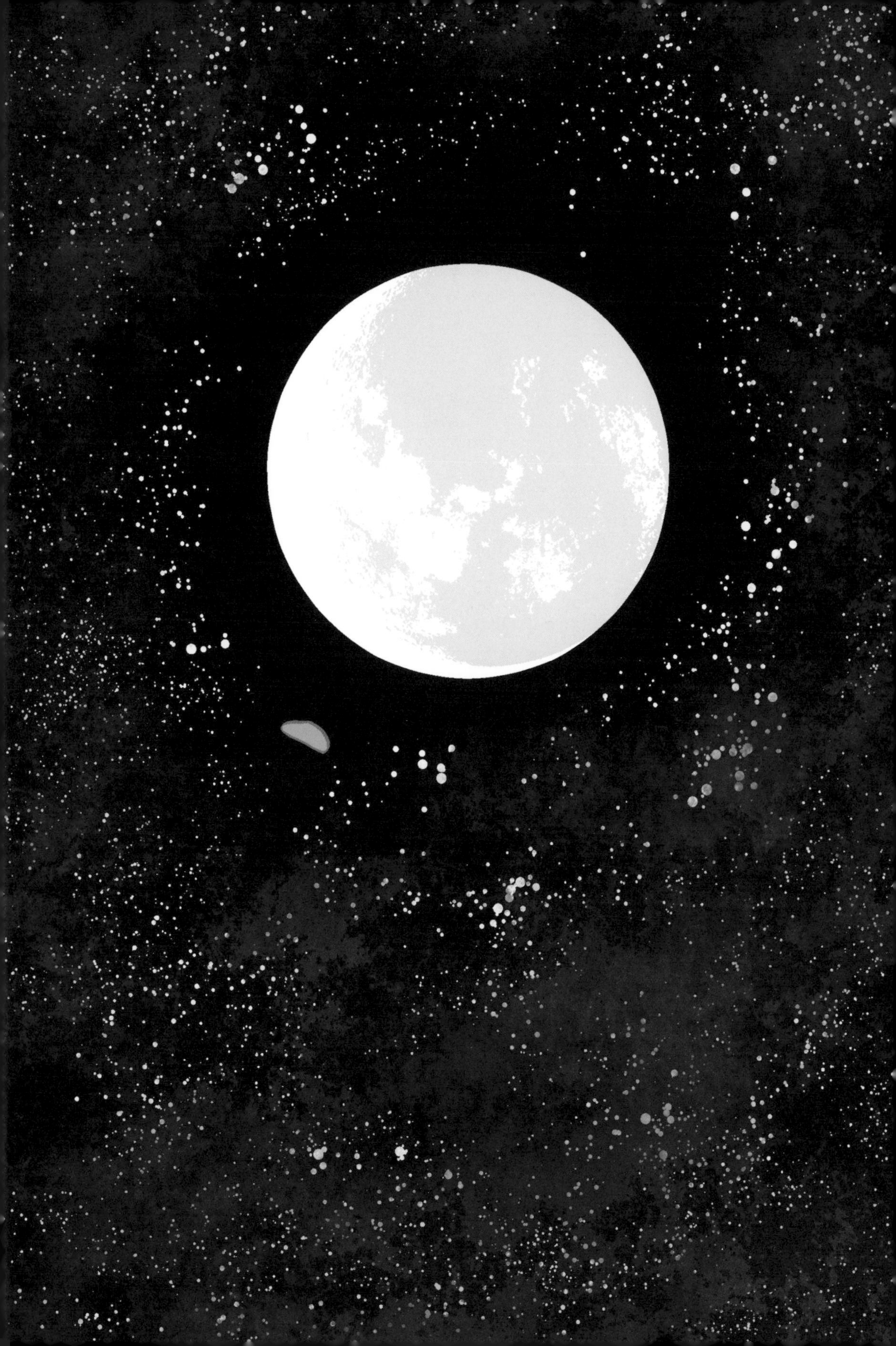

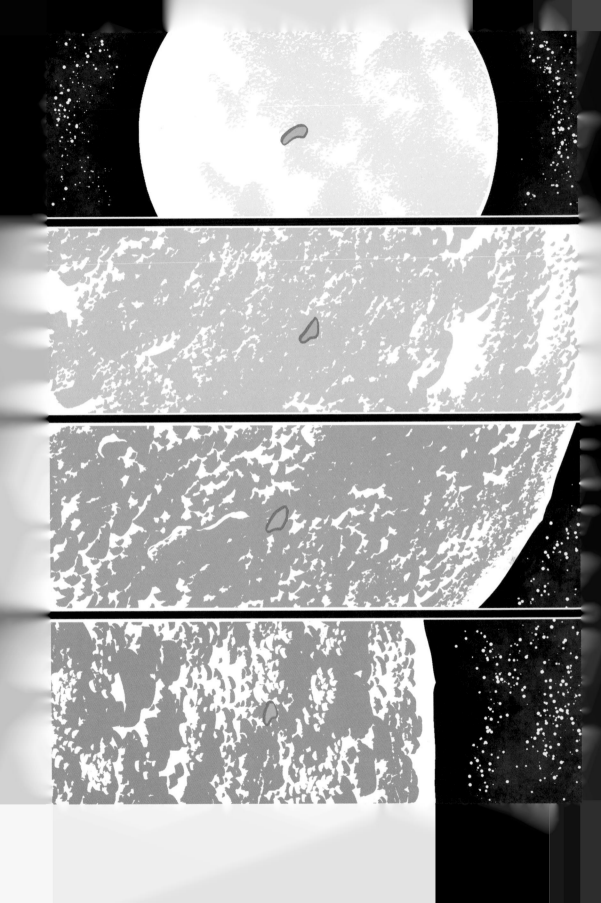

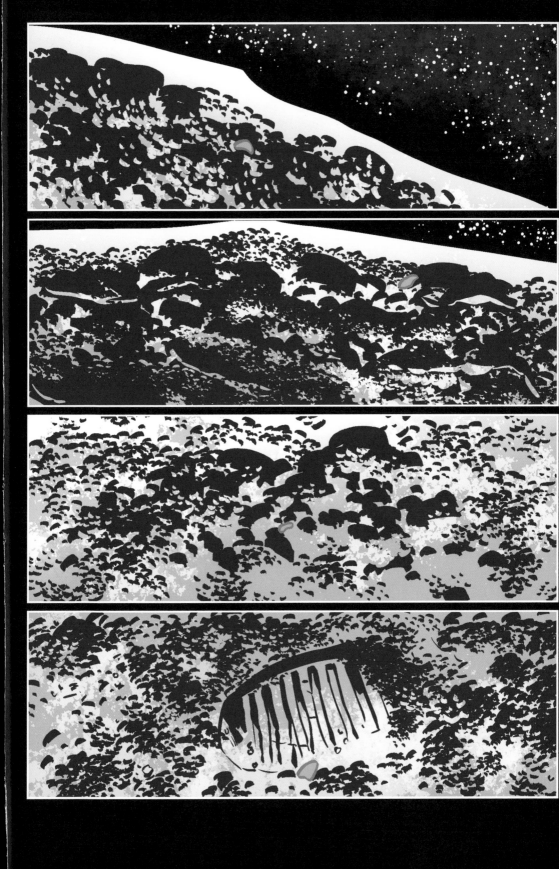

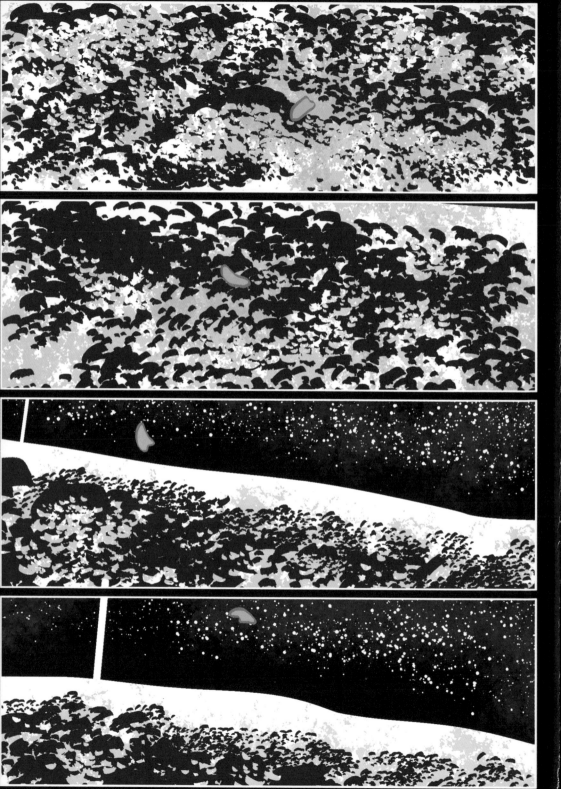

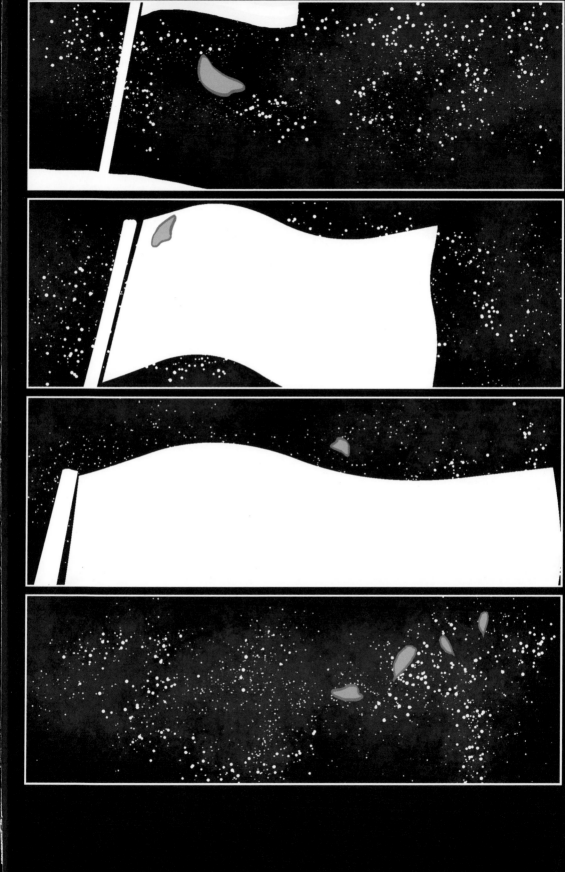

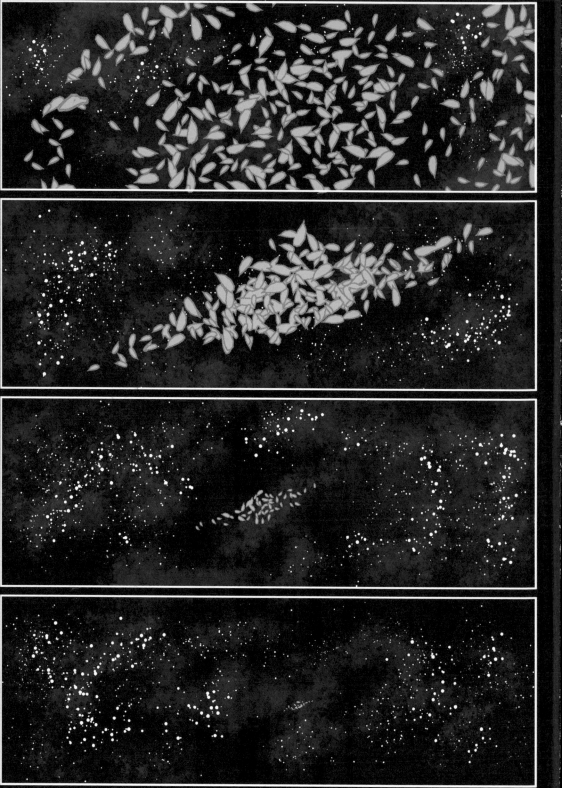

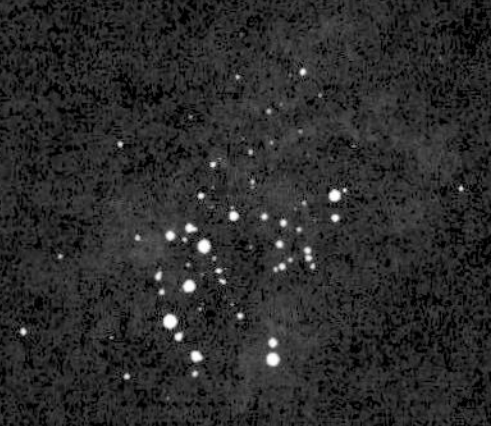